# *Manchester*
# *United*

## POCKET ANNUAL
## 1994-95

Edited by
Phil Bradley
Andy Bradley

# Manchester United Pocket Annual 1994-95

Copyright © Phil Bradley – 1994

ISBN: 1-898351-08-2

Typeset by Bruce Smith Books Ltd

All photographs supplied by Empics Ltd.
Cover Photo: Paul Ince

Statistics supplied by Football Information Services.

The right of Phil Bradley to be identified as the Author of the Work has been asserted by him in accordance with the *Copyright, Designs and Patents Act 1988.*

This is not an approved nor an official publication of Manchester United Football Club.

First published in 1994 by
*Words on Sport*

Words on Sport Ltd
PO Box 382
St. Albans
Herts, AL2 3JD

Registration Number: 2917013

Registered Office:
Worplesdon Chase, Worplesdon,
Guildford, Surrey, GU33LA

Printed and Bound in the Great Britain by
Ashford Colour Press Ltd. Gosport.

# CONTENTS

## Miscellaneous

# Acknowledgements

Many thanks to all those people who, in one way or another, have contributed something to this first *Manchester United Pocket Annual*. In particular, I would like to thank Andy Bradley for the many hours of work he put in to produce the statistics that the annual contains. To Carole, my wife, I would like to record my appreciation of her patience during the hours I spent working on the book and also to Erica for the numerous cups of tea. I would also like to take this belated opportunity of thanking John Earley, Dave Kibble and Jim Morrison for keeping me company on so many United travels in the sixties. To Alan Allcock for giving us a good laugh simply by supporting Manchester City and to Bruce Smith, Peter Fitzpatrick and Mark Webb of *Words on Sport* for making it all possible. Finally, I dedicate the hours spent on the book to Eveline who, sadly, did not live to see it published. God Bless.

## Disclaimer

In a book of this type it is inevitable that some errors will creep in. While every effort has been made to ensure that the details given in this annual are correct at the time of going to press, neither the editor nor the publishers can accept any responsibilities for errors within.

If you do notice any mistakes then please write in and we will try and rectify them for future issues. In addition, if there are other areas of information about Manchester United Football Club that you feel should be included in future editions then please let us know of your choices.

# Introduction

Manchester United are probably the best known football club in the world and, since the Munich Air Disaster, have held a special place in the hearts of most neutrals. No club has appeared in more FA Cup Finals, nor won the famous trophy on more occasions than the Old Trafford side. They have conquered not only the domestic scene but also, on two occasions, Europe.

The common denominator in all their successes has been flair. Many players such as Duncan Edwards, Bobby Charlton, Denis Law, and George Best have become household names, nowadays replaced with the likes of Eric Cantona and Ryan Giggs.

The bulk of the club's achievements have been made during the last fifty years within the dynasty founded by Sir Matt Busby in 1945 when he inherited a club with no ground and very little cash. Sadly 1994 witnessed the passing of Sir Matt but there could have been no tribute more fitting for one of football's greatest ambassadors than for the present team to become the first United side to land the double.

This first edition of the independent *Manchester United Pocket Annual* chronicles that success, match by match, blow by blow, goal by goal. But it contains much else besides, all the records, facts and statistics associated with this great football institution as well as how the world's most famous club were saved from extinction by a dog! Read on.

# The Season Reviewed

So they eventually did the double – a tremendous achievement by anybody's standards, yet so many were ready to castigate the side for failing to complete a three, or even more ludicrously, a four timer. The truth of the matter was that the treble was denied them only in the Final of the Coca-Cola Cup when an on-form Aston Villa met a below par United. Any United follower knew before the season started that success in Europe was not attainable but to hear Alan Hansen saying on television that, because they failed in Europe, they had failed to show they were as good as the Liverpool team that had dominated the European scene took some swallowing. The Liverpool teams he referred to would have had as much chance of victory in Europe under the present rules as the current United squad – zero. For the Anfield Reds had even more "foreign" players in their squad such as Dalglish, Souness, Case, Heighway, Toshack, and Hansen himself. United, with Hughes, Giggs, Keane, Irwin, and McClair, in addition to Schmeichel, Cantona and Kanchelskis. all classed as foreigners were never going to trouble the top European teams. The surprise was going out to Galatasary after gaining an early two goal lead. But on the night the Turks played well at Old Trafford and have beaten some mighty names in their own intimidating back yard. Unless the top clubs are successful in getting the present ridiculous European rules changed. United will have to buy English.

All that said. United in 1993-94 lost only four league games, the club's best since 1906 when they also lost just four games in a 38 match programme but only finished in second spot. four points behind Second Division champions Bristol City! In addition, they became the only club to ever win the championship and reach both domestic cup finals in the same season and made their record six major trophies in five years.

United started strongly in the League and from early on seemed likely to justify the bookies apparently ridiculous odds of 7-4 against the Reds winning the League. However silly the odds looked in August, the layers don't often get it wrong and they were proved to be right on the ball before the end of the season. Having fielded a weakened team in the Coca Cola Cup against Stoke and lost in the first leg. United's feelings towards this competition were significantly changed by the dismissal from Europe at the hands of Galatasary. It now figured on the Red's hit list. For a long time, the retention of the FA Carling Premiership title looked to be a foregone conclusion as the Reds strung together a run of 22 matches unbeaten in the League in between Chelsea inflicting the first defeat of the season on the Reds at Stamford Bridge in September and the second campaign reversal in the return encounter at Old Trafford in March. Indeed, United during October and November looked unstoppable as they chalked up eight wins on the bounce before being suffocated by an Ipswich Town side that never ventured out of their own half in Old Trafford's worst game of the season.

The Ipswich performance, however, was significant in that better teams suddenly realised that United could be human after all and chinks suddenly began to appear. Norwich showed what could be achieved when they attacked United to force a very creditable 2-2 draw at Old Trafford and Newcastle followed up at St James' Park by securing their second 1-1 draw of the season against the Reds. Two games later, United were somewhat fortunate to keep their unbeaten run intact when Blackburn had all but beaten them until Ince scored a last gasp equaliser with only his second goal of the campaign – his first had been the point clincher at Newcastle a few days earlier! Leeds gave a New Year's Day defensive display almost as boring as Ipswich's had been except that the Yorkshire side's tactics were more difficult to understand as victory was their last chance of keeping in with even a slim chance of the title. The next game saw United squander a three goal lead at Liverpool and United had taken just 18 points from 30 since the failure to break down Ipswich.

Nerves were definitely beginning to show as United moved into FA Cup action against Sheffield United and Hughes, after being provoked for most of the game, got himself sent off for retaliation close to the end of a game he had won with the only goal. With the hindsight of what was to develop later, it was significant that Alex Ferguson supported his player when, in truth, it was an act of reckless folly that had resulted in Hughes' dismissal. It quickly became apparent that United's players felt they had their manager's blessing to react to provocation – certainly they suddenly needed very little niggling to become involved in situations that two months earlier they would have walked away from. Progress, however, had also been made in the Coca Cola Cup with the defeat by Stoke City, being overcome in the second leg at Old Trafford. In fact, after the Stoke reverse United were to play another 35 games before tasting defeat again. United's run in the League Cup saw them comprehensively dismiss Leicester City and then Everton. But after the League scares of December and January followed by the Hughes dismissal, United were to receive another shock when Portsmouth held the Reds at Old Trafford in the fifth round of the Coca Cola. Within days, Sir Matt Busby had passed away and that sad event seemed at last to galvanise United with victories against Everton and Queens Park Rangers in the League, a replay success over Portsmouth followed by a Semi Final first leg Coca Cola Cup victory at the expense of Sheffield Wednesday and FA Cup successes over Norwich and Wimbledon. The treble, once thought impossible, now seemed very much on the cards.

February ended with Ince once again grabbing a last ditch equaliser, this time at his former club West Ham United on his first return to Upton Park since joining United. It was thought at the time that this latest escape was proof of just how resilient the team were and, sure enough, as March opened, United reached Wembley with an awesome display against Sheffield Wednesday in a 4-1 second leg Coca Cola Cup victory. United fans, and no doubt the players too, were full of themselves that night. What they didn't know was that their problems were just about to begin!

The 5th March saw Chelsea arrive at Old Trafford. Although in a lowly position in the Premiership, the London side were making steady progress in the FA Cup and were the only team to have lowered United's colours in the FA Premiership. Amazingly, lightning was to strike twice, with Chelsea not only winning 1-0 again but the goalscorer being the same Gavin Peacock! In the next game, an FA Cup tie against Charlton Athletic, Peter Schmeichel was sensationally dismissed when, without needing to do so, he ran a long way out of his goal area before bringing down a Charlton player. The indiscretion cost him a place in the Coca Cola final. A 5-0 victory over a weakened Sheffield Wednesday steadied the nerves again but it was only the calm before the storm.

There could not have been a bigger gap in the FA Premiership between United and Swindon Town when the Reds visited the County Ground for the first time ever in a League match. It was obviously an away banker but, unfortunately for United, somebody had forgotten to read the script to the Swindon players. United were grateful to hang on for a point at the end but, even worse, had seen Eric Cantona dismissed for stamping on an opponent to become the second United player to be dismissed in three games. Three days later, Cantona was off again after being booked twice at Highbury against Arsenal. This time, it was universally accepted that he was extremely unfortunate with the second booking as he definitely appeared to be jumping out of the way of a lunging tackle from Adams but the question has to be asked as to why he was not substituted after the first caution given the previous week's events. So it was now three United dismissals in four games, an unheard of figure in United history and definitely not the warm up needed for the Coca Cola Cup Final against Aston Villa.

With two dismissals against him in the previous two matches, it was hardly surprising that Cantona did not light up Wembley, indeed he appeared frightened to be in the action in case he notched a hat-trick of the wrong type. One could not help but think that the events of the previous few games had taken their toll on United and it was a lack lustre display that conceded the treble. But there was to be one final kick in the teeth for United. With Cantona subdued and Schmeichel missing due to suspension, Kanchelskis became United's third foreign player to be dismissed and United's fourth dismissal in five games when he was shown the red card for a hand ball offence in the dying seconds of the game. United must have thought the World was against them.

If March had been a bad month, April started just as disastrously with a defeat at nearest rivals Blackburn Rovers. Alan Shearer's two goals proved the difference and people began to wonder if United's failure to sign him from Southampton would return to haunt them. Not so much for the goals he would undoubtedly have scored for the Reds but for the goals he wouldn't have been able to score for Rovers had he been at Old Trafford. Shearer had netted almost half of Rovers' goals on the day they beat the Reds. United's 16 point lead in January had now been whittled away to the stage that if Rovers won their game in hand they would be level and United were left with what looked to be the more difficult run in. Alex Ferguson responded by saying the pressure that had been United's was now Blackburn's and that it would be interesting to see how they coped. Nobody believed him but he was to be proved right. As Shearer's goals dried up so their challenge faltered. With a lot of league football still to be played, United now had a little matter of an FA Cup semi-final at Wembley against Oldham Athletic to contend with. Still goalless after ninety minutes, Schmeichel dropped the ball in extra time to gift Oldham the lead, an advantage they held until injury time. Even then, there didn't seem much danger as McClair hooked the ball, more in hope than anything else, towards where he thought Hughes might be. The Welshman proceeded to score a stunning goal with a volley right out of the top drawer that not only saved the game but probably United's season. After six weeks of seeing their dreams crumbling, United were suddenly given a lifeline which they grabbed with both hands. From that moment on, very little went wrong for the Reds.

Kanchelskis, suspended from the first game, destroyed Oldham in the replay to book a date with United's tormentors in chief, Chelsea. Meanwhile, Blackburn were, as Alex Ferguson had suggested, finding it difficult to cope with the pressure. They were given a good hiding by Wimbledon, lost at Southampton, and could only manage a point at home to Queens Park Rangers. True, United also slipped up at Wimbledon but there were fine wins over Manchester City, Leeds United and Ipswich Town to restore a breathing space. Blackburn's poor run-in continued with defeat at Coventry City and the title stayed at Old Trafford with two games to spare. Strangely, it was exactly a year to the day, 2nd May, that United had been handed the 1992-93 Championship without playing when Oldham Athletic defeated Aston Villa. United's next day defeat of Southampton gave them the top flight's all time record number of points and, by now, even BBC's Alan Hansen was forced to admit the team had a bit of something special. There was, however, still an old score to settle with Chelsea.

United were after the double but the London side were after their own treble. Having beaten the Reds twice in the League they were intent on becoming the first side since 1954-55 to inflict three defeats on the Old Trafford outfit in the League and FA Cup – the last team almost forty years ago to achieve this had been Manchester City. But the pendulum of luck that had seemingly deserted United in March and early April had now swung decidedly back in their favour. Outplayed in the first half they were grateful to see Pallister clear off the line and breathed a huge sigh of relief when Peacock's shot smacked Schmeichel's crossbar. Chelsea had had their chance but the extent to which they were punished for failing to accept it was totally unjust. Two penalties from Cantona put the game out of their reach and they collapsed but the 4-0 scoreline was a harsh price to pay for a side that had pushed the favourites every inch of the way for an hour.

At the end of the day, United were just one match from completing a historic treble but as the rain beat down on Wembley and the team's celebrations at completing the double, surely there was somebody up there in the heavens wearing a satisfied smile. It was a fitting tribute to Sir Matt Busby that the club should achieve the double for the first time in the year of his passing.

Despite the success, however, Old Trafford would never be quite the same. There was the announcement that Bryan Robson would be taking up one of the numerous Player/Manager roles he had been offered and, sadly, the biggest Old Trafford name of all would no longer be with us – Sir Matt Busby.

# 'Red Devils' Diary 1993-94

*25th*    United go down 2-0 to Arsenal in South Africa but worse still is the South African referee's decision to dismiss Bryan Robson for something the player said. The referee's appalling performance prompts manager Alex Ferguson to say *"I don't know what Robson said to the referee but whatever it was, it was worth it."*

*28th*    United draw 1-1 in South Africa with Kaiser Chiefs. Dion Dublin scores his first goal since breaking his leg ten months previously.

## August

*2nd*    Record signing Roy Keane makes a disappointing home debut in the friendly against Benfica to commorate the 25th anniversary of United's success over the Portuguese team at Wembley in the 1968 European Cup Final. The £3.75m buy looks far from fit in a 1-0 defeat.

*4th*    Keane is left out of United's starting line up against Celtic but gets on as a second half substitute. He looks in better shape but manager Alex Ferguson misses the game due to a virus. United win 1-0 with an Andrei Kanchelskis shot deflecting off Celtic defender Dariusz Wdowdzyk past Pat Bonner. Ryan Giggs suffers a freak accident in the dressing room when he bends down to fasten his boot and Clayton Blackmore kicks him in the face as he chooses the same moment to do a leg stretch. Giggs needs two stitches above his eye.

*7th*    United take the FA Charity Shield in a penalty shoot out after a classic encounter finishes 1-1. The club also announce that Denis Irwin has signed a new three year contract.

*8th*    United win their second trophy of the weekend when their Under-19s take the prestigious Sunderland Soccer Festival. They defeat Werder Bremen 4-0 and Feyenoord 5-2 to capture the City of Sunderland Challenge Cup. Paul Scholes is voted Player of the Tournament as well as lifting the Top Scorer of the Tournament award.

*9th*    Steve Bruce receives the inaugural FA Carling Premiership No.1 Award. The prize is for the player, official or supporter who is adjudged to have made the biggest impact on the League – Bruce takes the award for his "leadership and commitment". United announce their "squad numbers" with Bryan Robson losing his favourite number 7 – he is to wear the number 12. A sign of things to come?

*10th*  United's first assault on the Lancashire Cup in twenty-four years ends in failure when a side containing no fewer than eight players who made first team appearances in the previous season lose 1-0 in the final to Blackpool. Scholes who was on top of the world two days earlier comes down to earth with a bump – he is taken to hospital having fractured both cheekbones. United's first team beat Brondby 2-0 in Denmark in yet another pre-season friendly in a game that is part of the Peter Schmeichel transfer deal.

*15th*  United win their first game in defence of their championship when they outplay Norwich at Carrow Road: 2-0.

*16th*  FIFA announce that they are banning Bryan Robson for two matches as a result of his sending off in South Africa. This despite a plea from the South African FA that they felt the sending off was sufficient punishment.

*17th*  United let it be known that they will accept offers in the region of £750,000 for their manager's son Darren Ferguson who made 15 appearances in the previous season's Championship side. Oldham are interested but only as a loan deal which is not allowed by the FA Premier League.

*18th*  United are presented with the inaugural FA Premier League Championship flag prior to their game with Sheffield United. They celebrate by winning 3-0. After his flop in his home debut against Benfica, Roy Keane makes a much more favourable impression in his first Old Trafford league match, scoring twice.

*21st*  Paul Ince is presented with his Supporters' Player of the Year award before the game with Newcastle United which ends in a 1-1 draw.

*23rd*  The bookies drop the odds on United to keep their title to as low as 5-4 after a stunning 2-1 win over Aston Villa.

*28th*  Cantona returns to United's line up for the first time this season for the match against Southampton after playing for France in midweek without suffering any reaction to the knee injury that had kept him sidelined. He scores with a precision lob, United win 3-1.

## September

*1st*  Pat McGibbon, who has yet to play in the first team, is named in the Northern Ireland squad to play Latvia in a World Cup qualifier. The club receive a slap on the wrist from the FA over United's decision to withdraw, along with Leeds United, nine players from England's Youth tour of Scandinavia at the end of last season. The mildness of the punishment – merely a warning about their future conduct – suggests that the FA tribunal agreed with the two clubs defence that they were only acting in the best interests of the players. 15 out of 32 boys at Lilleshall Scool of Excellence had failed medicals due to stress fractures of the spine having played too much soccer.

*4th*    Alex Ferguson is named as the FA Premier League's Manager of the Month for August after his side's blistering start to the new campaign. He wins a cheque for £750 plus a magnum of champagne.

*8th*    United have no fewer than eleven players on World Cup duty for seven different countries.

*11th*    United lose a competitive game for the first time this season as they stumble to a 1-0 defeat to Chelsea at Stamford Bridge. It is their first league defeat for six months and dashes the hopes of supporters who had backed the Reds to go through the season unbeaten. The bookies had originally offered 2,000-1 against the feat but the sheer weight of money had forced those odds down to just 12-1 in recent weeks.

*15th*    Alex Ferguson says *"I don't even want to talk about it"* when asked if he would be interested in becoming Scotland's manager after the resignation of Andy Roxburgh.

*20th*    Alex Ferguson announces that Brian McClair, who made 41 appearances in last season's Championship side, would make his first start of the season in the following day's Coca-Cola cup-tie at Stoke.

*21st*    Manchester United lose 2-1 to Stoke City of the First Division.

*22nd*    The Football League issues a statement saying they are to ask United for an explanation of the wholesale changes to their team for the Coca-Cola cup-tie the previous night. Only four of the team that beat Arsenal three days earlier to go top of the league turned out in the cup-tie. Ferguson says *"I don't anticipate any problems with an inquiry – I fielded ten internationals"*.

*23rd*    Former United inside forward, Tommy Bogan, dies aged 73 on Wilmslow Golf Course after a heart attack. Bogan played for the Reds in 1949/50 after moving from Celtic and went on to Preston, Blackburn and Southampton.

*24th*    United announce they are to offer Brian McClair a new three year contract which the player indicates he will certainly accept. Sheffield Wednesday make an approach for forgotten 1990 FA Cup Final hero, Lee Martin.

*27th*    United announce they are to offer Alex Ferguson an undisclosed, but massive, pay rise in a new four year contract.

**1st**     In a draw that they think favourable United are paired with the Turkish champions Galatasary in the next stage of their European assault. The Turks captured their league title on goal difference by winning their last game 8-0 away to cause a storm of controversy. Cork City secretary Bill Kenny warns United *"It is very intimidating in Instanbul"* – Cork had lost their second leg game there 1-0.

**4th**     Older United fans are shattered by the death of *"Six foot two, eyes of blue, Big Jim Holton's after you"* at the age of 42. He had been signed from the relative obscurity of Shrewsbury Town for £80,000 in 1973 by Tommy Docherty and went on to win 15 Scottish caps. His career was virtually ended by a broken leg in United's Division Two Championship side although he went on to play for Sunderland and Coventry City. On retiring from the game he had taken over a pub. He was thought to have suffered a heart attack when returning home in his car from a training run.

**6th**     United reveal record breaking profits topping £8m before the buying of players. This profit was achieved on a turnover of £25m with the accounts showing the Reds had more than £7m in the bank. The actual profit after transfers was £4.25m and with dividends of 19.5p a share being announced, Chairman Martin Edwards stands to pick up a dividend pay out of £287,000 in addition to his salary.

**7th**     United announce they have given new five year deals to Ryan Giggs and Lee Sharpe which are thought to put the youngsters into the £6,000 a week bracket.

**9th**     Old Trafford earns the nickname "Sold Trafford" with yet another sell out – only this time it is for a boxing match as Chris Eubank and Paul Ince's cousin Nigel Benn meet in what has been termed "Judgement Day". The fight ends in a controversial draw.

**13th**     United have four players in action in England's ill fated World Cup game which ends in a 2-0 defeat by Holland. Paul Parker, Gary Pallister, Paul Ince and Lee Sharpe give the Reds a four player representation in the England starting line-up for the first time in over 36 years. The last occasion was in May 1957 when Duncan Edwards, Roger Byrne, Tommy Taylor and David Pegg played in a 1-1 draw in Dublin against the Republic of Ireland.

**15th**     Danny Wallace signs for Birmingham City in a cut price £170,000 move. He had cost United £1.2m when signed in 1989 but made just over 50 appearances in his time at Old Trafford. Peter Schmeichel is

|        | the latest player to be offered a new five year contract reported to be worth in the region of £2m. |
|--------|---|
| *21st* | United surrender a two goal lead to Galatasary needing a late goal by Cantona to salvage a 3-3 draw in the European Cup. |
| *22nd* | United announce that they are to close their membership list as it has reached 90,000. The members have poured more than £500,000 into the club's treasure chest with membership costing £10, half price for juniors. |
| *27th* | Hi-Tec Sports announce that Roy Keane has signed a deal reputed to be worth £200,000 to wear their boots for the next three seasons. |
| *28th* | United threaten to pull out of the Pontin's League as they say are getting little cooperation from the organisers. The Reds are unhappy at being ordered to play their Reserve team games at Old Trafford instead of at Bury FC where they played the previous season. The switch had benefitted Bury financially and allowed United to get Old Trafford's pitch into good condition. |

## November

| *1st* | United arrive at Istanbul Airport to a welcome party holding banners up such as "Welcome to Hell", "This is your last 48 hours on earth" and several more unprintable ones. Two years ago when the Republic of Ireland played at Galatasary the home crowd set fire to the stand housing Irish supporters and stoned the players' coach. United take no fewer than six of last season's Youth team as a flu bug hits the club. The players to hit the big time are Gary Neville, Chris Casper, David Beckham, Nicky Butt, Ben Thornley and Simon Davies. |
|--------|---|
| *2nd* | Both Robson and Pallister are rated "extremely doubtful" for the crunch 2nd Leg game with Galatasary thus leaving manager Ferguson with an ever increasing problem as he juggles with his side to conform to the European rules on foreign players. |
| *3rd* | United draw 0-0 against Galatasaray and go out of the European Cup on the away goals rule as the match ends in controversy. United players are attacked in the players' tunnel by the Turkish police, Cantona is sent off after the game by the referee who says the Frenchman alleged he had been "bought" and tales begin to emerge of United fans being treated horrendously by Turkish officialdom. Supporters, including a 71 year old man, had been dragged from their hotel beds in the early hours of the morning and either deported or jailed. They were told there had been overbooking and the authorities were taking them to another hotel. Their passports were stamped |

"Deportee". Outside the ground, supporters with tickets for the game were refused admission and taken to jail when they protested.

*4th*    UEFA announce they are to hold a discplinary hearing over Cantona's remarks that the referee had been bribed. The hearing will be by the same commision that handed out a five year ban from all international football for club or country at their last meeting to a Bulgarian, Georgy Donkov, after he had alleged bribery and then spat at the referee. Cantona said *"Banning me is simply hiding from what happened in the tunnel. UEFA are very fortunate nothing more serious happened to me or the other United players because then they really would have a problem".*

*7th*    United put their European problems behind them to come back from two down to beat Man City 3-2 in a thrilling 119th Manchester derby. But, incredibly, for the second time in five days United fans with valid tickets are locked out of a game. City promise a full scale inquiry.

*9th*    United send off a hard hitting defence of Cantona to UEFA. Ferguson says *"It's unbelievable. Horrific things happened to our supporters inside and outside the ground, and our players are assaulted in the tunnel by the police, yet UEFA are only concerned about hauling Eric Cantona over the coals."* The Foreign Office announce they have been inundated with complaints by United fans who suffered at the hands of the Turkish police.

*10th*    United Reserves play out a goalless draw with Liverpool and lose two seasonal records. The result dents their 100% home record as well as it being the first time they have failed to score in any of their games this campaign. United announce that Paul McGuinness, the son of former boss, Wilf McGuinness, will be the club's new Director of the United School of Excellence in succession to Nobby Stiles who left to further his after dinner speaking career.

*11th*    Cantona receives a four match European ban which leaves him free to play for France.

*12th*    United are notified that they have been fined £2,260 by UEFA for their fans alleged "unruly behaviour". Galatasary are fined the same amount for having insufficient after-match security and a further £6,748 for allowing fireworks to be set off prior to the game.

United are infuriated by the slur on their supporters who quite blatantly were wronged rather than wrongdoers. United said they would not appeal against the fine but were to make a protest through Government channels at the way supporters were treated. UEFA disciplinary chief, Rene Eberle, is reported as saying *"Before we* would have kicked Galatasary out of the competition, we would have thrown United out for the disgraceful behaviour of their fans"!

13th     The FA nominate Old Trafford as their choice of venue should England be asked to stage a European cup final this season. It is the first time a club ground in this country has been nominated as Wembley has previously held a monopoly. Eberle apologises for his astonishing outburst of the previous day saying that he had spoken out in temper.

17th     Disaster day for the home countries in the World Cup with all four eliminated. The Republic of Ireland, however, go to the USA on the back of a late goal from a United reject, Alan McLoughlin, who was given a free transfer out of Old Trafford in 1987. In France, Cantona gives his side the lead against Bulgaria but they too go out when the Bulgarians hit back with two goals, the winner coming in the dying seconds.

20th     United's third choice 'keeper, Gary Walsh, stars for Oldham Athletic who come under a fierce bombardment from West Ham United in a 2-0 defeat. Walsh, who hasn't seen first team action in almost two years, had answered an SOS to go on loan to Oldham.

22nd     A real shock for United's all conquering Youth Team. Winners of the FA Youth Cup in 1992 and runners-up in 1993 they are humbled 2-0 in their first appearance of the 1993/94 competition by Bradford City. The last time the two clubs met in the FA Youth Cup was in 1962/63 when United won 15-0!

24th     For the first time this season United have cash admission at the turnstiles with about 4,000 tickets unsold prior to the game with Ipswich Town.

29th     Ryan Giggs loses his title as the most gifted teenager in the game and that's official! He celebrates his 20th birthday.

## December

1st     Following intense lobbying of the Government by United, the last six supporters detained in Istanbul without being charged with any offence are released and return home. United's Reserves lose for the first time since February. They go down 3-2 at the Baseball Ground to end a fine run of 16 victories and nine draws.

2nd     United are presented with what seems to be a passport to the semi-finals of the Coca-Cola League Cup when they are paired with the winners of the Portsmouth or Peterborough tie in the quarter-finals.

3rd     Martin Edwards says the club will not break their rigid pay structure for Paul Ince and Peter Schmeichel who refuse to sign new contracts binding them to the club for six and four years respectively. They are the only two senior players now on extended contracts at Old Trafford. Edwards said *"They would be foolish not to sign because we have a good thing going. All the other players have accepted new contracts at vastly improved terms."*

*4th* Steve Bruce's chance of playing in the World Cup Final Stages collapse when FIFA rules that his appearances for the England Youth team bar him from selection for the Republic of Ireland. It had come to light that his one appearance for England B was not held against him as it had been in a friendly and the Irish were keen to enlist his services through his qualification of having an Irish mother.

*8th* Ince says he will be committing himself to the Old Trafford cause by signing the new six year contract on offer. The move leaves only Peter Schmeichel of the first team squad still to sign.

*11th* Alex Ferguson is voted the World's best manager in a poll conducted by *World Soccer* magazine. United are placed third in the Best Club in the World poll and the only British player to figure in the world's top twenty is Ryan Giggs at number six. His team-mate, Eric Cantona is just behind at number seven.

*16th* Portsmouth beat Peterboro with a goal in the 119th minute of their replayed Coca-Cola Cup tie to secure a quarter-final trip to Old Trafford.

*18th* United's souvenir shop announce takings of £250,000 in just one week in the run up to Christmas.

*19th* Bobby Charlton was named in the all-time Best World Cup squad announced at the draw for the 1994 World Cup. In the 22 were two others from the 1966 winning side, Gordon Banks and Bobby Moore.

*27th* The FA announce that Old Trafford has been pencilled in as a venue for some games in an end of season tournament to take place at the end of next season. As well as England and Scotland, it is hoped that Germany, Italy, Brazil, a Scandinavian country, a top African nation and a Far East side will make up the eight nation challenge.

*29th* United beat Oldham Athletic 5-2 to register over 100 points in the calender year. It is also United's record away score in the FA Premiership.

*31st* Alex Ferguson and Steve Bruce both celebrate their birthdays although Bruce insists he isn't quite as old as the boss!

*4th*    Roy Keane's £18,000 Volkswagen Corrado is involved in a 130 mph car chase through three counties whilst United's record signing plays against Liverpool. The car was stolen in Hale Barns and chased by cars from the Greater Manchester Constabulary before Cheshire Police and the Lancashire Police also got involved.

*5th*    Dion Dublin beats England 'keeper Chris Woods to score the only goal of the Reserves match against Sheffield Wednesday. Nicky Butt, however, is dismissed for dissent to become the second United youngster to be sent off in successive Pontin League fixtures. David Beckham received his marching orders in the previous game against Derby County.

*9th*    Mark Hughes is sent off in a bad tempered third round FA Cup tie at Sheffield claiming he was not given any protection by the referee.

*10th*    Sheffield United manager, Dave Bassett says he is going to ask the FA to bring charges of "bringing the game into disrepute" against Hughes and United boss, Alex Ferguson who supported the player's allegations.

*12th*    Manager's son Darren Ferguson signs for Wolverhampton Wanderers in a deal that pockets United £500,000. Mark Hughes' bad week continues – he misses three chances against Portsmouth that he would normally bury and is substituted.

*13th*    Bassett states he is not taking his complaint any further because *"Ryan Giggs has kept a promise to send my daughter a signed photo"*. It is now United's turn to complain to the FA. They are furious at the Norwich decision to allocate only 1700 tickets to United for the forthcoming FA cup-tie when FA rules say at least 25% should be made available to visiting clubs.

*15th*    A disastrous week for Hughes culminates in him being injured and substituted against Spurs. It was, however, almost much worse as his goalbound shot for the only goal of the game quite clearly took a deflection off a Spurs defender. Given the sort of luck Hughes has experienced in this traumatic week, it must have come as a pleasant surprise for him when the authorities decided he should be credited with the goal.

*18th*    Lee Martin, goal hero of the 1-0 FA Cup final triumph over Crystal Palace in 1990, moves to Celtic for a fee to be decided by tribunal.

*19th*    United receive a set back with the news that Lee Sharpe, who has already missed the last five games, will be out for another six weeks

|        | after undergoing a hernia operation. |
|--------|--------------------------------------|
| *20th* | Old Trafford in particular, and football in general, is in mourning at the death of Sir Matt Busby, aged 84. Old Trafford's forecourt is covered in flowers and scarves as the football world grieves. |
| *27th* | Thousands line the route of Sir Matt's cortege which makes a stop at Old Trafford. Players and officials from all over the country attend with Paddy Crerand reading the sermon. |
| *30th* | Alex Ferguson is involved in a war of words with BBC's Jimmy Hill who had described Cantona's behaviour in the televised FA Cup tie with Norwich as despicable. Ferguson says Hill is a prat and that the BBC presenters are the "Liverpool Supporters Club". |
| *31st* | BBC TV announce that they will not be covering United's next FA Cup tie against Wimbledon. They deny it has anything to do with Ferguson's response to Hill's remarks. |

## February

| | |
|--------|--------------------------------------|
| *1st* | A 41 year old man is arrested for taking unauthorised photographs of Sir Matt Busby in his coffin. It is also alleged that the man, an employee of the funeral parlour that undertook arrangements for Sir Matt's burial, took locks of hair from the body. |
| *9th* | Arsenal, Leeds United, and Newcastle United all crash out of the FA Cup to lower Division opposition in replays. The evening before, Blackburn Rovers had also been turfed out by Charlton Athletic at Ewood Park. The bookies' reaction is to cut United's odds for the treble to as low as 7-2. United's Youth team reach the Final of the Lancashire Youth Cup by beating Wigan Athletic 2-1. At Leicester City a crowd of 14,419 turn out to see United's second string in a Pontin's League fixture! |
| *15th* | United announce that Lee Sharpe has made an earlier than expected recovery and is in line for a Reserve team outing at Newcastle only for the game to be called off because of frost. |
| *16th* | Tranmere Rovers take a surprise 3-1 lead in their Coca Cola Cup first leg semi-final tie against Aston Villa to give themselves a great opportunity of meeting United at Wembley if the Reds can maintain their one goal lead over Sheffield Wednesday. |
| *19th* | As United have a day off to prepare for their FA Cup tie against Wimbledon, a late goal gives Blackburn Rovers a home win over Newcastle United cutting United's lead to seven points, the first time since November their lead has been in single figures. |
| *20th* | The latest second favourites behind United in the FA Cup, Aston |

Villa, crash out at Bolton as United beat Wimbledon and are drawn against either Bristol City or Charlton Athletic to contest a semi-final spot. The bookies' reaction is to make United odds on at 5-6 for the Cup and to offer just 6-4 against the Reds completing the treble.

22nd   United's title hopes are given a big boost as their only challengers, Blackburn Rovers only manage a 2-2 draw against a ten man Norwich City. The result leaves United six points clear with a game in hand.

23rd   United's Coca-Cola Cup semi-final, second leg tie with Sheffield Wednesday is snowed off at Hillsborough.

24th   United finally win the battle with the Pontin's League to play their Reserve games at Bury after months of wrangling.

26th   Although United only scrape a draw with West Ham, there is better news from Highbury where the Gunners beat Blackburn Rovers 1-0. United increase their lead to seven points with a game in hand. 18 year old Ben Thornley makes his first team debut at Upton Park.

27th   Former United 'keeper Mark Bosnich is the hero for Aston Villa as he saves three spot kicks in a penalty shoot out against Tranmere Rovers to earn his side a place in the Coca Cola League Cup Final at Wembley. Many experts, however, believe he should have not been on the pitch as he should have been dismissed in the first period for bringing down Tranmere's John Aldridge.

## March

2nd   United join Villa in the Coca-Cola Final with a comprehensive 4-1 victory at Sheffield Wednesday to win 5-1 on aggregate.

3rd   Alex Ferguson is fined £250 by the FA for comments made to a referee after an "A" team match against Blackburn Rovers.

4th   United lose the toss for choice of colours in the Coca Cola Cup Final. It means Aston Villa can play in their normal claret and blue while United turn to their green and gold – their black kit is ruled out because of a clash with the referee's kit.

5th   United lose at home for the first time in seventeen months when Chelsea win 1-0 at Old Trafford. The defeat also ends a run of 34 games unbeaten. A dismal start, therefore, to his Old Trafford career for United's latest signing, 16 year old England schoolboy captain John Curtis who is introduced to the packed crowd just prior to the kick off. United's forgotten man, Giuliano Maiorana, who thrilled the crowd in his eight first team appearances in 1989 before picking up an horrendous knee injury plays his first comeback game in a "B" match at Everton.

| 7th | United's agreement to loan 'keeper Gary Walsh to Aberdeen, who have lost both their first and second choice custodians to long term injury, is scuppered by the Scottish FA who say the Scottish title hopefuls still have a goalkeeper already on their books in 20 year old third team goalie Derek Stillie and that they must use his services. |
|---|---|
| 9th | Eric Cantona's autobiography is released and Leeds United manager, Howard Wilkinson who sold Cantona to the Reds, immediately says he is considering legal action against the Frenchman for certain statements in the book. |
| 12th | Lee Sharpe begins his fight back from injury in an "A" team fixture. Ten man United reach the FA Cup semi-final beating Charlton Athletic 3-1 without Peter Schmeichel sensationally just dismissed just before half-time. |
| 13th | United are drawn against neighbours Oldham Athletic to contest a FA Cup Final appearance. |
| 14th | The FA decree the venue for United against Oldham will be Wembley. United immediately lodge an objection on behalf of their fans because of the extra expense involved. A tribunal decides Celtic will pay United £350,000 for Lee Martin for whom United had asked £500,000 with Celtic offering £200,000. |
| 15th | Oldham do not support United's appeal to play the semi-final nearer the North-West and the FA say the game will go ahead as planned at Wembley. |
| 17th | United announce that they will pay half the coach fare of any fans going to the Wembley semi-final providing they can produce a Coca Cola Cup Final ticket to show they will be making two trips inside the fortnight. United say *"If the FA won't help the fans by keeping the semi-final in the North then we will try to do our bit in an expensive period for our supporters"*. The players, meanwhile, make a recording with Status Quo titled "Come on you Reds". The last time the club issued a record it got to number ten in the charts during the late eighties. |
| 18th | Stockport County announce they are the latest side to be interested in Cantona's brother. Joel and offer him a contract until the end of the season. |
| 19th | The latest player to attempt a comeback after a long lay-off is Clayton Blackmore who starts back at the bottom of the pile in a "B" team fixture against Manchester City. The Welsh international, who had not started a first team game for sixteen months has had a long history of hernia trouble. Cantona is sent off at Swindon for stamping on an opponent. |

| | |
|---|---|
| *21st* | Alex Ferguson fines Cantona two weeks wages – thought to be in the region of £16,000 – for his indiscretion against Swindon. |
| *22nd* | Roy Keane's booking against Arsenal rules him out of the FA Cup Semi-final against Oldham Athletic but even worse is the news that Cantona is sent off for the second consecutive game earning him a further two game ban on top of the three received for his offence against Swindon. |
| *23rd* | Another blow comes to United when Andrei Kanchelskis announces he is 70% certain to leave Old Trafford at the end of the season. He is very unhappy at *"always being the one to be left out for European matches."* |
| *25th* | Ferguson fines Roy Keane £5,000 for the number of cautions the player has received during the season. |
| *26th* | Blackburn Rovers beat Swindon Town 3-1 to reduce United's lead to just three points. |
| *27th* | A bad week for United ends with disaster as they are beaten 3-1 by Villa in the Coca Cola Cup Final at Wembley and have Andrei Kanchelskis sent off into the bargain. Former United 'keeper Mark Bosnich makes a crucial save from Mark Hughes with the score 2-1 to prevent United gaining a late equaliser that could have turned the game their way. |
| *28th* | United shares drop 30p as the Stock Market takes a dim view of their defeat by Villa. |
| *29th* | Better news for United as Blackburn, who could have gone level on points with the Reds had they won, slump 4-1 at Wimbledon. |
| *30th* | After the possibility only 24 hours earlier of being level on points with Blackburn, United go six points clear after a 1-0 victory over Liverpool. |
| *31st* | Goal crazy – that was United Reserves who, just one week after hammering Leeds United 7-0 away in a Pontins League match, blast six past Sheffield Wednesday's England international 'keeper, Chris Woods, at Hillsborough without reply in the same competition. |

## April

| | |
|---|---|
| *2nd* | Blackburn beat United 2-0 to close the gap at the top to just three points with seven games left. |
| *6th* | Disaster strikes for one of United's most promising youngsters, Ben Thornley, who is thought to have suffered cruciate ligament injuries after a bad tackle by a Blackburn Rovers player in a Reserve match. United juniors, Phil Neville, Terry Cooke and David Johnson are |

selected for an FA Youth XI in the annual challenge match against an English Schools Under 18 side. United also announce record half year profits of £7.6m

| | |
|---|---|
| *10th* | Eric Cantona wins the PFA Player of the Year award but his team-mates only draw with Oldham Athletic in the FA Cup semi final and are not allowed to attend the awards dinner by manager Alex Ferguson. United have four players, Ince, Irwin, Pallister and Cantona voted into the PFA's Premier League XI. Ryan Giggs comes third in the Young Player of the Year voting behind Andy Cole and Chris Sutton. |
| *11th* | Blackburn Rovers beat Aston Villa 1-0 to go level on points with United. |
| *12th* | Eric Cantona invites further wrath on himself when he calls referee Vic Callow, who sent him off against Arsenal, *"a little boy"* adding *"I don't think he'll ever grow up"* in an interview with a French newspaper. |
| *13th* | The FA say they do not propose to take any action against Cantona over his comments unless there is a complaint by Mr Callow. |
| *20th* | Clayton Blackmore, "the forgotten man" of Old Trafford, marks the start of his Testimonial Year by being recalled to the Welsh team against Sweden. Bad news, however, for young United reserve Keith Gillespie. After making the Northern Ireland squad for the European qualifier against Lichenstein. Gillespie is ruled out with a broken wrist. |
| *21st* | The first Trophy of the season to land up at Old Trafford comes courtesy of the Youth team who beat Burnley 4-2 in the Final of the Lancashire Youth Cup at Turf Moor. Keeping things neutral was fomer Burnley and United winger John Connolly who made the presentations. |
| *22nd* | Manchester City player, Terry Phelan, says *"We will wind Cantona up in the Derby match. Steve McMahon will let him know he's been in a game"*. |
| *23rd* | Eric Cantona's reply to Phelan's comments is to score both goals in the Manchester derby. Phelan doesn't make the starting line up but manager Horton refuses to say why whilst McMahon is booked! |
| *24th* | Queens Park Rangers do United a big favour by equalising late on to deprive Blackburn of two valuable points. Their goal in the 1-1 draw is scored by Karl Ready, his first ever in the FA Premier League and leaves United needing just seven points from their last four games to retain the title. |
| *27th* | United Reserves win the Pontin's League (formerly the Central |

League) when they defeat Bolton Wanderers Reserves 3-0. It is the first time since 1960 that the club has landed this particular title. Meanwhile, the first team edge closer to retaining their title by beating Leeds United.

28th  United's pop single release "Come on you Reds" makes it in to the nation's top ten.

## May

1st  United record their first ever FA Premiership victory over Ipswich Town to leave themselves needing just one point from their last two matches to clinch the Championship if Blackburn win both their last two games.

2nd  United are handed the title by Coventry City. Two goals from former Bolton Wanderers midfielder, Julian Darby are enough to see off Blackburn. Amazingly, it is twelve months to the day that United were handed the title in similar circumstances when Oldham beat Aston Villa.

4th  Having qualified for the European Cup, United indicate they are considering pulling out of the Coca-Cola Cup to avoid fixture congestion. The authorities are not at all impressed. On the field, United set a new all time record number of points for the top flight of English football when the win over Southampton gives them a tally of 91.

8th  Bryan Robson plays his last game for United after thirteen years of loyal service. There is no fairy tale ending as the game with Coventry City ends in a goalless stalemate.

10th  Andrei Kanchelskis announces he is now happy to sign a new contract to keep him at Old Trafford. He acknowledges the part the fans have played in making up his mind.

13th  Alex Ferguson lands the title of Carling Manager of the Year for a second successive season. He takes a cheque for £7,500 in addition to the Trophy that goes with the award.

14th  United beat Chelsea 4-0 in the FA Cup Final to round off their memorable season by becoming only the fourth team this century to complete the double.

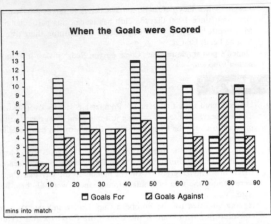

**When the Goals were Scored**

Goals For | Goals Against

mins into match

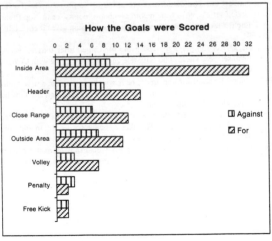

**How the Goals were Scored**

Against | For

Inside Area
Header
Close Range
Outside Area
Volley
Penalty
Free Kick

26

***Manchester United – Double Winners 1993-94***
*The picture that has only been taken four times this century.*

*Mark Hughes sparks life back into the season as he scores a dramatic late
equaliser against Oldham Athletic in the FA Cup Semi-Final at Wembley.*

*Andrei Kanchelskis tries to go past Chelsea's Mark Stein during
United's 4-0 FA Cup Final win.*

# *The Season*
## *Match by Match*

# RESULTS SUMMARY

| Date | Type | Opponents | | Scores | Scorers | Att |
|------|------|-----------|---|--------|---------|-----|
| 25/07/93 | friendly | Arsenal | (n) | 0-2 | | |
| 28/07/93 | friendly | Kaizer Chiefs | (a) | 1-1 | Dublin | 55,000 |
| 31/07/93 | friendly | Benfica | (h) | 0-1 | | 25,000 |
| 04/08/93 | friendly | Celtic | (h) | 1-0 | Kanchelskis | 25,000 |
| 07/08/93 | Char.Sh'd | Arsenal | (n) | 1-1 | Hughes | 66,519 |
| | | *Utd won 5-4 on pens* | | | | |
| 10/08/93 | friendly | Brondby | (a) | 2-0 | Bruce (pen), Hughes. | 15,000 |
| 15/08/93 | FAPL | Norwich City | (a) | 2-0 | Giggs, Robson. | 19,705 |
| 18/08/93 | FAPL | Sheffield Utd | (h) | 3-0 | Keane 2, Hughes | 41,949 |
| 21/09/93 | FAPL | Newcastle Utd | (h) | 1-1 | Giggs | 41,829 |
| 23/09/93 | FAPL | Aston Villa | (a) | 2-1 | Sharpe 2 | 39,624 |
| 28/09/93 | FAPL | Southampton | (a) | 3-1 | Sharpe, Cantona, Irwin. | 16,189 |
| 01/09/93 | FAPL | West Ham Utd | (h) | 3-0 | Sharpe, Cantona (pen), Bruce. | 44,613 |
| 11/09/93 | FAPL | Chelsea | (a) | 0-1 | | 37,064 |
| 15/09/93 | EC1 | Kispest Honved | (a) | 3-2 | Keane 2, Cantona. | 9,000 |
| 19/09/93 | FAPL | Arsenal | (h) | 1-0 | Cantona | 44,009 |
| 22/09/93 | FLC2 | Stoke City | (a) | 1-2 | Dublin | 23,327 |
| 25/09/93 | FAPL | Swindon Town | (h) | 4-2 | Kanchelskis, Cantona, Hughes 2 | 44,583 |
| 29/09/93 | EC1 | Kispest Honved | (h) | 2-1 | Bruce (2). | 35,781 |
| 02/10/93 | FAPL | Sheffield Wed. | (a) | 3-2 | Hughes (2), Giggs. | 34,548 |
| 06/10/93 | FLC2 | Stoke City | (h) | 2-0 | Sharpe, McClair | 41,387 |
| 16/10/93 | FAPL | Tottenham Hot. | (h) | 2-1 | Keane, Sharpe. | 44,655 |
| 20/10/93 | EC2 | Galatasary | (h) | 3-3 | Robson, Hakam (og), Cantona | 39,396 |
| 23/10/93 | FAPL | Everton | (a) | 1-0 | Sharpe. | 35,430 |
| 27/10/93 | FLC3 | Leicester City | (h) | 5-1 | Bruce 2. McClair, Sharpe, Hughes | 41,344 |
| 30/10/93 | FAPL | QPR | (h) | 2-1 | Cantona, Hughes. | 44,663 |
| 03/11/93 | EC2 | Galatasary | (a) | 0-0 | | 40,000 |
| 07/11/93 | FAPL | Manchester City | (a) | 3-2 | Cantona 2, Keane | 35,155 |
| 20/11/93 | FAPL | Wimbledon | (h) | 3-1 | Pallister, Hughes, Kanchelskis | 44,748 |
| 24/11/93 | FAPL | Ipswich Town | (h) | 0-0 | | 43,300 |
| 27/11/93 | FAPL | Coventry City | (a) | 1-0 | Cantona | 17,020 |
| 30/11/93 | FLC4 | Everton | (a) | 2-0 | Hughes, Giggs | 34,052 |
| 04/12/93 | FAPL | Norwich City | (h) | 2-2 | Giggs, McClair | 44,694 |
| 07/12/93 | FAPL | Sheffield United | (a) | 3-0 | Hughes, Sharpe, Cantona | 26,744 |
| 11/12/93 | FAPL | Newcastle Utd | (a) | 1-1 | Ince | 36,388 |

| Date | Type | Opponents | | Scores | Scorers | Att |
|------|------|-----------|---|--------|---------|-----|
| 19/12/93 | FAPL | Aston Villa | (h) | 3-1 | Cantona 2, Ince | 44,449 |
| 26/12/93 | FAPL | Blackburn Rovers | (h) | 1-1 | Ince | 44,511 |
| 29/12/93 | FAPL | Oldham Athletic | (a) | 5-2 | Kanchelskis, Bruce, Cantona pen, Giggs 2 | 16,708 |
| 01/01/94 | FAPL | Leeds United | (h) | 0-0 | | 44,724 |
| 04/01/94 | FAPL | Liverpool | (a) | 3-3 | Bruce, Giggs, Irwin | 42,795 |
| 09/01/94 | FAC3 | Sheffield United | (a) | 1-0 | Hughes | 22,019 |
| 12/01/94 | FLC5 | Portsmouth | (h) | 2-2 | Giggs, Cantona | 43,794 |
| 15/01/94 | FAPL | Tottenham Hot. | (a) | 1-0 | Hughes | 31,343 |
| 22/01/94 | FAPL | Everton | (h) | 1-0 | Giggs | 44,750 |
| 26/01/94 | FLC5 | Portsmouth | (a) | 1-0 | McClair | 24,950 |
| 30/01/94 | FAC4 | Norwich City | (a) | 2-0 | Keane, Cantona | 21,060 |
| 05/02/94 | FAPL | QPR | (a) | 3-2 | Kanchelskis, Cantona, Giggs | 21,267 |
| 13/02/94 | FLCSF1 | Sheffield Wed. | (h) | 1-0 | Giggs | 43,294 |
| 20/02/94 | FAC5 | Wimbledon | (a) | 3-0 | Cantona, Ince, Irwin | 27,511 |
| 26/02/94 | FAPL | West Ham Utd | (a) | 2-2 | Hughes, Ince | 28,832 |
| 02/03/94 | FLCSF2 | Sheffield Wed. | (a) | 4-1 | McClair, Kanchelskis, Hughes 2 | 34,878 |
| 05/03/94 | FAPL | Chelsea | (h) | 0-1 | | 44,745 |
| 12/03/94 | FAC6 | Charlton Athletic | (h) | 3-1 | Hughes, Kanchelskis 2 Cantona | 44,347 |
| 16/03/94 | FAPL | Sheffield Wed. | (h) | 5-0 | Giggs, Hughes, Ince, | 43,669 |
| 19/03/94 | FAPL | Swindon Town | (a) | 2-2 | Keane, Ince | 18,102 |
| 22/03/94 | FAPL | Arsenal | (a) | 2-2 | Sharpe 2. | 36,203 |
| 27/03/94 | FLC | Aston Villa | (n) | 1-3 | Hughes | 77,231 |
| 30/03/94 | FAPL | Liverpool | (h) | 1-0 | Ince | 44,751 |
| 02/04/94 | FAPL | Blackburn Rovers | (a) | 0-2 | | 20,866 |
| 04/04/94 | FAPL | Oldham Athletic | (h) | 3-2 | Giggs, Dublin, Ince | 44,686 |
| 10/04/94 | FAC | Oldham Athletic | (n) | 1-1 | Hughes | 56,399 |
| 13/04/94 | FAC | Oldham Athletic | (n) | 4-1 | Irwin, Kanchelskis, Robson, Giggs | 32,211 |
| 16/04/94 | FAPL | Wimbledon | (a) | 0-1 | | 28,553 |
| 23/04/94 | FAPL | Manchester City | (h) | 2-0 | Cantona 2 | 44,333 |
| 27/04/94 | FAPL | Leeds United | (a) | 2-0 | Kanchelskis, Giggs | 41,125 |
| 30/04/94 | FAPL | Ipswich Town | (a) | 2-1 | Cantona, Giggs | 22,559 |
| 04/05/94 | FAPL | Southampton | (h) | 2-0 | Kanchelskis, Hughes | 44,705 |
| 08/05/94 | FAPL | Coventry City | (h) | 0-0 | | 44,717 |
| 14/05/94 | FAC | Chelsea | (n) | 4-0 | Cantona 2pens, Hughes, McClair | 79,634 |

# The Pre-season Friendlies

United's campaign began with a series of friendly matches which didn't exactly set the football world alight. The Reds, minus quite a few stars, jetted off to South Africa at the end of July. Their season got off to the worst possible start when they lost 2-0 to Arsenal and had Bryan Robson sent off in controversial fashion in a showpiece game in which the local referee decided he would be the star. In addition to the sending off, both goals were the result of dubious penalty awards which Wright converted for the Gunners. The referee was to later turn down United appeals for a spot kick resulting in Robson's dismissal when he passed comment to the official. The game marked the first appearance of United's record signing, Roy Keane who looked far from being fit.

The second game of the mini-tour was against South Africa's top team, Kaizer Chiefs. It was played in front of a 55,000 crowd who were ecstatic as their local heroes gave the Reds a hard time. The first period was a poor affair but approaching the hour mark Dion Dublin scored his first goal since breaking his leg ten months previously. As the game progressed, however, the altitude began to take its toll and the Chiefs came into the game with a late equaliser from Lesanyane.

United's next game was back home at Old Trafford in a match to commemorate the 25th anniversary of the Reds' European Cup victory over Benfica. Only George Best was missing from the team that beat Benfica in 1968 and Matt Busby led the victorious team out before the kick off. When they got under way, United looked jet-lagged and Benfica obviously saw the game as nothing more than a practice jaunt. They made no fewer than nine substitutions during the match and, despite Dublin hitting the bar in a grandstand finish, the Portuguese won with a goal from Mostovoi, one of their many substitutes, after 56 minutes.

United finally got off the mark in their fourth friendly when they beat visiting Celtic thanks to a polished performance from Kanchelskis. Celtic's travelling support gave the meeting plenty of atmosphere but there was no goal action after Kanchelskis had given United a lucky eighth minute lead. The Russian had tried a long range effort but it carried little venom until it took a wicked deflection off Wdowdzyk to leave Bonner stranded. Even then. the shot required the aid of Bonner's left hand post to help it on its way. A bizarre incident at half time left United without Ryan Giggs for the second period. Apparently as he bent down to tie his boots back up, the Welshman was caught in the face by Clayton Blackmore's boot as he began to do some warm up exercises! The resulting injury left Giggs dazed and requiring two stitches above the eye.

After the Charity Shield penalty success against Arsenal, United played their last warm up game in Denmark where they visited Peter Schmeichel's former club, Brondby, for a game that was part of the transfer deal which brought the Great Dane to Old Trafford. Giggs, obviously recovered from his half time shock against Celtic and from being substituted in the Charity Shield, put on a superb performance to turn the Danes inside out in an easy 2-0 victory.

# Arsenal     **(1) 1**
# Manchester United     **(1) 1**

Match One

Saturday, 7th August 1993, Wembley     Att.: 66,519

## ARSENAL

| | | |
|---|---|---|
| 1 | David | Seaman |
| 2 | *Lee* | *Dixon (\*45)* |
| 3 | Nigel | Winterburn |
| 4 | Paul | Davis |
| 5 | Andy | Linighan |
| 6 | Tony | Adams |
| 7 | Kevin | Campbell |
| 8 | Ian | Wright |
| 10 | Paul | Merson |
| 15 | *Anders* | *Limpar (+74)* |
| 17 | John | Jensen |

*Subs*

| | | |
|---|---|---|
| 14 | *Martin* | *Keown (\*45)* |
| 11 | *Eddie* | *McGoldrick (+74)* |
| 22 | Ian | Selley |
| 25 | Neil | Heaney |

## MANCHESTER UNITED

| | | |
|---|---|---|
| 1 | Peter | Schmeichel |
| 2 | Paul | Parker |
| 3 | Denis | Irwin |
| 4 | Steve | Bruce |
| 6 | Gary | Pallister |
| 7 | Eric | Cantona |
| 8 | Paul | Ince |
| 10 | Mark | Hughes |
| 11 | *Ryan* | *Giggs (\*68)* |
| 14 | Andrei | Kanchelskis |
| 16 | Roy | Keane |

| | | |
|---|---|---|
| 12 | *Bryan* | *Robson (\*68)* |
| 9 | Brian | McClair |
| 5 | Lee | Sharpe |
| 18 | Darren | Ferguson |

---

### *Match Facts*

- United's 14th FA Charity Shield appearance of which they have only lost three.
- United's first ever penalty shoot out victory.

### *Score Sheet*

M. HUGHES 7 min – 0-1
I. WRIGHT 40 min – 1-1

*Referee:*
Mr G. Ashby (Worcester)

# Penalty Success at Last

United began the Charity Shield game in great style with a goal after only eight minutes and it has to be said that it was a goal fit to grace the Wembley stage. Irwin crossed to Cantona who chipped the ball back across the goal for Hughes to hit on the volley from a mid-air horizontal position. He might not score as many goals as some say he should, but the ones he does get are invariably worth the admission money – this was no exception.

Kanchelskis continued his good pre-season form with strong runs and was a constant early danger to the Gunners. After another such surge, the Russian created a good chance after 17 minutes for Cantona but the Frenchman screwed his shot wide of Seaman. United were well on top with Kanchelskis going close and Ince firing a screamer just over the Arsenal bar but then Giggs, who was having a distinctly quiet game, sliced an attempted clearance straight to Paul Davis who set up Ian Wright for an equaliser that, if anything was even better than United's opener.

Having given away the lead four minutes before half time, United began the second period looking very much second best with both Merson and Campbell going close. With his side struggling, none more so than Giggs on his first Wembley appearance, Ferguson clearly had to do something and his answer was to remove the Welsh youngster from the fray and replace him with the old warhorse, Robson. United immediately perked up and Cantona left the Gunners in his wake to put Keane in with a chance to restore the lead but the new signing was denied by a fabulous one-handed save from Seaman. Less than a minute later Ince was in on goal when he appeared to have been tripped by Jensen. The referee was having none of it. The same Arsenal player also stopped a Kanchelskis cross with his hand but again the referee waved play on. The match thus ended all square with the referee now having no choice about penalties.

United approached the ensuing shoot-out with some trepidation for they had lost their three previous penalty confrontations – twice in Europe and once in the FA Cup. Ince and Bruce's conversions were wiped out by Winterburn and Jensen and then United looked to be heading for a fourth shoot out defeat when Irwin saw his rather casual effort saved by Seaman. Although Keane and Cantona scored their spot kicks it was all down to Ian Wright whose goal earlier in the afternoon was his 57th in just 80 appearances. However, Wright who some days before had issued a pop single entitled *"Do the right thing"* did the wrong thing, at least as far as Arsenal supporters were concerned, and shot hopelessly wide. Robson stepped up to convert the first sudden death penalty and then Seaman – *"He is usually good at taking penalties in practice"* said Graham afterwards – came out of goal to take the Arsenal reply. It was tame and Schmeichel had no trouble ensuring United went home with the Shield.

# Norwich City
# Manchester United

**(0) 0**
**(1) 2**

Sunday, 15th August 1993, Carrow Road                    Att.: 19,705

## NORWICH CITY

| | | |
|---|---|---|
| 1 | Bryan | Gunn |
| 5 | Ian | Culverhouse |
| 17 | Ian | Butterworth |
| 10 | John | Polston |
| 3 | Rob | Newman |
| 2 | Mark | Bowen |
| 4 | Ian | Crook |
| 11 | Jeremy | Goss |
| 14 | Ruel | Fox |
| 22 | Chris | Sutton |
| 12 | Mark | Robins (*71) |

*Subs*

| | | |
|---|---|---|
| 7 | Efan | Ekoku (*71) |
| 18 | Robert | Ullathorne |
| 13 | Scott | Howie (gk) |

## MANCHESTER UNITED

| | | |
|---|---|---|
| 1 | Peter | Schmeichel |
| 2 | Paul | Parker |
| 3 | Denis | Irwin |
| 4 | Steve | Bruce |
| 6 | Gary | Pallister |
| 8 | Paul | Ince |
| 10 | Mark | Hughes |
| 11 | Ryan | Giggs |
| 12 | Bryan | Robson |
| 14 | Andrei | Kanchelskis |
| 16 | Roy | Keane |

| | | |
|---|---|---|
| 13 | Les | Sealey (gk) |
| 5 | Lee | Sharpe |
| 9 | Brian | McClair |

## *Match Facts*

- Only the second time Bryan Robson had played in the opening game of a campaign in the last five years.
- This was Roy Keane's league debut for United.

## *Score Sheet*

R. GIGGS 25 min – 0-1
B. ROBSON 44 min – 0-2

*Referee:*
Mr. K. Hackett (Sheffield)

**Result of this Season's Fixture**

Norwich City
Manchester Utd

The start of United's defence of their championship was delayed by 24 hours so that their trip to Carrow Road could be covered by satellite television. Never usually a happy hunting ground for the Reds, Carrow Road last season saw the most brilliant display put on by Ferguson's championship side. Indeed, many say the title was won on the night that United brushed aside what had been, until then, a highly commendable challenge by Norwich.

United went into the opening game without Cantona who was still troubled with a hamstring which gave Bryan Robson the chance to stake a claim. Ferguson stated he wanted 25 games out of his midfielder, Robson stated during the course of this performance he was intending to play many more. The former England captain's body may well have endured two decades of punishment but his contribution to a United performance had class written all over it – he was irrepressible.

If United's build up in the pre-season games had been sketchy, then it had to be acknowledged that Ferguson had got them to peak at exactly the right time. The way his side was ripped apart in last season's encounter had left an indelible impression on Norwich boss Mike Walker, since he decided to play a sweeper to counteract United's venom. Playing Culverhouse behind two defenders who only had Hughes to mark seemed to be overdoing things and, in the event, the question was whether he should pick up Giggs or allow Fox to mark him. Fox also seemed confused and both Giggs and Irwin enjoyed themselves down that flank.

The biggest surprise was that it took so long for the first goal to arrive – 25 minutes to be precise. When it did come it was Bryan Robson who made the initial surge forward to win a corner. Denis Irwin swung it over, Keane got a header down and Hughes banged in a shot which Gunn somehow got onto the bar. The rebound fell to Giggs and he gleefully accepted the chance to hit home an angled drive.

The game was put out of reach of the home side after 57 minutes with Robson supplying the coup de grace. Ince cut in to pass to Hughes who, with a deft back heel, threw the defence to open the way for Robson to make one of his typical "Rambo" style incursions into enemy territory. By the time he reached the edge of the 18 yard box, Robson was in full flight enabling him to power the ball, right footed, past a bemused and helpless Gunn. The goal set the seal on an impressive performance that was going to make it difficult for Feguson to discard Robson when Cantona regained fitness.

## League Record

| | Home | | | | | | Away | | | | |
|---|---|---|---|---|---|---|---|---|---|---|---|
| | P | W | D | L | F | A | W | D | L | F | A |
| FAPL 93/94 | 1 | 0 | 0 | 0 | 0 | 0 | 0 | 0 | 0 | 2 | 0 |
| All Time FAPL | 43 | 14 | 5 | 2 | 39 | 14 | 11 | 7 | 4 | 30 | 17 |
| All Time FL/FAPL | 3599 | 1050 | 415 | 334 | 3589 | 1798 | 543 | 469 | 788 | 2436 | 3074 |

| | Home | Away | Total |
|---|---|---|---|
| Attendances | — | 19,705 | 19,705 |

# Manchester United (2) 3
# Sheffield United (0) 0

Match Three

Wednesday, 18th August 1993, Old Trafford                    Att.: 41,949

| MANCHESTER UNITED | | | SHEFFIELD UNITED | | |
|---|---|---|---|---|---|
| 1 | Peter | Schmeichel | 1 | Alan | Kelly |
| 2 | Paul | Parker | 14 | David | Tuttle – *Booked* |
| 3 | Denis | Irwin | 3 | Tom | Cowan |
| 4 | Steve | Bruce | 20 | John | Pemberton – *Booked* |
| 6 | Gary | Pallister | 8 | *Paul* | *Rogers (+66)* |
| 8 | Paul | Ince | ** | Willie | Falconer |
| 10 | Mark | Hughes | 17 | Carl | Bradshaw |
| 11 | Ryan | Giggs | 26 | *Jamie* | *Hoyland – B'ked (*59)* |
| 12 | *Bryan* | *Robson (*71)* | 22 | Andy | Scott |
| 14 | Andrei | Kanchelskis | 18 | Dane | Whitehouse – *Booked* |
| 16 | Roy | Keane – *Booked* | 11 | Mitch | Ward |

*Subs*

| 9 | *Brian* | *McClair (*71)* | 21 | *Alan* | *Cork (*59)* |
|---|---|---|---|---|---|
| 13 | Les | Sealey (gk) | 2 | *Kevin* | *Gage (+66) – Booked* |
| 5 | Lee | Sharpe | 13 | Carl | Muggleton (gk) |

<table>
<tr><td>

### *Match Facts*

• United's 3,600th game in the Football League/FA Premier League.

• A two goal home debut for record signing Roy Keane.

</td><td>

### *Score Sheet*

R. KEANE 16 min – 1-0

R. KEANE 43 min – 2-0

M. HUGHES 85 min – 3-0

#### *Referee:*
Mr. G. Ashby (Worcester)

</td></tr>
</table>

**Result of this
Season's Fixture**

Manchester Utd
Sheffield United

# Keane as Mustard

What a home league debut for United's record signing and certainly the headlines made the most of it with slogans such as "Keane as Mustard" and, in reference to his squad number "Sweet Sixteen". The former Nottingham Forest midfielder scored two goals with aplomb, nearly made it a hat-trick and even managed to get referee Gerald Ashby to enquire about his name.

United's plan seemed to involve Keane and Hughes constantly swapping positions so that the Sheffield defenders were forever confused as to who and where they should be picking up the United dangermen. United took the lead in the 16th minute when a long ball from Ince was back headed by Giggs. It wrong footed the Yorkshire outfit's defence leaving Keane to slot the ball home. Before half time he was celebrating again after Hughes brilliantly held the ball up while waiting for support to arrive. After keeping defenders at bay on the edge of the area with his back to goal, the Welshman spotted Keane thundering up and a deft lay off into the path of his new team mate gave Keane the opportunity to shoot across Kelly in the Sheffield goal and into the back of the net.

The second half continued in much the same manner with United playing all the football and Sheffield doing their best to upset the Champions' rhythm. In the 70th minute Keane was denied a hat-trick as Kelly brought off a fine save but, as the United man turned away he was confronted by Sheffield full-back, Tom Cowan. After an eyeball to eyeball confrontation, Keane pushed Cowan away only to see the Blades defender collapse like a ton of bricks with the result that Keane was booked. Manager Alex Ferguson said afterwards *"Cowan was acting, but he wouldn't have won any Oscars, he was poor at it"*. Much to his credit, Sheffield manager Dave Bassett did not try to condone his player's action in getting Keane booked and said *"Tom was stupid, I have no time for what he did and I shall be having words with him. It might even cost him his place"*.

In the last few minutes, United threatened to turn their superiority into an outright riot as first Irwin and then Giggs almost punished crude fouls with shots that thudded against the woodwork. But the Red's still had the last laugh with a superb coup de grace, a move that ran the entire length of the pitch. The ball was cleared from inside United's six yard box to Giggs, still well within his own half on the left. The flying youngster must have made at least sixty yards, leaving stricken defenders in his wake before unleashing a precision cross to Hughes to smash the ball home at the far post.

## League Record

| | | | Home | | | | | | Away | | | |
|---|---|---|---|---|---|---|---|---|---|---|---|---|
| | P | W | D | L | F | A | W | D | L | F | A |
| FAPL 93/94 | 2 | 1 | 0 | 0 | 3 | 0 | 1 | 0 | 0 | 2 | 0 |
| All Time FAPL | 44 | 15 | 5 | 2 | 42 | 14 | 11 | 7 | 4 | 30 | 17 |
| All Time FL/FAPL | 3600 | 1051 | 415 | 334 | 3592 | 1798 | 543 | 469 | 788 | 2436 | 3074 |

| | Home | Away | Total |
|---|---|---|---|
| Attendances | 41,949 | 19,705 | 61,654 |

# Manchester United (1) 1
# Newcastle United (0) 1

Saturday, 21st August 1993, Old Trafford                    Att.: 41,829

## MANCHESTER UNITED

| 1 | Peter | Schmeichel |
| 2 | *Paul* | *Parker (+85)* |
| 3 | Denis | Irwin |
| 4 | Steve | Bruce |
| 6 | Gary | Pallister |
| 8 | Paul | Ince |
| 10 | Mark | Hughes |
| 11 | Ryan | Giggs |
| 12 | Bryan | Robson |
| 14 | *Andrei* | *Kanchelskis (*71)* |
| 16 | Roy | Keane |

*Subs*

| 9 | *Brian* | *McClair (*71)* |
| 5 | *Lee* | *Sharpe (+85)* |
| 13 | Les | Sealey (gk) |

## NEWCASTLE UNITED

| 1 | Pavel | Srnicek |
| 19 | Steve | Watson |
| 2 | Barry | Venison |
| 5 | Kevin | Scott – *Booked* |
| 3 | John | Berisford |
| 7 | Robert | Lee |
| 4 | Paul | Bracewell |
| 16 | Liam | O'Brien |
| 17 | Niki | Papavasiliou |
| 10 | Lee | Clark |
| 9 | Andy | Cole |

| 13 | Tommy | Wright (gk) |
| 24 | Rob | Appleby |
| 21 | | Allen |

---

### Match Facts.

• Newcastle have not won at Old Trafford since 12th February 1972.

### Score Sheet

R. GIGGS 40 min – 1-0

A. COLE 71 min – 1-1

*Referee:*
K. Morton (Bury St Edmunds)

---

## FA Carling Premiership

| | | P | W | D | L | F | A | Pts |
|---|---|---|---|---|---|---|---|---|
| 1 | Everton | 3 | 3 | 0 | 0 | 7 | 2 | 9 |
| 2 | Ipswich Town | 3 | 3 | 0 | 0 | 5 | 0 | 9 |
| 3 | **Manchester Utd** | **3** | **2** | **1** | **0** | **6** | **1** | **7** |
| 4 | Coventry City | 3 | 2 | 1 | 0 | 6 | 2 | 7 |
| 5 | Liverpool | 3 | 1 | 0 | 2 | 5 | 1 | 7 |

### Result of this Season's Fixture

Manchester Utd

Newcastle Utd

# Cole Fires up Geordies

With United boasting six points from six, five goals for and none against whilst the visiting Magpies had lost both opening matches, the Red legions turned up to watch the slaughter of the innocents. The saying goes that you don't take coals to Newcastle but Kevin Keegan did just that and his new boy Cole proved to be the star of the game.

Alex Ferguson had no hesitation in naming an unchanged team for the third successive game and was rewarded with another gem of a goal from wonder boy Giggs. This time he spotted Newcastle 'keeper Pavel Srnicek poorly positioned and hit a beautifully judged free-kick into the top corner after Robson had been shoved off the ball to give United a 40th minute lead.

Newcastle, however, had been playing much better than their previous two results suggested as last season's champions took on last season's First Division top dogs. The Magpies had not won at Old Trafford for 21 years but nobody seemed to have told them that as they set about United with gusto and a fair amount of creative football. Pallister in particular looked shaky against Andy Cole but last season's First Division sensation fired over when let in by the England centre-back. Keane once again received notification that he is on most manager's lists for being given special treatment and Scott was booked for a crashing tackle on the record signing. The former Notts Forest player, however, still had a great opportunity to give United the lead after 37 minutes when a flicked header from Giggs left him with only the 'keeper to beat but, after his mid-week scoring heroics against Sheffield United, Keane made a hash of his shot.

Keegan's half time answer was to throw more men forward to chase the equaliser and straight after the interval, Cole again left Pallister standing only to miscue. The Reds hit straight back only to find Kanchelskis shooting at the 'keeper with Giggs completely unmarked but Newcastle were driving United back more and more into their own territory with Cole causing all sorts of problems for the United rearguard. After beating Pallister yet again he shot narrowly wide and then unleashed a tremendous cross which Clark only just failed to convert. Just when it began to look like Ferguson's men would weather the storm, Cole finally made them pay when a weak Pallister clearance fell to the impressive Greek, Niki Papavasiliou who set up Cole for the kill.

## League Record

| | Home | | | | | | Away | | | | |
|---|---|---|---|---|---|---|---|---|---|---|---|
| | P | W | D | L | F | A | W | D | L | F | A |
| FAPL 93/94 | 3 | 1 | 1 | 0 | 4 | 1 | 1 | 0 | 0 | 2 | 0 |
| All Time FAPL | 45 | 15 | 6 | 2 | 40 | 15 | 11 | 7 | 4 | 30 | 17 |
| All Time FL/FAPL | 3601 | 1051 | 416 | 334 | 3593 | 1799 | 543 | 469 | 788 | 2436 | 3074 |

| | Home | Away | Total |
|---|---|---|---|
| Attendances | 83,778 | 19,705 | 103,483 |

# Aston Villa     (1) 1
# Manchester United     (1) 2

 Match Five

Monday, 23rd August 1993, Villa Park      Att.: 39,624

| ASTON VILLA | | |
|---|---|---|
| 1 | Nigel | Spink |
| 2 | Earl | Barrett |
| 5 | Paul | McGrath |
| 4 | Shaun | Teale |
| 23 | Bryan | Small |
| 7 | *Ray* | *Houghton (+79)* |
| 8 | Garry | Parker – *Booked* |
| 6 | Kevin | Richardson |
| 3 | *Steve* | *Staunton (*77) – B'ked* |
| 10 | Dalian | Atkinson |
| 9 | Dean | Saunders |

*Subs*

| 13 | Mark | Bosnich (gk) |
|---|---|---|
| 22 | *Guy* | *Whittingham (+79)* |
| 12 | *Stephen* | *Froggatt (*77)* |

| MANCHESTER UNITED | | |
|---|---|---|
| 1 | Peter | Schmeichel |
| 2 | Paul | Parker |
| 3 | Denis | Irwin |
| 4 | Steve | Bruce |
| 5 | Lee | Sharpe |
| 6 | Gary | Pallister |
| 8 | Paul | Ince |
| 14 | Andrei | Kanchelskis – *Booked* |
| 16 | Roy | Keane |
| 10 | Mark | Hughes |
| 11 | Ryan | Giggs |

| 13 | Les | Sealey (gk) |
|---|---|---|
| 14 | Brian | McClair |
| 18 | Darren | Ferguson |

---

### *Match Facts*

• The second Premiership visit of United to Villa Park updated that ground's Premiership record crowd of 39,063, also set against the Reds on 7th November 1992.

• Lee Sharpe's brace of match winning goals was achieved in his first full league outing of the season.

---

### *Score Sheet*

L. SHARPE 17 min – 0-1

D. ATKINSON 44 min – 1-1

L. SHARPE 74 min – 1-2

*Referee:*
Mr. D. Ellery (Harrow)

---

### FA Carling Premiership

| | | P | W | D | L | F | A | Pts |
|---|---|---|---|---|---|---|---|---|
| 1 | **Manchester United** | 4 | 3 | 1 | 0 | 8 | 2 | 10 |
| 2 | Liverpool | 3 | 3 | 0 | 0 | 10 | 1 | 9 |
| 3 | Everton | 3 | 3 | 0 | 0 | 7 | 2 | 9 |
| 4 | Ipswich | 3 | 3 | 0 | 0 | 5 | 0 | 9 |

**Result of this Season's Fixture**

Aston Villa

Manchester Utd

# Lee's Sharpe

With Brian Robson suspended as a result of being sent off in South Africa, manager Alex Ferguson had a quandary as to whether to give his place to Brian McClair or Lee Sharpe. In the event it went to the latter and the decision paid rich dividends as the England winger put on a display that could only increase Ferguson's future selection problems.

This was an enthralling game which had everything from pace to skill, from vision to ferocity. It was end to end but it was United who came closest to scoring when Giggs rapped the inside of an upright when put clear by Paul Ince. The near miss only served to drive United on and they gained their reward in the 18th minute when Sharpe, playing his first full game of the season, latched on to Ince's through ball to tuck away with some aplomb.

Villa, however, levelled just before half-time with a great strike from Dalian Atkinson after Keane had failed to cut out a ball which left central defenders Bruce and Pallister struggling. The finish gave Schmeichel no chance. At the start of the second period, Villa looked the more likely winners as they took the game to United and it was only Schmeichel at his very best who kept them level when he somehow managed to get a cannonball effort from Saunders round the post. From the corner, however, Richardson went even closer, rocking an upright with the United 'keeper well beaten.

United, though, are made of sterner stuff than a couple of years ago and they weathered the storm to set up their own offensive. Sixteen minutes from time another telling through ball from Ince put Sharpe in on goal and again he made no mistake, keeping a cool head in a cauldron of atmosphere to put the ball beyond the reach of Spink for a winner that was clinically executed.

Without doubt, United had withstood the kind of assault from Villa that would have surely over-run lesser teams. Their reward was to move back to the top of the table above Liverpool. Later in the week there was better news still as several of their nearest rivals went down. The bandwagon was rolling!

## League Record

|  | Home | | | | | Away | | | | |
|---|---|---|---|---|---|---|---|---|---|---|
|  | P | W | D | L | F | A | W | D | L | F | A |
| FAPL 93/94 | 4 | 1 | 1 | 0 | 4 | 1 | 2 | 0 | 0 | 4 | 1 |
| All Time FAPL | 46 | 15 | 6 | 2 | 43 | 15 | 12 | 7 | 4 | 32 | 18 |
| All Time FL/FAPL | 3602 | 1051 | 416 | 334 | 3593 | 1799 | 544 | 469 | 788 | 2438 | 3075 |

|  | Home | Away | Total |
|---|---|---|---|
| League Attendances | 83,778 | 59,329 | 143,107 |

# Southampton (1) 1
# Manchester United (2) 3

Saturday, 28th August 1993, The Dell                    Att.: 16,189

## SOUTHAMPTON

| | | |
|---|---|---|
| 1 | Tim | Flowers |
| 2 | Jeff | Kenna |
| 3 | Micky | Adams |
| 17 | *Kevin* | *Moore (+68)* |
| 6 | Ken | Monkou |
| 7 | Matthew | Le Tissier |
| 8 | *Glen* | *Cockerill (*56)* |
| 9 | Iain | Dowie |
| 10 | Neil | Maddison – *Booked* |
| 25 | Neal | Barlett |
| 11 | Francis | Benali |

*Subs*

| | | |
|---|---|---|
| 14 | *Simon* | *Charlton (+68)* |
| 16 | *Nicky* | *Banger (*56)* |
| 13 | Ian | Andrews(gk) |

## MANCHESTER UNITED

| | | |
|---|---|---|
| 1 | Peter | Schmeichel |
| 2 | Paul | Parker |
| 3 | Denis | Irwin – *Booked* |
| 4 | Steve | Bruce |
| 5 | Lee | Sharpe |
| 6 | Gary | Pallister |
| 7 | Eric | Cantona |
| 8 | Paul | Ince – *Booked* |
| 16 | *Roy* | *Keane (+74)* |
| 10 | Mark | Hughes |
| 11 | *Ryan* | *Giggs (*66)* |

| | | |
|---|---|---|
| 14 | *Andrei* | *Kanchelskis (+74)* |
| 9 | *Brian* | *McClair (*66)* |
| 13 | Les | Sealey (gk) |

---

## *Match Facts*

- Denis Irwin's goal was his first since his title winning goal the previous season.
- Lee Sharpe's goal, officially timed at 4.48 minutes was the third fastest Premier League goal of the season to date.
- United's fifteenth consecutive Premier League game without defeat.

## *Score Sheet*

L. SHARPE 4 min – 0-1
N. MADDISON 14 min – 1-1
E. CANTONA 14 min – 1-2
D. IRWIN 49 min – 1 3

*Referee:*
Mr. A. Gunn (Sussex)

---

## FA Carling Premiership

| | | P | W | D | L | F | A | Pts |
|---|---|---|---|---|---|---|---|---|
| 1 | **Manchester United** | 5 | 4 | 1 | 0 | 11 | 3 | 13 |
| 2 | Liverpool | 5 | 4 | 0 | 1 | 13 | 3 | 12 |
| 3 | Arsenal | 5 | 4 | 0 | 1 | 6 | 4 | 12 |
| 4 | Norwich City | 5 | 3 | 1 | 1 | 8 | 4 | 10 |
| 5 | Ipswich Town | 5 | 3 | 1 | 1 | 6 | 2 | 10 |

**Result of this Season's Fixture**

Southampton
Manchester Utd

# Saints Given French Lesson

Having gone back to the top of the table after the win against Aston Villa, United gave a first league outing of the season to Frenchman, Eric Cantona, but it was a player with England international aspirations that set the Reds on the way to victory. Lee Sharpe wasted no time before making it three goals in two games since he came back into the side when he converted Irwin's cross in the fourth minute. Irwin had been set free by a deft flick from Cantona and when he slung the ball over, Sharpe met it in mid-air to volley a brilliant goal. Even before that, Giggs and Ince had both gone close and after 10 minutes Hughes forced Flowers into a great save. It was all United but they then fell for a sucker punch. Cockerill and Le Tissier undid the Red's defence to leave Maddison in the clear to equalise.

It took United little time to hit back as Ince, not for the first time, dispossessed Moore in midfield and his pass found Cantona on the left hand side of the Saints box. The Frenchman saw Flowers off his line and in a flash had sized up the situation to place a delicate "pomme frite" over the Southampton keeper's outstretched arms for a gem of a goal.

United began the second period in total command and after Hughes had squandered a chance, Irwin added to the lead with his first goal of the season. Giggs, in a fairly deep position, picked the ball up and moved forward before releasing Irwin down the left. The full-back's overlapping run was timed to perfection and he made no mistake as he closed in and beat Flowers in the 49th minute.

The home side were now looking a well beaten outfit and United should have made it four when Keane chose to shoot with Cantona completely unmarked to his right and the goal at his mercy. Even the introduction of both outfield substitutes failed to help Southampton's cause and United were so confident that Alex Ferguson took off Giggs and Keane to give McClair and Kanchelskis a run. It was an awesome sign to rival managers of just how powerful this machine is but the move almost backfired on the United supremo when Ince took a knock on the shoulder he injured against Villa and had to play on until the final whistle clutching his shoulder and looking in considerable pain.

## League Record

| | | | Home | | | | | | Away | | |
|---|---|---|---|---|---|---|---|---|---|---|---|
| | P | W | D | L | F | A | W | D | L | F | A |
| FAPL 93/94 | 4 | 1 | 1 | 0 | 4 | 1 | 2 | 0 | 0 | 4 | 1 |
| All Time FAPL | 46 | 15 | 6 | 2 | 43 | 15 | 12 | 7 | 4 | 32 | 18 |
| All Time FL/FAPL | 3602 | 1051 | 416 | 334 | 3593 | 1799 | 544 | 469 | 788 | 2438 | 3075 |

| | Home | Away | Total |
|---|---|---|---|
| League Attendances | 83,778 | 59,329 | 143,107 |

# Manchester United   (2) 3
# West Ham United     (0) 0

Wednesday, 1st September 1993, Old Trafford      Att.: 44,630

## MANCHESTER UNITED

| | | |
|---|---|---|
| 1 | Peter | Schmeichel |
| 2 | Paul | Parker |
| 3 | Denis | Irwin |
| 4 | Steve | Bruce |
| 5 | Lee | Sharpe |
| 6 | Gary | Pallister |
| 7 | Eric | Cantona |
| 8 | *Paul* | *Ince (+70)* |
| 16 | Roy | Keane |
| 14 | *Andrei* | *Kanchelskis (*70)* |
| 11 | Ryan | Giggs |

*Subs*

| | | |
|---|---|---|
| 13 | Les | Sealey (gk) |
| 12 | *Bryan* | *Robson (*70)* |
| 9 | *Brian* | *McClair (+79)* |

## WEST HAM UNITED

| | | |
|---|---|---|
| 1 | Ludek | Miklosko |
| 2 | Tim | Breaker |
| 4 | Steve | Potts |
| 22 | Colin | Foster |
| 3 | Julian | Dicks |
| 11 | *Dale* | *Gordon (+70)* |
| 6 | *Martin* | *Allen (*45)* |
| 12 | Matt | Holmes |
| 23 | Keith | Rowland – *Booked* |
| 9 | Trevor | Morley |
| 10 | Clive | Allen |

| | | |
|---|---|---|
| 13 | Gerry | Peyton (gk) |
| 7 | *Mark* | *Robson (+70)* |
| 16 | *Tony* | *Gale (*45)* |

### *Match Facts*

• The attendance of 44,613 was the biggest gate of the season anywhere in the country and set a record Premiership attendance figure for Old Trafford.

### *Score Sheet*

L. SHARPE 7 min – 1-0

CANTONA 44 min Pen – 2-0

S. BRUCE 88 min – 3-0

*Referee:*
Mr. R. Milford (Bristol)

## FA Carling Premiership

| | | P | W | D | L | F | A | Pts |
|---|---|---|---|---|---|---|---|---|
| 1 | Manchester United | 6 | 5 | 1 | 0 | 14 | 3 | 16 |
| 2 | Arsenal | 6 | 4 | 1 | 1 | 7 | 5 | 13 |
| 3 | Liverpool | 6 | 4 | 0 | 2 | 13 | 4 | 12 |
| 4 | Coventry City | 6 | 3 | 3 | 0 | 11 | 6 | 12 |
| 5 | Norwich City | 6 | 3 | 2 | 1 | 11 | 7 | 11 |

**Result of this Season's Fixture**

Manchester Utd

West Ham Utd

# Hammered

Manager Alex Ferguson scored a psychological advantage over all his other rivals before a ball was kicked in this confrontation with West Ham. With Mark Hughes unavailable for the forthcoming European Cup game, Ferguson left out his No 1 striker only days after substituting Keane and Giggs against Southampton thus demonstrating the strength in depth that other challengers are facing. It must have sent a shiver up the spines of Ferguson's contemporaries!

With or without Hughes, newly promoted West Ham were never a match for a United side oozing confidence and the game as a contest was too one-sided for a neutral to really enjoy. For the United faithful, however, it was another extravaganza of chances created, most missed, three converted. The outcome was never in doubt from the moment Lee Sharpe flung himself in front of Eric Cantona to open the scoring in the seventh minute with a header of such power from an Andrei Kanchelskis cross that the West Ham 'keeper Miklosko probably never saw it.

In preparation for United's European challenge, Giggs played in the role vacated by Hughes and the Hammers had no answer to his scintillating runs. The nearest the young Welsh wizard came to scoring was hitting the crossbar but he ran the Londoners ragged. It was following another surging run from him that Miklosko brought down Keane. If the usual penalty taker, Steve Bruce, thought he was going to take it he had another think coming. Cantona, having been deprived of one goal already by Sharpe, had the ball placed and was in position to take the kick before Bruce was half way to the penalty area.

The second period saw numerous other chances squandered with the biggest culprit being Sharpe who, with a bit of luck or on another night, could have had six. He did, however, make amends with a cross for Bruce to head home two minutes from time to make up for the penalty that Cantona pinched from him just before half-time. The after match verdict from all present appeared to be that the first half performance was as polished as anything since the team began to take a grip on the Premier League title last year.

## League Record

| | P | W | D | L | F | A | W | D | L | F | A |
|---|---|---|---|---|---|---|---|---|---|---|---|
| | | | **Home** | | | | | | **Away** | | |
| FAPL1993/94 | 6 | 2 | 1 | 0 | 7 | 1 | 3 | 0 | 0 | 7 | 2 |
| All Time FAPL | 48 | 16 | 6 | 2 | 46 | 15 | 13 | 7 | 4 | 35 | 19 |
| All Time FL/FAPL | 3604 | 1052 | 416 | 334 | 3596 | 1799 | 545 | 469 | 788 | 2441 | 3076 |

| | *Home* | *Away* | *Total* |
|---|---|---|---|
| League Attendances | 128,391 | 75,518 | 203,909 |

# Chelsea (0) 1
# Manchester United (0) 0

Saturday, 11th September 1993, Stamford Bridge          Att.: 37,054

## CHELSEA

| | | |
|---|---|---|
| 1 | Dmitri | Kharin |
| 12 | Steve | Clarke |
| 26 | *Andy* | *Dow (+81)* |
| 20 | Glen | Hoddle |
| 6 | Frank | Sinclair – *Booked* |
| 35 | Jakob | Kjeldbjerg |
| 15 | Mal | Donaghy |
| 6 | *Tony* | *Cascarino (*46)* |
| 10 | Gavin | Peacock |
| 11 | Dennis | Wise |
| 18 | Eddie | Newton |

*Subs*

| | | |
|---|---|---|
| 13 | Kevin | Hitchcock |
| 14 | *Gareth* | *Hall (+81)* |
| 19 | Neil | Shipperley (*46)* |

## MANCHESTER UNITED

| | | |
|---|---|---|
| 1 | Peter | Schmeichel |
| 2 | Paul | Parker |
| 3 | Denis | Irwin |
| 4 | Steve | Bruce |
| 5 | Lee | Sharpe – *Booked* |
| 6 | Gary | Pallister |
| 7 | Eric | Cantona |
| 8 | Paul | Ince |
| 16 | Roy | Keane |
| 12 | *Bryan* | *Robson (*79)* |
| 11 | Ryan | Giggs |

| | | |
|---|---|---|
| 13 | Les | Sealey |
| 9 | *Brian* | *McClair (*79)* |
| 14 | Andrei | Kanchelskis |

---

### *Match Facts*

• United's first Premier League defeat in 17 outings. The attendance also broke the record Premier League gate for Stamford Bridge which United had set on their previous visit in December 1992.

---

### *Score Sheet*

G. PEACOCK 47 min – 1-0

*Referee:*
Mr. P. Foakes (Essex)

---

## FA Carling Premiership

| | | P | W | D | L | F | A | Pts |
|---|---|---|---|---|---|---|---|---|
| 1 | **Manchester United** | 7 | 5 | 1 | 1 | 14 | 4 | 16 |
| 2 | Arsenal | 7 | 5 | 1 | 1 | 11 | 5 | 16 |
| 3 | Coventry City | 7 | 3 | 4 | 0 | 11 | 6 | 13 |
| 4 | Liverpool | 6 | 4 | 0 | 2 | 13 | 4 | 12 |
| 5 | Aston Villa | 7 | 3 | 3 | 1 | 9 | 5 | 12 |

### Result of this Season's Fixture

Chelsea
Manchester Utd

# A Bridge Too Far

Stamford Bridge proved a bridge too far for the Reds as Chelsea striker Gavin Peacock, a summer signing from Newcastle United, plucked United's feathers. Pre match conversation surrounded Ferguson's decision to leave out Mark Hughes as he would be suspended for United's mid-week trip to Hungary in the European Cup and the United boss wanted to give his European side a chance to gel. It is easy to be wise after the event and so much had come off for Ferguson with his selections, but perhaps it really should have been a case of one game at a time.

Newcastle caused United severe problems at Old Trafford earlier this season and it was a Newcastle old boy, Peacock, who presented them with a new set of problems at Stamford Bridge. Chelsea had won only one game in this campaign under new boss Glen Hoddle, but it was the skill and guile of the veteran midfield maestro that undid the Reds. Chelsea set about United from the start and gave warning that they meant business when Pallister had to head out a Cascarino effort from under the bar with Schmeichel nowhere. Although it would not have counted as the referee had spotted an infringement, it served notice that Chelsea were not going to stand back and admire the Reds, a point hammered home when Sinclair was booked as early as the ninth minute for a scything tackle on Giggs. But then United were unlucky when Kharin raced out of his penalty area to head the ball clear. It fell into the path of Cantona whose lob hit the bar and bounced into the arms of the stranded Kharin as he ran back to his net.

Play switched to the other end where a shot from Steve Clarke forced Schmeichel into a save that he couldn't hold onto and Peacock pounced to put the rebound beyond the Dane. United came more into the game as half-time approached but their frustration began to show when Sharpe was booked for a wild lunge at Dennis Wise.

United began the second period in resolute mood and on the hour produced the best move of the game. Irwin sent Sharpe flying down the wing and his cross met Cantona's head as the Frenchman arrived in the box at great speed. Unfortunately for United the header flashed inches wide.

At the end of the day, one had to say that United were a pale shadow of themselves and were beaten by a team that looked fresh. The reason probably was not hard to find – of United's team no fewer than eight had been on mid-week international duty.

## League Record

| | Home | | | | | | Away | | | | |
|---|---|---|---|---|---|---|---|---|---|---|---|
| | P | W | D | L | F | A | W | D | L | F | A |
| FAPL1993/94 | 7 | 2 | 1 | 0 | 7 | 1 | 3 | 0 | 1 | 7 | 3 |
| All Time FAPL | 49 | 16 | 6 | 2 | 46 | 15 | 13 | 7 | 5 | 35 | 20 |
| All Time FL/FAPL | 3605 | 1052 | 416 | 334 | 3596 | 1799 | 545 | 469 | 789 | 2441 | 3077 |

| | Home | Away | Total |
|---|---|---|---|
| League Attendances | 128,391 | 112,582 | 240,973 |

# Kispest Honved (1) 2
# Manchester United (3) 3

Match Nine

Wednesday, 15th September 1993, Jozef Bozsik Stadium, Budapest     Att.: 7,000

## KISPEST HONVED

| | | |
|---|---|---|
| 1 | Istvan | Brockhauser |
| 2 | Jozsef | Szabados |
| 3 | Tibor | Csehi |
| 4 | Janos | Banfi |
| 5 | Gabor | Halmai |
| 6 | Attila | Plokai |
| 7 | Bela | Illes |
| 8 | Istvan | Hamar |
| 9 | Jozsef | Duro |
| 10 | Istvan | Stefanov |
| 11 | Istvan | Vincze |

*Subs*

| | | |
|---|---|---|
| 12 | Ferenc | Rott (gk) |
| 13 | Ferenc | Orosz |
| 14 | Istvan | Salloi |
| 15 | Attila | Dragoner |
| 16 | Mibaly | Toth |

## MANCHESTER UNITED

| | | |
|---|---|---|
| 1 | Peter | Schmeichel |
| 2 | Paul | Parker |
| 3 | Denis | Irwin |
| 4 | Steve | Bruce |
| 5 | Gary | Pallister |
| 6 | Roy | Keane |
| 7 | Paul | Ince |
| 8 | Bryan | Robson |
| 9 | Lee | Sharpe |
| 10 | Eric | Cantona |
| 11 | *Ryan* | *Giggs (\*80)* |

| | | |
|---|---|---|
| 12 | Lee | Martin |
| 13 | Les | Sealey (gk) |
| 14 | *Mike* | *Phelan (\*80)* |
| 15 | Dion | Dublin |
| 16 | Nicky | Butt |

## *Match Facts*

• Only United's second win in nine attempts on Hungarian soil. The first was in 1990 when they beat Pecsi Munkas 1-0 with a goal from Brian McClair.

## *Score Sheet*

R. KEANE 9 min – 0-1
J. SZABADOS 39 min – 1-1
R. KEANE 42 min – 1-2
E. CANTONA 42 min – 1-3
I. STEFANOV 68 min – 2-3

*Referee:*
Mr. P. Ceccarini (Italy)

## European Record

| | Home | | | | | | Away | | | | |
|---|---|---|---|---|---|---|---|---|---|---|---|
| | P | W | D | L | F | A | W | D | L | F | A |
| European Cup | 42 | 19 | 1 | 0 | 64 | 13 | 8 | 6 | 8 | 39 | 34 |
| All European Comps | 102 | 37 | 12 | 0 | 127 | 30 | 18 | 15 | 20 | 77 | 76 |

# Many Happy Returns

This game marked the return to European Cup action for United following a 25 year absence and to celebrate the occasion there were gifts galore. In the fourth minute Pallister tried to reward the Hungarian's hospitality with a suicidal square ball across the edge of the penalty area and Schmeichel had to pull off a smart stop to save Pallister's blushes. At the other end a Giggs cross was played by a Honved defender straight to Keane who slotted home the opening goal.

In the next ten minutes United could have gone an amazing four goals up. First, Giggs looked suspiciously offside but was allowed to play on with only the keeper to beat but the youngster screwed his shot wide and then Cantona gave Sharpe a splendid opportunity but the England player took too long and the chance was gone. Within a minute, however, a poor throw from the Honved 'keeper gave Cantona the chance to cross but Ince put his header over.

Having seen United spurn these chances, the 13 times Hungarian champions, managed by a Finn and with a Belgian as major shareholder, began to look as if they would make the Reds pay. Schmeichel had to make a couple of smart saves but then Parker made an absolute hash of a clearance to gift Szabados an easy equaliser. The hospitality of the Hungarians, though, knew no bounds and, having got back on equal terms, they showered United with more gifts. Slack marking enabled Sharpe to get up full speed and he left three men for dead before crossing for the incoming Keane to restore the United lead. Then we were treated to a piece of Giggs' Welsh wizardry which sent him clear on the left. He spoiled his act, however, with a poor cross only to see a Hungarian slip with nobody near him to let in Cantona for another easy strike right on the half-time whistle.

After 67 minutes United could have had the tie well and truly wrapped up when, yet again, a Honved defender slipped and let in Giggs on the right. Cutting in, he had only the keeper to beat but unselfishly rolled the ball across the face of the goal to Cantona who was thus presented with an open net some six yards out. Unfortunately, just as the Frenchman was about to make contact, the ball took a bad bobble and Cantona not only contrived to get the ball over the crossbar, he managed to clear it by some ten feet! The Hungarian reply was swift and decisive, although once again questions about the defensive capabilities of United's rearguard would have to be asked. Honved caught United's left side napping to break clear but was there any real need for Schmeichel to race so far out of his area? Certainly Stefanov was grateful his task of stabbing the ball past United's 'keeper was made that much easier and, suddenly, from the possibility of taking a 4-1 lead, United now found themselves looking at playing the last 20 minutes with their noses only just in front at 3-2. The goal obviously shook some sanity into the Reds and they actually began to play with some defensive cohesion for the first time in the game. There was little further goalmouth activity although substitute Phelan must have gone home wondering how Brockhauser kept out his point blank header in time added on.

| | Home | Away | Total |
|---|---|---|---|
| European Attendances | – | 7,000 | 7,000 |

# Manchester United (1) 1
# Arsenal (0) 0

Sunday, 19th September 1993, Old Trafford · Att.: 44,009

## MANCHESTER UNITED

| | | |
|---|---|---|
| 1 | Peter | Schmeichel |
| 2 | Paul | Parker |
| 3 | Denis | Irwin |
| 4 | Steve | Bruce |
| 5 | Lee | Sharpe |
| 6 | Gary | Pallister |
| 7 | Eric | Cantona |
| 8 | Paul | Ince |
| 10 | *Mark* | *Hughes – B'ked (\*89)* |
| 11 | Ryan | Giggs |
| 16 | Roy | Keane – *Booked* |

*Subs*

| | | |
|---|---|---|
| 9 | Brian | McClair *(\*89)* |
| 13 | Les | Sealey (gk) |
| 14 | Andrei | Kanchelskis |

## ARSENAL

| | | |
|---|---|---|
| 1 | David | Seaman |
| 14 | Martin | Keown – *Booked* |
| 5 | Andy | Linighan |
| 11 | Eddie | McGoldrick |
| 6 | Tony | Adams |
| 3 | Nigel | Winterburn |
| 17 | John | Jensen |
| 18 | *David* | *Hillier (\*78)* |
| 10 | *Paul* | *Merson (+78)* |
| 8 | Ian | Wright |
| 7 | Kevin | Campbell |

| | | |
|---|---|---|
| 4 | Paul | Davis *(\*78)* |
| 9 | Alan | Smith *(+78)* |
| 13 | Alan | Miller (gk) |

---

### *Match Facts*

- The win put United three points clear at the top of the Premier League but results elsewhere left Coventry City as the only undefeated team in the League.

- The attendance took Premier League crowds beyond the two million mark for the season.

### *Score Sheet*

E. CANTONA 37 min – 1-0

*Referee:*
Mr. V. Callow (Solihull)

---

## FA Carling Premiership

| | | P | W | D | L | F | A | Pts |
|---|---|---|---|---|---|---|---|---|
| 1 | **Manchester United** | 8 | 6 | 1 | 1 | 15 | 4 | 19 |
| 2 | Arsenal | 8 | 5 | 1 | 2 | 11 | 6 | 16 |
| 3 | Aston Villa | 8 | 4 | 3 | 1 | 11 | 6 | 15 |
| 4 | Everton | 8 | 5 | 0 | 3 | 10 | 6 | 15 |
| 5 | Tottenham Hotspur | 8 | 4 | 2 | 2 | 12 | 6 | 14 |

**Result of this Season's Fixture**

Manchester Utd
Arsenal

# Gunners Hit By Cannonball

The game, even at this early stage of the campaign, assumed an importance that generally only occurs as the Championship enters its final run in. United's defeat against Chelsea, however, had enabled the Gunners to draw level at the top with the Reds, so a victory was of vital importance to United although one suspected that the Gunners may well have been happy to return home with a point. It was against this scenario that the match kicked off at a breathtaking pace with Arsenal adopting the spoiling tactics that they have so often frustrated United with at Old Trafford in recent years and it looked at the start as though the plan to play McGoldrick as a sweeper would again upset United's rhythm.

United, however, now have skill in such abundance that it always seems that just one moment of pure genius will turn the game and so it proved to be. Although it was Giggs and Sharpe who provided the way past the visitor's defence it was Cantona, with a shot that deflected wide, and Hughes with a header that were closest to opening the scoring. Then, after 37 minutes, Hillier obstructed Giggs just outside the box to give the Reds an indirect free-kick. The kick was lined up in arguably the same position that Ryan Giggs has been so lethal at, although he was around the ball when Ince touched it to one side, it was Eric Cantona who latched on to it. If Giggs' free kicks are a cocktail of swerve and bend then this was a positive missile of Exocet proportions. The ball was still rising as it hit the back of Seaman's net to the keeper's right. Even in this season of United's exotic wares, this was a special moment, one of those that the memory savours into old age. As Ferguson said afterwards *"Young Giggs is under pressure now at free kicks!"*.

In the second period both Ince and Sharpe should have added to the lead but both were guilty of poor finishes. Arsenal seemed to sense from these misses that United had let them off the hook and could be vulnerable themselves. The London side now began to play with some confidence and certainly with more than they had done in the first period when United were down to ten men for eight minutes whilst Bruce had five stitches put in a head wound. During that spell the best effort they had managed was a sliced Paul Parker clearance that Schmeichel did well to keep out. In the second half, Campbell was thwarted by Irwin and Schmeichel twice whilst the Dane also had to be alert to prevent Wright grabbing an equaliser. In fairness, however, the score didn't really reflect United's superiority and they deserved their victory.

## League Record

| | | | Home | | | | | | Away | | |
|---|---|---|---|---|---|---|---|---|---|---|---|
| | P | W | D | L | F | A | W | D | L | F | A |
| FAPL 93/94 | 8 | 3 | 1 | 0 | 8 | 1 | 3 | 0 | 1 | 7 | 3 |
| All Time FAPL | 50 | 17 | 6 | 2 | 47 | 15 | 13 | 7 | 5 | 35 | 20 |
| All Time FL/FAPL | 3606 | 1053 | 416 | 334 | 3597 | 1799 | 545 | 469 | 789 | 2441 | 3077 |

| | Home | Away | Total |
|---|---|---|---|
| League Attendances | 172,400 | 112,582 | 284,982 |

# Stoke City      (1) 2
# Manchester United      (0) 1

Wednesday, 22nd September 1993, Victoria Ground     Att.: 23,327

| STOKE CITY | | | MANCHESTER UNITED | | |
|---|---|---|---|---|---|
| 1 | Mark | Prudhoe | 1 | Peter | Schmeichel |
| 2 | Ian | Clarkson | 3 | Denis | Irwin |
| 4 | Ian | Cranson | 23 | *Mike* | *Phelan (+78)* |
| 5 | Vince | Overson – *Booked* | 6 | Gary | Pallister |
| 3 | Lee | Sandford | 21 | Lee | Martin |
| 6 | Thor | Orlygsson | 14 | Andrei | Kanchelskis |
| 8 | Steve | Foley | 9 | Brian | McClair |
| 7 | Mick | Gynn | 12 | *Bryan* | *Robson (*45)* |
| 11 | Nigel | Gleghorn | 18 | Darren | Ferguson |
| 9 | Mark | Stein – *Booked* | 10 | Mark | Hughes |
| 10 | Martin | Carruthers | 20 | Dion | Dublin – *Booked* |

*Subs*

| 12 | David | Kevan | 4 | *Steve* | *Bruce (+78)* |
|---|---|---|---|---|---|
| 14 | Kenny | Lowe | 5 | *Lee* | *Sharpe (*45)* |
| 15 | Carl | Muggleton (gk) | 13 | Les | Sealey (gk) |

## *Match Facts*

• Stoke make it four League Cup matches against United without defeat. United also failed to beat Stoke in two FA Cup meetings since last winning against them in January 1967.

## *Score Sheet*

M. STEIN 33 min – 1-0
D. DUBLIN 72 min – 1-1
M. STEIN 74 min – 2-1

*Referee:*
Mr. J. Kay (Sheffield)

# League Cup Cropper

Manager Alex Ferguson took a chance in this Coca-Cola Second Round, First Leg tie by playing several of his squad not so far used on a regular basis this season. Nevertheless, an observer still had to look hard to find a man that had not been recognised at International level with nine such players appearing over the ninety minutes. Lee Martin and Dion Dublin both made their first start to a competitive match in over twelve months whilst the manager's son, Darren, also made a rare appearance. They found that "old boy" Lou Macari, who played for the Reds between 1973 to 1984, had certainly wound his charges up for the game and United were in trouble from the start.

The team that topped the Premier Division simply didn't look as if they knew each other and Stoke took full advantage, particularly down their right side where full back, Ian Clarkson must have been unable to believe the room he was given until the half time introduction of Lee Sharpe stopped his frolics. Quite predictably, Stoke's opening goal in the 33rd minute came from the right flank when Martin was caught out as Stein cut in. Pallister was left stranded and the Stoke striker, an attraction to many Premier Division managers, beat Schmeichel from some 15 yards.

The half time introduction of Sharpe steadied the United boat and they began to come more into the match without ever really threatening to score. When Dublin did eventually get the ball into the net after 72 minutes, it was the Reds' first real effort on target and it was Sharpe who provided the cross for a downward header. If United thought they had got out of jail, however, they had another rude awakening from the man of the match, Mark Stein, just two minutes later. The goal could have been straight out of United's own text book for specialty strikes with Stein collecting the ball outside the Reds' penalty area, shaking off the attentions of three defenders and then ramming the ball with unerring accuracy past a helpless Schmeichel. It was a goal of true quality and Stein deserved to enjoy his celebrations with the Stoke faithful. What a shame, therefore, that referee Mr John Key saw fit to book the striker for "excessive celebration and possibly inciting crowd trouble".

The last word goes to Macari who said after the game *"That'll do for me, three years ago we couldn't beat Wigan"*.

## League Cup Record

| | Home | | | | | | Away | | | | |
|---|---|---|---|---|---|---|---|---|---|---|---|
| | P | W | D | L | F | A | W | D | L | F | A |
| League Cup | 113 | 41 | 10 | 8 | 124 | 50 | 19 | 14 | 21 | 71 | 71 |

| | Home | Away | Total |
|---|---|---|---|
| Cup Attendances | – | 23,327 | 23,327 |

# Manchester United (2) 4
# Swindon Town (0) 2

Saturday, 25th September 1993, Old Trafford          Att.: 44,583

| MANCHESTER UNITED | | | SWINDON TOWN | | |
|---|---|---|---|---|---|
| 1 | Peter | Schmeichel | 1 | Fraser | Digby |
| 2 | Paul | Parker | 2 | Nicky | Summerbee |
| 3 | Denis | Irwin | 3 | Paul | Bodin |
| 4 | Steve | Bruce | 4 | Micky | Hazard |
| 6 | Gary | Pallister | 5 | Luc | Nijholt |
| 16 | Roy | Keane | 6 | Shaun | Taylor |
| 8 | Paul | Ince | 7 | *John* | *Moncur (+71)* |
| 14 | *Andrei* | *Kanchelskis (+79)* | 9 | *Jan* | *Fjortoft (*55)* |
| 10 | Mark | Hughes | 10 | Martin | Laing |
| 7 | Eric | Cantona | 25 | Andy | Mutch |
| 5 | *Lee* | *Sharpe (*55)* | 26 | Terry | Fenwick |

*Subs*

| 11 | *Ryan* | *Giggs (+79)* | 8 | Ross | *Maclaren (+71)* |
|---|---|---|---|---|---|
| 9 | *Brian* | *McClair (*55)* | 12 | Steve | *White (*55)* |
| 13 | Les | Sealey (gk) | 23 | Nicky | Hammond (gk) |

## *Match Facts*

• Swindon Town's first ever visit to Old Trafford for either a Football League or FA Premier League match. • Hughes' first goal was United's 3,600th at home in the Football and FA Premier Leagues and their 50th goal at Old Trafford in the FA Premier League. • Swindon's first goal was the 1,800th the Reds have conceded at Old Trafford in the same two competitions.

## *Score Sheet*

KANCHELSKIS 4 min – 1-0

E. CANTONA 40 min – 2-0

M. HUGHES 50 min – 3-0

A. MUTCH 78 min – 3-1

P. BODIN 87 min Pen – 3-2

M. HUGHES 89 min – 4-2

### *Referee:*

Mr.J Worrall (Warrington)

## FA Carling Premiership

| | | P | W | D | L | F | A | Pts |
|---|---|---|---|---|---|---|---|---|
| 1 | **Manchester United** | 9 | 7 | 1 | 1 | 19 | 6 | 22 |
| 2 | Arsenal | 9 | 6 | 1 | 2 | 12 | 6 | 19 |
| 3 | Aston Villa | 9 | 4 | 4 | 1 | 12 | 7 | 16 |
| 4 | Leeds United | 9 | 7 | 1 | 3 | 10 | 10 | 16 |
| 5 | Norwich City | 9 | 4 | 3 | 2 | 18 | 11 | 15 |

### Result of this Season's Fixture

Manchester Utd

Swindon Town

# Too Casual For Comfort

If United boss, Alex Ferguson needed to defend himself against FA allegations of fielding a weakened team at Stoke in mid-week, then all he had to do was produce a video of this match for it demonstrated once more the capability of his side to have a lazy Old Trafford Saturday afternoon whenever the mood takes them. Clearly they had underestimated Newcastle United earlier in the campaign and, equally clearly, they had failed to learn from the lesson. This was the home banker to end all home bankers, top versus bottom with Swindon still awaiting their first ever Premier League victory but United made hard work of it despite the obvious difference in class.

As early as the fourth minute Kanchelskis scored his first goal of the season with a low shot past former United reserve Fraser Digby and the crowd sat back to watch the slaughter of the innocents. It was, however, not to be as Taylor, Mutch , Fjortoft and Summerbee made Schmeichel the hardest working player on the park but just when it looked as if the visitors must get a reward for their efforts, Cantona made it five goals in his last six games with a cool finish after he was set free by Sharpe. Thus Fraser touched the ball for the second time in the game after 40 minutes, both times to retrieve it from the net!

Two up at half time, it didn't take the Reds long to add to their interval lead after the break with a flying header from Mark Hughes. Now when you are three down with fifteen minutes to go, the last thing a team in bottom place must want to see is the sight of Ryan Giggs warming up to come on as substitute but that was the view that presented itself to the leg weary Swindon outfit. Far from finishing them off, however, the arrival of Giggs seemed to inspire the Wiltshire team to even greater effort and they obtained what everybody thought would be merely a consolation goal through Mutch after 78 minutes. With three minutes remaining, pulses began to pump faster and heartbeats thump louder as Bruce brought down White in the area to give Swindon a penalty which Bodin converted. Could the unbelievable happen and another goal come in the last three minutes to deprive United of the spoils? There was certainly time left for another goal but thankfully it was Mark Hughes who sealed the match in the last minute. A far from happy Ferguson said afterwards *"It appears the players have not learned their lessons from the Newcastle match – I would have been quite happy if we had not won today, it might have got the message through to them"*.

## League Record

|  | Home | | | | | | Away | | | | |
|---|---|---|---|---|---|---|---|---|---|---|---|
|  | P | W | D | L | F | A | W | D | L | F | A |
| FAPL 1993/94 | 9 | 4 | 1 | 0 | 12 | 3 | 3 | 0 | 1 | 7 | 3 |
| All time FAPL | 51 | 18 | 6 | 2 | 51 | 17 | 13 | 7 | 5 | 35 | 20 |
| All time FL/FAPL | 3607 | 1054 | 416 | 334 | 3601 | 1801 | 545 | 469 | 789 | 2441 | 3077 |

|  | Home | Away | Total |
|---|---|---|---|
| League Attendances | 216,983 | 112,582 | 329,565 |

# Manchester United (0) 2
# Kispest Honved (0) 1

Wednesday, 29th September 1993, Old Trafford          Att.: 35,781

---

## MANCHESTER UNITED

| | | |
|---|---|---|
| 1 | Peter | Schmeichel |
| 2 | Paul | Parker |
| 3 | *Denis* | *Irwin (\*69)* |
| 4 | Steve | Bruce |
| 5 | Lee | Sharpe |
| 6 | Gary | Pallister |
| 7 | Bryan | Robson |
| 8 | *Paul* | *Ince (+79)* |
| 9 | Eric | Cantona |
| 10 | Mark | Hughes |
| 11 | Ryan | Giggs |

*Subs*

| | | |
|---|---|---|
| 12 | *Mike* | *Phelan (+79)* |
| 13 | Les | Sealey (gk) |
| 14 | *Lee* | *Martin (\*69)* |
| 15 | Dion | Dublin |
| 16 | Nicky | Butt |

## KISPEST HONVED

| | | |
|---|---|---|
| 1 | Istvan | Brockhauser |
| 2 | Jozsef | Szabados |
| 3 | Jozsef | Csabi |
| 4 | Janos | Banfi |
| 5 | Attila | Plokai |
| 6 | *Tibor* | *Csehi (\*28)* |
| 7 | Istvan | Vincze |
| 8 | Bela | Illes |
| 9 | Gabor | Halmai |
| 10 | Istvan | Salloi |
| 11 | *Istvan* | *Hamar (+61)* |

| | | |
|---|---|---|
| 12 | *Jozsef* | *Duro (\*28)* |
| 13 | *Ferenc* | *Orosz (+61)* |
| 14 | Attila | Dragoner |
| 15 | Mibaly | Toth |
| 16 | Ferenc | Rott (gk) |

---

## *Match Facts*

- This was United's 50th home European tie and maintained their proud record of never having lost at home in any of the three European competitions.

- Another unusual fact was the lack of any bookings in the tie.

## *Score Sheet*

S. BRUCE 55 min – 1-0
S. BRUCE 64 min – 2-0
I. SALLOI 78 min – 2-1

*Referee:*
Mr. A. Lopez-Nieto (Spain)

# United Head On

Much of the pre-match build up surrounded who Alex Ferguson would leave out of the side to comply with European rules. Kispest must have either been perplexed or grateful, or even both, when the United supremo decided on the two goal hero of the first leg – record signing Roy Keane! United gave Honved no chance to settle down and as early as the second minute a four man move of pace and one touch football left Giggs the chance to make United's 3-2 lead from the first game unassailable. However, the young Welsh international set the tone for the evening by slicing his effort wide of Brockhauser's left hand post. Before another two minutes had elapsed, both Ince and Robson had fired shots off target and then in the fifth minute a Hughes cross eluded three United predators. Bruce was next to go near but he couldn't quite get enough height to direct his header from a Giggs centre. United's approach work, at times, was breathtaking but Banfi, in a sweeper role, was playing well and United couldn't match their build up with anything like the same effectiveness in the area.

The second period began as much as the first had ended with the Reds well on top. In the 50th minute both Cantona and Sharpe confirmed the inability of United to convert easy chances and then Robson fired in a rare right foot effort that seemed to bring the best out of Brockhauser. Unfortunately for United, it wasn't as the 'keeper was saving that for when the assault on his goal became even more intense. Brockhauser was, in fact, now rapidly overtaking Banfi as the Hungarian's man of the match and he brought off another marvellous stop this time from Robson's more favoured left foot. The save was, however, wasted as from the resulting corner, the 'keeper was baulked by one of his own defenders, leaving Steve Bruce to do what his forwards couldn't manage as he found the back of the net with a looping header. Ten minutes later Bruce scored his sixth goal in European combat with another header. When Sharpe was brought down along the left, he simply picked himself up, dusted himself down and then proceeded to drop a pin point cross in the path of Bruce whose powerful downward header gave Brockhauser no chance at all. With the game well and truly over, United began to relax and were caught cold, vainly appealing for an offside that the linesman couldn't give because of Parker loitering on the far side of the field.

## European Cup Record

|  | | Home | | | | | Away | | | | |
|---|---|---|---|---|---|---|---|---|---|---|---|
|  | P | W | D | L | F | A | W | D | L | F | A |
| European Cup | 43 | 20 | 1 | 0 | 66 | 14 | 8 | 6 | 8 | 39 | 34 |
| All European Comps | 103 | 38 | 12 | 0 | 129 | 31 | 18 | 15 | 20 | 77 | 76 |

|  | Home | Away | Total |
|---|---|---|---|
| European Cup Attendances | 35,781 | 7,000 | 42,781 |

# Sheffield Wednesday (0) 2
# Manchester United (0) 3

Saturday, 2nd October 1993, Hillsborough                    Att.: 34,548

| SHEFFIELD WEDNESDAY | | | MANCHESTER UNITED | | |
|---|---|---|---|---|---|
| 1 | Chris | Woods | 1 | Peter | Schmeichel |
| 2 | Roland | Nilsson | 2 | Paul | Parker |
| 4 | Carlton | Palmer | 3 | Denis | Irwin |
| 8 | Chris | Waddle | 4 | Steve | Bruce |
| 10 | Mark | Bright | 5 | Lee | Sharpe |
| 11 | John | Sheridan | 6 | Gary | Pallister |
| 14 | Chris | Bart-Williams | 7 | Eric | Cantona |
| 15 | Andy | Sinton | 8 | Paul | Ince |
| 16 | Graham | Hyde | 10 | Mark | Hughes |
| 17 | Des | Walker | 11 | Ryan | Giggs |
| 18 | Phil | King | 16 | Roy | Keane |

*Subs*

| 12 | Andy | Pearce | | 9 | Brian | McClair |
|---|---|---|---|---|---|---|
| 21 | Ryan | Jones | | 14 | Andrei | Kanchelskis |
| 13 | Kevin | Pressman (gk) | | 13 | Les | Sealey (gk) |

## *Match Facts*

• The win put United five points clear of their nearest rivals, Arsenal.

## *Score Sheet*

BART-WILLIAMS 47 min – 1-0
M. HUGHES 50 min – 1-1
M. HUGHES 66 min – 1-2
R. GIGGS 71 min – 1-3
M. BRIGHT 86 min – 2-3

*Referee:*
Mr. D Allison (Lancaster)

## FA Carling Premiership

| | | P | W | D | L | F | A | Pts |
|---|---|---|---|---|---|---|---|---|
| 1 | Manchester United | 10 | 8 | 1 | 1 | 22 | 8 | 25 |
| 2 | Arsenal | 10 | 6 | 2 | 2 | 12 | 6 | 20 |
| 3 | Leeds United | 10 | 6 | 1 | 3 | 14 | 10 | 19 |
| 4 | Norwich City | 10 | 5 | 3 | 2 | 19 | 11 | 18 |
| 5 | Blackburn Rovers | 10 | 5 | 3 | 2 | 14 | 10 | 18 |

**Result of this Season's Fixture**

Sheffield Wed

Manchester Utd

# Welsh Duo Hit Treble

It was just like old times as United came from behind against Sheffield Wednesday thanks to a triple strike from their Welsh wizards, Mark Hughes and Ryan Giggs. Last season their come-backs against Wednesday probably won them the title. Boxing Day had seen them three down before staging a remarkable fight back to grab a point whilst at Old Trafford, Steve Bruce's brace of injury time goals set the Reds up for the final push that saw them romp home.

Prior to the last campaign, Wednesday had held something of a hoodoo on United and the first half suggested a return to that pattern was imminent with the Yorkshire side believing their lowly position with some attractive football that had the United defence at full stretch on more than one occasion. United, however, weathered the storm and as half time approached look to be getting more and more into their stride with Cantona sending a header flashing just over from Sharpe's corner.

If United thought they had come through the rough waters without damage they were in for a rude shock two minutes into the restart when Bart-Williams put Wednesday into the lead. Pallister had fouled Sinton near the touchline, and when the resultant free-kick was squared to Bart-Williams, he hit it from outside the box with such strength that it seemed to simply power its way through Schmeichel's hands. United, however, have shown they are at their best when threatened and they hit back brilliantly. Keane came out of defence to send Sharpe clear down the left. The strong running winger hit a perfect cross to Hughes who dribbled wide of Woods before stroking home the equaliser. With just over twenty minutes remaining, Hughes made it four goals in his last two league outings when Cantona hurt Wednesday out on the left before nonchalantly rolling the ball into the path of Hughes. The Reds certainly had their tails up now and within five minutes had added another. Again it was Cantona who did the damage with a through ball down the middle that ripped the Wednesday defence apart for Giggs to use his pace and make it three.

A lapse in the United back four saw them concede another set-piece goal when Bright flicked in a header from Waddle's free-kick but, with only four minutes left, it was too little, too late. At the post-match interviews, however, it seemed that Sheffield manager, Trevor Francis has sussed out where his team are going wrong against United. He said *"We keep making the mistake of upsetting United by scoring first against them"*.

## League Record

|  | Home | | | | | | Away | | | | |
|  | P | W | D | L | F | A | W | D | L | F | A |
|---|---|---|---|---|---|---|---|---|---|---|---|
| FAPL 1993/94 | 10 | 4 | 1 | 0 | 12 | 3 | 4 | 0 | 1 | 10 | 5 |
| All Time FAPL | 52 | 18 | 6 | 2 | 51 | 17 | 14 | 7 | 5 | 38 | 22 |
| All Time FL/FAPL | 3608 | 1054 | 416 | 334 | 3601 | 1801 | 546 | 469 | 789 | 2444 | 3079 |

|  | Home | Away | Total |
|---|---|---|---|
| League Attendances | 216,983 | 147,130 | 364,113 |

# Manchester United (0) 2
# Stoke City (0) 0

Wednesday, 6th October 1993, Old Trafford          Att.: 41,387

## MANCHESTER UNITED

| 1 | Peter | Schmeichel |
| 3 | Denis | Irwin |
| 4 | Steve | Bruce |
| 5 | Lee | Sharpe |
| 6 | Gary | Pallister |
| 21 | *Lee* | *Martin (\*85)* |
| 14 | Andrei | Kanchelskis |
| 16 | Roy | Keane |
| 12 | Bryan | Robson |
| 9 | Brian | McClair |
| 10 | Mark | Hughes |

*Subs*

| 11 | *Ryan* | *Giggs (\*85)* |
| 13 | Les | Sealey (gk) |
| 18 | Darren | Ferguson |

## STOKE CITY

| 1 | Carl | Muggleton |
| 2 | Ian | Clarkson – *Booked* |
| 3 | Tom | Cowan |
| 4 | Ian | Cranson |
| 5 | Vince | Overson |
| 6 | Thor | Orlygsson |
| 7 | Micky | Gynn – *Booked* |
| 8 | Steve | Foley |
| 9 | Mark | Stein |
| 10 | Nigel | Gleghorn |
| 11 | *Simon* | *Sturridge (\*69)* |

| 12 | Martin | Carruthers *(\*69)* |
| 13 | Mark | Prudhoe (gk) |
| 14 | David | Kevan |

## *Match Facts*

• This was United's first ever League Cup success over Stoke City. It had taken five attempts.

## *Score Sheet*

L. SHARPE 46 min – 1-0
B. McCLAIR 88 min – 2-0

*Referee:*
Mr. K. Cooper (Swindon)

61

# Reds Crack Stoke Hoodoo

United went into this Coca-Cola Cup tie not only a goal down from the first leg but with the knowledge that they had never beaten Stoke in a Football League Cup match in any of its various guises. It was, therefore, something of a surprise to find manager Alex Ferguson again not picking what many considered to be his best side. After all, an appearance in the Final of this competition still provides a lucrative pay-day but all Ferguson would say on the matter was that he had picked what he considered to be the best team for this particular game. Many people, however, were not convinced and Ferguson had not allayed their suspicions that this competition was low down on his list of priorities.

Stoke themselves were hardly at full strength with 'keeper Carl Muggleton and Simon Sturridge both making their first full appearances. The game was virtually one way traffic towards the Stoke goal apart from the odd foray into United territory but United's play in the final one third of the pitch lacked the vision that Cantona and Giggs supply. In fact, it had to be said that, despite all their possession United looked nothing out of the ordinary and certainly never appeared likely to breach Muggleton's line. When the half-time whistle went with only the minor scares to worry them, the 10,000 visiting fans definitely had the scent of taking United's scalp.

On the restart it took the Reds 45 seconds to put the first 45 minutes behind them with a spectacular Lee Sharpe goal. From the kick off, United pushed forward on the right with McClair hitting a ball into the area. It appeared destined to miss everybody until suddenly from nowhere, Sharpe appeared from the left to hit a stunning volley past the bemused Muggleton who had no chance with the shot from about ten yards.

What should have proved the catalyst for United to explode from however, proved to be no more than a damp squib as the game resumed its pattern of the first half. Plenty of United attacking with little penetration. There was never any danger of Stoke scoring but there was certainly the prospect of extra-time and Giggs was introduced five minutes from the end to see if his particular brand of magic could save United from overtime. He made little impact but by now Stoke's legs were clearly wilting from the chasing and harrying they been doing. Orlygsson could only divert a pass which fresh legs would have intercepted into the path of McClair who swept through a weary defence to tuck the ball away to Muggleton's right and Stoke were left to think of what might have been.

## League Cup Record

|  |  | Home |  |  |  |  | Away |  |  |  |  |
|---|---|---|---|---|---|---|---|---|---|---|---|
|  | P | W | D | L | F | A | W | D | L | F | A |
| League Cup record | 114 | 42 | 10 | 8 | 126 | 50 | 19 | 14 | 21 | 71 | 71 |

|  | Home | Away | Total |
|---|---|---|---|
| League Cup Attendances | 41,387 | 23,327 | 64,714 |

# Manchester United (0) 2
# Tottenham Hotspur (0) 1

Saturday, 16th October 1993, Old Trafford          Att.: 44,655

## MANCHESTER UNITED

| 1 | Peter | Schmeichel |
| 2 | Paul | Parker |
| 3 | Denis | Irwin |
| 4 | Steve | Bruce |
| 5 | Lee | Sharpe |
| 6 | Gary | Pallister |
| 7 | Eric | Cantona |
| 12 | *Bryan* | *Robson (\*69)* |
| 16 | Roy | Keane |
| 10 | Mark | Hughes |
| 11 | *Ryan* | *Giggs (+79)* |

*Subs*

| 9 | *Brian* | *McClair (\*69)* |
| 13 | Les | Sealey (gk) |
| 19 | *Nicky* | *Butt (+79)* |

## TOTTENHAM HOTSPUR

| 1 | Eric | Thorstvedt |
| 22 | David | Kerslake |
| 23 | Sol | Campbell |
| 4 | Vinny | Samways |
| 6 | Gary | Mabbutt |
| 14 | Steve | Sedgeley |
| 12 | Jason | Dozzell |
| 20 | Darren | Caskey – *Booked* |
| 7 | Nicky | Barmby |
| 10 | *Teddy* | *Sheringham (\*23)* |
| 15 | David | Howells |

| 3 | *Justin* | *Edinburgh (+69)* |
| 13 | Ian | Walker (gk) |
| 24 | *Paul* | *Moran (\*23)* |

---

### *Match Facts*

• The attendance of 44,655 set a new FA Premier League record.

• Spurs substitute Paul Moran was himself substituted after 69 minutes.

### *Score Sheet*

R. KEANE 65 min – 1-0

L. SHARPE 70 min – 2-0

D. CASKEY 73 min – 2-1

*Referee:*
Mr. K. Burge (Tonypandy)

---

## FA Carling Premiership

| | | P | W | D | L | F | A | Pts |
|---|---|---|---|---|---|---|---|---|
| 1 | **Manchester United** | 11 | 9 | 1 | 1 | 24 | 9 | 28 |
| 2 | Norwich City | 11 | 6 | 3 | 2 | 21 | 12 | 21 |
| 3 | Arsenal | 11 | 6 | 3 | 2 | 12 | 6 | 21 |
| 4 | Leeds United | 10 | 6 | 1 | 3 | 14 | 10 | 19 |
| 5 | Tottenham Hotspur | 11 | 5 | 3 | 3 | 18 | 12 | 18 |

### Result of this Season's Fixture

Manchester Utd
Tottenham H.

# Reds Beat International Blues

This match immediately followed England's World Cup defeat by Holland in which four United players appeared whilst a further five were on International duty elsewhere. The last time United had so many players away for mid-week internationals they had crashed to their only defeat of the season in the first game on their return. With Spurs arriving on the back of a seven match unbeaten run and Paul Ince missing due to an injury sustained on England duty there were justified fears that United might slip up. Coming in for his first league start for a month was Bryan Robson whilst with Kanchelskis, Phelan, and Dublin all out of the reckoning with injuries, Nicky Butt claimed one of the substitute spots.

Robson was to play a significant part in the outcome of the game as it appeared he had been detailed to mark Spurs danger man, Teddy Sheringham, scorer of over half the Londoner's goals up to this match. By the 23rd minute Sheringham was no longer a threat to United as Robson tackled him for something like the sixth and final time leaving the Spurs striker nursing a damaged knee. Until then, United had shown little but in the 30th minute Cantona looked incredulous as neither Hughes or Keane were able to get a touch to a cross from the Frenchman that seemed to skim across the goal line. Spurs hit back and Schmeichel had to be in his best form to keep out Sedgley with a superb one handed save.

The game livened up in the second half. United missed a great chance when Cantona set Giggs away but when Thorstvedt dived to thwart the youngster he found himself in a tangle with Hughes and as the ball fell free Sharpe blazed wildly over the top when it appeared easier to hit the net. Pallister then joined the culprits when he cleared the bar from five yards from an Irwin free kick but in the 65th minute the breakthrough arrived. Sharpe had moved to his more favoured left wing with Giggs going into the middle and it was the England international who got in a cross which fell into the path of Keane with the help of a deflection. He hit his fifth goal of the campaign just inside the post. Four minutes later United were two up when Howells made a complete hash of his attempted clearance and was robbed by the alert Sharpe, who living up to his name, pounced on the bewildered Spurs defender right in front of goal before shooting past Thorstved.

As often seems to be the case, however, United decided they had the game won and the Reds certainly made life difficult for themselves when they stood back and allowed Edinburgh to set up Caskey to reduce the lead. It made for an interesting last ten minutes but at the end of the day, the best team won.

## League Record

|  | Home | | | | | | Away | | | | |
|  | P | W | D | L | F | A | W | D | L | F | A |
|---|---|---|---|---|---|---|---|---|---|---|---|
| FAPL 1993/94 | 11 | 5 | 1 | 0 | 14 | 4 | 4 | 0 | 1 | 10 | 5 |
| All Time FAPL | 53 | 19 | 6 | 2 | 53 | 18 | 14 | 7 | 5 | 38 | 22 |
| All Time FL/FAPL | 3609 | 1055 | 416 | 334 | 3603 | 1802 | 546 | 469 | 789 | 2444 | 3079 |

|  | Home | Away | Total |
|---|---|---|---|
| League Attendances | 261,638 | 147,130 | 408,768 |

# Manchester United (2) 3
# Galatasary (2) 3

Thursday, 21st October 1993, Old Trafford          Att.: 39,396

## MANCHESTER UNITED

| 1 | Peter | Schmeichel |
|---|---|---|
| 2 | Lee | Martin |
| 3 | Lee | Sharpe |
| 4 | Steve | Bruce |
| 5 | Gary | Pallister |
| 6 | Roy | Keane |
| 7 | *Bryan* | Robson *(*65)* |
| 8 | Paul | Ince |
| 9 | Eric | Cantona – *Booked* |
| 10 | Mark | Hughes |
| 11 | Ryan | Giggs |

*Subs*

| 12 | *Mike* | Phelan *(*65)* |
|---|---|---|
| 13 | Les | Sealey (gk) |
| 14 | Dion | Dublin |
| 15 | Gary | Neville |
| 16 | Nicky | Butt |

## GALATASARY

| 1 | Demirbas | Hayrattin |
|---|---|---|
| 2 | Kaya | Ugar |
| 3 | Reinhard | Stumpf – *Booked* |
| 4 | Falko | Gotz |
| 5 | Korkmaz | Bulent |
| 6 | H. | Hamza |
| 7 | Erdem | Arif |
| 8 | K. | Tugay |
| 9 | Kaya | Suat |
| 10 | *T.* | *Kubilay* – B'ked *(*77)* |
| 11 | Sukur | Hakan |

| 12 | *Keser* | Erdal *(*77)* |
|---|---|---|
| 13 | Korkmaz | Mert |
| 14 | Altintas | Yusuf |
| 15 | Sukar | Arsla |
| 16 | Bologlu | Nezihi (gk) |

## *Match Facts*

• United's 51st home game without defeat in Europe but Galatasary became the first team since Real Madrid in United's first ever European Cup tie at Old Trafford in 1957 to prevent United winning a home leg in the European Cup. They also became the first club ever to score three goals at Old Trafford in the European Cup. • Kubilay will certainly remember his first visit to Old Trafford – he scored twice, was booked, and was substituted! • United's shares fell 44p each when the Stock Market opened for business the following morning!

## *Score Sheet*

B. ROBSON 3 min – 1-0

HAKAN 13min o.g. – 2-0

E. ARIF 16 min – 2-1

T. KUBILAY 31 min – 2-2

T. KUBILAY 63 min – 2-3

E. CANTONA 81 min 3-3

*Referee:*
Mr. P. Mikkelsen (Denmark)

# Turkish Delight

United had been reckoned by many to have drawn the easy option when the draw for the 2nd Round had been made but the Reds were to be in for a big surprise. Their problems began with the team selection forced on Alex Ferguson by the European eligibility conditions and Paul Parker going down with flu added to the manager's decision to leave out Eire international Denis Irwin meant that United were to play without either of their regular full backs. With Lee Sharpe being pulled to left back it also meant that United were without their two normal wingers.

There was no hint of disaster as Hughes read a deep Giggs cross better than anybody else to get the ball back to Cantona whose attempted pass hit a defender to deceive everybody and leave Robson to gleefully poke the ball left footed past Hayrattin after three minutes. Ten minutes later and United's passage was surely booked when Hakan, under pressure from the massive presence of Pallister, could only glance a Giggs corner kick past his own keeper.

Three minutes after conceding the own goal, the Turks hit back with a spectacular 25 yarder from Arif that caught Schmeichel off his line. Just after the half-hour Arif tried to thread the ball into the path of Kubilay. Martin, sensing the danger tried to cut it out but couldn't stretch far enough with the result that he turned the ball past Schmeichel. It was destined to be an own goal until Kubilay applied the final coup de grace.

The team who made all the early running in the second period were Galatasary who were proving to be anything but the easy option. They were duly rewarded for their enterprise after 62 minutes with a third goal that stunned Old Trafford and endangered United's proud unbeaten home record in Europe. Again it was Arif and Kubilay involved with Arif's shot beating Schmeichel but not the post and Kubilay finding the empty net, although this time from an angle, from the rebound.

Ferguson, brought off Robson, sent on Phelan to fill the right back position, switched Martin to left back which released Sharpe to take up his normal attacking left side role. Immediately Sharpe caused the Turks problems and they replied by taking off their two goal striker and replacing him with an extra defender to take care of Sharpe. United however looked more of a team and Cantona got on the end of a Keane cross to mishit a shot from six yards past Hayrattin. Then, in the final minute, United almost gave themselves breathing space for the return leg when Keane beautifully chested down a cross and unleashed a venomous shot at the Turkish goal only to see it heartbreakingly clip the post.

## European Cup Record

|  | | Home | | | | | Away | | | | |
|---|---|---|---|---|---|---|---|---|---|---|---|
|  | P | W | D | L | F | A | W | D | L | F | A |
| European Cup | 44 | 20 | 2 | 0 | 69 | 17 | 8 | 6 | 8 | 39 | 34 |
| All European Comps | 104 | 38 | 13 | 0 | 132 | 34 | 18 | 15 | 20 | 77 | 76 |

|  | Home | Away | Total |
|---|---|---|---|
| European Cup Attendances | 75,177 | 7,000 | 82,177 |

# Everton       (0) 0
# Manchester United   (0) 1

Saturday, 23rd October 1993, Goodison Park      Att.: 35,430

## EVERTON

| 1 | Neville | Southall |
|---|---|---|
| 12 | Paul | Holmes |
| 3 | Andy | Hinchliffe |
| 14 | John | Ebbrell |
| 5 | Dave | Watson |
| 6 | Gary | Ablett |
| 7 | Mark | Ward |
| 10 | Barry | Horne |
| 9 | Tony | Cottee |
| 19 | Stuart | Barlow |
| 11 | Peter | Beagrie |

## MANCHESTER UNITED

| 1 | Peter | Schmeichel |
|---|---|---|
| 21 | Lee | Martin |
| 3 | Denis | Irwin |
| 4 | Steve | Bruce |
| 5 | Lee | Sharpe |
| 6 | Gary | Pallister |
| 7 | Eric | Cantona |
| 8 | Paul | Ince |
| 9 | Brian | McClair |
| 10 | Mark | Hughes |
| 16 | Roy | Keane |

*Subs*

| 2 | Matthew | Jackson |
|---|---|---|
| 13 | Jason | Kearton(gk) |
| 16 | | Preki |

| 11 | Ryan | Giggs |
|---|---|---|
| 13 | Les | Sealey(gk) |
| 23 | Mike | Phelan |

---

### *Match Facts*

• Sharpe's goal, his seventh of the campaign, made him United's top scorer.

### *Score Sheet*

L. SHARPE 53 min – 0-1

*Referee:*
Mr. K. Hackett (Sheffield)

---

## FA Carling Premiership

| | | P | W | D | L | F | A | Pts |
|---|---|---|---|---|---|---|---|---|
| 1 | Manchester United | 12 | 10 | 1 | 1 | 25 | 9 | 31 |
| 2 | Norwich City | 12 | 6 | 4 | 2 | 21 | 12 | 22 |
| 3 | Arsenal | 12 | 6 | 4 | 2 | 12 | 6 | 22 |
| 4 | Leeds United | 12 | 6 | 3 | 3 | 17 | 13 | 21 |
| 5 | QPR | 12 | 6 | 2 | 4 | 23 | 19 | 20 |

### Result of this Season's Fixture

Everton

Manchester Utd

# Razor Sharpe

A drab game was lit up by one moment of magnificence from Lee Sharpe who described his goal, the only one of a drab match, as *"the best I've ever scored"*. Manager Alex Ferguson got proceedings under way even before a ball had been kicked by announcing Ryan Giggs would be on the substitutes bench with his place going to Brian McClair, a signal perhaps that the boss was trying to put the accent back on team work.

The Reds were in worse shape for this game than against the Turkish champions and only Schmeichel stood between them and defeat even allowing for Sharpe's tremendous strike. The Great Dane kept United level as early as the 13th minute when a dreadful error by Roy Keane left Barlow with only the 'keeper to beat. Fortunately the youngster showed his inexperience and gave Schmeichel the split second he needed to close Barlow down and block the shot with his legs leaving Pallister to finish the good work off by clearing Cottee's follow up from the rebound.

United's cup of tea appeared to have perked them up when they resumed after the interval with Keane trying to get in behind Ablett and then Cantona lobbing Southall only to see the effort finish just off target. Then, in the 53rd minute, came a goal as exciting as the match had been poor. The goal came from an overlapping run down the left flank by full back Lee Martin who was making his first full league start of the season. Martin did well to reach Cantona's nicely weighted pass and threw over a good cross. Everton's Watson, however, seemed to have dealt effectively with the situation when he headed the ball away from danger. The defender had every right to be dismayed as he watched Sharpe hit the clearance on the volley from three or four yards outside the area into the net with a stunning goal that will remain etched in Sharpe's memory well into old age. The shot was hit with such power that the ball hit the back of the net before Southall, one of the world's top 'keepers, had moved a muscle.

But Everton were not finished and still looked the better team. Beagrie got past Bruce but then fired over and then, with fifteen minutes left, Schmeichel again saved United. Cottee burst through with only the 'keeper to beat but Schmeichel blocked the effort. The Dane also had to pull out all the stops to prevent Beagrie equalising and, for once, United were very grateful to hear the full time whistle.

## League Record

| | Home | | | | | Away | | | | |
|---|---|---|---|---|---|---|---|---|---|---|
| | P | W | D | L | F | A | W | D | L | F | A |
| FAPL 1993/94 | 12 | 5 | 1 | 0 | 14 | 4 | 5 | 0 | 1 | 11 | 5 |
| All Time FAPL | 54 | 19 | 6 | 2 | 53 | 18 | 15 | 7 | 5 | 39 | 22 |
| All Time FL/FAPL | 3610 | 1055 | 416 | 334 | 3603 | 1802 | 547 | 469 | 789 | 2445 | 3079 |

| | Home | Away | Total |
|---|---|---|---|
| League Attendances | 261,638 | 182,560 | 444,198 |

# Manchester United (2) 5
# Leicester City (0) 1

Wednesday, 28th October 1993, Old Trafford          Att.: 41,344

| MANCHESTER UNITED | | | LEICESTER CITY | | |
|---|---|---|---|---|---|
| 1 | Peter | Schmeichel – *Booked* | 1 | Gavin | Ward |
| 23 | Mike | Phelan | 2 | Simon | Grayson |
| 21 | Lee | Martin | 3 | Mike | Whitlow |
| 4 | Steve | Bruce | 4 | Colin | Hill |
| 5 | *Lee* | *Sharpe (+61)* | 5 | *Neil* | *Lewis (\*75)* |
| 6 | *Gary* | *Pallister (\*28)* | 6 | David | Oldfield |
| 14 | Andrei | Kanchelskis | 7 | Steve | Thompson |
| 16 | Roy | Keane | 8 | Steve | Agnew |
| 12 | Bryan | Robson | 9 | Ian | Ormondroyd |
| 10 | Mark | Hughes | 10 | David | Speedie |
| 9 | Brian | McClair | 11 | Julian | Joachim |

*Subs*

| 11 | *Ryan* | *Giggs (+61)* | 12 | Kevin | Poole (gk) |
|---|---|---|---|---|---|
| 3 | *Denis* | *Irwin (\*28)* | 14 | Brian | Carey |
| 13 | Les | Sealey (gk) | 15 | *Gary* | *Mills (\*75)* |

## *Match Facts*

• The first ever meeting between the two sides in the League Cup.

• United have never lost to Leicester in a cup competition.

• Steve Bruce's goals took his career total of goals to 101 – a fantastic figure for a defender.

## *Score Sheet*

S. BRUCE 7 min – 1-0
B. McCLAIR 9 min – 2-0
L. SHARPE 53 min – 3-0
M. HUGHES 62 min – 4-0
C. HILL 64 min – 4-1
S. BRUCE 86 min – 5-1

### *Referee:*
Mr. T. Holbrook (Walsall)

# Firing On All Cylinders

From the first minute United dominated this game and Leicester, although pushing for promotion to the FA Premier were outclassed from the start. Within the first minute McClair had a header cleared off the line and within seven minutes central defenders Gary Pallister and Steve Bruce had linked up to put the Reds in front. A bad mistake by Whitlow needlessly gave away a corner and from the kick Pallister put the ball back across for his defensive partner to head home. United fans had to hold their breath, however, when it seemed that Schmeichel must be sent off when he clearly brought down Speedie who was in on goal just outside the penalty area. The Gods, or rather Mr Holbrook, shone on United when the colour of the card produced was yellow and United's keeper escaped not only the sending off but a suspension which would have proved much more expensive in the long term than just on the night. Within minutes of the incident the game as a contest, but not as a spectacle, was over. Leicester's defence failed to cut out a Sharpe cross and McClair was presented with an easy opportunity. The half ended with Leicester somehow surviving a torrid examination as Hughes had an effort cleared off the line whilst Keane trod on the ball when it seemed easier to score!

The second half began as much as the first had ended and after 53 minutes United increased their lead with a magnificent goal. Kanchelskis ran almost the length of the pitch before crossing to Hughes who quickly moved the ball to his left for Sharpe to blast home a rather special goal. McClair glanced a Sharpe centre wide when it seemed impossible to miss and the Leicester defenders couldn't have known whether to laugh or cry when Ferguson took Sharpe off, only to replace him with Giggs! Within seconds of being introduced to the fray, Giggs had set up a goal, crossing to the far post where McClair headed back for Hughes to convert at close range. A Leicester free kick gave them a consolation goal with two players blatantly offside but, in this all action performance from the Reds, there wasn't time to ponder that little point as the ball was soon back down at the Leicester end where it had been almost all night. A brilliant Giggs run ended when he was brought down but he simply picked himself up and pinpointed the free kick on to the head of Steve Bruce for his second and United's fifth goal of the game. With only four minutes now left Bruce vacated his central defensive position to look for his first ever hat-trick but time ran out on him.

## League Cup Record

|  | P | W | D | L | F | A | W | D | L | F | A |
|---|---|---|---|---|---|---|---|---|---|---|---|
|  |  | **Home** |  |  |  |  | **Away** |  |  |  |  |
| League Cup record | 115 | 43 | 10 | 8 | 131 | 51 | 19 | 14 | 21 | 71 | 71 |

|  | Home | Away | Total |
|---|---|---|---|
| League Cup Attendances | 82,731 | 23,327 | 106,058 |

# Manchester United (0) 2
# Queens Park Rangers (1) 1

Saturday, 30th October 1993, Old Trafford          Att.: 44,663

## MANCHESTER UNITED

| 1 | Peter | Schmeichel |
|---|---|---|
| 2 | Paul | Parker |
| 3 | Denis | Irwin |
| 4 | Steve | Bruce |
| 5 | Lee | Sharpe |
| 23 | Mike | Phelan |
| 7 | Eric | Cantona |
| 8 | Paul | Ince |
| 16 | Roy | Keane |
| 10 | Mark | Hughes |
| 11 | Ryan | Giggs |

*Subs*

| 13 | Les | Sealey (gk) |
|---|---|---|
| 14 | Andrei | Kanchelskis |
| 21 | Lee | Martin |

## QUEENS PARK RANGERS

| 13 | Jan | Stejskal |
|---|---|---|
| 2 | David | Bardsley |
| 3 | Clive | Wilson |
| 4 | Ray | Wilkins |
| 5 | Darren | Peacock |
| 6 | Alan | McDonald |
| 7 | Andrew | Impey |
| 14 | Simon | Barker – *Booked* |
| 9 | Les | Ferdinand |
| 10 | Bradley | Allen |
| 11 | Trevor | Sinclair |

| 1 | Tony | Roberts (gk) |
|---|---|---|
| 8 | Ian | Holloway |
| 24 | Steven | Yates |

## *Match Facts*

- The crowd of 44,663 set a new record for the FA Premiership.
- United had begun October two points clear at the top of the league. They finished the month eleven points clear, the biggest ever table topping margin in the history of the Premiership.

## *Score Sheet*

B. ALLEN 8 min – 0-1

E. CANTONA 53 min – 1-1

M. HUGHES 57 min – 2-1

*Referee:*
Mr. S. Lodge (Barnsley)

## FA Carling Premiership

| | | P | W | D | L | F | A | Pts |
|---|---|---|---|---|---|---|---|---|
| 1 | **Manchester United** | 13 | 11 | 1 | 1 | 27 | 10 | 34 |
| 2 | Norwich City | 13 | 6 | 5 | 2 | 21 | 12 | 23 |
| 3 | Arsenal | 13 | 6 | 5 | 2 | 12 | 6 | 23 |
| 4 | Blackburn Rovers | 13 | 6 | 5 | 2 | 18 | 13 | 23 |
| 5 | Aston Villa | 13 | 6 | 5 | 2 | 15 | 10 | 23 |

### Result of this Season's Fixture

Manchester Utd

QPR

# Second Half Storm

QPR came to Old Trafford having proved to be a jinx team on their last two visits. In 1991/92 they had hammered the Reds 4-1 and last season forced a goalless stalemate. There was no chance therefore that United would take them lightly and Giggs was back in the starting line up although Pallister was missing due to the ankle injury picked up in the previous game against Leicester City. Paul Parker came into the side and promptly took Pallister's place at the heart of the defence. After United, QPR were the leading goalscorers in the FA Premier League at the start of play and it didn't take them long to show why. England striker Les Ferdinand fired in a cracker of a shot which had Schmeichel at full stretch to get away for a corner. Unfortunately for the Reds, Schmeichel's great save counted for nothing. The ball was cleared but only as far as the edge of the area on the right where Bardsley was positioned to sling the ball back into the centre. Ferdinand headed the ball down and Bradley Allen did the rest from close range.

It was time to see what the Reds were made of but it was QPR who came closest to scoring when Ferdinand had the ball in the net only for the effort to be ruled offside. On first sight it certainly looked offside but television freeze frames afterwards clearly showed Ferdinand had a good yard to spare.

United started the second period looking like a rejuvenated team. Stejskal denied Cantona straight from the kick off and then Ince was only just off target. But United in this mood were not to be denied and Cantona scored a wonderful equaliser. Picking the ball up on the half-way line he jinked past his marker and then gladly accepted the space to run to the edge of the area as the defence retreated before him. He then hit the ball sweetly into the corner of Stejskal's net from 20 yards.

United were all over their opponents and five minutes later were in front when in Sharpe's corner kick was headed on by Keane for Hughes to score at point blank range. United were in the sort of mood that the crowds love and Giggs looked extra special when he picked the ball up just inside his own half before beating three men to race clear down the left. He looked up and planted an inch perfect cross into the path of Lee Sharpe who should have scored but for poor control. Giggs then whipped over a cross from the right wing which Bruce's head thumped against the outside of a post as United piled on the pressure. Credit was due to QPR's overworked defence who stood firm after the second goal even though they must have been one of few teams a goal down to be relieved to hear the final whistle!

## League Record

| | Home | | | | | | Away | | | | |
|---|---|---|---|---|---|---|---|---|---|---|---|
| | P | W | D | L | F | A | W | D | L | F | A |
| FAPL 93/94 | 13 | 6 | 1 | 0 | 16 | 5 | 5 | 0 | 1 | 11 | 5 |
| All Time FAPL | 55 | 20 | 6 | 2 | 55 | 19 | 15 | 7 | 5 | 39 | 22 |
| All Time FL/FAPL | 3611 | 1056 | 416 | 334 | 3605 | 1803 | 547 | 469 | 789 | 2445 | 3079 |

| | Home | Away | Total |
|---|---|---|---|
| League Attendances | 306,301 | 182,560 | 488,861 |

# Galatasary (0) 0
# Manchester United (0) 0

Wednesday, 3rd November 1993, Ali Sami Yen Stadium    Att.: 40,000

## GALATASARY

| | | |
|---|---|---|
| 1 | Demirbas | Hayrattin – *Booked* |
| 2 | Altintas | Yusuf |
| 3 | Falko | Gotz |
| 4 | Reinhard | Stumpf |
| 5 | H. | Hamza |
| 6 | *Erdem* | *Arif (*85)* |
| 7 | Kaya | Suat |
| 8 | K. | Tugay |
| 9 | Korkmaz | Bulent |
| 10 | T. | Kubilay |
| 11 | Sukur | Hakan |

*Subs*

| | | |
|---|---|---|
| 12 | *Kaya* | *Ugor (*85)* |
| 13 | Bologlu | Nezihi (gk) |
| 14 | Korkmaz | Mert |
| 15 | Keser | Cihat |
| 16 | Ariz | Mustafa |

## MANCHESTER UNITED

| | | |
|---|---|---|
| 1 | Peter | Schmeichel |
| 2 | *Mike* | *Phelan (+84)* |
| 3 | Denis | Irwin |
| 4 | Steve | Bruce – *Booked* |
| 5 | Lee | Sharpe |
| 6 | Paul | Parker – *Booked* |
| 7 | Bryan | Robson |
| 8 | Paul | Ince – *Booked* |
| 9 | Eric | Cantona – *Sent off* |
| 10 | *Roy* | *Keane (*72)* |
| 11 | Ryan | Giggs |

| | | |
|---|---|---|
| 12 | Lee | Martin |
| 13 | Les | Sealey (gk) |
| 14 | Dion | Dublin *(*72)* |
| 15 | Nicky | Butt |
| 16 | Gary | Neville *(+84)* |

## *Match Facts*

• United never got one shot on target during the ninety minutes.

• Galatasary have not been beaten at home in over ten years of European competition. Teams such as St Etienne, Roma, and Bayern Munich having been beaten in the Ali Sami Yen stadium.

• United's first goalless draw of the season.

• Shares in the club dropped a massive 42p on the Stock Exchange as City brokers saw United kiss goodbye to some £6m.

## *Score Sheet*

*Referee:*
Mr. Rothlisberger
(Switzerland)

# Down and Out

United faced an enormous task if they were to continue in their quest for European glory with the odds stacked against them. The Turkish FA had excused Galatasary from playing a game since the 3-3 in order to give their champions the best possible chance. The Reds had been met at the airport with banners reading *"Welcome to Hell"* and others that are not printable. The stadium was full to capacity some six or seven hours before kick off as United, needing to win, started off in reasonable fashion and as early as the first minute Sharpe had the ball in the net only to be ruled fractionally offside. Indeed, it looked as if Sharpe would be the man to unlock the Turkish defence with him trying to get on the end of long through balls but each time he was caught, marginally, offside. United, too, had their let offs, and Schmeichel was well beaten with a free kick that whistled perilously close to his left hand post. The home side began to gradually get on top, however, and it was Schmeichel to the rescue after 31 minutes when he made a brilliant one handed stop to his left only for the ball to run loose. Parker made an awful hash of his attempted clearance and Schmeichel, now back on his feet made a world class save from Hakan's point blank shot. The Turks closed in for the kill and minutes later Schmeichel was in action again just doing enough to put Kubilay off after a delicate chip from Tugay had left the United 'keeper exposed once more. In the liveliest period of the game, United hit back and after 35 minutes Robson got Giggs away down the left. As he cut in, Giggs let go with an angled drive that beat Hayrattin but also, unfortunately, the far post before it rolled teasingly across the face of an empty net.

United started the second period in a more upbeat mood and a Giggs corner after 48 minutes was headed down by Bruce. It looked as if it would fall into the path of Sharpe but the ball ran away from him at the last second. From then on United subsided into mediocrity and the longer the game went, the less likely they appeared to be able to break the deadlock. Cantona, a major disappointment on the night, didn't see it that way and told the referee so. Unfortunately, Mr Rothlisberger is a French teacher and understood every word that Cantona said which resulted in a red card after the final whistle had gone. In the uproar that followed in the player's tunnel, United players were set on by the Turkish police and Cantona received a hit on the head from a riot shield whilst Robson, who went to his aid, needed two stitches in a hand wound received as he tried to defend the Frenchman. It was little wonder that United's players had lost their nerve on the night.

## European Cup Record

|  | | Home | | | | | Away | | | | |
|---|---|---|---|---|---|---|---|---|---|---|---|
|  | P | W | D | L | F | A | W | D | L | F | A |
| European Cup | 45 | 20 | 2 | 0 | 69 | 17 | 8 | 7 | 8 | 39 | 34 |
| All European Comps | 105 | 38 | 13 | 0 | 132 | 34 | 18 | 16 | 18 | 77 | 76 |

|  | Home | Away | Total |
|---|---|---|---|
| European Cup Attendances | 75,177 | 47,000 | 122,177 |

# Manchester City (2) 2
# Manchester United (0) 3

Sunday, 7th November 1993, Maine Road                    Att.: 35,155

| MANCHESTER CITY | | | MANCHESTER UNITED | | |
|---|---|---|---|---|---|
| 1 | Tony | Coton | 1 | Peter | Schmeichel |
| 22 | Richard | Edgehill | 2 | Paul | Parker |
| 3 | Terry | Phelan | 3 | Denis | Irwin |
| 4 | Steve | McMahon | 4 | Steve | Bruce |
| 5 | Keith | Curle – *Booked* | 5 | Lee | Sharpe |
| 6 | Michel | Vonk | 6 | Gary | Pallister |
| 15 | Alan | Kernaghan | 7 | Eric | Cantona |
| 7 | David | White – *Booked* | 8 | Paul | Ince |
| 8 | Mike | Sheron | 10 | Mark | Hughes – *Booked* |
| 9 | Niall | Quinn | 14 | *Andrei* | *Kanchelskis (\*76)* |
| 10 | Garry | Flitcroft | 16 | Roy | Keane |

*Subs*

| | | | | | |
|---|---|---|---|---|---|
| 21 | Steve | Lomas | 11 | *Ryan* | *Giggs (\*76)* |
| 25 | Andy | Dibble (gk) | 12 | Bryan | Robson |
| 11 | Carl | Griffiths | 13 | Les | Sealey (gk) |

## *Match Facts*

● It was exactly seven years to the day that Alex Ferguson had taken charge of United side for the first time. That game, against Oxford United, also saw his team trailing by two goals but that time they didn't come back to win.

## *Score Sheet*

N. QUINN 22 min – 1-0
N. QUINN 32 min – 2-0
E. CANTONA 52 min – 2-1
E. CANTONA 78 min – 2-2
R. KEANE 87 min – 2-3

### *Referee:*
Mr. R. Hart (Darlington)

## FA Carling Premiership

| | | P | W | D | L | F | A | Pts |
|---|---|---|---|---|---|---|---|---|
| 1 | **Manchester United** | 14 | 12 | 1 | 1 | 30 | 12 | 37 |
| 2 | Norwich City | 14 | 7 | 5 | 2 | 23 | 13 | 26 |
| 3 | Aston Villa | 14 | 7 | 5 | 2 | 17 | 11 | 26 |
| 4 | Leeds United | 14 | 7 | 4 | 3 | 24 | 17 | 25 |
| 5 | Liverpool | 14 | 7 | 2 | 5 | 22 | 12 | 23 |

### Result of this Season's Fixture

Manchester City
Manchester Utd

# Reds and Blues White Hot

United and City put on the most exciting derby match for several seasons with City playing their part to the full in a first period when they were a yard quicker to the ball and had their fans in jubilant mood. That mood had begun prior to the match when local shops sold out of bars of Turkish Delight which the City fans threw to the United players as they came out to remind them – should they need reminding – of their dismal trip to Istanbul a few days previously. City hit the Reds with a right and left combination to take a 2-0 interval lead. The first goal was a simple affair as Irwin made a mistake on the edge of City's area. Sheron sped some 60 yards down the right to the other end where he floated the ball over for Quinn to place a header past Schmeichel who thought ball was going wide.

Just after half an hour, City were two up as Steve McMahon's cross, this time from the left, was headed home again by Quinn with questions having to be asked about Schmeichel's positioning once more. But if the Great Dane was caught out, he certainly made up for it a few minutes later when he performed wonders to deny White.

The second half, however, was a different story as the Reds upped their game. Despite United's superiority in the second period, it still needed a slice of monumental luck to get them back in the game. Vonk made a dreadful hash of a header-back to Coton and found only Cantona. The City 'keeper did everything right but the Frenchman made his finish just inside the far post look a great deal simpler than it was. Then with less than 15 minutes remaining, Ferguson made the move that the United fans had been waiting for when he introduced Giggs to the action. Incredibly, within seconds and with his first touch, Giggs sent a first time ball, weighted to perfection across the City goalmouth for Cantona to gleefully score the equaliser from almost point blank range after he himself had set the initial move up with one of his deft flicks. Three minutes from time Sharpe set Irwin free and it appeared that City had escaped when Hughes couldn't quite make contact with an open net yawning. City's hopes of a reprieve, however, were dashed as Keane roaring in behind his team mate cracked the ball into the empty net about an inch inside the post. United had triumphed by the skin of their teeth.

## League Record

| | Home | | | | | | Away | | | | |
|---|---|---|---|---|---|---|---|---|---|---|---|
| | P | W | D | L | F | A | W | D | L | F | A |
| FAPL 93/94 | 14 | 6 | 1 | 0 | 16 | 5 | 0 | 1 | 1 | 14 | 7 |
| All Time FAPL | 56 | 20 | 6 | 2 | 55 | 19 | 16 | 7 | 5 | 42 | 24 |
| All Time FL/FAPL | 3612 | 1056 | 416 | 334 | 3605 | 1803 | 548 | 469 | 789 | 2448 | 3081 |

| | Home | Away | Total |
|---|---|---|---|
| League Attendances | 306,301 | 217,715 | 524,016 |

# Manchester United (0) 3
# Wimbledon (0) 1

Saturday, 20th November 1993, Old Trafford          Att.: 44,748

## MANCHESTER UNITED

| 1 | Peter | Schmeichel |
|---|-------|-----------|
| 2 | Paul | Parker |
| 3 | Denis | Irwin |
| 4 | Steve | Bruce |
| 5 | Lee | Sharpe |
| 6 | Gary | Pallister |
| 7 | Eric | Cantona |
| 8 | Paul | Ince |
| 12 | Bryan | Robson |
| 10 | Mark | Hughes |
| 14 | Andrei | Kanchelskis |

*Subs*

| 11 | Ryan | Giggs |
| 13 | Les | Sealey (gk) |
| 23 | Mike | Phelan |

## WIMBLEDON

| 1 | Hans | Seger |
|---|------|-------|
| 2 | Warren | Barton |
| 3 | Brian | McAllister |
| 4 | Vinny | Jones |
| 6 | Scott | Fitzgerald |
| 8 | Robbie | Earle |
| 9 | John | Fashanu |
| 10 | Dean | Holdsworth |
| 15 | John | Scales |
| 17 | Roger | Joseph |
| 18 | Steve | Talboys |

| 7 | Andy | Clarke |
| 37 | Perry | Digweed (gk) |
| 26 | Neal | Ardley |

---

### *Match Facts*

• The attendance of 44,748 set yet another Premier League record, giving Wimbledon the unusual record of both the highest and the lowest attendance records for the League – just 3,039 against Everton in January 1993. The three points took United's total to 103 in their last 42 games (a full season).

---

### *Score Sheet*

G. PALLISTER 53 min – 1-0
J. FASHANU 64 min – 1-1
KANCHELSKIS 64 min – 2-1
M. HUGHES 66 min – 3-1

*Referee:*
Mr. J. Lloyd (Wrexham)

---

## FA Carling Premiership

| | | P | W | D | L | F | A | Pts |
|---|---|---|---|---|---|---|---|-----|
| 1 | **Manchester United** | 15 | 13 | 1 | 1 | 33 | 13 | 40 |
| 2 | Aston Villa | 15 | 8 | 5 | 2 | 18 | 11 | 29 |
| 3 | Norwich City | 15 | 7 | 6 | 2 | 24 | 14 | 27 |
| 4 | QPR | 15 | 8 | 2 | 5 | 28 | 21 | 26 |
| 5 | Leeds United | 15 | 7 | 5 | 3 | 25 | 18 | 26 |

### Result of this Season's Fixture

Manchester Utd
Wimbledon

# Another Second Half Show

Wimbledon came to Old Trafford as the last of only two teams to have beaten United at home in the FA Premier League. Roy Keane dropped out just prior to the kick off with a groin strain, his position being taken by Robson but Kanchelskis held his place with Giggs on the bench again.

Although it wasn't the Reds at their best, they still managed to control the first forty-five minutes with Kanchelskis probably the best player on the pitch. However, it was Wimbledon who had the first chance after 11 minutes but Schmeichel was out quickly to beat Holdsworth to the ball whilst at the other end Cantona hit back with a shot and a header that were both off target. Sharpe, though, forced a great save from Segers when put through by Ince and Hughes. Wimbledon were generally defending well and looked dangerous on the odd occasion they mounted an attack. Holdsworth made a good run down the left to get over a cross from which Earle should have done better than turn the ball wide. Five minutes from the interval it seemed that United had taken the lead when Ince again got Sharpe away to score nonchalantly but the linesman had spotted a marginal offside.

Wimbledon almost started the second period with a bang as Joseph crossed for Fashanu to slam in a rocket shot from which Schmeichel produced a spectacular save. United then got the goal their territorial advantage deserved with Pallister getting the better of Fashanu in an aerial battle to plant a header home from Sharpe's flag kick after 53 minutes. Kanchelskis almost made it two but Segers tipped the Russian's blockbuster to safety with the help of a post but just when it appeared that United would take the Londoner's apart, the visitors hit back to stun the Old Trafford crowd. Ten minutes after United's opener, a cross from Holdsworth ballooned over the stranded Schmeichel for Fashanu to nod home.

To their credit, United once more showed the major difference between the current team and two years ago is their ability to immediately overcome set backs and within a minute they were back in front. Cantona was the architect but Hughes simply doesn't seem to believe in scoring easy goals. Almost all are spectacular and this goal ranked amongst his best as he volleyed home whilst horizontal three feet off the ground. Ten minutes from time Kanchelskis capped a fine individual performance with a surge in from the right wing before transferring the ball to his left to slip it past Segers and put the game beyond the reach of the Dons.

## League Record

|  | Home | | | | | | Away | | | | |
|---|---|---|---|---|---|---|---|---|---|---|---|
|  | P | W | D | L | F | A | W | D | L | F | A |
| FAPL 93/94 | 15 | 7 | 1 | 0 | 19 | 6 | 6 | 0 | 1 | 14 | 7 |
| All Time FAPL | 57 | 21 | 6 | 2 | 58 | 20 | 16 | 7 | 5 | 42 | 24 |
| All Time FL/FAPL | 3613 | 1057 | 416 | 334 | 3608 | 1804 | 548 | 469 | 789 | 2448 | 3081 |

|  | Home | Away | Total |
|---|---|---|---|
| League Attendances | 351,049 | 217,715 | 568,764 |

# Manchester United (0) 0
# Ipswich Town (0) 0

Wednesday, 25th November 1993, Old Trafford          Att.: 43,300

| MANCHESTER UNITED | | | IPSWICH TOWN | | |
|---|---|---|---|---|---|
| 1 | Peter | Schmeichel | 1 | Craig | Forrest |
| 2 | Paul | Parker | 2 | Mick | Stockwell |
| 3 | Denis | Irwin | 16 | Eddie | Youds |
| 4 | Steve | Bruce | 5 | John | Wark |
| 5 | Lee | Sharpe | 6 | David | Linighan |
| 6 | Gary | Pallister | 15 | Phil | Whelan |
| 7 | Eric | Cantona | 4 | *Paul* | *Mason* (*84) |
| 8 | Paul | Ince | 18 | Steve | Palmer |
| *14* | *Andrei* | *Kanchelskis* (*57) | 3 | Neil | Thompson |
| *12* | *Bryan* | *Robson* (+83) | 10 | Ian | Marshall |
| 10 | Mark | Hughes | 11 | Chris | Kiwomya |

*Subs*

| 13 | Les | Sealey (gk) | 19 | *Frank* | *Yallop* (*84) |
|---|---|---|---|---|---|
| 18 | *Darren* | *Ferguson* (+83) | 23 | Philip | Morgan (gk) |
| 11 | *Ryan* | *Giggs* (*57) | 17 | Simon | Milton |

## *Match Facts*

• First time United failed to score at Old Trafford since Arsenal held them 0-0 in March 1993. • Ipswich unbeaten against United in three FA Premier League games, the only team apart from newly promoted Newcastle United not to have been beaten by the Reds in the new Premier League.

## *Score Sheet*

*Referee:*
Mr. T. Holbrook (Walsall)

## FA Carling Premiership

| | | P | W | D | L | F | A | Pts |
|---|---|---|---|---|---|---|---|---|
| 1 | Manchester United | 16 | 13 | 2 | 1 | 33 | 13 | 41 |
| 2 | Blackburn Rovers | 16 | 8 | 5 | 3 | 22 | 15 | 29 |
| 3 | Aston Villa | 16 | 8 | 5 | 3 | 18 | 13 | 29 |
| 4 | Newcastle United | 16 | 8 | 4 | 4 | 31 | 15 | 28 |
| 5 | Norwich City | 15 | 7 | 6 | 2 | 24 | 14 | 27 |

### Result of this Season's Fixture

Manchester Utd
Ipswich Town

# Road Block

United found the road to the Ipswich Town goal completely blocked and when they tried to find alternative routes these too were full of traffic – all heading in the same direction.

During the course of the ninety minutes, the East Anglian outfit strayed into the United half just twice but, strangely could have inflicted an even bigger miscarriage of justice as a result of both sorties. In the first period, Youds went very close with a header that seemed to have Schmeichel beaten as it went dangerously close to the 'keeper's right hand post. When Giggs had been introduced to the action in the derby game with Manchester City two weeks earlier, his first touch had set up a goal. His first touch here, after he had emerged from the bench in the 57th minute, also nearly produced a goal only it was at the United end. When the young Welshman tried a quick flick it was intercepted for Mason to run at the Reds defence and unleash a shot that sped across the face of Schmeichel's net.

Apart from those two encroachments, the game was played exclusively in the Town half of the field but Ipswich defended resolutely whilst United looked for the key to unlock the formidable barrier in front of them. The nearest they came was a free kick from Giggs that beat both the wall and Forrest in the Ipswich goal but not the crossbar. The pattern for the game was set in the first minute with a knock down from Bruce getting Ince into a shooting position but his effort was blocked. After the Youds scare, a move of sheer poetry between Cantona and Kanchelskis got Hughes in on goal but again the Ipswich ranks closed quickly to deny a clear chance. The same two foreign players again combined brilliantly to enable the Russian to close in from the right and send a snap shot across the beckoning goal but nobody was there to apply the required touch.

The second half began in the same vein with Ipswich under constant pressure but Forrest was having an inspired game whilst Wark and Linighan were winning most of the aerial battles. As the half wore on, however, it seemed that United began to believe that it was not going to be their night and, although the crowd chanted *"Boring, boring Ipswich"*, the East Anglians will have returned home well satisfied with their night's work.

## League Record

| | P | W | D | L | F | A | W | D | L | F | A |
|---|---|---|---|---|---|---|---|---|---|---|---|
| | | **Home** | | | | | | **Away** | | | |
| FAPL 93/94 | 16 | 7 | 2 | 0 | 19 | 6 | 6 | 0 | 1 | 14 | 7 |
| All Time FAPL | 58 | 21 | 7 | 2 | 58 | 16 | 16 | 7 | 5 | 42 | 24 |
| All Time FL/FAPL | 3614 | 1057 | 417 | 334 | 3608 | 1804 | 548 | 469 | 789 | 2448 | 3081 |

| | Home | Away | Total |
|---|---|---|---|
| League Attendances | 394,349 | 217,715 | 612,064 |

# Coventry City     (0) 0
# Manchester United     (0) 1

Saturday, 27th November 1993, Highfield Road     Att.: 17,020

| COVENTRY CITY | | | MANCHESTER UNITED | | |
|---|---|---|---|---|---|
| 1 | Steve | Ogrizovic | 1 | Peter | Schmeichel |
| 4 | Peter | Atherton | 2 | Paul | Parker |
| 20 | Phil | Babb | 3 | Denis | Irwin |
| 6 | David | Rennie | 4 | Steve | Bruce – *Booked* |
| 3 | Steve | Morgan | 5 | Lee | Sharpe |
| 18 | Sean | Flynn | 6 | Gary | Pallister |
| 16 | Willie | Boland | 7 | Eric | Cantona |
| 25 | Julian | Darby | 8 | Paul | Ince – *Booked* |
| 17 | Roy | Wegerle | 10 | Mark | Hughes |
| 10 | Mick | Quinn | 11 | Ryan | Giggs |
| 12 | Peter | Ndlovu | 18 | Darren | Ferguson |

*Subs*

| | | | | | |
|---|---|---|---|---|---|
| 23 | Jonathon | Gould (gk) | 9 | Brian | McClair |
| 7 | John | Williams | 12 | Brian | Robson |
| | Chris | Marsden | 13 | Les | Sealey (gk) |

### *Match Facts*

- First league start of the season for manager's son Darren Ferguson.
- The win put United 14 points clear, a new record for the FA Premier League.
- The result left Coventry still looking for their first FA Premier League goal against the Reds.

### *Score Sheet*

E. CANTONA 60 min – 0-1

*Referee:*
Mr. S. Lodge (Barnsley)

## FA Carling Premiership

| | | P | W | D | L | F | A | Pts |
|---|---|---|---|---|---|---|---|---|
| 1 | **Manchester United** | 17 | 14 | 2 | 1 | 34 | 13 | 44 |
| 2 | Leeds United | 17 | 8 | 6 | 3 | 29 | 19 | 30 |
| 3 | Arsenal | 17 | 8 | 6 | 3 | 17 | 9 | 30 |
| 4 | Blackburn Rovers | 17 | 8 | 5 | 4 | 22 | 16 | 29 |
| 5 | Aston Villa | 16 | 8 | 5 | 3 | 18 | 13 | 29 |

### Resultsof this Season's Fixture

Coventry City
Manchester Utd

# Cantona Celebration

Exactly one year ago to the day, Manchester United surprised the football critics by plunging what became the bargain of the decade, £1.2m on Eric Cantona and by way of celebration the Frenchman scored United's winner against Coventry City just when it was beginning to look like a second goalless draw in succession for the Reds. Nevertheless, the party was only possible because of four super saves from Peter Schmeichel as United turned in a much under par performance.

Sharpe seemed United's main hope in the early skirmishes as he forced Ogrizovic into the first save of the match and then crossed for Cantona to head wide. After 25 minutes, however, came the first of Schmeichel's excellent saves as Quinn looked certain to open the scoring. Roy Wegerle had squeezed a path along the by-line to cross to Quinn who appeared to have the goal at his mercy but as he shot, Schmeichel somehow got his legs in the way. Within five minutes the great Dane had blocked another almost certain goal bound effort from Quinn, this time with his body, to leave the former Newcastle player shaking his head.

The Reds certainly looked a brighter outfit on the resumption and Irwin, who scored the only goal goal of the corresponding game last year with a 25 yard rocket shot, tried to emulate the performance but was denied by a tremendous save by Ogrizovic who turned the effort round the post. Bruce was booked for a late tackle on Quinn but this was the prelude to the turning point of the game. Atherton did well down the right and his cross was volleyed with tremendous force from close range by Ndlovu only for Schmeichel, who was turning in a tremendous performance, to get his body in the way and parry the shot on to a post. From this let off, play switched to the opposite end where only Giggs realised the ball might hit the corner flag rather than go out of play. Whilst others stopped, he chased and found himself with the ball as it did, indeed, come back off the flag. With five yards of breathing space, Giggs played the ball back to Irwin who picked out Cantona with an inch perfect cross for the Frenchman to nod home at close range. The goal opened up the game somewhat as Coventry had to start becoming more adventurous and the Reds began to look a better side as they found more space. Nevertheless, it was the Reds 'keeper, Schmeichel, to the rescue again at the death as Flynn's cross found substitute Marsden in front of goal. His shot from close range had equaliser written all over it but Schmeichel got a touch to get it onto the crossbar and eventual safety.

## League Record

|  | Home | | | | | | Away | | | | |
|  | P | W | D | L | F | A | W | D | L | F | A |
|---|---|---|---|---|---|---|---|---|---|---|---|
| FAPL 93/94 | 17 | 7 | 2 | 0 | 19 | 6 | 7 | 0 | 1 | 15 | 7 |
| All Time FAPL | 59 | 21 | 7 | 2 | 58 | 20 | 17 | 7 | 5 | 43 | 24 |
| All Time FL/FAPL | 3615 | 1057 | 417 | 334 | 3608 | 1804 | 549 | 469 | 789 | 2449 | 3081 |

|  | Home | Away | Total |
|---|---|---|---|
| League Attendances | 394,349 | 234,735 | 629,084 |

# Everton
# Manchester United

**(0) 0**
**(1) 2**

Tuesday, 30th November 1993, Goodison Park          Att.: 34,052

## EVERTON

| | | |
|---|---|---|
| 1 | Neville | Southall |
| 2 | Matthew | Jackson |
| 5 | Dave | Watson |
| 6 | Gary | Ablett |
| 3 | Andy | Hinchliffe |
| 10 | Barry | Horne |
| 4 | *Ian* | *Snodin (+68)* |
| 14 | John | Ebbrell |
| 7 | *Mark* | *Ward (*51)* |
| 8 | Graham | Stuart |
| 9 | Tony | Cottee |

*Subs*

| | | |
|---|---|---|
| 13 | Jason | Kearton (gk) |
| 19 | *Stuart* | *Barlow (*51)* |
| 16 | | *Preki (+68)* |

## MANCHESTER UNITED

| | | |
|---|---|---|
| 1 | Peter | Schmeichel |
| 2 | Paul | Parker |
| 3 | Denis | Irwin |
| 4 | Steve | Bruce |
| 6 | Gary | Pallister |
| 7 | Eric | Cantona |
| 8 | Paul | Ince |
| 10 | Mark | Hughes |
| 11 | Ryan | Giggs |
| 12 | *Bryan* | *Robson (*77)* |
| 14 | Andrei | Kanchelskis |

| | | |
|---|---|---|
| 13 | Les | Sealey (gk) |
| 9 | Brian | McClair |
| 18 | *Darren* | *Ferguson (*77)* |

## *Match Facts*

- United's first ever win in either the FA Cup or League Cup at Goodison Park.

- It was the first victory for the Reds over Everton in the League Cup after defeats in 1984-85 and 1976-77 at Old Trafford.

## *Score Sheet*

M. HUGHES 13 min – 0-1

R. GIGGS 46 min – 0-2

*Referee:*
Mr. P. Wright (Northwich)

# Everton "Schmeicheled" Again

If Everton thought lightning couldn't strike twice, they were very much mistaken for, after United 'keeper Peter Schmeichel had held them at bay in the League game at Goodison in October, the Great Dane put on another world class display of keeping. The opening ten minutes was mundane stuff but when Pallister blocked Cottee's path for Schmeichel to clear to Ince, there was certainly nothing ordinary about Hughes' opening goal. A brilliant 40 yard pass from Ince was taken magnificently on the chest by the Welsh striker at the edge of the Everton penalty area. Sensing Southall to be off his line, Hughes, almost in the same movement lobbed the ball under the bar for an exquisite strike.

Within a minute of the restart, United were two up as Giggs cleared his lines way back in his own half. His clearance to the half way line found Cantona whose first time touch sent Kanchelskis flying down the right wing. As he cut in he let loose but Southall was able to parry the shot only to see it loop up in the air so high that it easily cleared the on rushing Hughes. Right behind, however, coming up like an express train was Giggs who must have made 70 yards from his clearance to smash the ball home from six yards.

From thereon in, the game virtually became the Peter Schmeichel one man show. Almost immediately Gary Pallister bundled Stuart over in clumsy fashion and, although the big central defender disagreed vehemently, there seemed little alternative but for the referee to award the spot kick. Schmeichel dived quickly to his right to push the well struck penalty for a corner from which Everton must have thought they had got another spot kick when Pallister clearly handled the ball but United escaped when Mr Wright adjudged Pallister to have been fouled. Schmeichel was then down bravely and, brilliantly, at the feet of substitute Barlow before he was finally beaten by a snorter of a shot from Snodin. Unfortunately for Everton the effort whistled just wide. In a period of intense Merseyside pressure, Schmeichel and Barlow were almost having a personal duel and once again the Great Dane beat out a fierce shot from the Evertonian. He then proceeded to make a triple save from Barlow, Stuart and Cottee.

In a rare United excursion in to the Everton goalmouth, Bruce appeared to have put the game beyond recall for the Goodison outfit when he beat Southall in the air to nod home but the effort was disallowed, somewhat questionably, for a shove on the Welsh 'keeper. It was then back to the Schmeichel versus Barlow battle but United still had time to bounce back in the dying stages to have efforts by Giggs and Cantona ruled out by close offside decisions.

## League Cup Record

|  | P | W | D | L | F | A | W | D | L | F | A |
|---|---|---|---|---|---|---|---|---|---|---|---|
|  |  | **Home** |  |  |  |  | **Away** |  |  |  |  |
| All time League Cup | 116 | 43 | 10 | 8 | 131 | 51 | 20 | 14 | 21 | 73 | 71 |

|  | Home | Away | Total |
|---|---|---|---|
| League Cup Attendances | 82,731 | 57,379 | 183,904 |

# Manchester United (2) 2
# Norwich City (1) 2

Saturday, 4th December 1993, Old Trafford      Att.: 44,694

## MANCHESTER UNITED

| 1 | Peter | Schmeichel |
|---|-------|-----------|
| 2 | Paul | Parker |
| 3 | Denis | Irwin |
| 4 | Steve | Bruce |
| 6 | Gary | Pallister |
| 7 | Eric | Cantona |
| 8 | Paul | Ince |
| 9 | Brian | McClair |
| 10 | *Mark* | *Hughes (\*73)* |
| 11 | Ryan | Giggs |
| 14 | Andrei | Kanchelskis |

*Subs*

| 13 | Les | Sealey (gk) |
|----|-----|-------------|
| 5 | *Lee* | *Sharpe (\*73)* |
| 18 | Darren | Ferguson |

## NORWICH CITY

| 1 | Bryan | Gunn – *Booked* |
|---|-------|-----------------|
| 2 | Mark | Bowen |
| 3 | Rob | Newman |
| 5 | Ian | Culverhouse |
| 8 | Colin | Woodthorpe |
| 9 | Gary | Megson |
| 11 | Jeremy | Goss |
| 14 | *Ruel* | *Fox (+78)* |
| 16 | Lee | Power |
| 17 | *Ian* | *Butterworth (\*45)* |
| 22 | Chris | Sutton |

| 15 | *Daryl* | *Sutch (\*45)* |
|----|---------|----------------|
| 13 | Scott | Howie (gk) |
| 20 | *Darren* | *Eadie (+78)* |

### *Match Facts*

• This was the first occasion United had failed to beat Norwich in the Premier League in four starts.

• Peter Schmeichel reached a century of League appearances for the Reds.

### *Score Sheet*

R. GIGGS 30 min – 1-0
C. SUTTON 31 min – 1-1
B. CLAIR 42 min – 2-1
R. FOX 47 min Pen– 2-2

*Referee:*
Mr. M. Bodenham (East Looe)

## FA Carling Premiership

| | | P | W | D | L | F | A | Pts |
|---|---|---|---|---|---|---|---|-----|
| 1 | **Manchester United** | 18 | 14 | 3 | 1 | 36 | 15 | 45 |
| 2 | Leeds United | 18 | 9 | 6 | 3 | 32 | 21 | 33 |
| 3 | Newcastle United | 18 | 9 | 4 | 5 | 34 | 18 | 31 |
| 4 | Arsenal | 18 | 8 | 6 | 4 | 17 | 10 | 30 |
| 5 | Aston Villa | 18 | 8 | 6 | 4 | 21 | 17 | 30 |

**Result of this Season's Fixture**

Manchester Utd
Norwich City

# Canaries Clip United Wings

Norwich quickly showed they were intent on cutting United's runaway lead at the top of the league and totally dominated the opening half-hour. But, against the run of play it was United who took the lead with a piece of opportunism seized by Giggs. There seemed little danger when Cantona slung over a high cross from the right but as the Norwich defence hesitated, Giggs came bursting in from the left to make their minds up for them. The Canaries hit back immediately with Fox forcing Schmeichel in to a good block but, as the ball broke loose Pallister, much as the Norwich defence had a minute earlier, hesitated and Sutton stepped in to rifle the ball home from the edge of the box with Schmeichel still stranded. It was no more than the visitors deserved but just before half-time United were back in front after an exciting seven man move. Parker started it on the right finding Cantona who looked to be in trouble before switching it to Irwin on the left flank. He turned it inside to Ince who passed forward to Giggs. The Welsh youngster simply stopped the ball, put his foot under it and lifted it over the Norwich defence on to the head of Cantona. The Frenchman headed the ball back across the goal for McClair, under pressure, to volley home.

The second half started with Norwich immediately pulling level as Pallister, in very similar fashion to three days earlier against Everton, bundled over his opponent in the area. Fox smacked the penalty straight at Schmeichel but unfortunately for the Reds, the 'keeper had departed to his left. If the first half belonged almost entirely to Norwich then this equaliser seemed to stir United into action at last and they dominated the remainder of the game. Hughes couldn't quite control a Giggs cross and Cantona suffered a similar fate when he tried to take another cross from the youngster on the chest when in space inside the area. The Frenchman was certainly in the thick of things now and was lucky not to get booked when he retaliated after being man handled to the ground by Culverhouse. Parker did very well down the right to get a cross over from which Giggs showed his talent lies in his feet and not his head as he allowed the ball to brush his hair when it seemed all he had to do to score was get his head on the ball. With time running out a game of two halves came to a stalemate ending when McClair saw his twenty yarder scrape the post but any other result would have been an injustice.

## League Record

|  | Home | | | | | | Away | | | | |
|  | P | W | D | L | F | A | W | D | L | F | A |
|---|---|---|---|---|---|---|---|---|---|---|---|
| FAPL 93/94 | 18 | 7 | 3 | 0 | 21 | 8 | 7 | 0 | 1 | 15 | 7 |
| All Time FAPL | 60 | 21 | 8 | 2 | 60 | 22 | 17 | 7 | 5 | 43 | 24 |
| All Time FL/FAPL | 3616 | 1057 | 418 | 334 | 3610 | 1806 | 549 | 469 | 789 | 2449 | 3081 |

|  | Home | Away | Total |
|---|---|---|---|
| League Attendances | 439,043 | 234,735 | 673,778 |

# Sheffield United     (0) 0
# Manchester United     (2) 3

Tuesday, 7th December 1993, Bramall Lane      Att.: 26,744

| SHEFFIELD UNITED | | | MANCHESTER UNITED | | |
|---|---|---|---|---|---|
| 1 | Alan | Kelly | 1 | Peter | Schmeichel |
| 2 | Kevin | Gage | 2 | Paul | Parker |
| 14 | David | Tuttle | 3 | Denis | Irwin – *Booked* |
| 16 | *Paul* | *Beesley (\*62)* | 4 | Steve | Bruce |
| 33 | Roger | Nilssen | 5 | Lee | Sharpe |
| 17 | Carl | Bradshaw – *Booked* | 6 | Gary | Pallister |
| 26 | Jamie | Hoyland | 7 | Eric | Cantona |
| ** | Willie | Falconer | 8 | Paul | Ince – *Booked* |
| 11 | Mitch | Ward | 9 | *Brian* | *McClair (\*72)* |
| 10 | Glyn | Hodges | 10 | Mark | Hughes |
| 22 | *Andy* | *Scott (+45)* | 11 | Ryan | Giggs |

*Subs*

| 8 | *Paul* | *Rogers (\*62)* | 14 | Andrei | Kanchelskis |
|---|---|---|---|---|---|
| 12 | *Jostein* | *Flo (+45)* | 16 | *Roy* | *Keane (\*72)* |
| 13 | Carl | Muggleton | 13 | Les | Sealey (gk) |

---

### *Match Facts*

• It was the first occasion since the introduction of squad numbers that United had lined up numbers 1 to 11 in FAPL.

• The victory also gave United another record – the 15 point gap it created at the top set a new biggest ever leading margin in the FA Premiership.

### *Score Sheet*

M. HUGHES 13 min – 0-1

L. SHARP 27 min – 0-2

E. CANTONA 60 min – 0-3

*Referee:*
Mr. A. Gunn (Sussex)

---

## FA Carling Premiership

| | | P | W | D | L | F | A | Pts |
|---|---|---|---|---|---|---|---|---|
| 1 | Manchester United | 19 | 15 | 3 | 1 | 39 | 15 | 48 |
| 2 | Blackburn Rovers | 19 | 10 | 5 | 4 | 26 | 17 | 35 |
| 3 | Leeds United | 18 | 9 | 6 | 3 | 32 | 21 | 33 |
| 4 | Newcastle United | 18 | 9 | 4 | 5 | 34 | 18 | 31 |
| 5 | Arsenal | 19 | 8 | 7 | 4 | 18 | 11 | 31 |

### Result of this Season's Fixture

Sheffield Utd

Manchester Utd

# All Bets Off

After United had beaten Sheffield United by a 3-0 score line for the second consecutive time in the season, the bookmakers announced that they were not taking any more bets on United for the title as the odds would be too prohibitive. Not surprising really, as the victory gave United a 15 point lead!

The Reds took the lead as early as the 13th minute when Schmeichel came out to hoof a pass back up field. Cantona tried to meet it on the half way line with his head but missed which left Hughes to pick the ball up in the centre-circle. He passed it out to Parker on the right who threaded the ball down the wing to McClair. When the Scot crossed to the edge of the area, Hughes had made up the ground to meet the ball first time and score from the right of the 18 yard line past Kelly's forlorn dive to his right.

The second, fourteen minutes later was just as sweetly put away with the executioner this time being Lee Sharpe. Again the move started in United's own half with Pallister picking up a loose ball and passing to Hughes on the half way line. The Welshman switched it quickly right and a tremendous through ball from Ince put Sharpe in the clear. With appeals for offside ringing in his ears Sharpe kept his cool and from a similar position to Hughes, he placed the ball left footed once more past Kelly's outstretched right arm.

If those goals were clinical then there can be no definition of the third for it took exactly 15 seconds for the ball to finish in the Sheffield net from when they, themselves, had taken a corner. A Schmeichel punch ballooned up in the area but it was Cantona who was first to react. His header, however, wasn't decisive and it took Sharpe to complete the clearance by getting it up to Giggs on the half way line. Cantona suddenly appeared at a fast rate of knots to run into the Sheffield half. Giggs timed his pass to perfection and there was simply no catching the Frenchman who closed in on Kelly from the left to score nonchalantly.

Adding insult to injury was the fact that Schmeichel's attempted punch which had begun the move also connected with opposing defender Paul Beesley to leave him unconscious and stretchered off to hospital with concussion. In between the second and third goals, Sheffield had shown they were capable of getting back in the game but Bradshaw wasted their best opportunity towards the end of the first period when he lacked composure whilst at the beginning of the second half, replies from Flo and Hodges came to nothing.

## League Record

|  | | Home | | | | | Away | | | | |
|  | P | W | D | L | F | A | W | D | L | F | A |
|---|---|---|---|---|---|---|---|---|---|---|---|
| FAPL 93/94 | 19 | 7 | 3 | 0 | 21 | 8 | 8 | 0 | 1 | 18 | 7 |
| All Time FAPL | 61 | 21 | 8 | 2 | 60 | 22 | 18 | 7 | 5 | 46 | 24 |
| All Time FL/FAPL | 3617 | 1057 | 418 | 334 | 3610 | 1806 | 550 | 469 | 789 | 2452 | 3081 |

|  | Home | Away | Total |
|---|---|---|---|
| League Attendances | 439,043 | 261,479 | 700,522 |

# Newcastle United (0) 1
# Manchester United (0) 1

Saturday, 11th December 1993, St James Park          Att.: 36,388

## NEWCASTLE UNITED

| 30 | Mike | Hooper |
| 2 | Barry | Venison |
| 4 | Paul | Bracewell |
| 6 | Steve | Howey |
| 7 | Robert | Lee |
| 8 | Peter | Beardsley |
| 9 | Andy | Cole |
| 10 | Lee | Clark |
| 11 | Scott | Sellars |
| 19 | Steve | Watson |
| 26 | Robert | Elliott |

## MANCHESTER UNITED

| 1 | Peter | Schmeichel |
| 2 | Paul | Parker |
| 3 | Denis | Irwin |
| 4 | Steve | Bruce |
| 5 | Lee | Sharpe |
| 6 | Gary | Pallister |
| 7 | Eric | Cantona |
| 8 | Paul | Ince |
| 9 | *Brian* | *McClair (+76)* |
| 10 | *Mark* | *Hughes (*55)* |
| 11 | Ryan | Giggs |

*Subs*

| 16 | Liam | O'Brien |
| 21 | Malcolm | Allen |
| 1 | Pavel | Srnicek (gk) |

| 13 | Les | Sealey (gk) |
| 14 | Andrei | Kanchelskis (*55) |
| 16 | Roy | Keane (+76) |

---

### *Match Facts*

• Ince's goal made him the 13th player to score for United in less than half a season. Only Paul Parker of the outfield players remained without a goal.

---

### *Score Sheet*

P. INCE 58 min – 0-1
A. COLE 72 min – 1-1

*Referee:*
Mr. K. Hackett (Sheffield)

---

## FA Carling Premiership

| | | P | W | D | L | F | A | Pts |
|---|---|---|---|---|---|---|---|---|
| 1 | Manchester United | 20 | 15 | 4 | 1 | 40 | 16 | 49 |
| 2 | Leeds United | 19 | 10 | 6 | 3 | 33 | 21 | 36 |
| 3 | Blackburn Rovers | 19 | 10 | 5 | 4 | 26 | 17 | 35 |
| 4 | Newcastle United | 19 | 9 | 5 | 5 | 35 | 19 | 32 |
| 5 | Arsenal | 19 | 8 | 7 | 4 | 18 | 11 | 31 |

**Result of this Season's Fixture**

Newcastle Utd
Manchester Utd

# Smash And Grab

Although the game failed to live up to its pre-match billing as the *Game of the Season* it certainly showed that Newcastle were genuine title contenders. Outplayed from almost start to finish, United were lucky to finish with a point.

The attendance was Newcastle's best of the season to date but the fans must have been bitterly disappointed with the efforts served up in the first period from two teams acknowledged as the best attacking sides in the country. Hughes was fortunate that Howey didn't dive when the Welshman clearly tripped him, otherwise he may not have been on the pitch to get United's only effort of the first half on target. Even then, his overhead kick from Sharpe's cross carried no power and was easily collected by Hooper. At the other end, Pallister's headed clearance fell straight at the feet of Beardsley whose powerful first time shot was beaten away spectacularly by Schmeichel.

If the first half had been a big disappointment, the second made up for it. Newcastle almost took the lead from the kick off when Beardsley cut in from the left but, with only Schmeichel to beat, he was unable to squeeze the ball past the giant 'keeper who spread himself across the angle brilliantly to smother the shot. Clark then forced another save from the Dane before manager Alex Ferguson decided it was time for change. In the 55th minute he brought on Kanchelskis for Hughes and with his first touch, the Russian set up the opening goal. Ince did well to set the winger free down the right who crossed to Giggs. The Welsh youngster brought the ball down with his right foot and laid it back with his left to the onrushing Ince who had made ground from his own half where he had started the move. Ince hit the ball sweetly with his left foot from the edge of the area to put United in front, very much against the run of play.

A few minutes later it was almost game, set and match as Cantona put Sharpe through the centre, only for him to shot straight at Hooper who beat the powerful effort away for a corner. With all the goal to aim at, Sharpe should have clinched the points and the Reds were made to pay dearly for the miss. In the move of the match, Beardsley sent a beautifully weighted ball inside the full back for Lee to run onto. In the meantime, Newcastle's goal machine, Andy Cole was making up ground down the centre. With a quick shuffle, completed without breaking stride, Cole sent Pallister away from him and when the cross came in from the right the Geordie striker was able to rise unchallenged to nod home the equaliser.

## League Record

|  | Home | | | | | | Away | | | | |
|  | P | W | D | L | F | A | W | D | L | F | A |
|---|---|---|---|---|---|---|---|---|---|---|---|
| FAPL 93/94 | 20 | 7 | 3 | 0 | 21 | 8 | 8 | 1 | 1 | 19 | 8 |
| All Time FAPL | 62 | 21 | 8 | 2 | 60 | 22 | 18 | 8 | 5 | 47 | 25 |
| All Time FL/FAPL | 3618 | 1057 | 418 | 334 | 3610 | 1806 | 550 | 470 | 789 | 2453 | 3082 |

|  | Home | Away | Total |
|---|---|---|---|
| League Attendances | 439,043 | 297,867 | 736,910 |

# Manchester United (1) 3
# Aston Villa (0) 1

Match 30

Sunday, 19th December 1993, Old Trafford                    Att.: 44,499

## MANCHESTER UNITED

| 1 | Peter | Schmeichel |
| 2 | Paul | Parker |
| 3 | Denis | Irwin |
| 4 | Steve | Bruce |
| 5 | Lee | *Sharpe (\*80)* |
| 6 | Gary | Pallister |
| 7 | Eric | Cantona |
| 8 | Paul | Ince |
| 10 | Mark | Hughes |
| 14 | Andrei | Kanchelskis |
| 16 | Roy | Keane |

*Subs*

| 9 | Brian | McClair |
| 11 | *Ryan* | *Giggs (\*80)* |
| 13 | Les | Sealey (gk) |

## ASTON VILLA

| 13 | Mark | Bosnich |
| 2 | Earl | Barrett |
| 4 | Shaun | Teale |
| 5 | Paul | McGrath |
| 6 | Kevin | Richardson |
| 8 | Gary | Parker |
| 9 | *Dean* | *Saunders (\*64)* |
| 10 | Dalian | Atkinson |
| 17 | Neil | Cox |
| 22 | Guy | Whittingham |
| 23 | Bryan | Small |

| 11 | *Tony* | *Daley (\*64)* |
| 15 | Gordon | Cowans |
| 1 | Nigel | Spink (gk) |

---

### *Match Facts*

• Villa have won only once at Old Trafford in 39 years. That was in 1983 thanks to two Peter Withe goals.

---

### *Score Sheet*

E. CANTONA 21 min – 1-0
E. CANTONA 89 min – 2-0
P. INCE 90 min – 3-0
N. COX 90 min – 3-1

*Referee:*
Mr. J. Worrall (Warrington)

---

## FA Carling Premiership

| | | P | W | D | L | F | A | Pts |
|---|---|---|---|---|---|---|---|---|
| 1 | **Manchester United** | **21** | **16** | **4** | **1** | **43** | **17** | **52** |
| 2 | Leeds United | 21 | 11 | 6 | 4 | 36 | 24 | 39 |
| 3 | Blackburn Rovers | 20 | 11 | 5 | 4 | 28 | 17 | 38 |
| 4 | Newcastle United | 20 | 10 | 5 | 5 | 37 | 19 | 35 |
| 5 | Arsenal | 21 | 9 | 7 | 5 | 20 | 13 | 34 |

### Result of this Season's Fixture

Manchester Utd
Aston Villa

# The Late, Late Show

United went into the game with the knowledge that Leeds United had cut their lead to ten points and the Reds set off as if determined to ensure the gap was increased back to thirteen.

Parker found Keane at the right of the box and the Irish international easily turned Atkinson. His low cross into the six yard box eluded no fewer than three defenders before finding Cantona at the back post. He gleefully smacked the ball home to punish some slack defending from four yards.

Relentless pressure built up on the Villa goal but the Midlanders dug in and, to their great credit, withstood everything United threw at them. The attacking was so incessant that even Bruce tried his luck with a 30 yarder but the nearest the Reds went to increasing their lead was when Ince dived full length to head another Kanchelskis cross powerfully at goal where Bosnich did well to parry. Keane had a good chance too, but was so surprised that he completely failed to react.

Whatever former United boss, Ron Atkinson, had to say at half-time worked wonders and the Villa side looked transformed. Not that they had played badly in the first period, they had simply been overrun, but there was a new determination as though they had decided they had weathered the worst of the storm. The longer the second period went, the more likely it looked that Villa would score the equaliser. In the 56th minute, Ince gave the ball away in the centre circle leaving Richardson with acres of room to go forward. When he slipped the ball through to Saunders it looked odds on a goal but it was Schmeichel to the rescue with a great diving stop. Some ten minutes from time, Ferguson at last introduced Giggs to the action in place of a strangely ineffectual Sharpe and immediately the Reds got back into the action. Both Giggs and Cantona went close in the dying minutes before the last seconds brought a flurry of goals.

Nothing much looked on when Hughes received the ball in his own half but a first time clearance found Cantona who burst forward. Despite a trip, the Frenchman stayed on his feet to put the ball past Bosnich and take the game away from Villa. Whilst they were still on their knees, Hughes played an in-off against a defenders legs to leave Ince with a half chance that he put past Bosnich at a reverse angle with his left foot. Not to be outdone, Villa went straight down to United's end and claimed a consolation goal which was no more than they deserved. United had once again come through a sticky patch with three points in the bag.

## League Record

| | Home | | | | | | Away | | | | |
|---|---|---|---|---|---|---|---|---|---|---|---|
| | P | W | D | L | F | A | W | D | L | F | A |
| FAPL 93/94 | 21 | 8 | 3 | 0 | 24 | 9 | 8 | 1 | 1 | 19 | 8 |
| All Time FAPL | 63 | 22 | 8 | 2 | 63 | 23 | 18 | 8 | 5 | 47 | 25 |
| All Time FL/FAPL | 3619 | 1058 | 418 | 334 | 3613 | 1807 | 550 | 470 | 789 | 2453 | 3082 |

| | Home | Away | Total |
|---|---|---|---|
| League Attendances | 483,542 | 297,867 | 781,409 |

# Manchester United   (0) 1
# Blackburn Rovers   (1) 1

Sunday, 26th December 1993, Old Trafford      Att.: 44,511

## MANCHESTER UNITED

| | | |
|---|---|---|
| 1 | Peter | Schmeichel |
| 2 | *Paul* | *Parker (\*78)* |
| 3 | Denis | Irwin |
| 4 | Steve | Bruce |
| 5 | Lee | Sharpe |
| 6 | Gary | Pallister |
| 7 | Eric | Cantona |
| 8 | Paul | Ince |
| 10 | *Mark* | *Hughes (+85)* |
| 11 | Ryan | Giggs |
| 16 | Roy | Keane |

*Subs*

| | | |
|---|---|---|
| 18 | *Darren* | *Ferguson (+85)* |
| 9 | *Brian* | *McClair (\*78)* |
| 13 | Les | Sealey (gk) |

## BLACKBURN ROVERS

| | | |
|---|---|---|
| 26 | Tim | Flowers |
| 20 | Henning | Berg |
| 2 | David | May |
| 5 | Colin | Hendry – *Booked* |
| 6 | Graeme | Le Saux |
| 7 | Stuart | Ripley |
| 4 | Tim | Sherwood |
| 23 | David | Batty – *Booked* |
| 8 | Kevin | Gallagher |
| 10 | *Mike* | *Newall (\*11)* |
| 9 | Alan | Shearer – Booked |

| | | |
|---|---|---|
| 1 | Bobby | Mimms (gk) |
| 11 | *Jason* | *Wilcox (\*11)* |
| 3 | Alan | Wright |

---

### *Match Facts*

• The first time that Brian McClair has not scored two goals for United on 26th December in four years.

• After failing to find the net all season, Ince had now scored in three consecutive games.

### *Score Sheet*

GALLAGHER 15 min – 0-1

P. INCE 89 min – 1-1

*Referee:*
Mr. D. Gallagher (Banbury)

---

## FA Carling Premiership

| | | P | W | D | L | F | A | Pts |
|---|---|---|---|---|---|---|---|---|
| 1 | **Manchester United** | 22 | 16 | 5 | 1 | 44 | 18 | 53 |
| 2 | Leeds United | 22 | 11 | 7 | 4 | 37 | 25 | 40 |
| 3 | Blackburn Rovers | 21 | 11 | 6 | 4 | 29 | 18 | 39 |
| 4 | Newcastle United | 21 | 10 | 6 | 5 | 38 | 20 | 36 |
| 5 | Arsenal | 21 | 9 | 7 | 5 | 20 | 13 | 34 |

**Result of this Season's Fixture**

Manchester Utd
Blackburn Rovers

# The Late, Late Show Continues

United received a blow before the kick off when Andrei Kanchelskis was sent home with flu for, on a frozen pitch, the flying Russian would surely have been a trump card. Blackburn set about United with such gusto that the Reds did not even cross the half way line until over four minutes had elapsed. Such was the pressure on United that it was to be a further five minutes before they managed another excursion into Blackburn territory.

After 11 minutes, Rovers lost Newall with a leg injury but soon after that Batty sent Gallagher off on a run that was to bring Kenny Dalglish's side a deserved lead. Pallister was all at sea on an icy pitch and as Bruce came across to cover he too was never fully balanced as he struggled with the conditions. Once past Bruce, Gallagher feinted left and then put the ball to his right past the advancing Schmeichel.

United were at last stung into action and their best move of the game so far between Ince, Giggs and Irwin brought a corner. Bruce powered in a header from the kick which beat Flowers only for substitute Wilcox to hack off the line. But Blackburn still took the game to United and after 24 minutes Sherwood hammered in a volley that, fortunately, was straight at Schmeichel.

United began the second period as they had finished the first and the game threatened to boil over as Blackburn hung on grimly. In the 55th minute Sharpe appeared to push his marker off the ball to give himself a clear shot at goal but he put the chance wide. Blackburn remonstrated fiercely with the referee about the incident and then Shearer took his own retribution on Pallister to earn a booking. Almost immediately Batty took three clearly defined kicks at Sharpe in one tackle and also got himself in the book as Mr Gallagher began to lose control. Schmeichel was then in action as he raced 40 yards from goal to deny Ripley whilst, at the other end, Giggs deceived Flowers with a chip from the wing only to see it float past the far post. It began to look as if Rovers had weathered the worst of the storm and Ferguson threw on both substitutes in quick succession. In the last minute, Sharpe got Giggs only for the defence to scramble the ball away for a corner. When the corner came over, even Schmeichel was in the Blackburn penalty area but it was Pallister who got his head to the ball. McClair's head helped the ball on its way at point blank range but, somehow, Flowers parried the effort and as the ball dropped Ince blasted it home for a late, late equaliser that preserved United's 14 month unbeaten Old Trafford record at the last gasp.

## League Record

| | P | W | D | L | F | A | W | D | L | F | A |
|---|---|---|---|---|---|---|---|---|---|---|---|
| | | **Home** | | | | | **Away** | | | | |
| FAPL 1993/94 | 22 | 8 | 4 | 0 | 25 | 10 | 8 | 1 | 1 | 19 | 8 |
| All Time FAPL | 64 | 22 | 9 | 2 | 64 | 24 | 18 | 8 | 5 | 47 | 25 |
| All Time FL/FAPL | 3620 | 1058 | 419 | 334 | 3614 | 1808 | 550 | 470 | 789 | 2453 | 3082 |

| | Home | Away | Total |
|---|---|---|---|
| League Attendances | 528,053 | 297,867 | 825,920 |

# Oldham Athletic (2) 2
# Manchester United (3) 5

Wednesday, 29th December 1993, Boundary Park          Att.: 16,708

## OLDHAM ATHLETIC

| | | |
|---|---|---|
| 13 | Jon | Hallworth |
| 2 | Craig | Fleming |
| 16 | Tore | Pedersen |
| 5 | Richard | Jobson |
| 22 | Chris | Makin |
| 7 | Gunnar | Halle |
| 10 | Mike | Milligan |
| 11 | Paul | Bernard |
| 23 | *Richard* | *Graham (*45)* |
| 25 | Rick | Holden |
| 14 | Graeme | Sharpe |

*Subs*

| | | |
|---|---|---|
| 1 | Paul | Gerrard (gk) |
| 8 | Andy | Ritchie |
| 12 | *Neil* | *Adams (*45)* |

## MANCHESTER UNITED

| | | |
|---|---|---|
| 1 | Peter | Schmeichel |
| 2 | Paul | Parker |
| 3 | Denis | Irwin |
| 4 | Steve | Bruce |
| 5 | Lee | Sharpe |
| 6 | Gary | Pallister |
| 7 | *Eric* | *Cantona (+64)* |
| 8 | *Paul* | *Ince (*64)* |
| 14 | Andrei | Kanchelskis |
| 11 | Ryan | Giggs |
| 16 | Roy | Keane – *Booked* |

| | | |
|---|---|---|
| 13 | Les | Sealey (gk) |
| 12 | *Bryan* | *Robson (*64)* |
| 9 | *Brian* | *McClair (+64)* |

### Match Facts

- United scored five goals away from home for the first time in the FA Premier League. It was also their record away win in the competition. • The result took their points total for 1993 past the century mark (in 43 games). • United have beaten all five teams who beat them in the 1993/94 campaign.
- Peter Schmeichel overtook Alex Stepney's record set in 1973/74 of 76 consecutive league matches in the United goal.

### Score Sheet

KANCHELSKIS 4 min – 0-1
G. SHARPE 15 min – 1-1
CANTONA 19 min Pen– 1-2
R. HOLDEN 26 min – 2-2
S. BRUCE 39 min –2-3
R. GIGGS 53 min –2-4
R. GIGGS 56 min –2-5

*Referee:*
Mr. V. Callow (Solihull)

## FA Carling Premiership

| | | P | W | D | L | F | A | Pts |
|---|---|---|---|---|---|---|---|---|
| 1 | **Manchester United** | 23 | 17 | 5 | 1 | 49 | 20 | 56 |
| 2 | Blackburn Rovers | 22 | 12 | 6 | 4 | 31 | 18 | 42 |
| 3 | Leeds United | 23 | 11 | 8 | 4 | 38 | 26 | 41 |

**Result of this Season's Fixture**

No Fixture

# Cantona Turns on the Gallic Charm

On Boxing Day 1991, this fixture produced a 6-3 thriller, and as half-time approached with the score poised at 3-2, the crowd were looking forward to another scoring spectacle. In the event, United added just two more with substitute McClair letting Oldham off lightly in the 25 minutes or so he was on the pitch.

The Reds took the lead after only four minutes when Lee Sharpe won a midfield tussle to get Kanchelskis free down the right. He clipped the ball into Cantona who stroked it back into the path of the flying Russian who proceeded to outstrip the Oldham defence before hitting his shot against Hallworth's legs. Fortunately for United, the ball bounced straight back in to the path of Kanchelskis and he made no mistake the second time.

Graeme Sharp has always proved to be a thorn in United's side wherever he has played and when Denis Irwin, on his return to his old stamping ground, made a complete hash of clearing a Rick Holden cross it was Sharp who was on hand to beat Schmeichel from 12 yards out. United bounced straight back to take the lead when Kanchelskis again outpaced the Oldham rearguard until he was crudely scythed down in the area by Pedersen. Cantona stepped up with the minimum of fuss to put the ball high to Hallworth's right as the 'keeper dived left.

Still Oldham were not to be outdone and, although there didn't look to be much danger from a position out near the right touchline, Holden floated a free-kick straight into the far corner over a bewildered Schmeichel. Six minutes before half-time, Bruce scored with as powerful a header from an Irwin corner as one could wish to see – certainly Hallworth didn't see it!

The game was over fifteen minutes into the second period and once again it was Cantona who had a hand in both goals with Giggs providing the finish. The fourth goal started on the half-way line with Cantona who released a reverse pass to the left wing as he was running to the right. The ball was in acres of space with Giggs haring after it. He caught it just inside the touchline and then cut in to score from an angle with the help of a deflection from Jobson.

If that didn't quite seal United's victory, the fifth goal on the hour certainly did. Parker nudged a free-kick three feet to Cantona who then deposited the ball thirty yards onto the head of Lee Sharpe at the far post. The England player directed the ball back across the face of goal to where Giggs and Keane were queuing up to apply the finishing touch with the Welshman getting there first.

## League Record

|  | Home | | | | | | Away | | | | |
|  | P | W | D | L | F | A | W | D | L | F | A |
|---|---|---|---|---|---|---|---|---|---|---|---|
| FAPL 93/94 | 23 | 8 | 4 | 0 | 25 | 10 | 9 | 1 | 1 | 24 | 10 |
| All Time FAPL | 65 | 22 | 9 | 2 | 64 | 24 | 19 | 8 | 5 | 52 | 27 |
| All Time FL/FAPL | 3621 | 1058 | 419 | 334 | 3614 | 1808 | 551 | 470 | 789 | 2458 | 3084 |

|  | Home | Away | Total |
|---|---|---|---|
| League Attendances | 528,053 | 314,575 | 842,628 |

# Manchester United (0) 0
# Leeds United (0) 0

Saturday, 1st January 1994, Old Trafford          Att.: 44,724

## MANCHESTER UNITED

| 1 | Peter | Schmeichel |
|---|---|---|
| 2 | Paul | Parker |
| 3 | Denis | Irwin |
| 4 | Steve | Bruce |
| 6 | Gary | Pallister |
| 7 | Eric | Cantona – *Booked* |
| 9 | Brian | McClair |
| 11 | Ryan | Giggs |
| 12 | Bryan | Robson – *Booked* |
| 14 | Andrei | Kanchelskis |
| 16 | Roy | Keane |

*Subs*

| 13 | Les | Sealey (gk) |
|---|---|---|
| 20 | Dion | Dublin |
| 18 | Darren | Ferguson |

## LEEDS UNITED

| 13 | Mark | Beeney |
|---|---|---|
| 22 | Gary | Kelly |
| 16 | Jon | Newsome |
| 5 | Chris | Fairclough |
| 3 | Tony | Dorigo |
| 7 | Gordon | Strachan |
| 10 | Gary | McAllister |
| 11 | *Steve* | *Hodge (*84)* |
| 4 | David | White |
| 9 | Brian | Deane |
| 12 | John | Pemberton |

| 1 | John | Lukic (gk) |
|---|---|---|
| 20 | *Kevin* | *Sharp (*84)* |
| 14 | David | Wetherall |

### *Match Facts*

• The thirteenth consecutive game in which Leeds have failed to beat United.

### *Score Sheet*

*Referee:*
Mr. D. Ellery (Harrow)

## FA Carling Premiership

| | | P | W | D | L | F | A | Pts |
|---|---|---|---|---|---|---|---|---|
| 1 | **Manchester United** | **24** | **17** | **6** | **1** | **49** | **20** | **57** |
| 2 | Blackburn Rovers | 23 | 13 | 6 | 4 | 32 | 18 | 45 |
| 3 | Arsenal | 24 | 12 | 7 | 5 | 30 | 13 | 43 |
| 4 | Leeds United | 24 | 11 | 9 | 4 | 38 | 26 | 42 |
| 5 | Newcastle United | 23 | 11 | 6 | 6 | 40 | 21 | 39 |

### Result of this Season's Fixture

Manchester Utd
Leeds United

# Stalemate

Both teams had pre-match problems with United losing Hughes, Ince, and Sharpe to injuries and Leeds almost as badly hit with the absence of leading goalscorers Gary Speed and Rod Wallace. The game began with Kanchelskis playing a delightful through ball to Giggs but the chance went when the young Welshman was blatantly held back by his marker Gary Kelly, an equally young Irishman of immense potential.

It was some considerable time before the next effort of any note – a Robson shot from a half chance outside the area which just cleared the angle to Beeney's right. Deane's elbow did sufficient damage to Bruce's face to warrant a six minute departure for stitches during which time Leeds still couldn't pressurise the Reds despite them being down to ten men. Indeed, it was still United with the bulk of the play and Pemberton could only stop Giggs after the Welsh wizard had beaten three players at the expense of a booking. Almost immediately he had to resort to pushing the youngster to the ground to stop another threat and was very lucky not to receive the red card.

United nearly broke down the Leeds resistance at the start of the second half when Bruce moved forward and found the defence retreating before him. He chipped the ball into the area where Robson cleverly directed his header to Keane but his shot flashed harmlessly across the the face of the goal. Keane was back in the action when he got his head to a Cantona cross to give Kanchelskis a good chance but the Russian slipped as he turned and the opportunity was gone. United's one minute of alarm came when Robson lost the ball on the half-way line and Cantona had no hesitation in retrieving the situation by dropping McAllister to the ground and earning himself a booking. It could have been much worse for when Dorigo took the resulting free-kick, Fairclough outjumped everybody to plant a looping header on to the United crossbar with Schmeichel beaten.

From then until the final whistle it was all United but there were so many bodies in the Leeds area that when half chances appeared for Cantona and Kanchelskis they rebounded off either defenders or team mates alike. It was difficult to guess who was the more content with the stalemate. Before the game, United would have settled for a point with Leeds, having been comprehensively outplayed, also happy to have eventually survived to take a point home. But an even bigger injustice would have been done had Fairclough's header been more decisive!

## League Record

| | P | W | D | L | F | A | W | D | L | F | A |
|---|---|---|---|---|---|---|---|---|---|---|---|
| | | | **Home** | | | | | | **Away** | | |
| FAPL 93/94 | 24 | 8 | 5 | 0 | 25 | 10 | 9 | 1 | 1 | 24 | 10 |
| All Time FAPL | 66 | 22 | 10 | 2 | 64 | 24 | 19 | 8 | 5 | 52 | 27 |
| All Time FL/FAPL | 3622 | 1058 | 420 | 334 | 3614 | 1808 | 551 | 470 | 789 | 2458 | 3084 |

| | Home | Away | Total |
|---|---|---|---|
| League Attendances | 572,777 | 314,575 | 887,352 |

# Liverpool
# Manchester United

**(2) 3**
**(3) 3**

Tuesday, 4th January 1994, Anfield                    Att.: 42,795

## LIVERPOOL

| | | |
|---|---|---|
| 1 | Bruce | Grobbelaar |
| 2 | Rob | Jones |
| 5 | Mark | Wright |
| 25 | Neil | Ruddock |
| 3 | Julian | Dicks |
| 7 | Nigel | Clough – *Booked* |
| 17 | Steve | McManaman (*77) |
| 15 | Jamie | Redknapp |
| 10 | John | Barnes |
| 9 | Ian | Rush |
| 23 | Robbie | Fowler |

*Subs*

| | | |
|---|---|---|
| 13 | David | James (gk) |
| 4 | Steve | Nicol |
| 20 | *Stig* | *Bjornebye* (*77) |

## MANCHESTER UNITED

| | | |
|---|---|---|
| 1 | Peter | Schmeichel |
| 2 | Paul | Parker |
| 3 | Denis | Irwin |
| 4 | Steve | Bruce |
| 6 | Gary | Pallister |
| 7 | Eric | Cantona |
| 8 | Paul | Ince – *Booked* |
| 9 | Brian | McClair |
| 11 | Ryan | Giggs |
| 14 | Andrei | Kanchelskis |
| 16 | Roy | Keane – *Booked* |

| | | |
|---|---|---|
| 12 | Bryan | Robson |
| 13 | Les | Sealey (gk) |
| 18 | Darren | Ferguson |

### *Match Facts*

• The 50th appearance for United of Eric Cantona during which he has been on the losing side only twice.

• Only the second ever 3-3 draw between the two sides at Anfield. After nearly a hundred years without such a scoreline in Liverpool, this game produced the second in five years.

### *Score Sheet*

S. BRUCE 9 min – 0-1

R. GIGGS 20 min – 0-2

D. IRWIN 24 min – 0-3

N. CLOUGH 25 min – 1-3

N. CLOUGH 38 min – 2-3

N. RUDDOCK 79 min – 3-3

*Referee:*
Mr. P. Don (Middlesex)

## FA Carling Premiership

| | | P | W | D | L | F | A | Pts |
|---|---|---|---|---|---|---|---|---|
| 1 | **Manchester United** | 25 | 17 | 7 | 1 | 52 | 23 | 58 |
| 2 | Blackburn Rovers | 23 | 13 | 6 | 4 | 32 | 18 | 45 |
| 3 | Arsenal | 25 | 12 | 8 | 5 | 30 | 13 | 44 |

### Result of this Season's Fixture

Liverpool
Manchester Utd

# United Stunned

Liverpool started like a house on fire and missed a great opportunity to go a goal up inside the first sixty seconds. A slick attack by Clough culminated in a shot which deflected off Bruce straight to Fowler but with the goal at his mercy, the young Anfield prodigy somehow contrived to get the ball over Schmeichel's crossbar. But after seven minutes of severe Liverpool pressure, United at last broke free and applied some of their own which won them successive corner kicks. The second of these was decisive with Cantona playing the ball in and Bruce giving Grobbelaar no chance with a powerful, downward header. In the 20th minute Wright again hesitated and Giggs pounced to dispossess him and calmly chipped the ball over a stranded Grobbelaar to put United very much in the driving seat.

Four minutes later, the match looked over as Irwin slotted home a free kick to give Alex Ferguson's side a dream start. Nigel Clough, however, had something to say about the game being finished. Straight from the kick off he progressed to within 30 yards of goal where he appeared to run out of ideas as to where to turn to next. He solved his problem by blasting a great shot past Schmeichel and restored some semblance of balance to the game. He was quickly in the thick of things again when he stopped Giggs with a horrendous challenge that brought him a caution but Keane clearly thought that was not sufficient punishment and the next time Clough latched on to the ball, the Irishman meted out his own brand of retribution to join him in the referee's notebook. Clough was certainly playing an instrumental part in the match and he reduced the arrears still further in the 39th minute. There seemed little danger as a Liverpool effort on goal appeared to be well covered but a deflection off Bruce changed all that. The ball fell to Clough and as United's rearguard hesitated, the Liverpool midfielder drove the ball into the bottom right hand corner of Schmeichel's net.

Ince lost patience and was booked whilst Schmeichel made a great save from Redknapp before treating a tremendous 25 yard drive from Dicks as though it was merely a back pass. When United broke away they found Grobbelaar in irrepressible mood and soon Liverpool were back in the United half and a diving header from Ince wasn't sufficient to clear an attack. The ball went to the Liverpool substitute, Bjornebye who with his first touch floated over a cross for Ruddock to head powerfully home. Indeed, had it not been for a last ditch tackle by Kanchelskis in a central defender's role, Liverpool would have gone on to take all three points.

## League Record

| | Home | | | | | | Away | | | | |
|---|---|---|---|---|---|---|---|---|---|---|---|
| | P | W | D | L | F | A | W | D | L | F | A |
| FAPL 93/94 | 25 | 8 | 5 | 0 | 25 | 10 | 9 | 2 | 1 | 27 | 13 |
| All Time FAPL | 67 | 22 | 10 | 2 | 64 | 24 | 19 | 9 | 5 | 55 | 30 |
| All Time FL/FAPL | 3623 | 1058 | 420 | 334 | 3614 | 1808 | 551 | 471 | 789 | 2461 | 3087 |

| | Home | Away | Total |
|---|---|---|---|
| League Attendances | 572,777 | 357,370 | 930,147 |

# Sheffield United     **(0) 0**
# Manchester United     **(0) 1**

Sunday, 11th January 1994, Bramall Lane      Att.: 22,019

| | | **SHEFFIELD UNITED** | | | **MANCHESTER UNITED** |
|---|---|---|---|---|---|
| 1 | Alan | Kelly | 1 | Peter | Schmeichel |
| 17 | Carl | Bradshaw | 2 | Paul | Parker |
| 14 | David | Tuttle – *Booked* | 3 | Denis | Irwin |
| 26 | *Jamie* | *Hoyland (\*70)* | 4 | Steve | Bruce |
| 16 | Paul | Beesley | 6 | Gary | Pallister |
| 11 | *Mitch* | *Ward (+79)* | 7 | Eric | Cantona |
| 10 | Glyn | Hodges | 8 | Paul | Ince |
| 23 | Chris | Kamara | 10 | Mark | Hughes – *B'kd/Sent Off* |
| 18 | Dane | Whitehouse | 11 | Ryan | Giggs |
| 12 | Jostein | Flo | 14 | Andrei | Kanchelskis |
| 2 | Kevin | Gage | 16 | Roy | Keane |

*Subs*

| | | | | | |
|---|---|---|---|---|---|
| 9 | *Roger* | *Nilsen (+79)* | 13 | Les | Sealey |
| 22 | *Andy* | *Scott (\*70)* | 12 | Bryan | Robson |
| 13 | Carl | Muggleton | 9 | Brian | McClair |

## *Match Facts*

• This victory was sweet revenge for the previous season's 2-1 knock out at Bramall Lane

## *Score Sheet*

M. HUGHES 62 min – 0-1

### *Referee:*
Mr. G. Ashby (Worcester)

# Dreadful

Having been twice beaten 3-0 by United earlier in the campaign it was perhaps, no surprise, that Dave Bassett's Sheffield side chose spoiling tactics to try to repeat their previous year's Bramall Lane FA Cup success over the Reds. As a result the game was a massive disappointment.

Tuttle, later to become an even bigger villain, was booked as early as the eighth minute but already about a dozen players had taken part in an unseemly pushing and shoving episode. United's open play was stifled but there was the odd moment of magic, especially when a delightful pass from Cantona to Kanchelskis took three defenders out at a stroke. Unfortunately, the Russian's final ball just eluded Hughes. Worse was to follow for the Welshman when he was booked in the 21st minute after a scuffle with Kamara who was certainly putting himself about. On the half hour, Kanchelskis powered in a drive but it was straight at Kelly.

If the first half had been poor then the second session was even worse with little of note happening until, right out of the blue, came a goal worthy of the most exciting contest imaginable. United moved the ball quickly with one touch football from man to man, starting a seven man move on the right. Hughes, having played a part on the right, finished it from the left with a cross shot that beat Kelly before hitting the post and rolling into the net. It was a goal of breathtaking proportions and certainly had no part in this dismal affair.

Sheffield hit back and should have equalised after 71 minutes when Ward picked his spot but failed to put the ball there as he scooped it hopelessly over the bar. In the last ten minutes, as Sheffield began to throw caution to the wind, the game at last became endurable. Ince deflected a good Whitehouse effort for a corner whilst at the other end a Kanchelskis cross was well met by Giggs but Kelly stopped the Reds increasing their lead with a fine save. Tuttle then scythed Hughes down on the half-way line with a dreadful tackle that should have brought the red card as he had already been booked but the referee chose to ignore it. With his side winning 1-0 and only three minutes to go, the Welshman should also have ignored it but didn't. The next time Tuttle got the ball, Hughes fell for the sucker punch and took a massive kick at him. As always, the player who retaliates is dismissed leaving the provoker still on the pitch but Hughes should have known better.

## FA Cup Record

|  | P | W | D | L | F | A | W | D | L | F | A |
|---|---|---|---|---|---|---|---|---|---|---|---|
|  |  | **Home** |  |  |  |  | **Away** |  |  |  |  |
| FA Cup record | 340 | 98 | 31 | 28 | 330 | 147 | 74 | 52 | 57 | 284 | 266 |

|  | Home | Away | Total |
|---|---|---|---|
| 93-94 FA Cup Attendances | – | 22,019 | 22,019 |

# Manchester United (1) 2
# Portsmouth (1) 2

Wednesday, 12th January 1994, Old Trafford          Att.: 43,794

## MANCHESTER UNITED

| | | |
|---|---|---|
| 1 | Peter | Schmeichel |
| 2 | Paul | Parker |
| 3 | Denis | Irwin |
| 4 | Steve | Bruce |
| 6 | Gary | Pallister |
| 7 | Eric | Cantona |
| 9 | *Brian* | *McClair (+90)* |
| 10 | *Mark* | *Hughes (*71)* |
| 11 | Ryan | Giggs |
| 12 | Bryan | Robson |
| 14 | Andrei | Kanchelskis |

*Subs*

| | | |
|---|---|---|
| 13 | Les | Sealey (gk) |
| 16 | *Roy* | *Keane (*74)* |
| 20 | *Dion* | *Dublin (+90)* |

## PORTSMOUTH

| | | |
|---|---|---|
| 1 | Alan | Knight |
| 2 | *Kit* | *Symons (*23)* |
| 3 | Tony | Dobson |
| 4 | Andy | Awford |
| 5 | Bjorn | Kristensen |
| 6 | John | Durnin |
| 7 | Alan | McLoughlin |
| 8 | *Mark* | *Stimpson (+85)* |
| 9 | Darryl | Powell |
| 10 | Paul | Walsh |
| 11 | Ray | Daniel |

| | | |
|---|---|---|
| 12 | *Mark* | *Chamberlain (*) B'kd* |
| 13 | Brian | Horne (gk) |
| 14 | *Stuart* | *Doling (+85)* |

## *Match Facts*

- Alan McLaughlin, rejected by United as a teenager, returned to Old Trafford for Portsmouth.

- The meeting was the fifth League Cup clash between the two teams with United remaining unbeaten.

- Giggs' opening goal was the first conceded by Portsmouth in 508 minutes of League Cup action this season.

- The third time Mr Barrett has refereed at Old Trafford – United are still to win a game when he has officiated there

## *Score Sheet*

R. GIGGS 29 min – 1-0
P. WALSH 32 min – 1-1
E. CANTONA 60 min – 2-1
P. WALSH 71 min – 2-2

### *Referee:*

Mr. K. Barrett (Coventry)

# Almost Knight, Knight

The opening fifteen minutes or so of this game was virtually Kanchelskis versus Portsmouth as the Russian threatened to take the southern outfit apart single-handedly. As early as the second minute he let fly from the right wing but was just past the far post with his effort. Next he sent in an inch perfect cross for Hughes who was unmarked on the edge of the six yard box only to head a great chance well over the bar. The Russian then hit the byeline to pull the ball back across the face of Knight's net but nobody was there to capitalise. Next it was his pace that took him clear of everybody but his shot from an angle was blocked by Knight.

After that, others began to get in on the act and an exquisite ball from McClair saw Hughes clip it just wide. Then after 29 minutes, United's intense pressure paid off when Giggs put the Reds in front with probably the easiest goal he will ever score. A long ball from Pallister found Giggs in the clear as Portsmouth pushed out looking for offside. Giggs didn't control the ball and it broke away from him to find Hughes who went down in a tangle with three Pompey defenders. The ball rolled out of the melee for Giggs to stroke into a completely open net from eight yards.

But Portsmouth had plenty of fight left in them and they won a free kick out on the right. Unbelievably it was Walsh, the smallest Pompey player, who headed past Schmeichel from six yards.

At the start of the second period, United were very fortunate to survive what looked to be a perfectly legitimate claim for a penalty when McLaughlin was clearly brought down by Parker but Mr Barrett thought otherwise. Then Pompey entered their best spell of the game putting United under considerable pressure. United's defence was at sixes and sevens with McClair actually hitting his own post with an attempted clearance. Gradually the Reds gathered their composure and took play down to the Portsmouth end. Kanchelskis put in a stinging effort which was kicked off the line only for it to fall to Hughes. The Welshman took the ball round Knight but then missed the target from an acute angle. Hughes was quickly back in the thick of things, winning the ball in midfield and passing to Parker on the right. His inch perfect cross found Cantona who only had to jerk his head back to rifle in a header which even the inspired Knight couldn't keep out.

Portsmouth, however, were not to be denied and Stimpson sprung the offside trap to free Powell on the left and, as the big striker closed in on goal, Schmeichel narrowed the angle but could only parry the shot. It bounced into the path of Walsh who again had the easy task of nodding the ball home.

## League Cup Record

|  | | Home | | | | | | Away | | | | |
|---|---|---|---|---|---|---|---|---|---|---|---|---|
|  | P | W | D | L | F | A | W | D | L | F | A |
| League Cup Record | 117 | 43 | 11 | 8 | 133 | 53 | 20 | 14 | 21 | 73 | 71 |

|  | Home | Away | Total |
|---|---|---|---|
| Coca-Cola Cup Att. 93-94 | 126,525 | 57,379 | 183,904 |

# Tottenham Hotspur    (0) 0
# Manchester United    (0) 1

Saturday, 15th January 1994, White Hart Lane     Att.: 31,343

## TOTTENHAM HOTSPUR

| 13 | Ian | Walker |
| 3 | *Justin* | *Edinburgh (\*56)* |
| 4 | Vinny | Samways |
| 5 | Colin | Calderwood – *Booked* |
| 7 | *Nick* | *Barmby (+64)* |
| 9 | Darren | Anderton |
| 14 | Steve | Sedgeley |
| 16 | Micky | Hazard |
| 20 | Darren | Caskey |
| 22 | David | Kerslake |
| 23 | Sol | Campbell |

*Subs*

| 2 | *Dean* | *Austin (\*56)* |
| 25 | *John* | *Hendry (+64)* |
| 30 | Mervyn | Day (gk) |

## MANCHESTER UNITED

| 1 | Peter | Schmeichel |
| 2 | Paul | Parker |
| 3 | Denis | Irwin |
| 4 | Steve | Bruce |
| 6 | Gary | Pallister |
| 7 | Eric | Cantona |
| 8 | Paul | Ince |
| 10 | *Mark* | *Hughes (\*81)* |
| 11 | Ryan | Giggs |
| 14 | Andrei | Kanchelskis |
| 16 | Roy | Keane |

| 9 | *Brian* | *McClair (\*81)* |
| 20 | Dion | Dublin |
| 13 | Les | Sealey (gk) |

## *Match Facts*

• Tottenham hadn't won at White Hart Lane since 3rd October 1993.

## *Score Sheet*

M. HUGHES 48 min – 0-1

*Referee:*
Mr. R. Milford (Avon)

## FA Carling Premiership

| | | P | W | D | L | F | A | Pts |
|---|---|---|---|---|---|---|---|---|
| 1 | **Manchester United** | 26 | 18 | 7 | 1 | 53 | 23 | 61 |
| 2 | Blackburn Rovers | 24 | 14 | 6 | 4 | 34 | 19 | 48 |
| 3 | Arsenal | 26 | 12 | 9 | 5 | 30 | 13 | 45 |
| 4 | Leeds United | 25 | 11 | 10 | 4 | 38 | 26 | 43 |
| 5 | Newcastle United | 24 | 12 | 6 | 6 | 42 | 22 | 42 |

**Result of this Season's Fixture**

Tottenham H.
Manchester Utd

# Hughes on the Mark

Having suffered their only league defeat this season on a previous trip to London, United set off as if determined not to allow Spurs to repeat Chelsea's victory and could have gone in front as early as the first minute. Schmeichel's throw to Giggs was quickly moved inside to Ince, allowing the Welsh youngster to sprint into space down the left. Ince gave the ball back to Giggs who beat Kerslake to cross to the far post where United players were queueing. Roy Keane took the responsibility but his left foot shot hit Walker in the Spurs net and bounced to safety.

After Anderton had brought Schmeichel to his knees with a 35 yarder, Pallister calmly broke up a move in his own area and fed the ball wide to Giggs just outside the United area. The winger pushed the ball inside to Cantona and then set off for the return. When he got the ball back from the Frenchman, Giggs was advancing rapidly towards the Spurs box but his shot again hit Walker and fell safely, a move of breathtaking pace and skill. For all that, the London side almost took the lead when Campbell met a Darren Anderton free kick to send a header flashing past Schmeichel's left hand post. The only surprise of an entertaining first half was that there had been no goals.

United attacked again straight from the restart and put Ossie Ardiles's men under severe pressure with Kanchelskis causing most of the early problems. The Russian took the ball the length of the field before laying the ball back to Parker. The full back crossed superbly but Hughes missed his kick altogether. The ball now fell to Giggs whose rocket shot was palmed away for a corner by Walker. Parker found Keane down the right touchline and the Irishman easily turned Caskey to get in a cross to the near post. Hughes met the centre and clipped the ball firmly against Calderwood's legs and into the net. It was a goal much in line with the run of play and only served to fuel more United attacks.

Cantona now began to treat the crowd to a display of impromptu virtuosity with his delicate flicks and back heels but it was the raw power of Keane which next burst on the Spurs goal as the Irishman thundered in another strong shot which Walker did well to hold. Seconds later Walker, on the edge of the six yard box, couldn't hold another Keane piledriver and, after pushing it up in the air, the young 'keeper could only watch as it bounced into the roof of his unguarded net. As United celebrated what appeared to be a great strike, the referee consulted a linesman and then disallowed the goal for offside against Kanchelskis.

## League Record

| | Home | | | | | | Away | | | | |
|---|---|---|---|---|---|---|---|---|---|---|---|
| | P | W | D | L | F | A | W | D | L | F | A |
| FAPL 93/94 | 26 | 8 | 5 | 0 | 25 | 10 | 10 | 2 | 1 | 28 | 13 |
| All Time FAPL | 68 | 22 | 10 | 2 | 64 | 24 | 20 | 9 | 5 | 56 | 30 |
| All Time FL/FAPL | 3624 | 1058 | 420 | 334 | 3614 | 1808 | 552 | 471 | 789 | 2462 | 3087 |

| | Home | Away | Total |
|---|---|---|---|
| League Attendances | 572,777 | 388,713 | 961,490 |

# Manchester United (1) 1
# Everton (0) 0

Saturday, 22nd January 1994, Old Trafford          Att.: 44,750

## MANCHESTER UNITED

| | | |
|---|---|---|
| 1 | Peter | Schmeichel |
| 2 | Paul | Parker |
| 3 | Denis | Irwin |
| 4 | Steve | Bruce |
| 14 | Andrea | Kanchelskis |
| 6 | Gary | Pallister |
| 7 | Eric | Cantona |
| 8 | Paul | Ince |
| 16 | Roy | Keane |
| 10 | Mark | Hughes |
| 11 | Ryan | Giggs |

*Subs*

| | | |
|---|---|---|
| 9 | Brian | McClair |
| 20 | Dion | Dublin |
| 13 | Les | Sealey (gk) |

## EVERTON

| | | |
|---|---|---|
| 1 | Neville | Southall |
| 2 | Matthew | Jackson |
| 25 | Neil | Moore |
| 4 | Ian | Snodin |
| 14 | John | Ebbrell |
| 6 | Gary | Ablett |
| 8 | Graham | Stuart |
| 22 | Brett | Angell |
| 9 | *Tony* | *Cottee (\*15)* |
| 20 | *Robert* | *Warzycha (+80)* |
| 11 | Peter | Beagrie |

| | | |
|---|---|---|
| 3 | *Andy* | *Hinchliffe (+80)* |
| 19 | *Stuart* | *Barlow (\*45)* |
| 13 | Jason | Kearton (gk) |

---

### *Match Facts*

• Giggs' goal made him the third United player into double figures behind Cantona and Hughes. • The attendance of 44,750 set a new Premiership record and took the season's league attendances for United games past the one million mark. • United's lead at the top extends to a record 16 points.

### *Score Sheet*

R. GIGGS 27 min – 1-0

*Referee:*
R. D. Gifford (Llanbradach)

---

## FA Carling Premiership

| | | P | W | D | L | F | A | Pts |
|---|---|---|---|---|---|---|---|---|
| 1 | **Manchester United** | 27 | 19 | 7 | 1 | 54 | 23 | 64 |
| 2 | Blackburn Rovers | 24 | 14 | 6 | 4 | 34 | 19 | 48 |
| 3 | Arsenal | 27 | 12 | 10 | 5 | 31 | 14 | 46 |
| 4 | Newcastle United | 26 | 13 | 6 | 7 | 45 | 25 | 45 |
| 5 | Liverpool | 26 | 12 | 7 | 7 | 44 | 32 | 43 |

### Result of this Season's Fixture

Manchester Utd
Everton

# A Mark of Respect

Old Trafford was in sombre mood for this match where the Premiership's record crowd was joined by spectators on every other ground in the country in observing a minute's silence as a mark of respect for Sir Matt Busby who had passed away 48 hours earlier. The teams had been piped out on to the pitch by a lone bagpiper playing "A Scottish Soldier" after which there was only the sound of silence as the stadium paid its silent tribute to the legend.

It was always going to be a difficult game for United but the Reds did it the way Sir Matt would have wanted – in style. He would have been particularly satisfied with the display put on by the latest youngster of world class, Ryan Giggs, who tore Everton apart on several occasions. The Welsh wizard ran half the length of the pitch in one early attack beating three defenders on his way before forcing Southall into a diving save.

A goal had to come and it was United who scored it with Parker working the ball through to Keane at the right of the penalty area. The Irishman easily turned Ablett and then crossed. Nobody seemed to be anywhere near it but Giggs made five yards on an astonished Matthew Jackson across the face of the goal to get in a glancing header that left Southall grasping at thin air.

The second half saw the Reds in full flow with Giggs and Cantona particularly prominent. When the youngster crossed from the left, Cantona chested the ball down before turning and lashing a shot against Southall's right hand post. Ince then set up Kanchelkis for a shooting opportunity from outside the area and his powerful effort smacked the crossbar after taking a deflection off Ablett. Another brilliant move saw the Russian fly past Ablett, who was having a torrid time, cross to Cantona who laid it off to Hughes and then took the return in his stride before firing his shot inches over the Everton bar. But even that moment of magic was surpassed with a surging run from inside his own half by Giggs which took him past five Everton defenders in a style that would have had Sir Matt's approval.

As United kept up the pressure, Hughes got Cantona away but once again he hit the woodwork as the Reds put on a display of style that was more than appropriate for the day. As Alex Ferguson commented afterwards *"I think the gaffer would have been pleased with the entertainment value but he might have asked why we didn't score more goals"*. The victory had been achieved the Matt Busby way.

## League Record

|  | Home | | | | | | Away | | | | |
|  | P | W | D | L | F | A | W | D | L | F | A |
|---|---|---|---|---|---|---|---|---|---|---|---|
| FAPL 93/94 | 27 | 9 | 5 | 0 | 26 | 10 | 10 | 2 | 1 | 28 | 13 |
| All Time FAPL | 69 | 23 | 10 | 2 | 65 | 24 | 20 | 9 | 5 | 56 | 30 |
| All Time FL/FAPL | 3625 | 1059 | 420 | 334 | 3615 | 1808 | 552 | 471 | 789 | 2462 | 3087 |

|  | Home | Away | Total |
|---|---|---|---|
| League Attendances | 617,527 | 388,713 | 1,006,240 |

# Portsmouth       (0) 0
# Manchester United    (1) 1

Wednesday, 26th January 1994, Fratton Park      Att.: 24,950

## PORTSMOUTH

| 1  | Alan   | Knight                        |
|----|--------|-------------------------------|
| 2  | Warren | Neill                         |
| 3  | Bjorn  | Kristensen                    |
| 4  | Andy   | Awford                        |
| 5  | Kit    | Symons                        |
| 6  | Ray    | Daniel                        |
| 7  | Alan   | McLoughlin                    |
| 8  | John   | Durnin – B'ked/Sent Off       |
| 9  | Mark   | Chamberlain (*45)             |
| 10 | Paul   | Walsh                         |
| 11 | Gerry  | Creaney                       |

*Subs*

| 12 | Daryl | Powell (*45)  |
| 13 | Brian | Horne (gk)    |
| 14 | Tony  | Dobson        |

## MANCHESTER UNITED

| 1  | Peter  | Schmeichel  |
|----|--------|-------------|
| 2  | Paul   | Parker      |
| 3  | Denis  | Irwin       |
| 4  | Steve  | Bruce       |
| 6  | Gary   | Pallister   |
| 7  | Eric   | Cantona     |
| 8  | Paul   | Ince        |
| 9  | Brian  | McClair     |
| 11 | Ryan   | Giggs       |
| 14 | Andrei | Kanchelskis |
| 16 | Roy    | Keane       |

| 13 | Les  | Sealey (gk) |
| 20 | Dion | Dublin      |
| 19 | Gary | Neville     |

---

### *Match Facts*

- McClair's goal was his third in the Coca-Cola Cup this season and the first conceded at home by Pompey in the competition this season in 327 minutes.
- The sixth meeting of the clubs in the competition with Portsmouth still to register a win.
- The home debut of Pompey's £500,000 signing from Celtic, Gerry Creaney.
- United have suffered just two defeats in their last 32 games in the competition.

### *Score Sheet*

B. McCLAIR 27 min – 0-1

*Referee:*
Mr. K.Cooper (Pontypridd)

# Strolling

The ground was packed to capacity a full hour before kick off as United mania hit the south coast. The home team soon gave their supporters something to cheer when they won a corner in the opening twenty seconds. Facing a gale force wind, United hit back immediately and within a minute they, too, had forced a corner.

The first real shot of venom saw McLoughlin bring Schmeichel to his knees after ten minutes but United were slowly but surely beginning to get the upper hand. On fourteen minutes a Kanchelskis cross was headed down by Cantona to Keane whose shot clearly took a deflection off John Durnin who was immediately booked for disputing the point. The stupidity of his action was to return to haunt him later in the game. From the corner, Ince fired a volley just over. Keane and Irwin linked up brilliantly down the left to allow Irwin to send in a low cross right across the face of goal but nobody was able to get on the end of the opportunity. Portsmouth, however, bounced back and Keane was forced to send a diving header past his own post before United finally took the lead after 27 minutes.

Symons headed the ball for a corner when it seemed the 'keeper had called for it but, following several corners to the near post that had produced nothing, it was somewhat surprising that Giggs elected to send yet another looping to the same area. His persistence, however, was rewarded when Cantona got a flick on with his head and McClair applied the finishing touch with a deft header from five yards.

It took Pompey until the 55th minute to trouble United when Schmeichel was bravely down at the feet of Symons. Two minutes later McLaughlin caused mayhem in the United defence before firing in a shot but in the 62nd minute the game was all over. Just as one sensed that Portsmouth's effort was petering out, Durnin scythed Ince down from behind and, as a result of his earlier indiscretion, found himself sent off. It had taken Pompey all their time to keep up with United with eleven, once they were down to ten they were simply chasing shadows.

McClair smacked a twenty yarder against the bar that wouldn't have counted as Kanchelskis was offside and then the crowd had the rare sight of Les Sealey warming up after Creaney had flattened Schmeichel. United were quite content to play keep ball and they passed the ball between themselves as though they were on a training session. The pitch was cutting up badly with huge divots playing havoc with the path of the ball and this, as much as anything, was responsible for United failing to add to their lead as the Reds played out time.

## League Cup Record

|  |  | Home |  |  |  |  | Away |  |  |  |  |
|---|---|---|---|---|---|---|---|---|---|---|---|
|  | P | W | D | L | F | A | W | D | L | F | A |
| League Cup Record | 118 | 43 | 11 | 8 | 133 | 53 | 21 | 14 | 21 | 74 | 71 |

|  | Home | Away | Total |
|---|---|---|---|
| League Cup Attendances | 126,525 | 82,329 | 208,854 |

# Norwich City      (0) 0
# Manchester United      (1) 2

Sunday, 30th January 1994, Carrow Road      Att.: 21,060

| NORWICH CITY | | | MANCHESTER UNITED | | |
|---|---|---|---|---|---|
| 1 | Brian | Gunn | 1 | Peter | Schmeichel |
| 10 | John | Polston | 2 | Paul | Parker |
| 8 | Colin | Woodthorpe | 3 | Denis | Irwin |
| 5 | Ian | Culverhouse | 4 | Steve | Bruce |
| 2 | Mark | Bowen | 6 | Gary | Pallister |
| 4 | *Ian* | *Crook (\*75)* | 7 | Eric | Cantona – *Booked* |
| 9 | Gary | Megson | 8 | Paul | Ince |
| 3 | Rob | Newman | 10 | *Mark* | *Hughes (\*79)* |
| 14 | Ruel | Fox | 11 | Ryan | Giggs |
| 13 | Jeremy | Goss | 14 | Andrei | Kanchelskis |
| 22 | Chris | Sutton | 16 | Roy | Keane – *Booked* |

*Subs*

| 13 | Scott | Howie (gk) | 9 | *Brian* | *McClair (\*79)* |
|---|---|---|---|---|---|
| 7 | *Efan* | *Ekoku (\*75)* | 13 | Les | Sealey (gk) |
| 17 | Ian | Butterworth | 20 | Dion | Dublin |

## *Match Facts*

• The attendance of 21,060 was Carrow Road's biggest of the season.

• United's first ever FA Cup success at Carrow Road following defeats there in 1991 and 1959 and their first FA Cup win over Norwich since 1906.

## *Score Sheet*

R. KEANE 18 min – 0-1
E. CANTONA 73 min – 0-2

*Referee:*
Mr. Durkin (Dorset)

# 5-1 for the Treble

Immediately following this latest success, the bookies slashed the odds of the Reds completing the treble to a miserly 5-1. But the game didn't begin on a particularly high note for United when Keane got himself booked in an off the ball scuffle with Polston after just five minutes. Three minutes later a Kanchelskis cross was missed by Newman but his error only served to take Hughes equally by surprise and a good opportunity went begging. Ten minutes later, after Sutton had failed to find the target from a rare Norwich opening, United took the lead with the sort of high quality strike that they are now famed for.

Giggs picked the ball up on the edge of his own eighteen yard box and set off on a counter-attack that left three defenders trailing in his wake. As he reached the Canaries' penalty area he crossed to the far wing where Kanchelskis put the ball into the path of the advancing Keane. The Irishman struck the ball firmly from sixteen yards across a diving Gunn to beat him at his right hand post for a goal of true quality.

United had a scare after 24 minutes when Schmeichel, somewhat untypically, dropped a corner but was saved by Ince who kicked Newman's stabbed shot off the line. Cantona was having a quiet game by his own high standards and perhaps it was the frustration of not seeing a great deal of the ball that caused him to show the other side of his character when he felled Goss with an outrageous tackle on the touchline. Certainly he was fortunate not to be dismissed.

The second period carried on where the first left off with Ferguson's men well on top. Indeed, the second half had been in progress for ten minutes before Schmeichel had a touch of the ball. This was to be the start of Norwich's best spell of the game and they rocked the Reds back on their heels as Bruce was forced to concede a corner and Schmeichel had to make a good catch under pressure. There then came Norwich's best chance of the game from which they should have equalised. Goss' shot from the right was only parried by the United 'keeper and it fell to Polston. He fired from close range at Schmeichel who again parried the effort without being able to get it away. The ball returned to Polston who, with Schmeichel now down, should have picked his spot instead of hammering it without any control.

United were not to be denied, however, although it took an amazing lack of defensive concentration to seal the tie for them. Newman was under absolutely no pressure what so ever when he suddenly passed the ball square along the edge of the penalty area to an absolutely delighted Cantona who simply does not miss those sort of gifts.

## FA Cup Record

|  | | Home | | | | | Away | | | | |
|---|---|---|---|---|---|---|---|---|---|---|---|
|  | P | W | D | L | F | A | W | D | L | F | A |
| FA Cup Record | 341 | 98 | 31 | 28 | 330 | 147 | 75 | 52 | 57 | 286 | 266 |

|  | Home | Away | Total |
|---|---|---|---|
| FA Cup Attendances | – | 43,079 | 43,079 |

# Queens Park Rangers (1) 2
# Manchester United (2) 3

Saturday, 5th February 1994, Loftus Road          Att.: 21,267

## QUEENS PARK RANGERS

| 13 | Jan | Stejskal |
|---|---|---|
| 2 | David | Bardsley |
| 3 | Clive | Wilson |
| 4 | Ray | Wilkins |
| 5 | Darren | Peacock |
| 24 | Steven | Yates |
| 14 | Simon | Barker |
| 8 | Ian | Holloway |
| 9 | Les | Ferdinand |
| 12 | Gary | Penrice |
| 11 | *Trevor* | *Sinclair (\*87)* |

*Subs*

| 22 | *Mike* | *Meaker (\*87)* |
|---|---|---|
| 15 | Rufus | Brevett |
| 1 | Tony | Roberts (gk) |

## MANCHESTER UNITED

| 1 | Peter | Schmeichel |
|---|---|---|
| 2 | Paul | Parker |
| 3 | Denis | Irwin |
| 4 | Steve | Bruce – *Booked* |
| 6 | Gary | Pallister – *Booked* |
| 7 | Eric | Cantona |
| 8 | Paul | Ince |
| 10 | Mark | Hughes |
| 11 | Ryan | Giggs |
| 14 | Andrei | Kanchelskis |
| 16 | Roy | Keane |

| 13 | Les | Sealey (gk) |
|---|---|---|
| 9 | Brian | McClair |
| 20 | Dion | Dublin |

## *Match Facts*

• First booking of the season for central defender Gary Pallister.

• The Reds unbeaten run in all competitions extends to 30 games.

## *Score Sheet*

KANCHELSKIS 19 min – 0-1

C. WILSON 44 min Pen – 1-1

E. CANTONA 45 min – 1-2

R. GIGGS 59 min – 1-3

L. FERDINAND 64 min – 2-3

### *Referee:*
Mr. G. Poll (Reading)

## FA Carling Premiership

| | | P | W | D | L | F | A | Pts |
|---|---|---|---|---|---|---|---|---|
| 1 | **Manchester United** | 28 | 20 | 7 | 1 | 57 | 25 | 67 |
| 2 | Blackburn Rovers | 26 | 16 | 6 | 4 | 39 | 20 | 54 |
| 3 | Arsenal | 27 | 12 | 10 | 5 | 31 | 14 | 46 |
| 4 | Newcastle United | 26 | 13 | 6 | 7 | 45 | 25 | 45 |
| 5 | Liverpool | 27 | 12 | 8 | 7 | 46 | 34 | 44 |

**Result of this Season's Fixture**

QPR

Manchester Utd

# Another Giggs Wonder Goal

In an absorbing encounter, Rangers had more of the running while United scored more of the goals. United's brilliant counter attacking skills won them the day and kept intact their thirteen point lead at the top of the table.

It wasn't until after two Ferdinand efforts had been saved that United got in their first strike with Kanchelskis closing in on goal from the right but Stejskal was equal to the effort at the foot of his post. The effort bucked the Reds up, however, and three minutes later they were in front. Schmeichel hurled one of his inch perfect throws up to Kanchelskis on the half-way line to set the Russian on a pacy run that took him past Yates before running square with two defenders along the edge of the area and unleashing a venomous shot past the outstretched Stejskal.

With the interval beckoning, the game erupted with two goals in ninety seconds. The equaliser for Rangers was somewhat dubious with the referee deciding that Keane's flying challenge on Penrice warranted a penalty kick and shortly after Irwin smacked a free kick against the Rangers wall but took hold of the rebound and made ground down the left. A magnificent cross to the far post found Cantona slipping his marker to head home his seventeenth goal of the campaign.

The second period started in much the same vein as the first with United relying on counter attacks to offset a fair bit of pressure. It was one such counter attack on the hour that saw United increase their lead with an exquisite goal from Giggs. The Welshman picked the ball up on the halfway line and set off on one of his left sided runs that took him past two defenders. After cutting inside as he approached the penalty area he suddenly veered left again with such effect that another defender was left running in the wrong direction whilst a fourth simply fell over his own feet as he tried to turn as quickly as Giggs who went to score to score his fifth goal in six league games with stunning nonchalance.

QPR, however, were not done for and their dangerman, Ferdinand hit back almost straight away. He feinted to go left and then hit the shot with his right foot to take Schmeichel by surprise. As the London side staged a grandstand finale, both Pallister and Bruce were booked whilst Schmeichel had to pull off a great save from a Ferdinand header as the Reds just hung on.

## League Record

|  | | | Home | | | | | Away | | |
|---|---|---|---|---|---|---|---|---|---|---|
|  | P | W | D | L | F | A | W | D | L | F | A |
| FAPL 93/94 | 28 | 9 | 5 | 0 | 26 | 10 | 11 | 2 | 1 | 31 | 15 |
| All Time FAPL | 70 | 23 | 10 | 2 | 65 | 24 | 21 | 9 | 5 | 59 | 32 |
| All Time FL/FAPL | 3626 | 1059 | 420 | 334 | 3615 | 1808 | 553 | 471 | 789 | 2465 | 3089 |

|  | Home | Away | Total |
|---|---|---|---|
| League Attendances | 617,527 | 409,980 | 1,027,507 |

# Manchester United (1) 1
# Sheffield Wednesday (0) 0

Sunday, 13th February 1994, Old Trafford          Att.: 43,294

| MANCHESTER UNITED | | | SHEFFIELD WEDNESDAY | | |
|---|---|---|---|---|---|
| 1 | Peter | Schmeichel | 13 | Kevin | Pressman |
| 2 | Paul | Parker | 2 | Roland | Nilsson |
| 3 | Denis | Irwin | 12 | Andy | Pearce – *Booked* |
| 4 | Steve | Bruce | 17 | Des | Walker |
| 6 | Gary | Pallister | 28 | Simon | Coleman |
| 7 | Eric | Cantona | 8 | *Chris* | *Waddle (\*71)* |
| 8 | Paul | Ince | 16 | Graham | Hyde |
| 10 | Mark | Hughes | 4 | Carlton | Palmer – *Booked* |
| 11 | Ryan | Giggs | 15 | Andy | Sinton |
| 14 | Anrei | Kanchelskis | 10 | Mark | Bright |
| 16 | Roy | Keane | 9 | David | Hirst |

*Subs*

| 13 | Les | Sealey (gk) | 1 | Chris | Woods (gk) |
|---|---|---|---|---|---|
| 9 | Brian | McClair | 20 | Gordon | Watson |
| 20 | Dion | Dublin | 14 | *Chris* | *Bart-Williams (\*71)* |

## *Match Facts*

• United's first ever League Cup victory over Wednesday.

## *Score Sheet*

R. GIGGS 19 min – 1-0

*Referee:*
Mr. K. Burge (Tonypandy)

# Everybody's Happy

Despite two attacking teams and recent confrontations between the two clubs producing exciting matches, a packed Old Trafford was served up with a typical semi-final of attrition. As might be expected in the home leg, United made the early running with both Giggs and Irwin involved in breaks down the left but on each occasion their crosses came to nothing. It was then the turn of Kanchelskis on the right to cause problems as he left Coleman for dead and cut in to hit a blistering drive that Pressman could only parry before his defence scrambled it away.

United kept the pressure up and Nilsson headed over his own 'keeper but was grateful to see the ball roll wide. The Wednesday defender wasn't so lucky the next time he tried to find Pressman as he sold his 'keeper short with his pass back. Speed merchant Giggs was quickly on to the mistake before rounding Pressman and finding the net from the most acute of angles. The Reds almost went two up when a long raking cross from Giggs found Kanchelskis who whipped over a fine cross that only needed a touch but unfortunately Keane's neck couldn't quite stretch far enough as he flung himself forward.

At last, after half an hour's play, Wednesday made their first real sortie into United territory and Bright had the ball in the net but was well offside.

Wednesday started the second period as they had finished the first and Keane was more than happy to whack the ball away for a corner. Although the resulting kick was cleared, the Yorkshire side stayed on the attack and Waddle's effort scraped the bar. United were beginning to lose patience and Parker was extremely fortunate to escape a booking when he scythed down Sinton. The incident served to help Ferguson's men regain their composure and both Ince and Kanchelskis proved troublesome down the right. After one cross from the Russian, Keane was mighty happy to see the linesman's flag go up for offside against him when he missed an absolute sitter and then the winger himself took a pot shot that almost landed at the feet of Cantona following a deflection. In the last twenty minutes, Wednesday made it obvious they were prepared to settle for a one goal first leg deficit and took off Waddle to tighten things up whilst both Pearce and Palmer received yellow cards.

## League Cup Record

|  | | Home | | | | | Away | | | | |
|---|---|---|---|---|---|---|---|---|---|---|---|
|  | P | W | D | L | F | A | W | D | L | F | A |
| League Cup Record | 119 | 44 | 11 | 8 | 134 | 53 | 21 | 14 | 21 | 74 | 71 |

|  | Home | Away | Total |
|---|---|---|---|
| League Cup Attendances | 169,819 | 82,329 | 252,148 |

# Wimbledon
# Manchester United

**(0) 0**
**(1) 3**

Sunday, 20th February 1994, Selhurst Park          Att.: 27,511

## WIMBLEDON

| | | |
|---|---|---|
| 1 | Hans | Seger |
| 2 | Warren | Barton |
| 4 | Vinny | Jones – *Booked* |
| 6 | Scott | Fitzgerald – *Booked* |
| 8 | Robbie | Earle – *Booked* |
| 9 | John | Fashanu |
| 10 | Dean | Holdsworth |
| 15 | John | Scales |
| 24 | Peter | Fear |
| 33 | Gary | Elkins |
| 36 | Gary | Blissett |

*Subs*

| | | |
|---|---|---|
| 5 | Dean | Blackwell |
| 7 | Andy | Clarke |
| 23 | Neil | Sullivan (gk) |

## MANCHESTER UNITED

| | | |
|---|---|---|
| 1 | Peter | Schmeichel |
| 2 | Paul | Parker |
| 3 | Denis | Irwin |
| 4 | Steve | Bruce |
| 6 | Gary | Pallister |
| 7 | *Eric* | *Cantona (+73)* |
| 8 | Paul | Ince |
| 10 | *Mark* | *Hughes (*73)* |
| 11 | Ryan | Giggs |
| 14 | Andrei | Kanchelskis |
| 16 | Roy | Keane |

| | | |
|---|---|---|
| 13 | Les | Sealey (gk) |
| 9 | *Brian* | *McClair (*73)* |
| 20 | *Dion* | *Dublin (+73)* |

---

### *Match Facts*

• The first ever FA Cup tie between the two clubs.

• Paul Ince made it three successive scoring appearances on his last three trips to Selhurst Park.

### *Score Sheet*

E. CANTONA 42 min – 0-1
P. INCE 63 min – 0-2
D. IRWIN 71 min – 0-3

*Referee:*
Mr. D. Ellery (Harrow)

117

# C'est Magnifique

United started as though they meant business and could have scored after only 25 seconds when Segers was relieved to get a smart shot from Hughes round his right hand post. It was almost all United from then on but a long throw from Jones found its way onto Blissett's head and Schmeichel had to be alert to keep the sides level. It was becoming a one sided affair and the Reds could have had a penalty when Keane half fell and was half brought down by Elkins.

Jones was then booked for a diabolical tackle on Cantona from which the Frenchman, for once, kept his head and walked away to avoid becoming embroiled. Certainly, it was not for lack of effort that Jones stayed on the pitch for he later committed several more dubious acts. Giggs was the next to cause Wimbledon problems but Barton made an invaluable clearance off the line.

Hughes was next in the thick of things taking the ball down brilliantly on his chest before putting a long cross in to the box from the left of midfield. Elkins headed it out but only as far as Cantona just outside the area. He controlled the ball on his instep and before it had time to fall to the ground the Frenchman had smacked it beyond a helpless Segers for a goal that sheer class written all over it.

From the restart, Giggs robbed Barton and made quick progression towards goal only to be crudely brought down by Fitzgerald who was lucky that the card was only yellow.

United stayed on the attack when the second half got under way but a rare Wimbledon sortie into the Reds half brought them their first corner of the match after 49 minutes! It was then a case of normal service being resumed with a Keane cross just touched off the toes of Kanchelskis by Barton when it looked as though the Russian must increase the lead. Keane then set Giggs free down the centre only for the Welshman's shot to richochet off Segers and on to the post.

There then came a goal of classic proportions with a fifteen pass move culminating in Irwin dancing past the last line of defence to send an angled shot past Segers' despairing left hand. It was a goal that in any other season would have been acclaimed as the goal of the season but so many of United's strikes this campaign could qualify for the title that scoring goals of such quality has become common place as United coasted to the finish.

## FA Cup Record

|  | P | W | D | L | F | A | W | D | L | F | A |
|---|---|---|---|---|---|---|---|---|---|---|---|
|  |  | **Home** |  |  |  |  | **Away** |  |  |  |  |
| FA Cup Record | 342 | 98 | 31 | 28 | 330 | 147 | 76 | 52 | 57 | 289 | 266 |

|  | *Home* | *Away* | *Total* |
|---|---|---|---|
| FA Cup Attendances | – | 70,590 | 70,590 |

118

# West Ham United   (0) 2
# Manchester United   (1) 2

Saturday, 26th February 1994, Upton Park      Att.: 28,832

## WEST HAM UNITED

| | | |
|---|---|---|
| 1 | Ludek | Mikloso |
| 2 | Tim | Breacker |
| 4 | Steve | Potts – *Booked* |
| 6 | Martin | Allen |
| 14 | Ian | Bishop |
| 16 | Matt | Holmes |
| 18 | Alvin | Martin |
| 25 | Lee | Chapman |
| 34 | Mike | Marsh |
| 33 | David | Burrows |
| 9 | Trevor | Morley |

*Subs*

| | | |
|---|---|---|
| 10 | Clive | Allen |
| 23 | Keith | Rowland |
| 13 | Gary | Kelly (gk) |

## MANCHESTER UNITED

| | | |
|---|---|---|
| 1 | Peter | Schmeichel |
| 2 | Paul | Parker – *Booked* |
| 3 | *Denis* | *Irwin (\*78)* |
| 4 | Steve | Bruce |
| 6 | Gary | Pallister |
| 7 | Eric | Cantona |
| 8 | Paul | Ince |
| 9 | Brian | McClair |
| 10 | Mark | Hughes |
| 14 | *Andrei* | *Kanchelskis (+85)* |
| 16 | Roy | Keane |

| | | |
|---|---|---|
| 13 | Les | Sealey (gk) |
| 20 | *Dion* | *Dublin (+85)* |
| 29 | *Ben* | *Thornley (\*78)* |

---

### *Match Facts*

- 18 year old Ben Thornley's League debut.
- Lee Chapman's scoring sequence against United continues – West Ham are the sixth club he has scored with against the Reds.
- The Bobby Moore Stand opens one year after his death. Moore made his debut against Man Utd at Upton Park in 1958.

### *Score Sheet*

M. HUGHES 6 min – 0-1
L. CHAPMAN 70 min – 1-1
T. MORLEY 73 min – 2-1
P. INCE 87 min – 2-2

*Referee:*
A. Wilkie (Chester-Le-Street)

---

## FA Carling Premiership

| | | P | W | D | L | F | A | Pts |
|---|---|---|---|---|---|---|---|---|
| 1 | **Manchester United** | 29 | 20 | 8 | 1 | 59 | 27 | 68 |
| 2 | Blackburn Rovers | 30 | 18 | 7 | 5 | 44 | 23 | 61 |
| 3 | Arsenal | 30 | 13 | 12 | 5 | 34 | 16 | 51 |
| 4 | Newcastle United | 29 | 14 | 6 | 9 | 51 | 30 | 48 |
| 5 | Liverpool | 30 | 13 | 8 | 9 | 49 | 40 | 47 |

**Result of this Season's Fixture**

West Ham Utd
Manchester Utd

# Ince Perfect

United fans received a shock only minutes before the start of the game with the news that Ryan Giggs was out with a hamstring strain, his place being taken by Brian McClair with young Ben Thornley on the bench. Paul Ince had been threatened with violence prior to the game and United employed a security guard to travel with him and the player stayed in the dressing room during the warm up.

When the game got under way it was the Hammers who made the early running but it was United who took a quick lead. Keane slung in a low cross from the right and Hughes reacted a split second faster than the Hammers 'keeper, Miklosko, to take the ball almost from his hands and into net from six yards. West Ham resumed their attacking and Chapman was just wide with a header but Morley went even closer when he headed against the post.

United seemed more composed in the second period and Mikloso had to save at the feet of Hughes who was giving Alvin Martin a torrid time. Kanchelskis then seemed to be very laid back when presented with a good opportunity by Ince and, instead of smacking a first time effort, he waited until surrounded by defenders and then tried a chip that was both high and wide.

As if to underline the profligacy of the Russian the next West Ham attack almost brought the equaliser. A free kick was touched to Burrows who hammered it goalwards only for Schmeichel to make a great one handed save. But the Hammers were not to be denied and hesitancy in the Reds rearguard contributed to their downfall. Burrows' cross from the right was chested down by Chapman who converted from a narrow angle over the top of Schmeichel's body as the 'keeper threw himself despairingly at the striker's feet. Three minutes later the Reds were looking defeat in the face after Bruce appeared to slip and lost possession. The cross from the left seemed destined for the arms of Schmeichel but, for once, Morley reacted quicker to score in almost similar fashion to Hughes earlier in the game albeit from a narrower angle.

But United had faced defeat before in this exciting campaign and come back. Ben Thornley was slung on for his debut in place of Irwin and then, in a last throw of the dice, Dublin came on for Kanchelskis but it was the man that the crowd had berated all afternoon, Paul Ince, who had the last laugh when he flung himself powerfully at a Keane cross to force the ball home from six yards and to keep the Reds unbeaten run of 33 games intact.

## League Cup Record

| | Home | | | | | Away | | | | |
|---|---|---|---|---|---|---|---|---|---|---|
| | P | W | D | L | F | A | W | D | L | F | A |
| FAPL 93/94 | 29 | 9 | 5 | 0 | 26 | 10 | 11 | 3 | 1 | 33 | 17 |
| All Time FAPL | 71 | 23 | 10 | 2 | 65 | 24 | 21 | 10 | 5 | 61 | 34 |
| All Time FL/FAPL | 3627 | 1059 | 420 | 334 | 3615 | 1808 | 553 | 472 | 789 | 2467 | 3091 |

| | Home | Away | Total |
|---|---|---|---|
| League Cup Attendances | 617,527 | 438,812 | 1,056,339 |

# Sheffield Wednesday (1) 1
# Manchester United (3) 4

Wednesday, 2nd March 1994, Hillsborough — Att.: 34,878

| SHEFFIELD WEDNESDAY | | | MANCHESTER UNITED | | |
|---|---|---|---|---|---|
| 13 | Kevin | Pressman | 1 | Peter | Schmeichel |
| 2 | Roland | Nillsen | 2 | Paul | Parker |
| 12 | Andy | Pearce | 3 | Denis | Irwin |
| 17 | Des | Walker | 4 | Steve | Bruce |
| 28 | Simon | Coleman | 6 | Gary | Pallister |
| 14 | Chris | Bart-Williams | 8 | Paul | Ince |
| 4 | Carlton | Palmer – *Booked* | 9 | Brian | McClair |
| 15 | Andy | Sinton | 10 | Mark | Hughes |
| 16 | Graham | Hyde | 11 | Ryan | Giggs |
| 10 | Mark | Bright | 14 | Andrei | Kanchelskis |
| 9 | David | Hirst – *Booked* | 16 | Roy | Keane – *Booked* |

*Subs*

| 23 | Lance | Key (gk) | 13 | Les | Sealey (gk) |
|---|---|---|---|---|---|
| 7 | Andy | Poric | 12 | Bryan | Robson |
| 20 | *Gordon* | *Watson* | 20 | Dion | Dublin |

## *Match Facts*

• Sheffield Wednesday commenced this semi-final tie needing to achieve what no team had found possible in the last 91 matches – beating United by two clear goals.

• The first goal conceded by United in the last five cup ties.

• The result gave United revenge for their 1991 League Cup Final defeat at the hands of Wednesday.

## *Score Sheet*

B. McCLAIR 9 min – 0-1

KANCHELSKIS 10 min – 1-2

D. HIRST 33 min – 1-2

M. HUGHES 38 min – 1-3

M. HUGHES 82 min – 1-4

*United win 5-1 on aggregate*

### *Referee:*
Mr. D. Ellery (Harrow)

# On the Way to Wembley

The tie was over almost before it had started when United, already one up from the first leg of this Coca-Cola Cup Semi-final, increased their lead with a goal after only four minutes. Walker lost out in midfield and Keane advanced down the left to cross for McClair to slide in at the far post. Pressman's first touch of the ball was to pick it out of the net! Wednesday and their supporters were stunned into inaction and silence respectively.

Six minutes later Kanchelskis picked the ball up on the half way line and quickly made ground down the centre before playing it wide to Giggs on the left. His chipped cross, floated to the far post where the Russian winger beat Hughes to get a header in. The ball bounced against Pressman to give him his second touch of the night as he scurried back across his line but the 'keeper could only watch helplessly as the ball rolled over the line.

Then, out of the blue came a ray of hope for Trevor Francis' embattled team.

Hyde's cross was dropped by Schmeichel as he appeared to be fouled by Bright and fell straight back to Hyde on the byeline. His attempt to cross was deflected by Ince who could only watch in horror as the ball ballooned over the United defence to the far post where Hirst made sure, although the ball had probably crossed the line already for a freak goal.

If the door had opened slightly for Wednesday it was almost immediately slammed shut in their face as United's reply was swift, although it shouldn't have been decisive. Irwin intercepted on the left and slipped the ball to Hughes at the edge of the area. He turned and worked an opening for a shot but when it came it was weak. Pressman, however, made an awful hash of his save and the ball rolled just inside his right hand post for a gift of a goal.

Wednesday gave the lost cause all they had on the resumption and for the first time in the game put in a prolonged period of attacking that pushed the Reds back. To end the show, United scored a goal of stunning simplicity as McClair, in the side for Cantona, produced an inch perfect chipped cross in the Frenchman's own style to pick out Hughes running in and it was 4-1, game, set and match.

## League Cup Record

|  | Home | | | | | Away | | | | |
|---|---|---|---|---|---|---|---|---|---|---|
|  | P | W | D | L | F | A | W | D | L | F | A |
| FAPL 93/94 | 4 | 1 | 1 | 0 | 4 | 1 | 2 | 0 | 0 | 4 | 1 |
| All Time FAPL | ? | ? | ? | ? | ? | ? | ? | ? | ? | ? | ? |
| All Time FL/FAPL | 120 | 44 | 11 | 8 | 134 | 53 | 22 | 14 | 21 | 78 | 71 |

|  | Home | Away | Total |
|---|---|---|---|
| League Cup Attendances | 169,819 | 117,207 | 287,026 |

# Manchester United (0) 0
# Chelsea (0) 1

Saturday, 5th March 1994, Old Trafford                    Att.: 44,745

| MANCHESTER UNITED | | | CHELSEA | | |
|---|---|---|---|---|---|
| 1 | Peter | Schmeichel | 1 | Dimitri | Kharine |
| 2 | *Paul* | *Parker (\*73)* | 12 | Steve | Clarke |
| 3 | Denis | Irwin | 35 | Jakob | Kjeldbjerg |
| 4 | Steve | Bruce | 5 | Erland | Johnsen |
| 6 | Gary | Pallister | 6 | Frank | Sinclair – *Booked* |
| 8 | Paul | Ince – *Booked* | 24 | Craig | Burley |
| 9 | *Brian* | *McClair (+84)* | 18 | Eddie | Newton |
| 10 | Mark | Hughes | 10 | Gavin | Peacock |
| 11 | Ryan | Giggs | 11 | Denis | Wise |
| 14 | Andrei | Kanchelskis | 21 | *Mark* | *Stein (\*86)* |
| 16 | Roy | Keane | 7 | John | Spencer |

*Subs*

| | | | | | |
|---|---|---|---|---|---|
| 12 | *Bryan* | *Robson (+84)* | 20 | ˙Glenn | Hoddle |
| 13 | Les | Sealey (gk) | 27 | *David* | *Hopkin (\*86)* |
| 20 | *Dion* | *Dublin (\*73)* | 13 | Kevin | Hitchcock (gk) |

## *Match Facts*

• United's first defeat at Old Trafford in seventeen months, their first defeat after 34 games.

## *Score Sheet*

G. PEACOCK 65 min – 0-1

*Referee:*
Mr. D. Gallagher (Banbury)

## FA Carling Premiership

| | | P | W | D | L | F | A | Pts |
|---|---|---|---|---|---|---|---|---|
| 1 | **Manchester United** | **30** | **20** | **8** | **1** | **59** | **28** | **68** |
| 2 | Blackburn Rovers | 31 | 19 | 7 | 5 | 44 | 23 | 64 |
| 3 | Arsenal | 31 | 14 | 12 | 5 | 39 | 17 | 54 |
| 4 | Newcastle United | 30 | 15 | 6 | 9 | 52 | 30 | 51 |
| 5 | Aston Villa | 30 | 13 | 10 | 7 | 38 | 28 | 49 |

**Result of this Season's Fixture**

Manchester Utd
Chelsea

# Peacock Struts Again

With Cantona still unfit, United kept the same side that had comprehensively
defeated Sheffield Wednesday the previous week but this game was to prove a
different story altogether. Neither team were quickly into their stride and the only
moment of interest in the first ten minutes was the sight of Sinclair being unable to
extricate himself from the advertising hoardings after sliding into them following a
tackle on Kanchelskis. With almost 15 minutes gone Parker, the only United
outfield player yet to score this season, advanced as the Chelsea defence obviously
considered him, given his record, to be of little threat and almost paid the price
when the right back thundered a great shot just wide with Kharine beaten. Ince was
booked for a wild tackle on Wise and then the Reds were let off the hook by
Sinclair. A long throw was completely mis-headed by Bruce and the ball sliced off
his head to leave Chelsea's Sinclair with a clear sight of goal. Fortunately, the big
defender seemed as surprised as everybody else that Bruce had made a mistake and
made a complete hash of his effort.

In the second half, after Peacock had been booked for felling Parker, Giggs
skimmed the crossbar with a header from a Kanchelskis cross and then Kharine
dealt confidently with an effort from Keane. Then, after 65 minutes, Chelsea took
the lead with a simple but brave goal. Mark Stein, whose goals for Stoke City had
beaten United in an early round of the Coca Cola cup prior to his move to the
London club, split the defence with a long through ball. Schmeichel at first seemed
to be favourite to beat Peacock to it but as the two players merged onto the ball it
became evident it was very much a 50/50 ball. Peacock bravely carried his
challenge through and just got his foot to the ball before Schmeichel's lunge could
block his path. The ball bounced agonisingly towards the unguarded net with Bruce
in a despairing chase unable to prevent it rolling over the line. The referee seemed
very tolerant of the Chelsea celebrations which went on for a full minute before Mr
Gallagher asked the Londoners to get on with the game. The Reds staged a
grandstand finish but having played their "get out of jail" cards against Blackburn
and West Ham earlier in the campaign there was no escape this time round.

## League Record

| | Home | | | | | | Away | | | | |
|---|---|---|---|---|---|---|---|---|---|---|---|
| | P | W | D | L | F | A | W | D | L | F | A |
| FAPL 93/94 | 30 | 9 | 5 | 1 | 26 | 11 | 11 | 3 | 1 | 33 | 17 |
| All Time FAPL | 72 | 23 | 10 | 3 | 66 | 25 | 21 | 10 | 5 | 61 | 34 |
| All Time FL/FAPL | 3628 | 1059 | 420 | 335 | 3615 | 1809 | 553 | 472 | 789 | 2467 | 3091 |

| | Home | Away | Total |
|---|---|---|---|
| League Attendances | 662,272 | 438,812 | 1,101,084 |

# Manchester United (0) 3
# Charlton Athletic (0) 1

Saturday 12th March 1994, Old Trafford                    Att.: 44,347

## MANCHESTER UNITED

| 1 | Peter | Schmeichel – *Sent off* |
| 2 | *Paul* | *Parker (\*44)* |
| 3 | Denis | Irwin |
| 4 | Steve | Bruce |
| 6 | Gary | Pallister |
| 7 | Eric | Cantona |
| 8 | Paul | Ince |
| 10 | Mark | Hughes |
| 11 | Ryan | Giggs |
| 14 | Andrei | Kanchelskis |
| 16 | Roy | Keane |

*Subs*

| 13 | *Les* | *Sealey (gk) (\*44)* |
| 9 | Brian | McClair |
| 12 | Bryan | Robson |

## CHARLTON ATHLETIC

| 22 | John | Vaughan |
| 24 | Steve | Brown |
| 11 | Scott | Minto |
| 15 | Alan | Pardew |
| 1 | Stuart | Balmer |
| 10 | Alan | McLeary |
| 16 | Darren | Pitcher |
| 27 | Mark | Robson |
| 8 | Carl | Leaburn |
| 6 | *Kim* | *Grant (\*57)* |
| 12 | Garry | Nelson |

| 23 | Phil | Chapple |
| 21 | Colin | *Walsh (\*57)* |
| 2 | Bob | Bolder (gk) |

## *Match Facts*

• Charlton Athletic's first appearance in the sixth round since they won the FA Cup in 1947 and their first game at Old Trafford since their last match in football's top flight on 5th May 1990.

• United had only met Charlton once before in the FA Cup – at Leeds Road in 1948 when United won 2-0 and went on to win the Cup.

## *Score Sheet*

M. HUGHES 46 min – 1-0
KANCHELSKIS 71 min – 2-0
KANCHELSKIS 75 min – 3-0
C. LEABURN 77 min – 3-1

*Referee:*
Mr. R. Hart (Darlington)

# Schmeichel Off

United welcomed back Eric Cantona as they met Charlton Athletic to dispute a semi-final place in the FA Cup. It was, however, the underdogs who were first to attack with Grant and Leaburn causing Schmeichel serious problems in a scramble near the corner flag when they intercepted a throw from Parker intended for the 'keeper. The Dane was then at full stretch to push away a free kick but United gradually got into their stride and began to exert pressure.

With the half-time interval beckoning, Grant beat Bruce in the air to an everyday type of clearance from Brown. As Bruce stumbled, Grant set off into the United half towards goal but it appeared as if either Pallister or Parker, or both, would be able to cut his route off. Then, out of the big blue yonder, Schmeichel appeared having left his goal like an Olympic sprinter. He hurled himself feet first at Grant who, on seeing the onrushing 'keeper, chipped the ball only to see it hit Schmeichel's right hand a split second before the big Dane clattered him to the ground. United didn't like the decision to send Schmeichel off but in the letter of the law, Mr Hart could have taken his pick of the handball offence or the foul tackle.

Paul Parker was the unlucky player to be substituted to make way for Les Sealey with the Reds dropping Keane in to the right-back position. The consensus of opinion at half-time was that the incident had levelled the sides up but United immediately put paid to that theory straight from the kick off. A Cantona shot was deflected for a corner which Giggs delivered deep into the area for Hughes to find a yard of space. His shot almost put Vaughan in the back of the net, never mind the ball, and the 'keeper was desperately unlucky that his block fell again to Hughes who made scoring from the acutest of angles look easy. Hughes blasted a good opportunity over but then Kanchelskis sealed the semi-final spot for United with two strikes in four minutes. He picked the ball up on the halfway line and set off at pace. With both Giggs and Hughes in good positions and screaming for the ball, the Ukranian kept going and unleashed a fierce drive from the edge of the area which Vaughan could only beat down on to the ground and then watch helplessly as it still flashed under his body into the net. Giggs then played a defence splitting pass with his so-called weak right foot which gave Kanchelskis another chance. He ran across the edge of the area before rounding Vaughan with some ease to roll the ball into the empty net. There was, however, still time for the London side to score the first goal against United in this season's competition but it was in truth only a consolation when Leaburn headed past Sealey from Robson's cross.

## FA Cup Record

|  |  | Home |  |  |  |  | Away |  |  |  |  |
|---|---|---|---|---|---|---|---|---|---|---|---|
|  | P | W | D | L | F | A | W | D | L | F | A |
| FA Cup Record | 343 | 99 | 31 | 28 | 333 | 148 | 76 | 52 | 57 | 289 | 266 |

|  | Home | Away | Total |
|---|---|---|---|
| FA Cup Attendances | 44,347 | 70,590 | 114,937 |

# Manchester United    (4) 5
# Sheffield Wednesday  (0) 0

Wednesday, 16th March 1994, Old Trafford          Att.: 43,669

## MANCHESTER UNITED

| | | |
|---|---|---|
| 1 | Peter | Schmeichel |
| 2 | Paul | Parker |
| 3 | Denis | Irwin |
| 4 | Steve | Bruce |
| 6 | Gary | Pallister |
| 7 | Eric | Cantona |
| 8 | Paul | Ince |
| 10 | Mark | Hughes |
| 11 | *Ryan* | *Giggs (\*45)* |
| 14 | *Andrei* | *Kanchelskis (+69)* |
| 16 | Roy | Keane |

*Subs*

| | | |
|---|---|---|
| 13 | Les | Sealey (gk) |
| 9 | *Brian* | *McClair (\*45)* |
| 12 | *Brian* | *Robson (+69)* |

## SHEFFIELD WEDNESDAY

| | | |
|---|---|---|
| 13 | Kevin | Pressman |
| 2 | *Roland* | *Nilssen (\*23)* |
| 28 | Simon | Coleman |
| 17 | Des | Walker |
| 12 | Andy | Preece |
| 14 | Chris | Bart-Williams |
| 18 | Phil | King |
| 15 | Andy | Sinton |
| 24 | Julian | Watts |
| 7 | Adam | Poric |
| 10 | Mark | Bright |

| | | |
|---|---|---|
| 1 | Chris | Woods (gk) |
| 20 | *Gordon* | *Watson (\*23)* |
| 19 | Nigel | Jemson |

### *Match Facts*

- The scoreline equalled two United records – their best FAPL win of 5-0 over Coventry City in 1992/93 and their best effort against Sheffield Wednesday in 1906.
- Eric Cantona's second goal was his 20th of the campaign, but he missed the opportunity to become the first United player to hit a Premiership hat-trick.

### *Score Sheet*

R. GIGGS 14 min – 1-0

M. HUGHES 15 min – 2-0

P. INCE 21 min – 3-0

E. CANTONA 45 min – 4-0

E. CANTONA 55 min – 5-0

*Referee:*

Mr. M. Bodenham (Cornwall)

## FA Carling Premiership

| | | P | W | D | L | F | A | Pts |
|---|---|---|---|---|---|---|---|---|
| 1 | **Manchester United** | 31 | 21 | 8 | 2 | 64 | 28 | 71 |
| 2 | Blackburn Rovers | 31 | 19 | 7 | 5 | 46 | 23 | 64 |
| 3 | Newcastle United | 31 | 16 | 6 | 9 | 59 | 31 | 54 |
| 4 | Arsenal | 31 | 14 | 12 | 5 | 39 | 17 | 54 |
| 5 | Leeds United | 32 | 13 | 13 | 6 | 46 | 32 | 52 |

### Result of this Season's Fixture

Manchester Utd

Sheffield Wed

# Rout

Sheffield Wednesday came to Old Trafford for this league game only days after being being whipped 4-1 at Hillsborough in the Coca-Cola Cup semi-final at Hillsborough and, to make matters worse, were without ten players through illness, injury or suspension. Things did not improve.

After only ten minutes, full back Roland Nilssen collapsed after an innocuous tackle involving Giggs and received treatment for several minutes. Within minutes of him resuming, United shrugged off a sluggish start as Cantona hit a magnificent 60 yard pass from just outside his own penalty area to Giggs. Against a fit Nilssen it may have been a close race, against a hobbling one it was no contest, all of which left Giggs to draw Pressman before caressing it past the exposed 'keeper.

The crowd had not had time to sit down again when United were two up through Hughes. Again Cantona was the provider with a deft header into the path of the Welshman. Hughes simply lashed the ball from fully 35 yards and it rocketed past Pressman, clipping the underneath of the bar on its way.

United gave their enthralled fans just six minutes in which to get their breath back before hitting a third. Kanchelskis played a short ball from the right to Ince. A defence that was now totally bemused, gave Ince the space to turn on the edge of the area and he shot low from the right into the far corner of the Wednesday net. As the half drew to a close, Watson forced Schmeichel into action for the Dane to make an excellent save especially as he had been a bystander for so long. Watson and Poric then advanced on the United goal but left the ball to one another just over the half way line to allow Cantona to pick up the loose ball. He played it wide to Parker who found Kanchelskis. The through ball to Cantona was inch perfect leaving the Frenchman to slip the ball nonchalantly under Pressman.

Ten minutes into the second period Parker played Ince into a good position but the midfielder unselfishly slipped the ball to Cantona who had time to change from right foot to left before driving home the fifth via Pressman's right hand post.

Keane missed a great chance to make it six but then United got their biggest fright of the night. A sudden snowstorm blanketed the ground and in no time at all the pitch markings were virtually obscured. Could the referee abandon the game with the Reds five up? Fortunately, the storm stopped almost as quickly as it started and the danger passed.

## League Record

| | | Home | | | | | Away | | | | |
|---|---|---|---|---|---|---|---|---|---|---|---|
| | P | W | D | L | F | A | W | D | L | F | A |
| FAPL 93/94 | 31 | 10 | 5 | 1 | 31 | 11 | 11 | 3 | 1 | 33 | 17 |
| All Time FAPL | 73 | 24 | 10 | 3 | 70 | 25 | 21 | 10 | 5 | 61 | 34 |
| All Time FL/FAPL | 3629 | 1060 | 420 | 335 | 3620 | 1809 | 553 | 472 | 789 | 2467 | 3091 |

| | Home | Away | Total |
|---|---|---|---|
| League Attendances | 705,941 | 438,812 | 1,144,753 |

# Swindon Town (1) 2
# Manchester United (1) 2

Saturday, 19th March 1994, The County Ground          Att.: 18,102

## SWINDON TOWN

| 1 | Fraser | Digby |
| 2 | Nicky | Summerbee |
| 5 | Luc | Nijholt |
| 6 | Shaun | Taylor |
| 7 | John | Moncur |
| 9 | Jan | Fjortoft |
| 14 | Adrian | Whitbread |
| 16 | *Kevin* | *Horlock (+78)* |
| 31 | Brian | Kilcline |
| 32 | *Frank* | *McAvennie (\*71)* |
| 33 | Lawrie | Sanchez – *Booked* |

*Subs*

| 10 | *Martin* | *Ling (+78)* |
| 27 | *Keith* | *Scott (\*71)* |
| 23 | Nicky | Hammond (gk) |

## MANCHESTER UNITED

| 1 | Peter | Schmeichel |
| 2 | Paul | Parker |
| 3 | Denis | Irwin |
| 4 | Steve | Bruce |
| 6 | Gary | Pallister |
| 7 | Eric | Cantona – *Sent off* |
| 8 | Paul | Ince |
| 9 | Brian | McClair |
| 10 | Mark | Hughes |
| 11 | Ryan | Giggs |
| 16 | Roy | Keane |

| 13 | Les | Sealey (gk) |
| 20 | Dion | Dublin |
| 23 | Mike | Phelan |

## *Match Facts*

• United's first ever league visit to the County Ground. • Former United Reserve team 'keeper Fraser Digby, in goal for Swindon, never managed a first team game at Old Trafford. • Mr Hill, who sent off Cantona, was the referee who last season Alex Ferguson requested should not be allowed to officiate any more United games.

## *Score Sheet*

R. KEANE 13 min – 0-1
L. NIJHOLT 36 min – 1-1
P. INCE 56 min – 1-2
J. FJORTOFT 83 min – 2-2

*Referee:*
B. Hill (Market Harborough)

## FA Carling Premiership

| | | P | W | D | L | F | A | Pts |
|---|---|---|---|---|---|---|---|---|
| 1 | Manchester United | 32 | 21 | 9 | 2 | 66 | 30 | 72 |
| 2 | Blackburn Rovers | 31 | 19 | 7 | 5 | 44 | 23 | 64 |
| 3 | Newcastle United | 32 | 17 | 6 | 9 | 63 | 33 | 57 |
| 4 | Arsenal | 32 | 15 | 12 | 5 | 43 | 17 | 57 |
| 5 | Leeds United | 33 | 14 | 13 | 6 | 47 | 32 | 55 |

### Result of this Season's Fixture

Swindon Town
Manchester Utd

# Ooh, Ouch, Cantona

With Swindon having been demolished 7-1 by Newcastle United in their last league outing and United having won their previous game 5-0, there could surely be only one outcome to this contest. But a game that was seen as a formality turned from restless slumber to fitful sleep before becoming a nightmare that the Reds were grateful to wake from with even a point to take home.

As early as the thirteenth minute, United took the lead. Cantona started the move, winning the ball on the halfway line and then releasing it quickly to Hughes . Hughes slipped Kilcline and the Welshman hit the left side of the area. The Swindon defence moved across in unison and Hughes slipped a looping cross to the far post where Keane was completely unmarked with an open goal to head into. There appeared to be little threat to the Reds defence when Nijholt picked the ball up some thirty yards out as United had plenty of defenders back. His long range shot, however, took a wicked deflection off one of the massed ranks of defenders to loop high over Schmeichel and just under the bar.

United missed an opportunity to regain the lead in the 56th minute when Hughes just failed to connect with a McClair cross after good spadework from Giggs but seven minutes later they did get their noses in front. From a very similar position to that of Nijholt when he equalised, Ince powered the ball home but, unlike Nijholt, he didn't need the assistance of a deflection as the shot, low and hard into Digby's bottom right hand corner, gave the 'keeper no chance. The goal only served to ignite passions and three minutes later disaster struck for United when Cantona was sent off. He was just inside the Swindon half when he tangled with Moncur who had a little tug at the Frenchman's shirt as he fell to the ground. Cantona, still on his feet, extricated his legs from the melee but then stamped on the chest of Moncur as he lay on the floor. Referee Hill was no more than five yards away but, still consulted his linesman to make sure his eyes had not lied to him. The red card was produced and. in all fairness to the referee who had made some pretty poor decisions against the Reds in the past, he had no choice but to dismiss Cantona.

For the second Saturday running, United were reduced to ten men and they paid the penalty in the 83rd minute when Fjortoft equalised in a goalmouth scramble after both Sanchez and Scott had miskicked. It could have been worse for Ferguson's men had Pallister not blocked a last minute goal bound shot from Sanchez.

## League Record

| | Home | | | | | | Away | | | | |
| | P | W | D | L | F | A | W | D | L | F | A |
|---|---|---|---|---|---|---|---|---|---|---|---|
| FAPL 93/94 | 32 | 10 | 5 | 1 | 31 | 11 | 11 | 4 | 1 | 35 | 19 |
| All Time FAPL | 74 | 24 | 10 | 3 | 70 | 25 | 21 | 11 | 5 | 63 | 36 |
| All Time FL/FAPL | 3630 | 1060 | 420 | 335 | 3620 | 1809 | 553 | 423 | 789 | 2469 | 3093 |

| | Home | Away | Total |
|---|---|---|---|
| League Attendances | 705,941 | 456,914 | 1,162,855 |

# Arsenal (1) 2
# Manchester United (1) 2

Tuesday, 22nd March 1994, Highbury                    Att.: 36,203

## ARSENAL

| 1 | David | Seaman |
|---|---|---|
| 2 | Lee | Dixon |
| 3 | Nigel | Winterburn |
| 12 | Steve | Bould |
| 6 | Tony | Adams |
| 10 | Paul | Merson – *Booked* |
| 17 | John | Jensen |
| 4 | *Paul* | *Davis (*68)* |
| 8 | Ian | Wright |
| 9 | Alan | Smith |
| 22 | Ian | Selley |

*Subs*

| 13 | Alan | Miller (gk) |
|---|---|---|
| 14 | Martin | Keown |
| 7 | *Kevin* | *Campbell (*68)* |

## MANCHESTER UNITED

| 1 | Peter | Schmeichel |
|---|---|---|
| 2 | Paul | Parker |
| 3 | Denis | Irwin |
| 4 | Steve | Bruce |
| 5 | *Lee* | *Sharpe (*81)* |
| 6 | Gary | Pallister |
| 7 | Eric | Cantona – *Sent Off* |
| 8 | Paul | Ince |
| 10 | Mark | Hughes |
| 11 | Ryan | Giggs |
| 16 | Roy | Keane – *Booked* |

| 13 | Les | Sealey |
|---|---|---|
| 12 | Bryan | Robson |
| 9 | *Brian* | *McClair (*81)* |

## *Match Facts*

- Sharpe scores a brace of goals in a come back game for the second time this season after also performing the feat against Aston Villa. • Cantona becomes the first United player to be sent off in successive games.
- Merson became the first Gunner to score against the Reds in the competition.

## *Score Sheet*

L. SHARPE 10 min – 0-1
PALLISTER 36 min o.g. – 1-1
L. SHARPE 53 min – 1-2
P. MERSON 78 min – 2-2

### *Referee:*
Mr. V. Callow (Solihull)

## FA Carling Premiership

| | | P | W | D | L | F | A | Pts |
|---|---|---|---|---|---|---|---|---|
| 1 | Manchester United | 33 | 21 | 10 | 2 | 68 | 32 | 73 |
| 2 | Blackburn Rovers | 32 | 20 | 7 | 5 | 48 | 24 | 67 |
| 3 | Arsenal | 33 | 15 | 13 | 5 | 45 | 19 | 58 |
| 4 | Newcastle United | 32 | 17 | 6 | 9 | 63 | 33 | 57 |
| 5 | Leeds United | 33 | 14 | 13 | 6 | 47 | 32 | 55 |

**Result of this Season's Fixture**

Arsenal
Manchester Utd

# Cantona Off Again

United's last game prior to their Coca Cola Cup Final saw them squander two more league points after twice leading and, more seriously, have a player sent off for the third time in four games. Things began brightly enough for them when Parker fed the ball into Hughes from the right and the Welshman hit a hard, but fairly straightforward, shot from 18 yards. Seaman, diving to his right failed to hold it and Sharpe, belying the fact that he had not played for 17 games reacted quicker than anybody to ram the ball home from close range.

In the 36th minute Bruce was judged extremely harshly to have handled a ball that he was unable to prevent hitting his shoulder! Merson's free-kick was close enough to the 'keeper, one would have thought, for Schmeichel to have come for but he didn't and a surprised Pallister could only look on aghast as the ball hit his shin and went in the net for a lucky equaliser.

United settled down well in the second period and eight minutes after half-time deservedly regained the lead with a classy move that needed a little bit of luck. Giggs, on the halfway line picked out Cantona some forty yards away to his left with a pass that was inch perfect. Cantona made ground down the left before cutting in and crossing low and hard into the area. The ball hit Giggs and rebounded straight in to the path of Sharpe who beat Seaman for the second time. Arsenal, to their credit, began to fight their way back into the game and it became both exciting and totally unpredictable. The pressure told, when Dixon hit a long ball into the path of Merson who cut in from the right to unleash an unstoppable shot past Schmeichel. It smashed against the inside of the far post and rebounded along the line before nestling just inside the near post. As the game reached frantic proportions Cantona was booked, rightly, for a two footed tackle on Selley, although the Arsenal man also went in hard. The action was now pulsating and it looked as though the Gunners had a grabbed a late winner when Wright scored after Schmeichel had dropped the ball under pressure from Smith but the referee ruled that Smith had fouled the Dane.

Then came a fatal second booking for Cantona. He had done well to win the ball from Selley in midfield and he advanced down the touchline where Adams came flying in. The Frenchman appeared to everybody but the referee to try jump over the high tackle and he and Adams went down in a heap. Mr Callow immediately went to his pocket and Cantona didn't wait to receive his dismissal.

## League Record

|  |  | Home |  |  |  |  | Away |  |  |  |  |
|---|---|---|---|---|---|---|---|---|---|---|---|
|  | P | W | D | L | F | A | W | D | L | F | A |
| FAPL 93/94 | 33 | 10 | 5 | 1 | 31 | 11 | 11 | 5 | 1 | 37 | 21 |
| All Time FAPL | 75 | 24 | 10 | 3 | 70 | 25 | 21 | 12 | 5 | 65 | 38 |
| All Time FL/FAPL | 3631 | 1060 | 420 | 335 | 3620 | 1809 | 553 | 424 | 789 | 2471 | 3095 |

|  | Home | Away | Total |
|---|---|---|---|
| League Attendances | 705,841 | 493,117 | 1,199,058 |

# Aston Villa
# Manchester United

**(1) 3**
**(0) 1**

Sunday, 27th March 1994, Wembley Stadium          Att.: 77,231

| MANCHESTER UNITED | | | ASTON VILLA | | |
|---|---|---|---|---|---|
| 13 | Les | Sealey | 13 | Mark | Bosnich |
| 2 | Paul | Parker | 2 | Earl | Barrett |
| 3 | Denis | Irwin | 3 | *Steve* | *Staunton (\*79)* |
| 4 | *Steve* | *Bruce (+82)* | 4 | Shaun | Teale |
| 6 | Gary | Pallister | 5 | Paul | McGrath |
| 7 | Eric | Cantona | 6 | Kevin | Richardson |
| 8 | Paul | Ince | 14 | Andy | Townsend |
| 10 | Mark | Hughes | 25 | Graham | Fenton |
| 11 | *Ryan* | *Giggs (\*61)* | 10 | Dalian | Atkinson |
| 14 | Andrei | Kanchelskis – *Sent Off* | 9 | Dean | Saunders |
| 16 | Roy | Keane | 11 | Tony | Daley |

*Subs*

| | | | | | |
|---|---|---|---|---|---|
| 5 | *Lee* | *Sharpe (\*61)* | 17 | *Neil* | *Cox (\*79)* |
| 9 | *Brian* | *McClair (+82)* | 1 | Nigel | Spink (gk) |
| 25 | Gary | Walsh (gk) | 7 | Ray | Houghton |

## *Score Sheet*

D. ATKINSON 25 min – 0-1
D. SAUNDERS 75 min – 0-2
M. HUGHES 82 min – 1-2
D..SAUNDERS 90 min – 1-3

*Referee:*
Mr. K. Cooper (Pontypridd)

# Treble Dreams Blasted

Starting well, United, playing in their gold and green strip, dominated the early play and it was ten minutes before Sealey got his first touch of the ball from a back pass. After 17 minutes it looked like the Reds had taken the lead as Giggs outsmarted Atkinson and Barrett to whip over a cross that Hughes hit first time, beating not only Bosnich but also the post by the narrowest of margins. Back on the offensive Hughes, Keane and Cantona combined well to get the Irishman through on goal only to get his header parried by Bosnich.

Bosnich was at the centre of the next incident when the Villa 'keeper body checked Keane outside the area. The referee ruled their was no infringement, upsetting the United followers given that Schmeichel was suspended for something not too dissimilar. Villa's first real threat came after 23 minutes when a nasty looking corner whipped under Sealey's bar, the stand-in 'keeper confidently pushing it over and touching the ball with his hands for the first time.

As United kept the pressure up one could sense that Villa were becoming more confident of holding them back. Richardson was winning his battle with Giggs and United were largely ineffective in a very crowded box. Then, completely against the run of play, Villa scored. Saunders got the ball for virtually the first time in the game and ran across United's back four line. Chipping the ball through, Atkinson beat Sealey by mishitting the ball with his right shin.

Parker's reply, a twenty yard drive that had goal written all over it swerved past the post at the last second. More dissapointment followed when Pallister was brought down a yard inside the box with the free kick awarded a yard outside.

With Sharpe substituted for the ineffective Giggs the second period started with United doing all the attacking without ever looking like scoring. Cantona set-up Kanchelskis on goal but the former United defender Paul McGrath made a saving tackle. United's best chance came as Cantona cleverly headed down to leave Sharpe, only six yards out, to beat Bosnich. Teale made a critical tackle and got the ball away for a corner. Then came the killer punch.

Parker tripped Daley just outside the United penalty area. The free-kick was whipped in low to the near post where an unmarked Saunders poked the ball home.

Uniteds fight back got the goal they deserved. Bosnich poorly punched clear Irwin's corner which fell to Keane. His drive was blocked by team-mate Hughes, who reacted quickly to turn and stab the ball home. Sensationally, United had Kanchelskis dismissed in the final minute for handling the ball on the goal line, Saunders converting the penalty to sink United's treble dreams once and for all.

## League Record

| | Home | | | | | | Away | | | | |
|---|---|---|---|---|---|---|---|---|---|---|---|
| | P | W | D | L | F | A | W | D | L | F | A |
| Cup record | 121 | 44 | 11 | 8 | 134 | 53 | 22 | 14 | 222 | 79 | 74 |

| | Home | Away | Total |
|---|---|---|---|
| Cup Attendances | 169,819 | 194,438 | 364,257 |

# Coca-Cola Cup Final

How they got to Wembley

## Manchester United

| Round | Opponents | home/away | Score | Scorers |
|---|---|---|---|---|
| 2nd Round, 1st Leg | v Stoke City | (a) | 1-2 | (Dublin) |
| 2nd Round, 2nd Leg | v Stoke City | (h) | 2-0 | (Sharpe, McClair) |
| 3rd Round | v Leicester City | (h) | 5-1 | (Bruce 2, McClair, Sharpe, Hughes) |
| 4th Round | v Everton | (a) | 2-0 | (Hughes, Giggs) |
| 5th Round | v Portsmouth | (h) | 2-2 | (Giggs, Cantona) |
| 5th Round Replay | v Portsmouth | (a) | 1-0 | (McClair) |
| Semi Final, 1st Leg | v Sheffield Wednesday | (h) | 1-0 | (Giggs) |
| Semi Final, 2nd Leg | v Sheffield Wednesday | (a) | 4-1 | (Hughes 2, McClair, Kanchelskis) |

Goals 18-6

## Aston Villa

| Round | Opponents | home/away | Score | Scorers |
|---|---|---|---|---|
| 2nd Round, 1st Leg | v Birmingham City | (a) | 1-0 | (Richardson) |
| 2nd Round, 2nd Leg | v Birmingham City | (h) | 1-0 | (Saunders) |
| 3rd Round | v Sunderland | (a) | 4-1 | (Atkinson 2, Richardson, Houghton) |
| 4th Round | v Arsenal | (a) | 1-0 | (Atkinson) |
| 5th Round | v Tottenham Hotspur | (a) | 2-1 | (Houghton, Barrett) |
| Semi Final, 1st Leg | v Tranmere Rovers | (a) | 1-3 | (Atkinson) |
| Semi Final, 2nd Leg | v Tranmere Rovers | (h) | 3-1† | (Saunders, Teale, Atkinson) |

†Villa won 5-4 on penalties

Goals 13-6

*Roy Keane, previously an amateur boxer, was brought in to eventually replace United's other fighting forward, Bryan Robson.*

# Manchester United (1) 1
# Liverpool (0) 0

Match 52

Wednesday, 30th March 1994, Old Trafford                  Att.: 44,751

## MANCHESTER UNITED

| | | |
|---|---|---|
| 1 | Peter | Schmeichel |
| 2 | Paul | Parker |
| 3 | Denis | Irwin |
| 4 | Steve | Bruce |
| 5 | Lee | Sharpe (*66) |
| 6 | Gary | Pallister |
| 7 | Eric | Cantona (+73) |
| 8 | Paul | Ince |
| 10 | Mark | Hughes |
| 14 | Andrei | Kanchelskis |
| 16 | Roy | Keane |

*Subs*

| | | |
|---|---|---|
| 12 | Bryan | Robson (+73) |
| 13 | Les | Sealey (gk) |
| 11 | Ryan | Giggs(*66) |

## LIVERPOOL

| | | |
|---|---|---|
| 13 | David | James |
| 2 | Rob | Jones |
| 25 | Neil | Ruddock |
| 4 | Steve | Nicol |
| 3 | Julian | Dicks |
| 15 | Jamie | Redknapp |
| 12 | Ronnie | Whelan |
| 17 | Steve | McManaman |
| 9 | Ian | Rush |
| 16 | Michael | Thomas (*80) |
| 10 | John | Barnes |

| | | |
|---|---|---|
| 7 | Nigel | Clough |
| 23 | Robbie | Fowler (*80) |
| 1 | Bruce | Grobbelaar (gk) |

---

### *Match Facts*

• The attendance set a new record for the FAPL of 44,751 beating by just one the figure set at Old Trafford for the visit of Everton in January. The result left Liverpool still looking for a first FA Premiership success over United. The game was referee Mr Hackett's last at Old Trafford before his retirement after a long and illustrious career.

### *Score Sheet*

P. INCE 6 min – 1-0

*Referee:*
Mr. K Hackett (Sheffield)

---

## FA Carling Premiership League

| | | P | W | D | L | F | A | Pts |
|---|---|---|---|---|---|---|---|---|
| 1 | **Manchester United** | 34 | 22 | 10 | 2 | 69 | 32 | 76 |
| 2 | Blackburn Rovers | 34 | 21 | 7 | 6 | 52 | 29 | 70 |
| 3 | Newcastle United | 35 | 19 | 7 | 9 | 69 | 34 | 64 |
| 4 | Arsenal | 34 | 16 | 13 | 5 | 46 | 19 | 61 |
| 5 | Leeds United | 34 | 14 | 13 | 7 | 47 | 33 | 55 |

**Result of this Season's Fixture**

Manchester Utd
Liverpool

After four dismissals in their last five matches and no win in their last three outings including the Coca Cola Cup Final defeat, United were given a welcome generally reserved for heroes. They were also due a change of luck. Liverpool played five across the midfield and quickly succeeded in reducing the noise from United's fans. They were also clearly frustrating United's attempts to play an open game and Hughes was lucky to escape a caution when he fouled Whelan. When Cantona did manage to get free of the congested midfield after a mistake by Nicol his attempted lob fell tamely into the waiting arms of James. Hughes then produced the best effort of the game so far with a 25 yard drive that whistled over the bar but the Reds were looking somewhat ragged. Then, as the rain came down in bucket loads, Kanchelskis popped up on the left wing to force a corner. Thomas cleared for another flag kick on the right. Sharpe's inswinging kick was difficult to defend against but Liverpool made it easier by failing to mark tightly. Ince was stationed between Barnes and McManaman but neither were close enough to him. The ball cleared Barnes and Ince was free to force a powerful glancing header home before McManaman could.

Having undone all their good work in holding United, Liverpool came out for the second period in the mood to be slightly more adventurous. Redknapp was the villain of the piece for the Anfield outfit when he got clear of the Red's defence. As he cut in from the right he chose to go for glory and tried to beat Schmeichel at the near post when a far better tactic would have been to lay it back to the unmarked Barnes. The game in general, however, was still bogged down in midfield and, for once, it seemed as if United had decided that the three points were more vital than the manner of performance. They battled it out and were content to sit on their lead as they were not being unduly worried at the back. Then, as the game drifted into mediocrity, came a decision that gave United a welcome change of luck. Thomas made ground down the Liverpool left and was tackled by Kanchelskis in the penalty area where they both fell in a heap. Referee Hackett had no hesitation in pointing to the spot but United persuaded him to have a word with the linesman, Brian Lowe of Doncaster. After a lengthy consultation, the referee reversed his decision and gave United a free kick – a strange move considering Mr Hackett was at least thirty yards closer to the incident than Mr Lowe.

## League Record

| | | | Home | | | | Away | | | | |
|---|---|---|---|---|---|---|---|---|---|---|---|
| | P | W | D | L | F | A | W | D | L | F | A |
| FAPL 93/94 | 34 | 11 | 5 | 1 | 32 | 11 | 11 | 5 | 1 | 37 | 21 |
| All Time FAPL | 76 | 25 | 10 | 3 | 71 | 25 | 21 | 12 | 5 | 65 | 38 |
| All Time FL/FAPL | 3632 | 1061 | 420 | 335 | 3621 | 1809 | 553 | 424 | 789 | 471 | 3095 |

| | Home | Away | Total |
|---|---|---|---|
| League Attendances | 750,592 | 493,117 | 1,243,709 |

# Blackburn Rovers (0) 2
# Manchester United (0) 0

Saturday, 2nd April 1994, Ewood Park                    Att.: 20,866

## BLACKBURN ROVERS

| 26 | Tim | Flowers |
| 20 | Henning | Berg |
| 2 | David | May |
| 5 | Colin | Hendry – *Booked* |
| 6 | Graham | Le Saux – *Booked* |
| 7 | Stuart | Ripley |
| 23 | David | Sherwood |
| 4 | Tim | Sherwood |
| 11 | Jason | Wilcox |
| 10 | *Mike* | *Newell – Booked (\*85)* |
| 9 | Alan | Shearer |

*Subs*

| 1 | Bobby | Mimms (gk) |
| 12 | *Nicky* | *Marker (\*85)* |
| 3 | Alan | Wright |

## MANCHESTER UNITED

| 1 | Peter | Schmeichel |
| 2 | *Paul* | *Parker (\*70)* |
| 3 | Denis | Irwin |
| 4 | Steve | Bruce |
| 5 | Lee | Sharpe |
| 6 | Gary | Pallister |
| 8 | Paul | Ince |
| 10 | Mark | Hughes – *Booked* |
| 11 | Ryan | Giggs |
| 14 | Andrei | Kanchelskis |
| 16 | Roy | Keane |

| 12 | Bryan | Robson |
| 13 | Les | Sealey (gk) |
| 9 | *Brian* | *McClair (\*70)* |

---

### *Match Facts*

- United still to score a goal at Ewood Park in the FA Premier League.
- United's first defeat at Ewood Park since 10th April 1962.
- United's first League match at Ewood Park since losing 4-3 in 1892.

### *Score Sheet*

A. SHEARER 46 min – 1-0

A. SHEARER 76 min – 2-0

*Referee:*
Mr R Milford (Bristol)

---

## FA Carling Premiership League

|   |   | P | W | D | L | F | A | Pts |
|---|---|---|---|---|---|---|---|-----|
| 1 | **Manchester United** | 35 | 22 | 10 | 3 | 69 | 34 | 76 |
| 2 | Blackburn Rovers | 35 | 22 | 7 | 6 | 54 | 29 | 73 |
| 3 | Newcastle United | 35 | 19 | 7 | 9 | 69 | 34 | 64 |
| 4 | Arsenal | 35 | 16 | 14 | 5 | 47 | 20 | 62 |
| 5 | Leeds United | 35 | 14 | 14 | 7 | 48 | 34 | 56 |

**Result of this Season's Fixture**

Blackburn Rovers
Manchester Utd

139

# United's Lead Sheared

With leading goalscorer Eric Cantona serving the first instalment of his five match ban, Alex Ferguson opted to play both Giggs and Sharpe, a ploy that had not worked particularly well in the past. This was a game that Blackburn had to win to have any hope of catching the Reds at the top of the table. For all the pre-match hype, the start of the most important Premiership game of the season was reduced to farce when the teams lined up with all three officials in place but with no ball!

The first forty-five minutes failed to live up to expectations with both sides committed to giving nothing away and neither 'keeper had a shot to save although Pallister went close for both sides. On both occasions many people in the ground thought the big United defender had scored as he first of all sliced Berg's low cross past Schmeichel and into the side netting and then, at the other end, showed attacking skills previously unlinked to his 6ft 4in frame as he skipped past three Blackburn defenders before unleashing a rocket shot that beat Flowers before getting stuck in the netting and the stanchion, unfortunately for United the wrong side of the goalpost. The game opened up with a goal almost immediately after the interval. From a throw-in Rovers knocked the ball around in a series of short passes on the right until it fell for Sherwood. The Blackburn captain's cross to the far post was unerring, Shearer unmarked, Blackburn one up. United briefly loosened the shackles put on their attacking ideas when Sharpe crossed from the left and Kanchelskis fired in a stunning volley that brought an equally stunning instinctive parry from Flowers. United were even more unlucky a few minutes later when Kanchelskis broke away down the right to cross low into the box. Giggs jumped over the ball which ran into the path of Ince whose miskick deceived Flowers only for the ball to bounce back into play off the post. The contest was all over when Blackburn scored their second with just fourteen minutes left. Newell flattened Pallister with an elbow in the face and was lucky to escape with only a caution. The free kick into the Blackburn half was cleared to Ripley well inside his own half and posing no apparent danger to United. But a long ball found Shearer whom Pallister had allowed to get the wrong side of him and from then on, the giant defender always had the problem of risking a sending off if he tackled him from behind. Shearer blasted the ball through Schmeichel but almost certainly Newell's elbow had contributed as much to the goal as anything as Pallister had obviously not completely recovered.

## League Record

| | | Home | | | | | Away | | | | |
|---|---|---|---|---|---|---|---|---|---|---|---|
| | P | W | D | L | F | A | W | D | L | F | A |
| 93/94 FAPL | 35 | 11 | 5 | 1 | 32 | 11 | 11 | 5 | 2 | 37 | 23 |
| All Time FAPL | 77 | 25 | 10 | 3 | 71 | 25 | 21 | 12 | 6 | 65 | 40 |
| All Time FL/FAPL | 3633 | 1061 | 420 | 335 | 3621 | 1809 | 553 | 424 | 790 | 2471 | 3097 |

| | Home | Away | Total |
|---|---|---|---|
| League Attendances | 750,592 | 513,983 | 1,264,575 |

# Manchester United (1) 3
# Oldham Athletic (0) 2

Match 54

Monday, 4th April 1994, Old Trafford                    Att.: 44,686

| MANCHESTER UNITED | | | OLDHAM ATHLETIC | | |
|---|---|---|---|---|---|
| 1 | Peter | Schmeichel | 13 | Jon | Hallworth |
| 3 | Denis | Irwin | 22 | *Chris* | *Makin (+70)* |
| 4 | Steve | Bruce | 6 | Steve | Redmond |
| 5 | Lee | Sharpe | 5 | Richard | Jobson |
| 6 | Gary | Pallister | 3 | Neil | Pointon |
| 8 | Paul | Ince | 21 | Sean | McCarthy |
| 9 | *Brian* | *McClair (*65)* | 2 | Craig | Fleming |
| 10 | Mark | Hughes | 20 | *Mark* | *Brennan (*70)* |
| 11 | Ryan | Giggs | 10 | Mike | Milligan |
| 14 | Andrei | Kanchelskis | 25 | Rick | Holden |
| 16 | Roy | Keane | 14 | Graeme | Sharpe |

*Subs*

| 12 | Bryan | Robson | 1 | Paul | Gerrard (gk) |
|---|---|---|---|---|---|
| 13 | Les | Sealey (gk) | 17 | *Darren* | *Beckford (*70)* |
| 20 | *Dion* | *Dublin (*65)* | 19 | *Roger* | *Palmer (+70)* |

### *Match Facts*

• United have not lost to Oldham at Old Trafford since 1934.

• Dion Dublin was in just his tenth minute of FAPL action this season when he scored United's second goal – his first in the FA Premiership in 93/94.

• Incredibly, Sharp's goal was his fifteenth against United!

### *Score Sheet*

R. GIGGS 17 min – 1-0
S. McCARTHY 49 min – 1-1
D. DUBLIN 66 min – 2-1
P. INCE 67 min – 3-1
G. SHARPE 70 min – 3-2

*Referee:*
Mr. P Durkin (Dorset)

### FA Carling Premiership League

| | | P | W | D | L | F | A | Pts |
|---|---|---|---|---|---|---|---|---|
| 1 | **Manchester United** | 36 | 23 | 10 | 3 | 72 | 46 | 79 |
| 2 | Blackburn Rovers | 36 | 23 | 7 | 6 | 57 | 29 | 76 |
| 3 | Newcastle United | 37 | 19 | 8 | 10 | 70 | 36 | 65 |
| 4 | Arsenal | 36 | 16 | 15 | 5 | 48 | 21 | 63 |
| 5 | Leeds United | 36 | 15 | 14 | 7 | 52 | 34 | 59 |

**Result of this Season's Fixture**

No Fixture

141

# Winning Warm-up

United warmed up for their FA Cup semi final match against Oldham Athletic by beating the Latics 3-2. The display, however, was not vintage United and many people felt that the Reds' decisive third goal was offside.

All began well for United and such was their dominance that it was 16 minutes before Peter Schmeichel even touched the ball. A minute later United's territorial advantage saw them take the lead as Bruce came forward to within 30 yards of goal and chipped the ball onto the edge of the six yard box. Giggs, not known for his heading prowess, quickened away from his marker, Makin, to score a rare headed goal beating Hallworth at his left hand post. The Reds' lead was almost shortlived as Pallister slipped with nobody near him to let in McCarthy. Fortunately for United the big Oldham striker lost control at the critical moment and the ball bounced tamely off his shin to the relieved Schmeichel. The big United 'keeper was also in action just before the interval making a fine save from Holden's cross shot.

Things took a definite turn for the worse immediately after the resumption with McCarthy making up for his earlier blunder by turning Bruce and slamming an unstoppable left foot shot across Schmeichel and into the net by the 'keeper's left hand post. With the news that Blackburn were winning 2-0 at Everton, United's lead at the top of the table was at this stage down to a single point. Giggs got clear down the left and skipped away from two Oldham defenders before playing a great ball into the centre only for McClair to make a complete hash of it. This brought about an all action five minute spell of three substitutions and as many goals. Ferguson removed McClair from the fray for his misdemeanour and replaced him with Dion Dublin. The move paid immediate dividends as United played the ball about in a series of passes. Giggs was involved in the move no fewer than four times before crossing it to where Kanchelskis knocked it down and, whilst everybody hesitated, Dublin gleefully pounced to restore United's lead with his first touch of the ball. Sixty seconds later it was 3-1 with Giggs set free by a through ball from Mark Hughes. Despite Oldham appeals the flag stayed down and Giggs slipped the ball to Ince who fired home from ten yards. Oldham's reply was to make a double substitution, and like United's five minutes earlier, the move paid an instant dividend. As the ball bounced around the United penalty area, Oldham's substitute, Darren Beckford, caused havoc with his presence enabling Graeme Sharp, who always finds the net against the Reds, to score from twelve yards.

## League Record

|  | Home | | | | | | Away | | | | | |
|  | P | W | D | L | F | A | W | D | L | F | A |
|---|---|---|---|---|---|---|---|---|---|---|---|
| 93/94 FAPL | 36 | 12 | 5 | 1 | 35 | 13 | 11 | 5 | 2 | 37 | 23 |
| All Time FAPL | 78 | 26 | 10 | 3 | 74 | 27 | 21 | 12 | 6 | 65 | 40 |
| All Time FAPL/FL | 3634 | 1062 | 420 | 335 | 3624 | 1811 | 553 | 424 | 790 | 2471 | 3097 |

|  | Home | Away | Total |
|---|---|---|---|
| League Attendances | 795,278 | 513,983 | 1,309,261 |

# Manchester United (0) 1
# Oldham Athletic (0) 1

Sunday, 10th April 1994, Wembley                    Att.: 56,399

| **MANCHESTER UNITED** | | | **OLDHAM ATHLETIC.** | | |
|---|---|---|---|---|---|
| 1 | Peter | Schmeichel | 13 | Jon | Hallworth |
| 2 | *Paul* | *Parker (+108)* | 22 | Chris | Makin |
| 3 | Denis | Irwin | 5 | Richard | Jobson |
| 4 | Steve | Bruce | 2 | Craig | Fleming |
| 5 | Lee | Sharpe | 3 | Neil | Pointon – *Booked* |
| 6 | Gary | Pallister | 11 | Paul | Bernard |
| 8 | Paul | Ince – *Booked* | 10 | Mick | Milligan |
| 9 | Brian | McClair | 4 | Nick | Henry – *Booked* |
| 10 | Mark | Hughes – *Booked* | 25 | Rick | Holden |
| 11 | Ryan | Giggs | 17 | Darren | Beckford |
| 20 | *Dion* | *Dublin (\*73)* | 14 | Graeme | Sharp |

*Subs*

| 12 | *Bryan* | *Robson (\*79)* | 1 | Paul | Gerrard (gk) |
|---|---|---|---|---|---|
| 13 | Les | Sealey (gk) | 20 | Mark | Brennan |
| 19 | *Nicky* | *Butt (+108)* | 8 | Andy | Ritchie |

## *Match Facts*

• This was United's nineteenth Semi Final appearance, Oldham's third. It was United's sixteenth post war semi. The goals conceded by United and Oldham were only the second by both teams in this year's competition.

## *Score Sheet*

N. POINTON 106 min – 0-1
M. HUGHES 119 min – 1-1

*Referee:*
Mr. P. Don (Middlesex)

# Hughes Special

Without Cantona, Keane and Kanchelskis, all suspended, manager Alex Ferguson opted to play Dion Dublin and Brian McClair and promoted young Nicky Butt to the substitutes bench for this FA Cup semi-final at Wembley. Oldham also had trouble with Redmond suspended and McCarthy cup-tied.

The game started slowly with Oldham ready to defend in depth and stifle United's attacking ambitions. Hughes was quite magnificent but lack of support proved his undoing and he was constantly "given the treatment" by the Oldham defence. The first shot came after eight minutes but the effort from Ince was hardly noteworthy as it cleared the crossbar by some way. His next attempt, a diving header from a Parker cross, was much closer and the beaten Hallworth much relieved to see it go just wide. Oldham were just as close at the other end when a cross from Holden was mishit by Sharp to deceive Schmeichel and go inches past his right hand post. That was the sum total of goalmouth action for the first period and the second half was even more barren with the only effort of any significance being a superb header from Hughes that Hallworth responded to with a brilliant diving flick over the bar.

Extra time began to make up for some of poor entertainment served up in the first ninety minutes but just when it looked as if United were getting on top, Oldham took the lead. Sharpe and Irwin stopped an attack from Chris Makin at the expense of a corner but Schmeichel dropped the resulting kick straight at the feet of Pointon who hit it into the unguarded net from about ten yards. United were left fourteen minutes to break down a defence they had failed to penetrate in over a hundred. In fact it went to the last seconds before Hughes struck one of his magical goals. Milligan headed clear a Sharpe lob only for young substitute Nicky Butt to play it straight back in. McClair, with his back to goal, chipped it over his head and Hughes, with all his body apart from his left leg on which he was standing horizontal, volleyed a goal that was quite exceptional even by the Welshman's own standards. United were saved.

## Cup Record

|  | P | W | D | L | F | A | W | D | L | F | A |
|---|---|---|---|---|---|---|---|---|---|---|---|
|  |  | **Home** |  |  |  |  | **Away** |  |  |  |  |
| All time Cup record | 344 | 99 | 31 | 28 | 333 | 148 | 76 | 53 | 57 | 290 | 267 |

|  | Home | Away | Total |
|---|---|---|---|
| Cup Attendances | 44,347 | 126,989 | 171,336 |

# Manchester United (2) 4
# Oldham Athletic (1) 1

Wednesday, 13th April 1994, Maine Road                Att.: 32,211

## MANCHESTER UNITED

| 1 | Peter | Schmeichel |
|---|---|---|
| 2 | Paul | Parker |
| 3 | Denis | Irwin |
| 4 | Steve | Bruce |
| 6 | Gary | Pallister |
| 8 | Paul | Ince |
| 10 | Mark | Hughes (+75) |
| 11 | Ryan | Giggs |
| 12 | Bryan | Robson |
| 14 | Andrei | Kanchelskis |
| 16 | Roy | Keane – Booked (*69) |

*Subs*

| 13 | Les | Sealey (gk) |
|---|---|---|
| 9 | Brian | McClair (*69) |
| 5 | Lee | Sharpe (+75) |

## OLDHAM ATHLETIC

| 13 | John | Hallworth |
|---|---|---|
| 22 | Chris | Makin |
| 5 | Richard | Jobson |
| 2 | Craig | Fleming |
| 3 | Neil | Pointon (*70) |
| 11 | Paul | Bernard – Booked |
| 10 | Mick | Milligan |
| 4 | Nick | Henry |
| 25 | Rick | Holden |
| 17 | Darren | Beckford (+70) |
| 14 | Graeme | Sharp |

| 1 | Paul | Gerrard (gk) |
|---|---|---|
| 6 | Steve | Redmond (*70) |
| 8 | Andy | Ritchie (+70) |

## *Match Facts*

• The win put United in their twelfth FA Cup Final, eleven of which have been post-war, and their seventh in nineteen years. The winning margin was United's biggest ever in a FA Cup semi-final.

## *Score Sheet*

D. IRWIN 9 min – 1-0

KANCHELSKIS 15 min – 2-0

N. POINTON 39 min – 2-1

B. ROBSON 62 min – 3-1

R. GIGGS 68 min – 4-1

### *Referee:*
Mr. M. Bodenham (Cornwall)

# Kanchelskis the Difference

United had both Andrei Kanchelskis and Roy Keane back from suspension for this FA Cup semi-final along with Bryan Robson as Ferguson tried desperately to shake his side out of their lacklustre form. The new formula worked to perfection with Kanchelskis, in particular, giving a breathtaking display of wing play which was to prove decisive. The Reds got what Sunday's game needed, an early goal for the Old Trafford outfit to make Oldham come out of their defensive ploy. United played the ball about in a series of passes until Robson, on the left of the Oldham penalty area, played a lightning one-two that put Irwin clear to volley with ease past the exposed Hallworth. Oldham barely had time to recover their composure before finding themselves two down. Kanchelskis was allowed to run from the right touchline across the entire length of the penalty area before turning and shooting left footed into the far corner of Hallworth's net for a superb solo strike. United began to coast and allowed Oldham back in the game when Robson made a bad mistake. Having done the difficult work in breaking up an Oldham attack, Robson hesitated a long time in clearing and was eventually forced to concede a corner. Beckford got a slight touch to Holden's kick and Pointon, who had scored Oldham's goal in the Wembley clash, scored his second goal of the season!

Oldham tried hard to get back on level terms in the second half but, as they pushed forward, Kanchelskis ran riot. After another attack set up by Kanchelskis, Oldham conceded a corner. When the cross arrived from Giggs, Hallworth went for it only to be stopped dead in his tracks by Jobson. Unable to thus reach the ball he could only look on in horror as the ball floated to Robson whose late arrival in the area left him unmarked to bundle the ball home via a combination of arms, legs and head. Now with a safety cushion, United began to play vintage football and the game threatened to become a rout. Jobson blocked a shot from Giggs but neither he nor Hallworth could do anything about the Welshman's follow up effort. The fact that the Reds failed to add to their tally was as much due to their profligacy in front of goal as to the Oldham rearguard.

## Cup Record

|  | | Home | | | | | Away | | | | |
|---|---|---|---|---|---|---|---|---|---|---|---|
|  | P | W | D | L | F | A | W | D | L | F | A |
| All time Cup record | 345 | 99 | 31 | 28 | 333 | 148 | 77 | 53 | 57 | 294 | 268 |

|  | Home | Away | Total |
|---|---|---|---|
| Cup Attendances | 44,347 | 159,211 | 203,547 |

# Wimbledon **(1) 1**
# Manchester United **(0) 0**

Saturday, 16th April 1994, Selhurst Park                    Att.: 28,553

## WIMBLEDON

| | | |
|---|---|---|
| 1 | Hans | Segers |
| 2 | Warren | Barton |
| 15 | John | Scales |
| 5 | Dean | Blackwell |
| 33 | Gary | Elkins |
| 24 | Peter | Fear |
| 4 | Vinny | Jones |
| 8 | Robbie | Earle |
| 20 | Marcus | Gayle |
| 10 | Dean | Holdsworth |
| 9 | John | Fashanu |

## MANCHESTER UNITED

| | | |
|---|---|---|
| 1 | Peter | Schmeichel |
| 2 | *Paul* | *Parker (+73)* |
| 3 | Denis | Irwin |
| 4 | Steve | Bruce |
| 6 | Gary | Pallister |
| 8 | Paul | Ince |
| 9 | Brian | McClair |
| 10 | Mark | Hughes |
| 11 | Ryan | Giggs |
| 12 | *Bryan* | *Robson (*64)* |
| 14 | Andrei | Kanchelskis |

*Subs*

| | | |
|---|---|---|
| 21 | Chris | Perry |
| 36 | Gary | Blisset |
| 23 | Neil | Sullivan (gk) |

| | | |
|---|---|---|
| 13 | Les | Sealey (gk) |
| 5 | *Lee* | *Sharpe (*64)* |
| 20 | *Dion* | *Dublin (+73)* |

---

### *Match Facts*

- Wimbledon unbeaten in the league at their adopted home since New Year's Day.

- Joe Kinnear received the Manager of the Month award for March just prior to kick off and became the first manager to receive the award twice in 93/94.

- Wimbledon became the first team to defeat the Reds in successive FAPL seasons.

---

### *Score Sheet*

J. FASHANU 21 min – 1-0

*Referee:*
Mr T.Holbrook (Walsall)

---

## FA Carling Premiership League

| | | P | W | D | L | F | A | Pts |
|---|---|---|---|---|---|---|---|---|
| 1 | **Manchester United** | 37 | 23 | 10 | 4 | 72 | 37 | 79 |
| 2 | Blackburn Rovers | 38 | 24 | 7 | 7 | 59 | 32 | 79 |
| 3 | Newcastle united | 38 | 20 | 8 | 10 | 72 | 36 | 68 |
| 4 | Arsenal | 37 | 17 | 15 | 5 | 49 | 21 | 66 |
| 5 | Leeds United | 36 | 15 | 14 | 7 | 52 | 34 | 59 |

### Result of this Season's Fixture

Wimbledon
Manchester Utd

# Slip Up

If United needed any encouragement to put on one of their best performances they
surely got it fifteen minutes prior to this 5.00pm kick off when the news filtered
through that nearest rivals Blackburn Rovers had crashed 3-1 at relegation
threatened Southampton. A win would all but wrap up the Championship.

Straight from the kick off, Wimbledon almost went into the lead when Fashanu
got between Bruce and Pallister and the ball broke for Gayle. Fortunately for Alex
Ferguson's men, the midfielder was unable to get more than a cursory toe on the
ball which finished up with Schmeichel. United hit back and a smart back heel from
Hughes almost got McClair through the the Dons' rearguard. Kanchelskis was then
freed by Parker but as the Londoners' defence closed him down, the Russian shot
hastily and the effort was both high and wide. Almost innocuously, McClair gave
the ball away on the halfway line but from little acorns grow big oak trees and that
mistake, harmless as it appeared at the time, proved to be the decisive moment of
the match. Peter Fear picked up McClair's errant pass and slipped the ball to
Fashanu in the centre circle. Jones was brought into the action with a quick ball
from the big striker and the man the crowds love to hate moved the play with equal
haste to Elkins making ground on the left. He hit the byeline and crossed hard and
low to the near post which Schmeichel, clearly expecting the centre to be pulled
back, had vacated and Fashanu did the rest.

United did get the ball in the net in the second half when Kanchelskis crossed to
Hughes who headed back across the face of the goal. Segers was at full stretch to
catch the ball but it was definitely in his hands when Ince's boot made contact to
force the ball home and the decision to disallow the effort appeared correct as
United failed to cash in on Blackburn's afternoon defeat.

## League Record

| | Home | | | | | | Away | | | | |
|---|---|---|---|---|---|---|---|---|---|---|---|
| | P | W | D | L | F | A | W | D | L | F | A |
| FAPL 93/94 | 37 | 12 | 5 | 1 | 35 | 13 | 11 | 5 | 3 | 37 | 24 |
| All Time FAPL | 79 | 26 | 10 | 3 | 74 | 27 | 21 | 12 | 7 | 65 | 41 |
| All Time FL/FAPL | 3635 | 1062 | 420 | 335 | 3624 | 1811 | 553 | 424 | 791 | 2471 | 3098 |

| | Home | Away | Total |
|---|---|---|---|
| League Attendances | 795,278 | 542,536 | 1,337,814 |

# Manchester United (2) 2
# Manchester City (0) 0

Saturday, 23rd April 1994, Old Trafford                    Att.: 44,333

## MANCHESTER UNITED

| 1 | Peter | Schmeichel |
|---|---|---|
| 2 | Paul | Parker |
| 3 | Denis | Irwin |
| 4 | Steve | Bruce |
| 5 | *Lee* | *Sharpe (* 72)* |
| 6 | Gary | Pallister |
| 7 | Eric | Cantona – *Booked* |
| 8 | Paul | Ince – *Booked* |
| 10 | Mark | Hughes |
| 14 | Andrei | Kanchelskis |
| 16 | Roy | Keane – *Booked* |

## MANCHESTER CITY

| 25 | Andy | Dibble |
|---|---|---|
| 2 | Andy | Hill |
| 18 | David | Brightwell |
| 4 | Steve | McMahon – *Booked* |
| 5 | Keith | Curle |
| 6 | Michel | Vonk |
| 7 | David | Rocastle – *Booked* |
| 30 | Paul | Walsh |
| 28 | Uwe | Rosler |
| 31 | *Steffen* | *Karl (* 57)* |
| 32 | Peter | Beagrie |

### Subs

| 25 | Gary | Walsh (gk) |
|---|---|---|
| 12 | Bryan | Robson |
| 11 | *Ryan* | *Giggs (*72)* |

| 12 | *Ian* | *Brightwell (*57)* |
|---|---|---|
| 13 | Martyn | Margetson (gk) |
| 21 | Steve | Lomas |

## *Match Facts*

● Although he only signed for United in November 1992, Cantona's second goal was his fifth against City. The victory increased the Red's advantage in the derby series to 43 wins against City's 30.

## *Score Sheet*

E. CANTONA 40 min – 1-0
E. CANTONA 45 min – 2-0

*Referee:*
K. Morton (Bury St Edmunds)

## FA Carling Premiership League

| | | P | W | D | L | F | A | Pts |
|---|---|---|---|---|---|---|---|---|
| 1 | **Manchester United** | 38 | 24 | 10 | 4 | 74 | 37 | 82 |
| 2 | Blackburn Rovers | 38 | 24 | 7 | 7 | 59 | 32 | 79 |
| 3 | Newcastle United | 39 | 21 | 8 | 10 | 75 | 38 | 71 |
| 4 | Arsenal | 39 | 18 | 16 | 5 | 52 | 23 | 70 |
| 5 | Leeds United | 38 | 16 | 15 | 7 | 55 | 35 | 63 |

### Result of this Season's Fixture

Manchester Utd
Manchester City

# Cantona Back

Eric Cantona was welcomed back after a five match suspension with City players warning that they were going to set out to "wind him up" in the words of Terry Phelan. The Frenchman delivered the perfect riposte with both United goals although some of the shine disappeared when Cantona was one of three United players to be needlessly booked in the last five minutes.

McMahon's attempts to wind Cantona up lasted just five minutes before his crude attempts were brought under control with a quick booking from Mr Morton for an attempted elbow strike. That effectively put paid to any hope McMahon had of destroying skill with brawn and the football was able to get underway.

It was certainly a lively start by City but as the half approached its conclusion, United struck and, love him or hate him, you simply cannot keep Cantona out of the headlines. Hughes started the move that brought the lead with a pass to Kanchelskis from within his own half. The Russian left Brightwell in a 40 yard sprint before cutting in and picking his spot beyond Dibble where Cantona was waiting to tap the ball home. In fairness to City, there looked to be a distinct possibility of offside about the Frenchman's position when he rolled the ball into the empty net. Right on the stroke of half time there was again the suspicion of offside against Cantona as he scored number two but this time without a shadow of doubt the officials had it exactly right with the culprit playing the Frenchman onside being Brightwell on the far touchline. Hughes' through ball was devasting, leaving Cantona with nobody to beat other than Dibble and the finish under Dibble's body was executed to perfection.

Sharpe lost an early chance in the second period to increase the lead when he was put through by Cantona but generally United appeared to be content simply to keep control rather than go looking to increase their advantage. City were restricted to long range efforts, with both Beagrie and Rosler well off target with optimistic shots.

## League Record

|  | Home | | | | | Away | | | | |
|---|---|---|---|---|---|---|---|---|---|---|
|  | P | W | D | L | F | A | W | D | L | F | A |
| FAPL 93/94 | 38 | 13 | 5 | 1 | 37 | 13 | 11 | 5 | 3 | 37 | 24 |
| All Time FAPL | 80 | 27 | 10 | 3 | 76 | 27 | 21 | 12 | 7 | 65 | 41 |
| All Time FL/FAPL | 3636 | 1063 | 420 | 335 | 3626 | 1811 | 553 | 424 | 791 | 2471 | 3098 |

|  | Home | Away | Total |
|---|---|---|---|
| League Attendances | 839,611 | 542,536 | 1,382,147 |

# Leeds United      (0) 0
# Manchester United      (0) 2

Wednesday, 27th April 1994, Elland Road      Att.: 41,125

## LEEDS UNITED

| 1 | John | Lukic |
| 22 | Gary | Kelly |
| 5 | Chris | Fairclough |
| 14 | *David* | *Weatherall (*75)* |
| 16 | Jon | Newsome |
| 3 | Tony | Dorigo |
| 7 | Gordon | Strachan |
| 10 | Gary | McAllister |
| 11 | Gary | Speed |
| 8 | Rod | Wallace |
| 9 | Brian | Deane |

*Subs*

| 13 | Mark | Beeney (gk) |
| 25 | *Noel* | *Whelan (*75)* |
| 12 | John | Pemberton |

## MANCHESTER UNITED

| 1 | Peter | Schmeichel |
| 2 | Paul | Parker |
| 3 | Denis | Irwin |
| 4 | Steve | Bruce |
| 6 | Gary | Pallister |
| 7 | Eric | Cantona |
| 8 | Paul | Ince |
| 10 | Mark | Hughes |
| 11 | Ryan | Giggs |
| 14 | Andrei | Kanchelskis |
| 16 | Roy | Keane |

| 25 | Gary | Walsh |
| 9 | Brian | McClair |
| 12 | Bryan | Robson |

### *Match Facts*

• Leeds have not beaten United in the 14 meetings since they came back into the top flight and have won only once in the last twenty-two years at Elland Road. • Leeds yet to score against United in the FA Premiership. • Attendance set Elland Road record for a Premiership game. • United's first away league victory since 5th February.

### *Score Sheet*

KANCHELSKIS 47min – 1-0

R. GIGGS 65 min – 2-0

*Referee:*
P. Don (Hanworth Park, Middx)

## FA Carling Premiership League

| | P | W | D | L | F | A | Pts |
|---|---|---|---|---|---|---|---|
| 1   **Manchester United** | 39 | 25 | 10 | 4 | 76 | 37 | 85 |
| 2   Blackburn Rovers | 40 | 25 | 8 | 7 | 62 | 34 | 83 |
| 3   Newcastle United | 41 | 22 | 8 | 11 | 80 | 41 | 74 |
| 4   Arsenal | 41 | 18 | 17 | 6 | 53 | 26 | 71 |
| 5   Leeds United | 40 | 17 | 15 | 8 | 58 | 37 | 66 |

**Result of this Season's Fixture**

Leeds Utd

Manchester Utd

# Crowd Ignored

Elland Road's record crowd for an FA Premiership game included just 1,600 United fans and was hostile in the extreme, before, during and after the game. United, however, gave a thoroughly professional performance which ignored the abuse hurled at them from the terraces and earned the tribute from Alex Ferguson of *"our best away display in terms of resilience of the season"*.

United were first on the attack with Cantona earning a free-kick but Irwin was wide with his shot from some 35 yards. Leeds hit back with a corner but it was the Reds who were controlling the game and Giggs was next away to get in a cross despite the attention of both Strachan and Kelly. Cantona got on the end of it but his powerful effort was directly at Lukic. Despite their dominance, United could have gone behind to a spectacular diving header from Speed whose quick run into the area caught United's defence off guard at a Strachan cross from the right. The ball certainly seemed destined for the net until Schmeichel made a brilliant save on the line.

Nothing much had been seen of Kanchelskis in the first period but he made up for lost time at the start of the second. He outpaced the Leeds defence down the right but nobody could get on the end of his cross. He then immediately launched another raid, this time in a more central position. As he approached the area, he slipped the ball left to Hughes who got a lucky bounce off his shin before playing it back into the Russian's path to hit the ball home under Lukic's body.

Five minutes from time, United made the game safe with a super goal from Giggs. Not many can outpace Leeds' teenage sensation Gary Kelly but Giggs did as he burst through on the left. The Welshman then played a quick one-two with Hughes and continued to outrun Kelly before putting the ball beyond Lukic.

## League Record

|  | | Home | | | | | Away | | | |
|---|---|---|---|---|---|---|---|---|---|---|
|  | P | W | D | L | F | A | W | D | L | F | A |
| FAPL 93/94 | 39 | 13 | 5 | 1 | 37 | 13 | 12 | 5 | 3 | 39 | 24 |
| All Time FAPL | 81 | 27 | 10 | 3 | 76 | 27 | 22 | 12 | 7 | 67 | 41 |
| All Time FL/FAPL | 3637 | 1063 | 420 | 335 | 3626 | 1811 | 554 | 424 | 791 | 2473 | 3098 |

|  | Home | Away | Total |
|---|---|---|---|
| League Attendances | 839,611 | 583,661 | 1,423,272 |

# Ipswich Town (1) 1
# Manchester United (1) 2

Sunday, 1st May 1994, Portman Road    Att.: 22,559

## IPSWICH TOWN

| | | |
|---|---|---|
| 1 | Craig | Forrest |
| 2 | Mick | Stockwell |
| 5 | John | Wark |
| 6 | David | Linighan |
| 15 | Phil | Whelan (+62) |
| 17 | Simon | Milton |
| 18 | Steve | Palmer |
| 7 | Gerraint | Williams |
| 8 | Gavin | Johnson (*48) |
| 10 | Ian | Marshall |
| 11 | Chris | Kiwomya |

*Subs*

| | | |
|---|---|---|
| 13 | Clive | Baker (gk) |
| 16 | Eddie | Youds (*48) |
| 9 | Bonicho | Guentchev (+62) |

## MANCHESTER UNITED

| | | |
|---|---|---|
| 1 | Peter | Schmeichel (*25) |
| 2 | Paul | Parker – Booked |
| 3 | Denis | Irwin |
| 4 | Steve | Bruce |
| 6 | Gary | Pallister |
| 7 | Eric | Cantona |
| 8 | Paul | Ince |
| 10 | Mark | Hughes |
| 11 | Ryan | Giggs (+83) |
| 14 | Andrei | Kanchelskis |
| 16 | Roy | Keane |

| | | |
|---|---|---|
| 25 | Gary | Walsh (gk) (*25) |
| 5 | Lee | Sharpe (+83) |
| 9 | Brian | McClair |

## *Match Facts*

• United's first FAPL victory over Ipswich meant they had now beaten every opponent they had faced in the first two seasons of the new competition. • The win was also United's 50th in the FAPL • Gary Walsh's first appearance in the first team since February 1992 when he kept a clean sheet in a goalless draw at Coventry.

## *Score Sheet*

C. KIWOMYA 20 min – 1-0

E. CANTONA 36 min – 1-1

R. GIGGS 47 min – 1-2

*Referee:*
Mr. A.Gunn (Burgess Hill)

## FA Carling Premiership League

| | | P | W | D | L | F | A | Pts |
|---|---|---|---|---|---|---|---|---|
| 1 | Manchester United | 40 | 26 | 10 | 4 | 78 | 38 | 88 |
| 2 | Blackburn Rovers | 40 | 25 | 8 | 6 | 62 | 34 | 83 |
| 3 | Newcastle United | 41 | 21 | 8 | 11 | 76 | 41 | 74 |
| 4 | Arsenal | 41 | 18 | 17 | 6 | 53 | 26 | 71 |
| 5 | Leeds United | 40 | 17 | 15 | 8 | 58 | 37 | 66 |

**Result of this Season's Fixture**

Ipswich Town

Manchester Utd

United came into this game knowing that victory would leave the Reds needing just one point from two Old Trafford fixtures to clinch the title. Ipswich, however, with six defeats in their last eight games, had slipped right into the relegation dog-fight and quickly showed they were not going to be an easy touch. They set off at a breakneck speed and United were never allowed to settle on the ball in the opening half-hour by which time they were a goal down and minus Peter Schmeichel.

The Dane was responsible for gifting the first goal of the match to Ipswich's Chris Kiwomya when he failed to hold on to a cross cum shot from Ian Marshall on the Ipswich right. As Schmeichel dived to his right to deal with the cross, there appeared to be no undue reason for concern but the ball squirmed away from him and his legs slipped in the heavily sanded area and Kiwomya pounced. Kiwomya was again involved with Schmeichel five minutes later as both attempted to get to a long through ball first. Just outside his area, Schmeichel managed to kick the ball clear but only a split second before Kiwomya arrived. In the inevitable collision, Schmeichel damaged his ankle ligaments which forced his substitution. The incident, however, served to inspire United into a more positive frame of mind whilst the long stoppage possibly broke Ipswich's concentration.

Cantona equalised with a goal of stunning simplicity. Wark and Whelan were involved in a monumental misunderstanding as they got in each other's way inside the penalty area to allow the ball to reach Kanchelskis on the right. The Russian's cross to the far post was pin-point and Cantona's head did the rest past Forrest's despairing right hand.

The second period began with United going straight in to the lead thanks to slack marking by the East Anglians' defence. Parker took a quick throw near the right hand corner flag which found Keane unmarked. He made ground into the area before crossing waist high in to the centre where Giggs pushed himself in front of a Town defender to get a foot on the ball and force it home from close range.

## League Record

|  | Home | | | | | | Away | | | | |
|---|---|---|---|---|---|---|---|---|---|---|---|
|  | P | W | D | L | F | A | W | D | L | F | A |
| FAPL 93/94 | 40 | 13 | 5 | 1 | 37 | 13 | 13 | 5 | 3 | 41 | 25 |
| All Time FAPL | 82 | 27 | 10 | 3 | 76 | 27 | 23 | 12 | 7 | 69 | 42 |
| All Time FL/FAPL | 3638 | 1063 | 420 | 335 | 3626 | 1811 | 555 | 424 | 791 | 2475 | 3099 |

|  | Home | Away | Total |
|---|---|---|---|
| League Attendances | 839,611 | 606,220 | 1,445,831 |

# Manchester United (0) 2
# Southampton (0) 0

Wednesday, 4th May 1994, Old Trafford          Att.: 44,705

## MANCHESTER UNITED

| 25 | Gary | Walsh |
| 2 | Paul | Parker |
| 3 | Denis | Irwin |
| 5 | Lee | Sharpe |
| 6 | Gary | Pallister |
| 7 | Eric | Cantona |
| 8 | Paul | Ince |
| 10 | Mark | Hughes |
| 11 | Ryan | Giggs |
| 14 | Andrei | Kanchelskis |
| 16 | Roy | Keane |

*Subs*

| 13 | Les | Sealey (gk) |
| 9 | Brian | McClair |
| 12 | Bryan | Robson |

## SOUTHAMPTON

| 1 | Dave | Beasant |
| 2 | Jeff | Kenna |
| 6 | Ken | Monkou |
| 21 | *Tom* | *Widdrington (*65)* |
| 11 | Francis | Benali |
| 14 | Simon | Charlton |
| 25 | Paul | Allen |
| 4 | Jim | Magilton |
| 10 | Neil | Maddison |
| 7 | Matthew | Le Tissier |
| 9 | Iain | Dowie |

| 13 | Ian | Andrews (gk) |
| 15 | Jason | Dodd |
| 8 | *Craig* | *Maskell (*65)* |

### *Match Facts*

• The win gave United a points record of 91 for the top flight of English football. It also maintained United's 100% FAPL record against Southampton and extended the Saints poor record at Old Trafford to just one win in over twenty visits since 1970. Paul Ince captained the side for the first time.

### *Score Sheet*

KANCHELSKIS 60 min – 1-0
M. HUGHES 89 min – 2-0

*Referee:*
Mr. T. Holbrook (Walsall)

## FA Carling Premiership League

| | | P | W | D | L | F | A | Pts |
|---|---|---|---|---|---|---|---|---|
| 1 | **Manchester United** | 41 | 27 | 10 | 4 | 80 | 38 | 91 |
| 2 | Blackburn Rovers | 42 | 25 | 9 | 8 | 63 | 36 | 84 |
| 3 | Newcastle United | 42 | 23 | 8 | 11 | 82 | 41 | 77 |
| 4 | Arsenal | 42 | 18 | 17 | 7 | 53 | 28 | 71 |
| 5 | Leeds United | 42 | 18 | 16 | 8 | 65 | 39 | 70 |

**Result of this Season's Fixture**

Manchester Utd
Southampton

# Simply the Best

United took to the pitch for this game in the knowledge that the Championship was staying at Old Trafford following Blackburn Rovers' defeat by Coventry City 48 hours earlier. Appropriately the music played was Tina Turner's "Simply the Best". Southampton, though, were out to spoil the party as they were desperate for points to save themselves from relegation.

United almost took the lead inside the first 45 seconds as Ince, Giggs and Keane linked up down the left to set up Giggs for a shot. Beasant parried the effort and the ball fell to Cantona but, from only five yards out, the Frenchman miskicked completely and sliced the ball wide of the open net. It was an incredible miss by anybody's standards, let alone Cantona's. Minutes later, an Irwin cross from the right saw Hughes miss his header from as close as Cantona had been. Then, from a Giggs corner, Keane headed the ball down so powerfully that it bounced over the crossbar. Until now it had been all United but Southampton at last responded with a Charlton raid down the left. He put in a telling cross and Dowie's header looked to be goal bound until Walsh produced a class save, diving to his right to palm the ball away for a corner.

The second period saw Southampton push the Reds back with Magilton trying his luck from distance and almost finding the range. Then a right wing cross from Le Tissier caused problems until Irwin headed over his own bar to clear the immediate danger. Another long range effort from Magilton was only just over but then, as so often before in 93/94, United proved to be at their most dangerous when being forced to defend. Giggs, on the halfway line, spread the ball wide to the right to Cantona who brought Irwin into the action. The Irishman continued his run down the right touchline before finding Kanchelskis in the inside right slot.

The Russian hit a blistering drive under Beasant's body at his left hand near post. Maddison hit straight back for the Saints but Irwin, now back in his defensive role, blocked the shot at the expense of a corner. In stoppage time Cantona made a strong run down the right before rolling a devastating ball into the path of Hughes. The Welshman fired unerringly past Beasant's flailing left hand for another of his spectaculars. United left the pitch to "We are the Champions".

## League Record

| | P | W | D | L | F | A | W | D | L | F | A |
|---|---|---|---|---|---|---|---|---|---|---|---|
| | | | **Home** | | | | | | **Away** | | |
| FAPL 93/94 | 41 | 14 | 5 | 1 | 39 | 13 | 13 | 5 | 3 | 41 | 25 |
| All Time FAPL | 83 | 28 | 10 | 3 | 78 | 27 | 23 | 12 | 7 | 69 | 42 |
| All Time FL/FAPL | 3639 | 1064 | 420 | 335 | 3628 | 1811 | 555 | 424 | 791 | 2475 | 3099 |

| | Home | Away | Total |
|---|---|---|---|
| League Attendances | 884,316 | 606,220 | 1,490,536 |

# Manchester United (0) 0
# Coventry City (0) 0

Sunday, 8th May 1994, Old Trafford                    Att.: 44,717

## MANCHESTER UNITED

| 25 | Gary | Walsh |
| 27 | Gary | Neville |
| 4 | *Steve* | *Bruce (\*57)* |
| 6 | Gary | Pallister |
| 5 | Lee | Sharpe |
| 3 | Denis | Irwin |
| 7 | Eric | Cantona |
| 17 | *Colin* | *McKee (+75)* |
| 9 | Brian | McClair |
| 20 | Dion | Dublin |
| 12 | Bryan | Robson |

*Subs*

| 13 | Les | Sealey (gk) |
| 2 | *Paul* | *Parker (\*57)* |
| 16 | *Roy* | *Keane (+75)* |

## COVENTRY CITY

| 1 | Steve | Ogrizovic |
| 2 | Brian | Borrows |
| 4 | Peter | Atherton |
| 20 | Phil | Babb |
| 3 | Steve | Morgan |
| 16 | Willie | Boland |
| 6 | David | Rennie |
| 25 | Julian | Darby |
| 22 | Leigh | Jenkinson |
| 12 | Peter | Ndlovu |
| 18 | Sean | Flynn |

| 23 | Jonathon | Gould (gk) |
| 10 | Mick | Quinn |
| 27 | Nick | Pickering |

## *Match Facts*

- Full FAPL debuts for Gary Neville and Colin McKee ● Coventry's first Premiership point against United but they are still to score against the Reds in the FAPL ● Attendance took United's 93/94 FAPL aggregate past the 1.5m mark. ● The game took the FAPL 11 game weekend programme to 320,755, the first time it had exceeded 300,000 in 93/94.

## *Score Sheet*

*Referee:*
Mr. S Lodge (Barnsley)

## FA Carling Premiership League

|   |   | P | W | D | L | F | A | Pts |
|---|---|---|---|---|---|---|---|---|
| 1 | Manchester United | 42 | 27 | 11 | 4 | 80 | 38 | 92 |
| 2 | Blackburn Rovers | 42 | 25 | 9 | 8 | 63 | 36 | 84 |
| 3 | Newcastle United | 42 | 23 | 8 | 11 | 82 | 41 | 77 |
| 4 | Arsenal | 42 | 18 | 17 | 7 | 53 | 28 | 71 |
| 5 | Leeds United | 42 | 18 | 16 | 8 | 65 | 39 | 70 |

### Result of this Season's Fixture

Manchester Utd
Coventry City

# Carnival Time

Celebration of United's second successive title began in earnest with the ground awash with red balloons given away by United's latest commercial enterprise, Fred the Red. The fifth highest crowd of the campaign turned out, not only to join in the party but to pay their homage to Bryan Robson, widely rumoured to be playing his last league game in a red shirt after thirteen stalwart years. Robson resumed his role of captain for one last time and ended the game by going up to collect the Championship trophy with Steve Bruce as happened the previous season.

United took the opportunity, with one eye on the FA Cup Final, to field a somewhat weakened team containing what could be argued as only five of their Championship regulars in the starting line up whilst giving FAPL debuts to full back Gary Neville and striker Colin McKee. The match itself was almost incidental to the celebrations but, whilst they were not prepared to give anything away, Coventry also resisted the temptation to gatecrash the party. True, Julian Darby, who with his two goals against Blackburn Rovers giving United the title, had been awarded honourary life membership of United's Supporters Club, almost had the honour rescinded immediately when he smacked the angle of Walsh's woodwork whilst Boland forced Walsh to make an excellent save and Peter Ndlovu went close after robbing Pallister. Those efforts apart, United were never going to lose and the day could have been even more memorable if Ogrizovic had been a bit more benevolent. When Irwin slung a long ball over from the left, McKee appeared to have done everything right when heading the ball powerfully down to the Coventry 'keeper's left only to be deprived of a debut goal by a good save. The 'keeper, surpassed that effort when he combined with Cantona to produce a moment of magical football. Cantona's overhead kick was as explosive and as fluent as Mark Hughes at his most extravagant. The ball seemed destined for the net and a truly memorable goal until Ogrizovic used every inch of his 6ft 5in frame to fingertip the ball to safety. United in fact manage to beat Ogrizovic twice but on both occasions the goals were disallowed. McKee's neat ball from the right flank was turned into his own net by Atherton only for Dublin to have been adjudged to have handled in trying to get to the ball before the Coventry defender and then, when Dublin's shot was parried by Ogrizovic, Keane's follow-up was ruled out by an offside flag. When the final whistle went, United had lost just four league games all season – the club's best performance since 1906 in a 38 match Second Division campaign.

## League Record

| | | | Home | | | | | | Away | | |
|---|---|---|---|---|---|---|---|---|---|---|---|
| | P | W | D | L | F | A | W | D | L | F | A |
| FAPL 93/94 | 4 | 14 | 6 | 1 | 39 | 13 | 13 | 5 | 3 | 39 | 25 |
| All Time FAPL | 84 | 28 | 11 | 3 | 78 | 27 | 23 | 12 | 7 | 69 | 42 |
| All Time FL/FAPL | 3640 | 1064 | 421 | 335 | 3628 | 1811 | 555 | 424 | 791 | 2475 | 3099 |

| | Home | Away | Total |
|---|---|---|---|
| League Attendances | 929,033 | 606,220 | 1,535,253 |

# Manchester United (0) 4
# Chelsea (0) 0

Saturday, 14th May 1994, Wembley                    Att.: 79,634

| | MANCHESTER UNITED | | | CHELSEA | |
|---|---|---|---|---|---|
| 1 | Peter | Schmeichel | 1 | Dmitri | Kharine |
| 2 | Paul | Parker | 12 | Steve | Clarke |
| 3 | *Denis* | *Irwin (* 86)* | 35 | Jakob | Kjeldbjerg |
| 4 | Steve | Bruce – *Booked* | 5 | Erland | Johnsen – *Booked* |
| 6 | Gary | Pallister | 6 | Frank | Sinclair |
| 7 | Eric | Cantona | 24 | *Craig* | *Burley (*67)* |
| 8 | Paul | Ince | 18 | Eddie | Newton |
| 10 | Mark | Hughes | 10 | Gavin | Peacock |
| 11 | Ryan | Giggs | 11 | Dennis | Wise |
| 14 | *Andrei* | *Kanchelskis (+ 86)* | 7 | John | Spencer |
| 16 | Roy | Keane | 21 | *Mark* | *Stein (+79)* |

*Subs*

| | | | | | |
|---|---|---|---|---|---|
| 25 | Gary | Walsh (gk) | 13 | Kevin | Hitchcock (gk) |
| 5 | *Lee* | *Sharpe (*86)* | 20 | *Glenn* | *Hoddle (*67)* |
| 9 | *Brian* | *McClair (+86)* | 9 | *Tony* | *Cascarino (+79)* |

---

## *Match Facts*

• Andrei Kanchelskis becomes the first Ukranian to play in the FA Cup Final, Chelsea's Kharine the first Russian and Eric Cantona the first Frenchman (Cyrille Regis was born in French Guyana) • Chelsea's fourth FA Cup Final and their third with an Old Trafford connection – they were beaten in the 1915 Final at Old Trafford but won there in the 1970 replay against Leeds United, after extra time • The last three Chelsea managers, Ian Porterfield, David Webb and Glenn Hoddle have all scored FA Cup winning goals.

---

## *Score Sheet*

CANTONA 61 min Pen – 1-0
CANTONA 67 min Pen – 2-0
M. HUGHES 69 min – 3-0
B. McCLAIR 90 min – 4-0

*Referee:*
Mr. D. Ellery (Harrow)

159

# United Double Up

When United took to the pitch at 3.00pm they equalled Arsenal's record twelve FA Cup Final appearances and, less than two hours later, equalled Tottenham Hotspur's record of eight FA Cup Final victories. For the opening forty-five minutes, Chelsea were the better team and, with a little bit of luck, could have won the game too.

After Mr Elleray let the Londoners know with his second minute booking of Johnsen for an outrageous challenge on a flying Giggs that he would not allow the Reds to be kicked out of it, Glenn Hoddle's side were more than a match for the Champions. Ince had a goal saving tackle and then Pallister cleared virtually from off the goal line. Peacock came close to scoring in the 26th minute when he quickly controlled a bouncing ball outside the area and unleashed a venomous, dipping shot that beat Schmeichel only to smack the crossbar and bounce back into play. United's only chance in the first period came when Cantona headed back across the face of the Chelsea goal to set up Hughes, only to find Kharine covering it safely.

United were grateful for the half-time whistle and to go off all square. Alex Ferguson's talk during the break rallied the Reds who returned looking as if they meant business. Arguments may rage about United's luck in getting two penalties in the space of six minutes on the hour but that would be to take credit away from them. Giggs did well down the left and, although he seemed to have lost the ball, recovered to stab it past Clarke to Irwin. The Irishman sidestepped Newton's challenge but was upended in no uncertain terms by the lateness of the tackle. Cantona stroked the ball to Kharine's left as the 'keeper went right. After only being awarded two spot kicks all season this was a welcome change and the season's number of United penalties was doubled in the 67th minute. This was a great deal more doubtful – there was certainly a push from Sinclair on Kanchelskis but equally certain was the fact that the challenge was outside the box. Whatever the argument, it resulted the same. Cantona kicked to the 'keeper's left as Kharine dived right. Within minutes, Sinclair's world collapsed as he slipped on the wet turf to present Hughes with a gift that the Welshman accepted with aplomb to notch his fourth goal in four 1993/94 Wembley appearances. Chelsea, to their credit, gamely rallied as United eased and Schmeichel had to make a couple of smart saves but then a brilliant injury time move started by Cantona on the right to Hughes saw the Londoners' defence clinically dissected by the Welshman's throughball to Ince. He rounded Kharine to an open goal but unselfishly pulled the ball back to McClair to roll into the empty net. For Chelsea it was very cruel as they didn't deserve to be on the end of a 4-0 scoreline. For United, the celebrations began in earnest.

## Cup Record

|  | Home | | | | | | Away | | | | |
|  | P | W | D | L | F | A | W | D | L | F | A |
|---|---|---|---|---|---|---|---|---|---|---|---|
| All time Cup record | 346 | 99 | 31 | 28 | 333 | 148 | 78 | 53 | 57 | 298 | 268 |

|  | Home | Away | Total |
|---|---|---|---|
| Cup Attendances | 44,347 | 238,845 | 283,192 |

# FA Cup Final 1994

How they got to Wembley

## Manchester United

| Round | Opponents | home/away | Score | Scorers |
|---|---|---|---|---|
| 3rd Round | v Sheffield United | (a) | 1-0 | Hughes |
| 4th Round | v Norwich City | (a) | 2-0 | Keane, Cantona |
| 5th Round | v Wimbledon | (a) | 3-0 | Cantona, Ince, Irwin |
| 6th Round | v Charlton Athletic | (h) | 3-1 | Hughes, Kanchelskis 2 |
| Semi Final | v Oldham Athletic | (n) | 1-1 | Hughes |
| Replay | v Oldham Athletic | (n) | 4-1 | Irwin, Kanchelskis, Robson, Giggs |

*Goals 14-4*

## Chelsea

| Round | Opponents | home/away | Score | Scorers |
|---|---|---|---|---|
| 3rd Round | v Barnet | (a) | 0-0 | *Played at Stamford Bridge* |
| Replay | v Barnet | (h) | 4-0 | Peacock, Shipperley, Stein, Burley |
| 4th Round | v Sheffield Wednesday | (h) | 1-1 | Peacock |
| Replay | v Sheffield Wednesday | (a) | 3-1 | Spencer, Peacock, Burley |
| 5th Round | v Oxford United | (a) | 2-1 | Spencer, Burley |
| 6th Round | v Wolves | (h) | 1-0 | Peacock |
| Semi Final | v Luton Town | (n) | 2-0 | Peacock 2 |

*Goals 13-3*

*Paul Ince's natural grace on the ball has won him many admirers.*

# Manchester United
# Player by Player

# Stephen Roger BRUCE

Date of Birth: 31st December 1960, Corbridge

Signed for United in 1987 for £800,000 and made his debut against Portsmouth in a
game he is unlikely to ever forget as he broke his nose and conceded a penalty in
United's 2-1 victory. In the early nineties he was probably the unluckiest player
never to win an England cap as Graham Taylor appeared to award them to almost
everybody else and his chances now seem to have gone. He does, however, have
international honours at both Youth and "B" levels and has been one of the most
consistent performers for the Reds over a long period. Many people reckon it was
Bruce's two goals during injury time against Sheffield Wednesday in April 1993
that landed United the elusive championship after twenty-six years of toil. Indeed,
Bruce has had the knack of scoring a big tally of goals for a central defender and in
1990/91 netted 19, a total many strikers would be proud of. Hailing from the North-
East where he learned his football in the famous Wallsend Boys Club youth sides,
Bruce began his Football League career with Gillingham and when he made his
debut against Blackpool in August 1979 he could hardly have dreamed of the
honours he would go on to win in United colours. He was, more or less, an ever-
present thereafter clocking up over 200 appearances before signing for Norwich
City in 1984 for a fee in the region of £125,000. Whilst at Carrow Road he
appeared at Wembley in the Canaries side which beat Sunderland in the 1985 Milk
Cup before gaining honours galore with United.

## Previous Clubs and Appearance Record

| Clubs | Signed | Fee | Appearances | | | Goals | | |
|---|---|---|---|---|---|---|---|---|
| | | | Lge | FLC | FAC | Lge | FLC | FAC |
| Gillingham | 10/78 | – | 203+2 | 15 | 14 | 29 | 6 | 1 |
| Norwich City | 8/84 | £125,000 | 141 | 20 | 9 | 14 | 5 | 1 |
| Man Utd | 12/87 | £800,000 | 161 | 19 | 21 | 26 | 4 | 1 |
| *FA Premier League Record* | | | | | | | | |
| 92/93 | | | 42 | 3 | 3 | 5 | | |
| 93/94 | | | 41 | 8/1 | 7 | 3 | 2 | |

There is little doubt that Bruce will finish his football career with United and it is
likely that he will be found a job on the coaching staff when his days are numbered.
In the unlikely event of him wanting to move on then United have a proven track
record of not standing in players way when they have given the sort of service that
Bruce has given. In view of this and his age, it is most unlikely that United would
insist on a fee.

## Estimated value: Free Transfer

# Eric CANTONA

Date of Birth: 24th May 1966, Paris

Many critics at the time considered his signing in November 1992 from Leeds United in exchange for £1.2m as confirmation that Alex Ferguson had finally flipped his lid in the frustration of not being able to land the coveted title. The signing of the wayward genius seemed totally out of character for Ferguson who had previously always erred on the side of caution. It was, however, to prove to be the final piece of the jigsaw as United with the talented, but erratic Frenchman, in their side mounted a charge up the table that was to prove unstoppable. The value of Cantona's presence in the side can be gauged by the fact that of his first sixty appearances in United colours, they only lost twice – a remarkable statistic. But Cantona had equal cause to be thankful to United. At last it seemed, after a nomadic football career, that the Frenchman had found peace of mind, at last playing on a stage he thought worthy of his skills. His peace, however, was shattered when he began to get irritated at the weekly treatment handed out to him and he was sent off against Swindon for a stamping offence. The matter was compounded when he was the victim of a great injustice in his next appearance when he was dismissed again when clearly trying to jump out of the way of a scything Tony Adams tackle. It remains to be seen whether he regains the enthusiasm for the game that his move to Old Trafford rekindled. He had arrived at Leeds in February 1992 on loan from Nimes via a week's training at Sheffield Wednesday, but the move was soon made permanent in a deal worth £900,000 and with him in their line up, Leeds overtook United to pinch the Championship from under the noses of the Old Trafford faithful. Cantona began his career with Auxerre in 1986 before moving to Marseille during 1988 in a £2.2m deal that was not successful with Cantona making just 40 appearances and spending time on loan at both Montpellier and Bordeaux before moving on to Nimes for £1m in June 1991. Eight months later he was at Leeds and nine months further down the road he was at Old Trafford where it seemed until his sendings off he had found stability for the first time. Even his international career led a chequered existence with him walking out of the French set up at one stage but one thing is for sure, United fans will always have a place in their heart for the man who became the only Frenchman to win English Championship medals with two different clubs

## Previous Clubs and Appearance Record

| Clubs | Signed | Fee | Appearances | | | Goals | | |
|---|---|---|---|---|---|---|---|---|
| | | | Lge | FLC | FAC | Lge | FLC | FAC |
| Auxerre | | | 81 | 23 | | | | |
| Martiques | | loan | – | – | | | | |
| Marseille | 1988 | £2.2m | 55 | 13 | | | | |
| Bordeaux | | loan | 11 | 6 | | | | |
| Montpellier | | loan | 33 | 10 | | | | |
| Nimes | 1991 | £1m | n/k | n/k | | | | |
| Leeds Utd | 2/92 | £900,000 | 16 | | | 3 | | |
| *FA Premier League Record* | | | | | | | | |
| Leeds Utd | | | 13 | 1 | | 6 | | |
| Man Utd | 11/92 | £1.2m | 22 | 1 | | 9 | | |
| | 93/94 | | 34 | 5 | 5 | 18 | 1 | 4 |

Because of his unpredictable nature it is difficult to assess how much a club would be prepared to risk on someone who could walk out after a few weeks. Without this side of his nature Cantona would be in the £10m class but anybody buying him from Old Trafford would almost certainly only want to pay a down payment and then so much per game.

**Estimated value: £7,500,000**

# Ryan Joseph GIGGS

Date of Birth: 29th November 1973, Cardiff

Although born in Cardiff, Ryan Giggs first came under the eye of United fans when he captained England Schoolboys against Scotland at Old Trafford under the name of Ryan Wilson having been brought up in Manchester when his father, good enough at his chosen sport to play for Great Britain, moved to the area to take up Rugby League after a successful Rugby Union career. The young Wilson was actually first spotted by Manchester City and played for one of their junior sides but it was to United that the gifted youngster turned on leaving school. At about this time his mother changed her name to Giggs and that name is now the one on everybody's lips. Giggs was quickly recognised as something very special and was elevated through the ranks at a surprisingly quick rate. He made his first team debut on 2nd March 1991 at the age of 17 when he came on as substitute against Everton in a 2-0 home defeat. By the following season he was a regular, making 38 league appearances and winning a League Cup medal against Notts Forest, a month before he won a FA Youth Cup winners medal against Crystal Palace. Giggs became the youngest ever Welsh full international when he played against Germany on 16th October 1991 aged 17 years 321 days to complete an unusual quartet of home country "youngest" records for United. Duncan Edwards had become the youngest player to play for England, Northern Ireland's Norman Whiteside was the youngest ever player to appear in the Final stages of the World Cup during his days at Old Trafford and the youngest player ever to turn out for Scotland, Denis Law, also later played for the Reds. Giggs also set another record when he became the first player to win the PFA's Young Player of the Year Award in successive seasons, a feat he achieved in 1992 and 1993. He also won the Barclay's Bank Young Eagle of the Year award in 1992.

## Previous Clubs and Appearance Record

| Clubs | Signed | Fee | Appearances | | | Goals | | |
|---|---|---|---|---|---|---|---|---|
| | | | Lge | FLC | FAC | Lge | FLC | FAC |
| Man Utd | 12/90 | | 30 | 8 | 1 | 4 | 3 | |
| *FA Premier League Record* | | | | | | | | |
| | 92/93 | | 41 | 2 | 2 | 9 | | 2 |
| | 93/94 | | 32+6 | 6+2 | 7 | 13 | 3 | 1 |

No British club could surely afford to prise Giggs away from Old Trafford but Continental clubs would also be looking at the youngster's form towards the end of the season when he didn't really look the finished article. His youth would boost the fee, however, although not to the reported £10m that Italian clubs were said to be prepared to pay.

## Estimated value: £7,500,000

# Leslie Mark HUGHES

Date of Birth: 1st November 1963, Wrexham

Although signed from Barcelona in June 1988 for £1,500,000 Hughes was a product of the United youth system playing in the same youth team as Norman Whiteside. Born in Wrexham Hughes made his debut for United when he came on as substitute for Whiteside in a League Cup tie against Port Vale in October 1983 but his league debut was delayed until January 1984 when he again made an appearance as substitute against QPR. Hughes scored in his first full league game against Leicester City in March that year, a feat he was to repeat only a couple of months later when he made his international debut on his home town ground against England, indeed it was the only goal of the game. In 1984/85 he completed a memorable year by being voted Young Player of the Year by the PFA after topping United's goalscoring charts and picking up a FA Cup winners medal against Brighton. At the end of the 1985/86 season, however, he was lured to the continent to play for Barcelona in a move worth £2,300,000 to United but his style never quite fitted in with Spanish football and his time there, by his own standards was somewhat disappointing. He had a loan spell with Bayern Munich but returned to the fold in 1988 and immediately hit top form. He was voted the PFA's Player of the Year at the end of the 1988/89 season and became the first player to win the accolade twice when taking the award again in 1991. In between he had scored two goals in the FA Cup Final against Crystal Palace and it was his two strikes that gave United victory over Barcelona in Rotterdam in May 1991 – sweet satisfaction indeed.

## Previous Clubs and Appearance Record

| Clubs | Signed | Fee | Appearances | | | Goals | | |
|---|---|---|---|---|---|---|---|---|
| | | | Lge | FLC | FAC | Lge | FLC | FAC |
| Man Utd | 11/80 | | 85/4 | 5/1 | 10 | 37 | 4 | 4 |
| Barcelona | 7/86 | £2.5m | 186 | 63 | | | | |
| Bayern Munich | 10/87 | loan | nk | | | | | |
| Man Utd | 7/88 | £1.5m | 141/4 | 21 | 20/1 | 47 | 6 | 7 |
| *FA Premier League Record* | | | | | | | | |
| | 92/93 | | 41 | 3 | 2 | 15 | 1 | 0 |
| | 93/94 | | 36 | 8 | 7 | 12 | 5 | 4 |

Despite his age he is still capable of scoring the most stunning of goals. His strong play is likely to see him figure for some years as a midfielder once his days as a forward are over.

## Estimated value: £2,200,000

168

# Andrei KANCHELSKIS

Date of Birth : 23rd January 1969, Kirovograd

For a winger, Kanchelskis weighs in a little on the heavy side at 12st 11lbs but this does not hinder his blistering pace that has given United an extra dimension. Born in the Ukraine, he opted to continue playing for Russia rather than his fledgling native country upon the break up of the communist bloc and his decision paid rich dividends when he was one of only three players from the Old Trafford dynasty to participate in the 1994 World Cup finals. Having started his career with Dynamo Kiev, Kanchelskis was actually playing for Shakhtyor Donetsk when Russia's need for foreign currency began an exodus of their top players to the West. Kanchelskis arrived at Old Trafford in April 1991 for trials and played in the final away game of the season at Crystal Palace on 11th May 1991. Nine days later United completed the formalities of a deal that cost them £650,000. The flying Russian, however, found it difficult to hold down a regular place and although he made 34 league appearances in 1991/92 many were as substitute, or if he did start the game he found himself the one to make way part way through the game. His worst fears were confirmed when he was the one foreigner who never got a chance when United played in Europe and he was looking at another frustrating season until Sharpe got injured. The popular Russian then came into his own with teams finding it difficult to cope with his speed but, more than that, he gave the team a great deal more balance with a natural right winger complementing the left wing wizardry of Giggs, something that was never achieved when Giggs and Sharpe, both natural left wingers played together. He won his first English honour when United lifted the League Cup against Forest in 1992 but when United were back in the League Cup Final in 1994, Kanchelskis became one of the few players to receive a Wembley dismissal when he handled the ball on the line but the sympathy exuded to him in the situation he found himself in also allowed him to become the first dismissed player in a Wembley final to go up the famous steps and collect his medal.

## Previous Clubs and Appearance Record

| Clubs | Signed | Fee | Appearances | | | Goals | | |
|---|---|---|---|---|---|---|---|---|
| | | | Lge | FLC | FAC | Lge | FLC | FAC |
| Donetsk | | | | | | | | |
| Man Utd | 5/91 | £650,000 | 35 | 4 | 2 | 4 | 2 | 1 |
| *FA Premier League Record* | | | | | | | | |
| 92/93 | | | 26 | 3 | 1 | 3 | | |
| 93/94 | | | 28+3 | 9 | 6 | 6 | 1 | 3 |

His true worth may only be known after this book is published as he was still not sure to sign a new contract when the book went to press. There is little doubt that he has proved a bargain buy and will definitely increase the fee the Reds paid for him.

## Estimated value: £3,000,000

# Roy KEANE

Roy Keane set a record for a transfer deal between English clubs when signing for United in the summer of 1993 for a £3.75m fee from Nottingham Forest. It gave Forest a massive profit on their lay out of £25,000 which it had cost them to bring the former amateur boxer over from Republic of Ireland outfit Cobh Ramblers. Manager Alex Ferguson saw his costliest player as the replacement for his ageing midfield general Bryan Robson, but the younger Keane looked far from that in his early games for United. He was quite definitely not match fit and looked positively overweight during the pre match friendlies and people were quick to question the wisdom of the outlay. As the season progressed, however, Keane's importance to the cause became apparent with his ability not only to win the ball but to then do something constructive with it. Equally vital Keane seems to have developed the knack of arriving late from deep positions to score goals, much like Robson. Having brought Keane over from the comparative obscurity of Cobh Ramblers in 1990, Brian Clough quickly pushed him into his first team line up and in his first full season Keane had a FA Cup runners-up medal after Spurs beat Forest 2-1 after extra-time. The following season he had another runners-up medal when Forest were beaten at Wembley in the League Cup Final by United but Forest did win the Zenith Data Systems Cup that year which led to the honours laden United team nick naming Keane "ZDS". He was, of course, to have the last laugh on most of his colleagues when he was one of only three United players to participate in the 1994 World Cup Finals in the USA. Keane, once at Forest, had not taken long to attract the attention of the Republic of Ireland's team boss, Jack Charlton, and he won his first cap against Chile on 22nd May 1991.

## Previous Clubs and Appearance Record

| Clubs | Signed | Fee | Appearances | | | Goals | | |
|-------|--------|-----|-----|-----|-----|-----|-----|-----|
| | | | Lge | FLC | FAC | Lge | FLC | FAC |
| Notts Forest | 5/90 | £25,000 | 74 | 12 | 14 | 16 | 5 | 2 |
| *FA Premier League Record* | | | | | | | | |
| Notts Forest | 92/93 | | 42 | 5 | 4 | 6 | 1 | 1 |
| Man Utd | 93/94 | | 34+3 | 6+1 | 6 | 5 | – | 1 |

Thought by many to be over priced when signed for £3.75m but has shown the figure to be about right. United would perhaps have to take a slight loss if they wished to part but it would not be a big drop.

## Estimated value: £3,500,000

# Paul Emerson Carlyle INCE

Date of Birth : 21st October 1967, Ilford

Paul Ince, a Londoner, joined West Ham on leaving school and made his debut for them at Newcastle in November 1986 in a 4-0 defeat. He went on to make 72 appearances, scoring 7 goals before United moved in during August 1989 to offer a fee in the region of £2M for his services. A medical examination, however, revealed a pelvic problem which appeared to have scuppered the deal but an agreement was reached whereby United paid £800,000 plus £5,000 for each appearance. The medical problem has never reared its head and Ince went on to become an important member of the engine room. He made his United debut against Millwall as the Reds put an end to the London club's surprise table topping start to life in the First Division with a 5-1 drubbing. Although a rare scorer of goals for West Ham, Ince scored twice in his second game in a United shirt against Portsmouth but hopes that this would lead to an increased output failed to materialise until scoring some vital goals in 93/94. When the goals came for him during 93/94 they tended to equate to points with him scoring in 1-1 draws against Newcastle and Blackburn, the 1-0 win over Liverpool and the 2-2 draws with his old club West Ham and Swindon Town. There were also doubts about his temperament but he gradually learned to control himself to the extent that he actually took over the England captaincy on England's USA 1993 summer tour to become the first coloured player to hold that position. He is also a keen follower of boxing and his cousin is the well known fighter Nigel Benn.

## Previous Clubs and Appearance Record

| Clubs | Signed | Fee | Appearances | | | Goals | | |
|---|---|---|---|---|---|---|---|---|
| | | | Lge | FLC | FAC | Lge | FLC | FAC |
| West Ham | 7/85 | – | 66+6 | 9 | 8+2 | 7 | 3 | 1 |
| Man Utd | 8/89 | See Text | 87+3 | 15+1 | 6+1 | 6 | 2 | 0 |
| *FA Premier League Record* | | | | | | | | |
| | 92/93 | | 41 | 3 | 2 | 6 | 0 | 0 |
| | 93/94 | | 39 | 6 | 6 | 8 | 0 | 1 |

Has now added goal power to his tackling ability. As a current international Ince would carry a high fee which would increase still further if he showed he could keep his feelings under control.

## Estimated value: £3,000,000

# Denis Joseph IRWIN

Date of Birth 31st October 1965, Cork

An established international and an important part of United's set up, he made his start by way of the junior ranks at Leeds United, making his debut against Fulham at Elland Road on 21st January 1984 just three months after signing professional forms. After playing some 80 games for the Yorkshire club he recieved a free transfer in the summer of 1986 from Leeds to Oldham Athletic and is quick to acknowledge the part played in his career by Oldham's Joe Royle and his assistant Willie Donachie. He became a vital part of the best team Oldham ever had and appeared in their 1990 League Cup Final defeat at the hands of Nottingham Forest. In the same season Oldham had two titanic duels against United in the semi-final of the FA Cup and Irwin impressed the United management throughout that campaign. By the end of the summer Ferguson had landed Irwin and he was to play in United's League Cup Finals in 1991 and 1992 to become the only player to appear in the first three League Cup Finals of the 1990's. He was later to make it four League Cup Finals in five years when playing against Aston Villa. By the time he left Boundary Park he was game short of 200 appearances. He had been signed as a right back, a position he plays in regularly when on international duty, and it was in that position that he made his debut for the Reds in August 1990 when United enjoyed a 2-0 home win over Coventry City. Ferguson, however, was struggling with his left back position with Mal Donaghy, Clayton Blackmore, a young Lee Sharpe, and Lee Martin all trying and failing to hold their place in that position. Paul Parker arrived from QPR, ostensibly as a central defender but he was soon converted to right back with Irwin asked to switch to the problematic left back slot, a position he has held ever since for United despite playing right back for his country! He made his international debut just after his move to Old Trafford on 12th September 1990 in Dublin against Morrocco and has been first choice ever since and one of only three players to represent United in the 1994 World Cup Finals. The full caps won by Irwin complete the full set as he had already played for his country at School, Youth and Under 21 levels.

## Previous Clubs and Appearance Record

| Clubs | Signed | Fee | Appearances | | | Goals | | |
|---|---|---|---|---|---|---|---|---|
| | | | Lge | FLC | FAC | Lge | FLC | FAC |
| Leeds United | 10/83 | – | 72 | 5 | 3 | 1 | | |
| Oldham Athletic | 5/86 | – | 167 | 19 | 13 | 4 | 3 | |
| Man Utd | 6/90 | £625,000 | 72 | 15 | 6 | 4 | | |
| *FA Premier League Record* | | | | | | | | |
| | 92/93 | | 40 | 3 | 3 | 5 | | |
| | 93/94 | | 42 | 8+1 | 7 | 2 | | 2 |

**Estimated value: £1,000,000**

# Brian John McCLAIR

Date of Birth : 8th December 1963, Bellshill

One of the few Scots currently on United's books, McClair joined the Old Trafford set up in 1987 for £850,000 after Celtic had originally been pushing for a fee of £2m. Whilst with Celtic he had netted 99 goals in 145 league appearances after joining the Glasgow club from Motherwell for £100,000 in 1983. Strangely, after dropping out of University to concentrate on making a career in football, McClair had failed to make the grade with his first club, Aston Villa, who were later to beat United in the 1994 Coca Cola Cup Final. After being leading goalscorer in all four seasons he was with Celtic, McClair immediately hit the goal trail at Old Trafford becoming, in his first season at the club, the first Red since George Best to hit twenty League goals in a campaign. However, after the arrival back home of United's prodigal son, Mark Hughes, McClair found goalscoring a lot more difficult and was gradually withdrawn to a more midfield role but still completed a century of goals in the United cause in the last game of the 1991/92 season against Spurs after making his debut at the Dell in a 2-2 draw. McClair played in all three of United's League Cup appearances in the nineties but his first winners medal with the club was in the 1990 FA Cup Final against Crystal Palace quickly followed by his place in the successful European Cup-winners Cup Final side. He won the first of thirty caps against Luxembourg in 1987 shortly before his move to United and was an ever present in the United side that regained the Championship in 1993. With the emergence of Giggs, the signing of Cantona, and the return from illness of Lee Sharpe, however, his role in 1993/94 was mainly as substitute and, given his list of success, it is a great tribute to his loyalty that he stayed throughout a season where he could have commanded a regular first team spot in almost any other FA Premiership side. Alex Ferguson said of him *"If sides were made up of thirteen players out on the pitch, he would be playing every game"*. McClair was voted Scottish Player of the Year in 1987.

## Previous Clubs and Appearance Record

| Clubs | Signed | Fee | Appearances | | | Goals | | |
|-------|--------|-----|-----|-----|-----|-----|-----|-----|
| | | | Lge | FLC | FAC | Lge | FLC | FAC |
| Aston Villa | 1980 | — | – | – | – | – | – | – |
| Motherwell | 1981 | — | 39 | 15 | | | | |
| Celtic | 1983 | £100,000 | 145 | 99 | | | | |
| Man Utd | 1987 | £850,000 | 190/3 | 28 | 24 | 70 | 14 | 11 |
| *FA Premier League Record* | | | | | | | | |
| | 92/93 | | 41/1 | 3 | 3 | 9 | | |
| | 93/94 | | 12+14 | 6+1 | 1+4 | 1 | 4 | 1 |

## Estimated value: £850,000

# Gary Andrew PALLISTER

Date of Birth: 30th June 1965, Ramsgate

When United signed Gary Pallister in August 1989 the fee of £2.3m was not only a club record but a British record. His early games at Old Trafford suggested to many people that he had been overpriced but once he was settled in and, perhaps even more importantly, the team began winning, Pallister went on to prove that he has been a sound investment. His early days were spent in non-league football with Billingham Town and Middlesbrough were the first full-time club to show interest in him. He joined Middlesbrough in November 1984 making his debut for them in August 1985 at Wimbledon in a 3-0 defeat. The Ayresome Park club, however, were in bad state at that time and were relegated that season to Division Three with Pallister going on loan to Darlington for whom he would have signed had the Feethams outfit been able to afford the £4,000 fee! He returned to Middlesbrough and was a virtual regular as they bounced straight back up with a club record points total of 94 to finish runners-up in 1986/87. By 1988 he had made his international debut against Holland and had also played against Saudi Arabia when United signed him. He made his United debut in a dreadful 2-0 home defeat by Norwich but by the end of his first season in United colours he was the proud owner of a FA Cup winners medal. He was also a member of the United sides that appeared in three League Cup Finals in four years and lifted the European Cup-winners Cup in Rotterdam. After his move to Old Trafford he lost his England place but when his form took an upturn along with United's, he came back into international reckoning with a substitute appearance against Cameroon in 1991 and since 1993 has been a regular member of the England set up to take his number of caps to well into double figures. Pallister was voted the PFA's Player of the Year in 1992.

## Previous Clubs and Appearance Record

| Clubs | Signed | Fee | Appearances | | | Goals | | |
|-------|--------|-----|-----|-----|-----|-----|-----|-----|
| | | | Lge | FLC | FAC | Lge | FLC | FAC |
| Middlesbrough | 11/84 | — | 156 | 10 | 10 | 5 | 1 | |
| Darlington | 10/85 | loan | 7 | | | | | |
| Man Utd | 8/89 | £2.3m | 111 | 20 | 14 | 4 | | |
| *FA Premier League Record* | | | | | | | | |
| | 92/93 | | 42 | 3 | 3 | 1 | | |
| | 93/94 | | 41 | 9 | 7 | 1 | | |

Many said United paid over the odds for Pallister but they have had the best out of him for some time now. Still looking as strong as ever and still has a good number of years service left in him.

## Estimated value: £2,800,000

# Paul Andrew PARKER

Date of Birth 4th April 1964, West Ham

"Capped" at Under 21, "B" and Full international levels by England, Paul Parker arrived at Old Trafford in August 1991 from QPR for a fee of £2m but it took him over eighteen months to register his first goal for the club which came in a 4-1 defeat of Spurs in January 1993. Born in West Ham, Parker made the short trip across London on leaving school to link up with Fulham for whom he made his debut at the age of 17 years and 21 days against Reading in a 2-1 home defeat. That was his only game that season and he managed only five more the following campaign but by 1984 he was a regular and in 1987 he moved the short distance to QPR for £300,000. He was noted as one of the fastest defenders in the game and he made his full international debut for England against Albania in 1989. He became a regular in the England set up and United moved for him in August 1991 but, strangely, after arriving at Old Trafford his international career went on the back burner after just one more appearance against Germany in September 1991. His United debut was against Notts County in a 2-0 Old Trafford victory and he picked up a League Cup winners medal in his first season when playing in the side that beat Notts Forest 1-0. He was also a regular in the side that lifted the Championship for the first time in 1992/93 and his performances during the early part of 1993/94 saw him win back his England shirt.

## Previous Clubs and Appearance Record

| Clubs | Signed | Fee | Appearances | | | Goals | | |
|-------|--------|-----|-----|-----|-----|-----|-----|-----|
| | | | Lge | FLC | FAC | Lge | FLC | FAC |
| Fulham | 4/82 | — | 153 | 16 | 11 | 2 | 1 | |
| QPR | 6/87 | £300,000 | 125 | 14 | 16 | 1 | | |
| Man Utd | 8/91 | £2m | 26 | 6 | 3 | | | |
| *FA Premier League Record* | | | | | | | | |
| | 92/93 | | 31 | 2 | 3 | 1 | | |
| | 93/94 | | 39+1 | 6 | 7 | | | |

United would almost certainly have to take a loss on what they paid for Parker due to his age. He has also lost his England place whilst at Old Trafford and is now the wrong side of 30.

## Estimated value: £1,000,000

# Peter Boleslaw SCHMEICHEL

Date of Birth: 18 th November 1968, Gladsaxe, Denmark

With respect to Les Sealey who was United's Number 1 when Alex Ferguson plunged for Peter Schmeichel in August 1991, the arrival of the Great Dane solved what has traditionally been a problem position at Old Trafford. Whilst truly great 'keepers such as Frank Swift and Bert Trautmann had prospered at rivals Manchester City, United had always struggled, by and large, in the custodian stakes. Paddy Roche, Pat Dunne, Dave Gaskell, and Ronnie Briggs are just some names that crop up in discussion about United 'keepers but there can be no arguing about Schmeichel's position as the best United 'keeper ever. When Alex Ferguson signed him in August 1991 for £850,000 Schmeichel was already an established Danish international but his best was still to come. After helping United to win the League Cup against Forest in his first season, Schmeichel was to become one of the stars of the 1992 European Nation's Championships when Denmark were let in by the backdoor just days prior to the start of the Championships. The fighting in Yugoslavia brought about the decision to expel them with the Danes taking their place. He kept a clean sheet against England in the Group matches and against Germany in the Final itself to become the first ever United player to win a European Nations' medal. He kept clean sheets in his first four games for the Reds and seventeen in the League in his first season, a figure he bettered by one in United's FA Premier Championship success the following campaign. As well as stopping goals, however, he has also set up on more than one occasion, goals with his magnificent throws to beyond the half way line. Indeed, the extrovert character was seen marauding in the opposing penalty area in the last seconds of the Old Trafford game against Blackburn as United desperately sought an equaliser!

## Previous Clubs and Appearance Record

| Clubs | Signed | Fee | Appearances | | | Goals | | |
|---|---|---|---|---|---|---|---|---|
| | | | Lge | FLC | FAC | Lge | FLC | FAC |
| Man Utd | 8/91 | £850,000 | 40 | 6 | 3 | | | |
| *FA Premier League Record* | | | | | | | | |
| | 92/93 | | 42 | 3 | 3 | | | |
| | 93/94 | | 40 | 8 | 7 | | | |

Possibly United's best buy in terms of value for money. Now acknowledged as the best in Europe if not the world and only the fact that there are so many good number 1's about would keep his value below £4m.

## Estimated value: £3,750,000

# Lee Stuart SHARPE

Date of Dirth: 27th May 1971, Halesowen

Although still not 23 at the end of the 93/94 season, Lee Sharpe's career has been blighted by a series of serious injuries and illnesses. It is testament to his ability that, despite the lengthy set backs he has taken, Sharpe has by still such a young age accumulated so many honours in the game. A native of Halesowen, Sharpe's first chance in football was as a YTS apprentice at Torquay United but United quickly spotted his potential and after only nine full games plus five more as substitute they plunged £185,000 in May 1988 for the unknown 17 year old. Sharpe signed professional forms for Torquay on his seventeenth birthday but within days was signing for United. He had played his first Football League game for Torquay coming on as substitute in the local "Derby" against Exeter City at the ripe old age of 16 in October 1987. Strangely, the first time he actually started a game was also against Exeter in the return fixture at Plainmoor the following February. If anybody harboured any thoughts about the new young signing being one to watch for the future they were quickly put in their place by a young man determined to make his way to the top in the shortest time possible. The 1988/89 season was just five games old when Sharpe was put in against Wst Ham United at Old Trafford where the Reds enjoyed a 2-0 victory and he was to play over twenty games that season. He also won the first of his eight Under 21 caps that season when he played against Greece in Patras on 7th February 1989 and he went on to become the most United player at Under 21 level other than former 'keeper Gary Bailey. But whereas Bailey won most of his caps as an "over age" player, Sharpe had won all his prior to his 20th Birthday. He missed the first big chunk of his fledgling career when he was out for the second half of the 1989/90 campaign but by September 1990 he was back and was to play a significant part in getting United to the League Cup Final, scoring against Liverpool, netting a hat-trick against Arsenal at Highbury and two of the three goals by which United beat Leeds in the semi-final. His form had not gone unnoticed at international level and he became the youngest player to represent England since the late Duncan Edwards when he played against the Republic of Ireland on 27/3/91, still two months short of his 20th birthday. Despite missing a further eight months between April 91 and November 91, and a total of six months during the first two FAPL competitions, Sharpe has still managed to total over 150 appearances for United. Sharpe was voted the PFA's *Young Player of the Year* in 1991.

# Previous Clubs and Appearance Record

| Clubs | Signed | Fee | Appearances | | | Goals | | |
|---|---|---|---|---|---|---|---|---|
| | | | Lge | FLC | FAC | Lge | FLC | FAC |
| Torquay United | 5/88 | — | 14 | — | — | 3 | — | — |
| Manchester Utd | 5/88 | £185,000 | 77 | 15 | 10 | 3 | 7 | |
| *FA Premier League Record* | | | | | | | | |
| 92/93 | | | 27 | — | 3 | 1 | | |
| 93/94 | | | 26+4 | 2+2 | 1+2 | 9 | 2 | 3 |

Very difficult to estimate his worth on the transfer market due to his history of injury and illness. Any buyer would probably insist on a down payment only with a fee per game thereafter.

## Estimated value: £3,000,000

# Season's Records 1993-94

## Attendances by Number – FA Premier League

| Home | | | Away | | |
|---|---|---|---|---|---|
| 30/03/94 | Liverpool | 44,751 | 1/01/94 | Liverpool | 42,795 |
| 22/01/94 | Everton | 44,750 | 27/04/94 | Leeds United | 41,125 |
| 6/11/93 | Wimbledon | 44,748 | 23/08/93 | Aston Villa | 39,624 |
| 5/03/94 | Chelsea | 44,745 | 11/09/93 | Chelsea | 37,064 |
| 1/01/94 | Leeds United | 44,724 | 11/12/93 | Newcastle United | 36,388 |
| 8/05/94 | Coventry City | 44,717 | 22/03/94 | Arsenal | 36,203 |
| 4/05/94 | Southampton | 44,705 | 23/10/93 | Everton | 35,430 |
| 4/12/93 | Norwich City | 44,694 | 7/11/93 | Manchester City | 35,155 |
| 4/04/94 | Oldham Athletic | 44,686 | 2/10/93 | Sheffield Wednesday | 34,548 |
| 30/10/93 | Queen's Park Rangers | 44,663 | 15/01/94 | Tottenham Hotspurs | 31,343 |
| 16/10/93 | Tottenham Hotspur | 44,655 | 26/02/94 | West Ham United | 28,832 |
| 1/09/93 | West Ham United | 44,613 | 16/04/94 | Wimbledon | 28,553 |
| 25/09/93 | Swindon Town | 44,583 | 7/12/93 | Sheffield United | 26,744 |
| 26/12/93 | Blackburn Rovers | 44,511 | 1/05/94 | Ipswich Town | 22,559 |
| 19/12/93 | Aston Villa | 44,499 | 5/02/94 | Queen's Park Rangers | 21,267 |
| 23/04/94 | Manchester City | 44,333 | 2/04/94 | Blackburn Rovers | 20,866 |
| 19/09/93 | Arsenal | 44,009 | 15/08/93 | Norwich City | 19,705 |
| 16/03/94 | Sheffield Wednesday | 43,669 | 19/03/94 | Swindon Town | 18,102 |
| 24/11/93 | Ipswich Town | 43,300 | 27/11/93 | Coventry City | 17,020 |
| 18/08/93 | Sheffield United | 41,949 | 29/12/93 | Oldham Athletic | 16,708 |
| 21/09/93 | Newcastle United | 41,829 | 28/08/93 | Southampton | 16,189 |

## Attendances by Number – European Cup

| Home | | | Away | | |
|---|---|---|---|---|---|
| 20/10/93 | Galatasary | 39,396 | 3/11/93 | Galatasary | 40,000 |
| 29/09/93 | Kispest Honved | 35,781 | 15/09/93 | Kispest Honved | 9,000 |

## Attendances by Number – Coca Cola Cup

| Home | | | Away | | |
|---|---|---|---|---|---|
| 12/01/94 | Portsmouth | 43,794 | 27/03/94 | Aston Villa at Wembley | 77,231 |
| 13/02/94 | Sheffield Wednesday | 43,294 | 2/03/94 | Sheffield Wednesday | 34,878 |
| 6/10/93 | Stoke City | 41,387 | 30/11/93 | Everton | 34,052 |
| 27/10/93 | Leicester City | 41,344 | 26/01/94 | Portsmouth | 24,950 |
| | | | 22/09/93 | Stoke City | 23,327 |

## Attendances by Number – FA Cup

| Home | | | Away | | |
|---|---|---|---|---|---|
| 12/03/94 | Charlton Athletic | 44,347 | 14/05/94 | Chelsea *at Wembley* | 79,634 |
| | | | 10/04/94 | Oldham Ath *at Wembley* | 56,399 |
| | | | 13/04/94 | Oldham Ath *at Maine Rd* | 32,211 |
| | | | 9/01/94 | Sheffield United | 22,019 |
| | | | 30/01/94 | Norwich City | 21,060 |
| | | | 20/02/94 | Wimbledon | 27,511 |

## Sending Offs

| | | | | | |
|---|---|---|---|---|---|
| Bryan | ROBSON | 25/07/93 | v | Arsenal | (n) |
| Eric | CANTONA | 3/11/93 | v | Galatasary | (a) |
| | | 19/03/94 | v | Swindon Town | (a) |
| | | 22/03/94 | v | Arsenal | (a) |
| Mark | HUGHES | 9/01/94 | v | Sheffield United | (a) |
| Peter | SCHMEICHEL | 12/03/94 | v | Charlton Athletic | (h) |
| Andrei | KANCHELSKIS | 27/03/94 | v | Aston Villa | (n) |

## Bookings

| | | | | | |
|---|---|---|---|---|---|
| Eric | CANTONA | 20/10/93 | v | Galatasary | (h) |
| | | 1/01/94 | v | Leeds United | (h) |
| | | 30/01/94 | v | Norwich City | (a) |
| | | 23/04/94 | v | Man City | (h) |
| Dion | DUBLIN | 22/09/93 | v | Stoke City | (a) |
| Mark | HUGHES | 19/09/93 | v | Arsenal | (h) |
| | | 7/11/93 | v | Manchester City | (a) |
| | | 2/04/94 | v | Blackburn Rovers | (a) |
| | | 10/04/94 | v | Oldham Athletic | (n) |
| Paul | INCE | 28/08/93 | v | Southampton | (a) |
| | | 3/11/93 | v | Galatasary | (a) |
| | | 27/11/93 | v | Coventry City | (a) |
| | | 7/12/93 | v | Sheffield United | (a) |
| | | 4/01/94 | v | Liverpool | (a) |
| | | 5/03/94 | v | Chelsea | (h) |
| | | 10/04/94 | v | Oldham Athletic | (n) |
| | | 23/04/94 | v | Man City | (h) |
| Denis | IRWIN | 28/08/93 | v | Southampton | (a) |
| | | 7/12/93 | v | Sheffield United | (a) |
| | | 19/03/94 | v | Swindon Town | (a) |
| Andrei | KANCHELSKIS | 23/08/93 | v | Aston Villa | (a) |
| | | 30/01/94 | v | Norwich City | (a) |

| Roy | KEANE | 18/08/93 | v | Sheffield United | (h) |
| | | 19/09/93 | v | Arsenal | (h) |
| | | 29/12/93 | v | Oldham Athletic | (a) |
| | | 4/01/94 | v | Liverpool | (a) |
| | | 30/01/94 | v | Norwich City | (a) |
| | | 2/03/94 | v | Sheffield Wed | (a) |
| | | 22/03/94 | v | Arsenal | (a) |
| | | 13/04/94 | v | Oldham Athletic | (n) |
| | | 23/04/94 | v | Man City | (h) |
| Lee | SHARPE | 11/09/93 | v | Chelsea | (a) |
| Peter | SCHMEICHEL | 27/10/93 | v | Leicester City | (h) |
| Steve | BRUCE | 3/11/93 | v | Galatasary | (a) |
| | | 27/11/93 | v | Coventry City | (a) |
| | | 5/02/94 | v | QPR | (a) |
| | | 14/05/94 | v | Chelsea | (n) |
| Paul | PARKER | 3/11/93 | v | Galatasary | (a) |
| | | 26/02/94 | v | West Ham United | (a) |
| | | 1/05/94 | v | Ipswich Town | (a) |
| Bryan | ROBSON | 1/01/94 | v | Leeds United | (h) |
| Gary | PALLISTER | 5/02/94 | v | QPR | (a) |

## Suspensions

| Bryan | ROBSON | 2 match ban | September 1993 |
| Mark | HUGHES | 1 match ban | January 1994 |
| Peter | SCHMEICHEL | 1 match ban | March 1994 |
| Eric | CANTONA | 3 match ban | April 1994 |
| | | 2 match ban | April 1994 |
| Roy | KEANE | 1 match ban | April 1994 |
| Andrei | KANCHELSKIS | 1 match ban | April 1994 |
| Paul | INCE | 1 match ban | April 1994 |

## List of Scores by Number (League Games Only)

| 0-0 | 1-0 | 0-1 | 1-1 |
| --- | --- | --- | --- |
| Ipswich T | Everton | Chelsea | Newcastle Utd |
| Leeds Utd | Arsenal | Chelsea | Newcastle Utd |
| Coventry City | Coventry City | Wimbledon | Blackburn Rovs. |
| | Tottenham H. | | Southampton |
| | Everton | | |
| | Liverpool | | |

| 2-0 | 0-2 | 2-1 | 1-2 |
|---|---|---|---|
| Norwich City | Blackburn R. | Tottenham H. | West Ham Utd |
| Man City | | Aston Villa | Arsenal |
| Leeds Utd | | QPR | |
| | | Ipswich T | |

| 2-2 | 3-0 | 3-1 | 3-2 |
|---|---|---|---|
| Norwich | Sheff.Utd | Southampton | Sheff Wed |
| West Ham Utd | Wimbledon | Aston Villa | Man City |
| Swindon T | Sheff.Utd | | QPR |
| | | | Oldham Ath. |

| 3-3 | 4-2 | 5-0 | 5-2 |
|---|---|---|---|
| Liverpool | Swindon Town | Sheff Wed | Oldham Ath |

## Summary of Appearances

| No. | Player | | Lge | EC | CCC | FAC |
|---|---|---|---|---|---|---|
| 1 | Peter | SCHMEICHEL | 40 | 4 | 8 | 7 |
| 2 | Paul | PARKER | 39/1 | 3 | 6 | 7 |
| 3 | Denis | IRWIN | 42 | 3 | 8/1 | 7 |
| 4 | Steve | BRUCE | 41 | 4 | 8/1 | 7 |
| 6 | Gary | PALLISTER | 41 | 3 | 9 | 7 |
| 12 | Bryan | ROBSON | 10/5 | 4 | 5 | 1/1 |
| 16 | Roy | KEANE | 34/3 | 3 | 6/1 | 6 |
| 8 | Paul | INCE | 39 | 3 | 6 | 6 |
| 14 | Andrei | KANCHELSKIS | 28/3 | – | 9 | 6 |
| 10 | Mark | HUGHES | 36 | 2 | 8 | 7 |
| 11 | Ryan | GIGGS | 32/6 | 4 | 6/2 | 7 |
| 9 | Brian | McCLAIR | 12/14 | – | 6/1 | 1/4 |
| 5 | Lee | SHARPE | 26/4 | 4 | 2/2 | 1/2 |
| 7 | Eric | CANTONA | 34 | 4 | 5 | 5 |
| 23 | Mike | PHELAN | –/1 | 1/3 | 2 | – |
| 20 | Dion | DUBLIN | 1/4 | –/1 | 1/1 | 1/1 |
| 18 | Darren | FERGUSON | 1/2 | – | 1/1 | – |
| 21 | Lee | MARTIN | 1 | 1/1 | 3 | – |
| 19 | Nicky | BUTT | –/1 | – | – | –/1 |
| 27 | Gary | NEVILLE | 1 | –/1 | – | – |
| 29 | Ben | THORNLEY | –/1 | – | – | – |
| 13 | Les | SEALEY | – | – | 1 | –/1 |
| 25 | Gary | WALSH | 2/1 | – | – | – |
| 17 | Colin | McKEE | 1 | – | – | – |

## Goalscorers

| No. | Player | | Lge | EC | CCC | FAC |
|---|---|---|---|---|---|---|
| 7 | Eric | CANTONA | 18 | 2 | 1 | 4 |
| 10 | Mark | HUGHES | 12 | – | 5 | 4 |
| 11 | Ryan | GIGGS | 13 | – | 3 | 1 |
| 5 | Lee | SHARPE | 9 | – | 2 | 3 |
| 14 | Andrei | KANCHELSKIS | 6 | – | 1 | 3 |
| 8 | Paul | INCE | 8 | – | – | 1 |
| 16 | Roy | KEANE | 5 | 2 | – | 1 |
| 4 | Steve | BRUCE | 3 | 2 | 2 | – |
| 9 | Brian | McCLAIR | 1 | – | 4 | 1 |
| 3 | Denis | IRWIN | 2 | – | – | 2 |
| 12 | Bryan | ROBSON | 1 | 1 | – | 1 |
| 6 | Gary | PALLISTER | 1 | – | – | – |
| 20 | Dion | DUBLIN | 1 | – | 1 | – |
| | Own | Goal | – | 1 | – | – |

## League Sequences

| | | | |
|---|---|---|---|
| Consecutive Wins | 8 | Consecutive Home Wins | 6 |
| Consecutive Away Wins | 5 | Games without defeat | 22 |
| Games without a Win | 2 | | |

## Transfers to Manchester Utd

| Player | | Date Bought | From | Fee |
|---|---|---|---|---|
| Roy | KEANE | July 1993 | Notts Forest | £3,750,000 |

## Transfers from Manchester Utd

| Player | | Date Sold | To | Fee |
|---|---|---|---|---|
| Brian | CAREY | July 1993 | Leicester City | £250,000 |
| Danny | WALLACE | October 1993 | Birmingham City | £170,000 |
| Darren | FERGUSON | January 1994 | Wolverhampton Wanderers | £500,000 |
| Lee | MARTIN | January 1994 | Glasgow Celtic | £350,000 |
| Les | SEALEY | May 1994 | | Free |
| Mike | PHELAN | May 1994 | | Free |
| Bryan | ROBSON | May 1994 | | Free |

## United's Record Against Other Clubs in the FAPL

| Club | P | W | D | L | F | A | W | D | L | F | A |
|---|---|---|---|---|---|---|---|---|---|---|---|
| Arsenal | 4 | 1 | 1 | 0 | 1 | 0 | 1 | 1 | 0 | 3 | 2 |
| Aston Villa | 4 | 1 | 1 | 0 | 4 | 2 | 1 | 0 | 1 | 2 | 2 |
| Blackburn Rovers | 4 | 1 | 1 | 0 | 4 | 2 | 0 | 1 | 1 | 0 | 2 |
| Chelsea | 4 | 1 | 0 | 1 | 3 | 1 | 0 | 1 | 1 | 1 | 2 |
| Coventry City | 4 | 1 | 1 | 0 | 5 | 0 | 2 | 0 | 0 | 2 | 0 |
| Crystal Palace | 2 | 1 | 0 | 0 | 1 | 0 | 1 | 0 | 0 | 2 | 0 |
| Everton | 4 | 1 | 0 | 1 | 1 | 3 | 2 | 0 | 0 | 3 | 0 |
| Ipswich Town | 4 | 0 | 2 | 0 | 1 | 1 | 1 | 1 | 0 | 3 | 3 |
| Leeds United | 4 | 1 | 1 | 0 | 2 | 0 | 1 | 1 | 0 | 2 | 0 |
| Liverpool | 4 | 1 | 1 | 0 | 3 | 2 | 1 | 1 | 0 | 5 | 4 |
| Manchester City | 4 | 2 | 0 | 0 | 4 | 1 | 0 | 1 | 1 | 4 | 3 |
| Middlesborough | 2 | 1 | 0 | 0 | 3 | 0 | 0 | 1 | 0 | 1 | 1 |
| Newcastle United | 2 | 0 | 1 | 0 | 1 | 1 | 0 | 1 | 0 | 1 | 1 |
| Norwich City | 4 | 1 | 1 | 0 | 3 | 2 | 2 | 0 | 0 | 1 | 5 |
| Nottingham Forest | 2 | 1 | 0 | 0 | 2 | 0 | 1 | 0 | 0 | 2 | 0 |
| Oldham Athletic | 4 | 2 | 0 | 0 | 6 | 2 | 1 | 0 | 1 | 5 | 3 |
| QPR | 4 | 1 | 1 | 0 | 2 | 1 | 2 | 0 | 0 | 6 | 3 |
| Sheffield United | 4 | 2 | 0 | 0 | 5 | 1 | 1 | 0 | 1 | 4 | 2 |
| Sheffield Wednesday | 4 | 2 | 0 | 0 | 7 | 1 | 1 | 1 | 0 | 6 | 5 |
| Southampton | 4 | 2 | 0 | 0 | 4 | 1 | 2 | 0 | 0 | 4 | 1 |
| Swindon Town | 2 | 1 | 0 | 0 | 4 | 2 | 0 | 1 | 0 | 2 | 2 |
| Tottenham Hotspur | 4 | 2 | 0 | 0 | 6 | 2 | 1 | 1 | 0 | 2 | 1 |
| West Ham United | 2 | 1 | 0 | 0 | 3 | 0 | 0 | 1 | 0 | 2 | 2 |
| Wimbledon | 4 | 1 | 0 | 1 | 3 | 2 | 1 | 0 | 1 | 2 | 2 |
| Total | 84 | 28 | 11 | 3 | 78 | 27 | 23 | 12 | 7 | 69 | 42 |

## Players Numbers 1993-94

| | | | | | |
|---|---|---|---|---|---|
| 1 | Peter SCHMEICHEL | 2 | Paul PARKER | 3 | Denis IRWIN |
| 4 | Steve BRUCE | 5 | Lee SHARPE | 6 | Gary PALLISTER |
| 7 | Eric CANTONA | 8 | Paul INCE | 9 | Brian McCLAIR |
| 10 | Mark HUGHES | 11 | Ryan GIGGS | 12 | Bryan ROBSON |
| 13 | Les SEALEY | 14 | Andrei KANCHELSKIS | 16 | Roy KEANE |
| 17 | Colin McKEE* | 18 | Darren FERGUSON | 19 | Nicky BUTT |
| 20 | Dion DUBLIN | 21 | Lee MARTIN | 23 | Mike PHELAN |
| 25 | Gary WALSH | 27 | Gary NEVILLE | 29 | Ben THORNLEY† |

†Ben Thornley made one appearance as substitute against West Ham (a) coming on in the 78th minute. * Colin McKee (No 17) made one appearance against Coventry City on 8th May 1994.

## Appearances – FA Carling Premiership

| Player's No | 1 | 2 | 3 | 4 | 5 | 6 | 7 | 8 | 9 | 10 | 11 | 12 | 13 | 14 | 16 | 18 | 19 | 20 | 21 | 23 | 27 | 25 |
|---|---|---|---|---|---|---|---|---|---|---|---|---|---|---|---|---|---|---|---|---|---|---|
| Norwich C (a) | * | * | * | * | * | * | – | * | S | * | * | * | S | * | * | – | – | – | – | – | – | – |
| Sheff Utd (h) | * | * | * | * | S | * | – | * | 71 | * | * | s | S | * | * | – | – | – | – | – | – | – |
| Newcastle U (h) | * | s | * | * | 85 | * | – | * | 71 | * | * | * | S | * | * | – | – | – | – | – | – | – |
| Aston Villa (a) | * | * | * | * | * | * | * | * | S | * | * | * | S | * | s | S | – | – | – | – | – | – |
| Southampton (a) | * | * | * | * | * | * | * | * | 66 | * | * | – | S | 74 | * | S | – | – | – | – | – | – |
| West Ham (h) | * | * | * | * | * | * | * | s | 79 | – | * | 70 | S | s | s | – | – | – | – | – | – | – |
| Chelsea (a) | * | * | * | * | * | * | * | * | 79 | s | * | s | S | S | – | – | – | – | – | – | – | – |
| Arsenal (h) | * | * | * | * | * | * | = | * | 89 | s | * | * | S | S | – | – | – | – | – | – | – | – |
| Swindon T (h) | * | * | * | * | s | * | * | * | 55 | 79 | s | – | S | S | – | – | – | – | – | – | – | – |
| Sheff Wed (a) | * | * | * | * | * | * | * | * | S | s | s | s | S | 85 | * | – | – | 79 | – | – | – | – |
| Spurs (h) | * | * | * | * | * | * | * | * | 69 | * | S | s | S | – | * | – | 79 | – | – | – | – | – |
| Everton (a) | – | – | * | * | * | – | * | * | * | * | * | – | S | S | * | * | – | – | * | – | – | – |
| QPR (h) | * | * | * | * | * | – | * | * | * | * | 76 | S | S | S | * | – | – | – | S | – | – | – |
| Man City (a) | * | * | * | * | * | * | * | * | – | * | 76 | s | s | * | s | 83 | – | – | – | – | – | – |
| Wimbledon (h) | * | * | * | * | * | * | * | * | – | s | S | s | s | * | – | * | – | – | – | 79 | – | – |
| Ipswich T (h) | * | * | * | * | * | * | * | * | – | * | 57 | S | S | s | – | – | – | – | – | – | – | – |
| Coventry C (a) | * | * | * | * | 73 | * | * | * | S | – | * | – | S | – | – | * | – | – | – | – | – | – |
| Norwich C (h) | * | * | * | * | * | * | * | * | s | * | * | – | s | S | – | S | S | – | – | – | – | – |
| Sheff Utd (a) | * | * | * | * | * | * | * | * | s | * | * | – | S | 55 | 72 | – | – | – | – | – | – | – |
| Newcastle U (a) | * | * | * | * | * | * | * | * | * | * | 80 | – | S | * | 76 | – | – | – | – | – | – | – |
| Aston Villa (h) | * | s | * | * | s | * | * | * | S | s | * | * | S | – | * | 85 | – | – | – | – | – | – |
| Blackburn R (a) | * | * | * | * | * | * | s | s | 78 | * | * | 64 | S | * | * | S | – | – | – | – | – | – |
| Oldham Ath (a) | * | * | * | * | * | s | s | s | 64 | – | * | * | S | – | * | S | – | – | – | 79 | – | – |
| Leeds Utd (h) | * | * | * | * | – | * | * | – | * | – | * | * | S | S | * | S | s | s | – | – | – | – |

185

| Player's No | 1 | 2 | 3 | 4 | 5 | 6 | 7 | 8 | 9 | 10 | 11 | 12 | 13 | 14 | 16 | 18 | 19 | 20 | 21 | 23 | 27 | 25 |
|---|---|---|---|---|---|---|---|---|---|---|---|---|---|---|---|---|---|---|---|---|---|---|
| Liverpool (a) | * | * | * | * | - | * | * | * | * | - | * | - | * | * | * | * | - | - | - | - | - | - |
| Spurs (a) | * | * | * | * | - | * | * | * | 81 | s | * | s | s | * | * | s | - | s | s | - | - | - |
| Everton (h) | * | * | * | * | - | * | * | * | s | s | * | - | s | * | * | s | s | s | - | - | - | - |
| QPR (h) | * | * | s | * | * | * | * | * | * | * | * | - | s | * | * | - | s | s | 85 | - | - | - |
| West Ham Utd (a) | * | * | * | * | * | * | * | - | * | * | * | 73 | s | s | * | - | - | - | 84 | - | - | - |
| Chelsea (h) | * | * | s | * | * | * | * | * | s | 45 | * | 69 | s | * | * | - | - | - | - | - | - | s |
| Sheff Wed (h) | * | * | * | * | - | * | - | * | * | * | * | s | s | * | * | - | - | - | - | - | - | * |
| Swindon T (a) | * | * | * | * | * | * | * | * | 81 | * | * | * | s | * | * | - | - | - | - | - | - | 25 |
| Arsenal (a) | * | * | * | * | * | * | * | * | - | 81 | * | s | s | * | * | - | - | - | - | - | - | * |
| Liverpool (h) | * | * | s | * | s | * | s | * | - | - | 66 | 73 | s | * | * | - | - | - | - | - | - | * |
| Blackburn Rovs (a) | * | s | * | * | * | * | - | * | 70 | * | * | s | s | * | * | - | - | 63 | - | - | - | s |
| Oldham Ath. (h) | * | * | s | * | * | * | - | * | s | s | * | s | s | * | * | - | - | 73 | - | - | - | - |
| Wimbledon (h) | * | s | * | 64 | * | * | * | * | * | * | * | s | * | * | - | - | - | - | - | - | - | s |
| Manchester C. (h) | * | * | * | * | s | * | * | * | - | s | 72 | s | s | * | * | - | - | - | - | - | - | - |
| Leeds United (a) | * | * | * | * | - | * | * | * | * | s | * | s | s | * | * | - | - | - | - | - | - | 25 |
| Ipswich Town (h) | s | * | * | 83 | * | * | * | * | s | s | * | s | s | * | * | - | - | - | - | - | - | * |
| Southampton (h) | - | * | * | - | * | * | * | * | s | s | - | * | s | * | * | - | - | - | - | - | - | * |
| Coventry City (h) | - | 57 | - | s | * | - | * | * | * | - | - | * | s | - | 75 | * | * | * | * | * | * | * |

## Appearances – European Champions' Cup

| Player's No | 1 | 2 | 3 | 4 | 5 | 6 | 7 | 8 | 9 | 10 | 11 | 12 | 13 | 14 | 16 | 18 | 19 | 20 | 21 | 23 | 27 | 25 |
|---|---|---|---|---|---|---|---|---|---|---|---|---|---|---|---|---|---|---|---|---|---|---|
| Honved (a) | * | * | * | * | * | * | * | * | - | - | s | * | * | * | - | - | - | s | s | 80 | - | - |
| Honved (h) | * | s | - | * | * | * | * | s | * | - | * | * | s | - | * | - | s | s | 69 | 79 | - | - |
| Galatasary (h) | * | - | * | * | * | * | s | * | - | * | * | * | * | * | * | - | s | s | * | 65 | s | s |
| Galatasary (a) | * | * | * | - | * | - | * | * | - | * | * | * | * | - | * | - | s | 72 | s | * | 84 | - |

# Appearances – FA Cup

| Player's No | | 1 | 2 | 3 | 4 | 5 | 6 | 7 | 8 | 9 | 10 | 11 | 12 | 13 | 14 | 16 | 18 | 19 | 20 | 21 | 23 | 27 | 25 |
|---|---|---|---|---|---|---|---|---|---|---|---|---|---|---|---|---|---|---|---|---|---|---|---|
| Sheff Utd | (a) | * | * | * | * | - | * | * | * | S | * | * | S | S | * | * | - | - | - | - | - | - | - |
| Norwich C | (a) | * | * | - | * | * | * | - | - | 79 | s | * | - | S | * | - | - | - | S | - | - | - | - |
| Wimbledon | (a) | * | * | * | * | - | * | s | - | 73 | s | * | - | S | * | - | - | - | 73 | - | - | - | - |
| Charlton A | (h) | s | * | * | * | * | * | = | * | S | * | * | S | 44 | * | s | - | - | - | - | - | - | - |
| Oldham Ath | (n) | * | * | * | * | 75 | * | - | * | s | * | * | 73 | S | s | s | - | 108 | s | - | - | - | - |
| Oldham Ath | (n) | * | * | s | * | 86 | * | - | * | 69 | s | * | * | S | s | s | - | - | - | - | - | - | - |
| Chelsea | (n) | * | * | s | * | 86 | * | - | * | 86 | * | * | - | - | * | * | - | - | - | - | - | - | S |

# Appearances – Coca Cola League Cup

| Player's No | | 1 | 2 | 3 | 4 | 5 | 6 | 7 | 8 | 9 | 10 | 11 | 12 | 13 | 14 | 16 | 18 | 19 | 20 | 21 | 23 | 27 | 25 |
|---|---|---|---|---|---|---|---|---|---|---|---|---|---|---|---|---|---|---|---|---|---|---|---|
| Stoke City | (a) | * | - | * | 78 | 45 | * | - | - | * | * | * | - | S | S | - | * | - | * | * | s | - | - |
| Stoke City | (h) | * | - | s | * | * | * | - | - | * | * | 85 | s | S | S | - | S | - | - | * | * | - | - |
| Leicester C | (h) | * | - | 28 | * | s | s | * | * | * | * | 61 | * | S | * | - | - | - | - | * | * | - | - |
| Everton | (a) | * | * | * | * | * | * | * | * | S | * | * | s | S | * | - | 77 | - | - | - | - | - | - |
| Portsmouth | (h) | * | * | * | * | * | * | * | - | s | * | * | - | S | 74 | 74 | - | - | 90 | - | - | - | - |
| Portsmouth | (a) | * | * | * | * | * | * | * | * | s | * | * | S | S | * | - | - | - | s | - | - | - | - |
| Sheff Wed | (h) | * | * | * | * | - | * | - | * | S | * | * | - | S | * | - | - | - | s | - | - | - | - |
| Sheff Wed | (a) | * | * | * | * | 61 | * | * | * | * | * | s | S | S | * | - | - | - | s | - | - | - | - |
| Aston Villa | (n) | - | - | * | s | * | * | - | * | 82 | * | s | - | - | * | - | - | - | - | * | * | - | S |

**Symbols** –

| | |
|---|---|
| * | played |
| S | Substitute who did not make an appearance |
| s | substituted |
| – | not in squad for this game |
| 75 | states the minute the player appeared as a substitute |

187

# General Records

## *Football Alliance*

| | | |
|---|---|---|
| **Biggest Home Win:** | 10-1 v Lincoln City | 21/11/1891 |
| **Biggest Away Win:** | 6-1 v Lincoln City | 02/04/1892 |
| **Biggest Home Defeat:** | 1-3 v Birmingham St George | 14/03/1891 |
| **Biggest Away Defeats:** | 0-7 v Grimsby Town | 08/02/1890 |
| | 2-8 v Notts Forest | 22/11/1890 |
| **Highest Home Attendance:** | 16,000 v Nottingham Forest (1-1) | 01/01/1892 |
| **Most Appearances:** | 62    WS Stewart | |
| **Leading Goalscorer:** | 25    AH Farman | |
| **Most Goals in a Season:** | 20    R Donaldson | 1891/1892 |
| **Most Consecutive Wins:** | 5    31/10/1891 to 12/12/1891 | |
| **Most Consecutive Defeats:** | 5    07/03/1891 to 12/09/1891 | |
| **Longest Run Without a Win:** | 6    21/02/1891 to 12/09/1891 | |
| **Longest Unbeaten Run:** | 15    19/09/1891 to 20/02/1892 | |

*United's longest unbeaten run in the Alliance came immediately after their longest sequence of defeats and their longest run without a win!*

## *Football League*

| | | |
|---|---|---|
| **Biggest Home Win:** | 10-1 v Wolverhampton Wanderers | 15/10/1892 |
| **Biggest Away Win:** | 7-0 v Grimsby Town | 26/12/1899 |
| **Biggest Home Defeat:** | 1-7 v Newcastle United | 10/09/1927 |
| | 0-6 v Aston Villa | 14/03/1914 |
| | v Huddersfield Town | 10/09/1930* |

*\* In their next home match on 13th September 1930, United were beaten 7-4 by Newcastle United which made a total of thirteen goals conceded at home in a period of four days! They had also conceded six goals at Chelsea in their previous away game.*

| | | |
|---|---|---|
| **Biggest Away Defeat:** | 0-7 v Blackburn Rovers | 10/04/1926 |
| | v Aston Villa | 27/12/1930 |
| | v Wolverhampton Wanderers | 26/12/1931* |

*\* This was United's second consecutive Christmas 7-0 defeat.*

| | | |
|---|---|---|
| **Highest Home Attendance:** | 70,504 v Aston Villa (lost 1-3) | 27/12/1920 |
| | 83,260 v Arsenal (1-1)* | 17/01/1948 |

*\* This game was played at Maine Road and set a record Football League attendance which still stands today*

| | | |
|---|---|---|
| **Most Appearances:** | 604 plus 2 as substitute  R Charlton | |
| **Leading Goalscorer:** | 199    R Charlton | |
| **Most Goals in a Season:** | 32    D Viollet | 1959/1960 |
| **Most Goals in a Game:** | There have been numerous instances of players scoring 4 in a game but nobody has achieved five or more. | |
| **Most Consecutive Wins:** | 14    15/10/1904 to 03/01/1905 | |
| **Most Consecutive Defeats:** | 14    26/04/1930 to 25/10/1930 | |

*The 12 consecutive defeats United suffered in this spell from the beginning of the 1930/31 season is still a Football League record for the number of defeats from the opening of a season.*

| | | |
|---|---|---|
| **Longest Unbeaten Run:** | 26    04/02/1956 to 13/10/1956 | |
| **Longest Run Without a Win:** | 16    19/04/1930 to 25/10/1930 | |
| | 03/11/1928 to 09/02/1929 | |

## *FA Premiership*

| | | |
|---|---|---|
| **Biggest Home Win:** | 5-0 *v* Coventry City | 28/12/92 |
| | 5-0 *v* Sheffield Wednesday | 16/03/94 |
| **Biggest Home Defeat:** | 0-3 *v* Everton | 19/08/93 |
| **Biggest Away Win:** | 5-2 *v* Oldham Athletic | 29/12/93 |
| **Biggest Away Defeat:** | 0-2 *v* Blackburn Rovers | 02/04/94 |
| **Highest Home Attendance:** | 44,750 v Everton (1-0) 22/01/94 | |
| **Lowest Home Attendance:** | 29,736 v Crystal Palace | 02/09/92 |
| **Most Appearances:** | 83 –  S. Bruce, G. Pallister | |
| **Leading Goalscorer:** | 27 –  E. Cantona, M. Hughes | |
| **Most Goals in a Season:** | 18 –  E. Cantona   1993/94 | |
| **Most Consecutive Wins:** | 9    05/04/1993 to 18/08/1993 | |
| **Games Without Defeat:** | 22    19/09/1993 to 26/02/1994 | |

*Note:- In 38 league games between 14/03/1993 and 26/03/1994 United lost just once*

## *FA Cup*

| | | |
|---|---|---|
| **Biggest Home Win:** | 8-0 *v* Yeovil Town – 5th Round | 12/02/1949 |
| **Biggest Away Win:** | 8-2 *v* Northampton Town – 5th Round | 07/02/1970 |
| **Biggest Home Defeat:** | 2-7 *v* Sheffield Wednesday | 01/02/1961 |
| | 4th Rnd replay | |
| **Biggest Away Defeat:** | 1-7 *v* Burnley – 1st Rnd replay | 13/02/1901 |
| | 0-6 *v* Sheffield Wednesday (2nd Round) | 20/02/1904 |

| Highest Home Attendance: | 81,565 v Yeovil Town – 5th Round | |
|---|---|---|
| | (at Maine Road) | 12/02/1949 |
| | 66,350 v Sheffield Wed – 5th Round | |
| | (at Old Trafford) | 20/02/1960 |
| Most Appearances: | 79 R Charlton | |
| Leading Goalscorer: | 34 D Law | |
| Most Goals in a Game: | 6 G Best v Northampton Town | 07/02/1970 |
| Longest Unbeaten Run: | 13 10/01/1948 to 26/03/1949 | |
| Longest Run Without a Win: | 5 12/02/1898 to 28/10/1899 | |
| | 31/01/1920 to 13/01/1923 | |
| | 24/01/1931 to 17/01/1934 | |

*Between January 1929 and January 1935 United won just one FA Cup tie – a replay against Liverpool. From 18th February 1928 to 16th January 1937 United failed to win a single FA Cup tie at Old Trafford.*

## Football League Cup

| Biggest Home Win: | 7-2 v Newcastle United | 27/10/1976 |
|---|---|---|
| Biggest Away Win: | 6-2 v Arsenal | 28/11/1990 |
| Biggest Home Defeat: | 0-3 v Everton | 01/12/1976 |
| | v Tottenham Hotspur | 25/10/1989 |
| Biggest Away Defeat: | 1-5 v Blackpool | 14/09/1966 |

*United's team for this game was virtually full strength with nine internationals*

| Highest Home Attendance: | 63,418 v Manchester City (2-2) | 17/12/1969 |
|---|---|---|
| | Semi-Final | |
| Most Appearances: | 52 B Robson | |
| Leading Goalscorer: | 18 B McClair | |
| Most Goals in a Game: | 3 G Hill, M Hughes (twice), B McClair and | |
| | L Sharpe | |
| Longest Unbeaten Run: | 10 25/09/1991 to 28/10/1992 | |
| Longest Run Without a Win: | 5 26/09/1979 to 28/10/1981 | |

## European Champions' Cup

| Biggest Home Win: | 10-0 v Anderlecht (at Maine Road) | 26/09/1956 |
|---|---|---|
| Biggest Win at Old Trafford: | 7-1 v Waterford | 02/10/1968 |
| Biggest Away Win: | 6-0 v Shamrock Rovers | 25/09/1957 |
| Biggest Home Defeat: | None | |
| Biggest Away Defeat: | 0-4 v AC Milan | 14/05/1958 |

*This was the first away tie after the Munich Air Crash*

| **Highest Home Attendance:** | 65,000 v Real Madrid (2-2) | 25/04/1957 |
| | Semi-Final | |

*The crowd was equalled for the visit of Atletico Bilbao on 6/2/1957 but that game was played at Maine Road.*

| **Most Appearances:** | 35 | W Foulkes | |
| **Most Goals:** | 14 | D Law | |
| **Most Goals in a Game:** | 4 | D Viollet v Anderlecht | 26/09/56 |
| | | D Law v Waterford | 02/10/68 |

*Law scored 7 in total during this tie having netted a hat-trick in the First Leg.*

| **Most Consecutive Wins:** | 6 | 22/09/1965 to 09/03/1966 |
| **Longest Unbeaten Run:** | 6 | 22/09/1965 to 09/03/1966 |
| | | 20/04/1966 to 28/02/1968 |
| | | 24/04/1968 to 13/11/1969 |
| **Longest Run Without a Win:** | 2 | on numerous occasions |

## *European Cup-Winners' Cup*

---

| **Biggest Home Win:** | 6-1 v Willem II | 15/10/1963 |

*United set their record score in this competition in their first home game – as they had done in the European Cup.*

| **Biggest Away Win:** | 3-1 v Legia Warsaw | 10/04/1991 |
| **Biggest Home Defeat:** | None | |
| **Biggest Away Defeat:** | 0-5 v SC Lisbon | 18/03/1964 |

*This result overturned a 4-1 lead that United held from the First Leg.*

| **Biggest Home Attendance:** | 60,000 v SC Lisbon (won 4-1) | 26/02/1964 |
| **Most Appearances:** | 16 | M Hughes | |
| **Leading Goalscorer:** | 6 | D Law | |
| **Most Goals in a Game:** | 3 | D Law v Willem II | 15/10/1963 |
| | | D Law v SC Lisbon | 26/02/1964 |
| **Most Consecutive Wins:** | 4 | 19/09/1990 to 07/11/1990 |
| **Longest Unbeaten Run:** | 11 | 19/09/1990 to 02/10/1991 |
| **Longest Run Without a Win:** | 2 | several occasions |

## *Inter Cities Fairs / UEFA Cup*

---

| **Biggest Home Win:** | 6-1 v Djurgardens | 27/10/1964 |

*This completed United's unusual hat-trick of recording their biggest home win in each of the three major European tournaments in their first home game in each respective competition.*

| | | | |
|---|---|---|---|
| **Biggest Away Win:** | 6-1 *v* Borrussia Dortmund | 11/11/1964 |
| **Biggest Home Defeat:** | None | |
| **Biggest Away Defeat:** | 0-3 *v* Juventus | 03/11/1976 |
| **Highest Home Attendance:** | 59,000 *v* Juventus (won 1-0) | 20/10/1976 |
| **Most Appearances:** | 11 | R Charlton |
| **Leading Goalscorer:** | 8 | R Charlton |
| **Most Goals in a Game:** | 3 | D Law *v* Djurgardens | 27/10/1964 |
| | | R Charlton *v* Borrussia Dortmund | 11/11/1964 |
| **Most Consecutive Wins:** | 3 | 27/10/1964 to 02/12/1964 |
| **Most Consecutive Defeats:** | 2 | 06/06/1965 to 16/06/1965 |

*Both defeats were by Hungarian side, Ferencvaros who thus became the first and, to date, only team to defeat United in consecutive European matches. The second defeat came in a play-off after the first two matches had failed to produce a winner.*

**Longest Unbeaten Run:**   9   23/09/1964 to 31/05/1965

*These were United's first nine games in the competition.*

**Longest Run Without a Win:**  5   30/11/1976 to 29/09/1982

# Manchester United

**Nickname:** Red Devils    **Colours:** Red Sirts, White Shorts
**Change:** All Black or Yellow / Green Halves
**Capacity:** 44,622    **Pitch:** 116yds x 76yds

## Officials

| | |
|---|---|
| **Chairman/Chief Executive:** | Martin Edwards |
| **Directors:** | J.M.Edelson, R.Charlton, E.M.Watkins, |
| | A.M.Midani, L.Olive, R.P.Launders. |
| **Manager:** | Alex Ferguson |
| **Assistant Manager:** | Brian Kidd |
| **Physio:** | Jim McGregor |
| **Secretary:** | Ken Merrett |

## Honours

| | |
|---|---|
| **FA Premier League Champions:** | 1992-93, 1993-94 |
| **Division 1 Champions:** | 1907-8, 1910-11, 1951-52, 1955-56, |
| | 1956-57, 1964-65, 1966-67 |
| **Division 1 Runners-up:** | 1946-47, 1947-48, 1948-49, 1950-51, |
| | 1958-59, 1963-64, 1967-68, 1979-80, |
| | 1987-88, 1991-92 |
| **Division 2 Champions:** | 1935-36, 1974-75 |
| **Division 2 Runners-up:** | 1896-97, 1905-06, 1924-25, 1937-38. |
| **FA Cup Winners:** | 1909, 1948, 1963, 1977, 1983, 1985, 1990 |
| **FA Cup Runners-up:** | 1957, 1958, 1976, 1979 |
| **Football League Cup Winners:** | 1991-92 |
| **Football League Cup Runners-up:** | 1982-83, 1990-91, 1993-94 |

## European Honours

| | |
|---|---|
| **European Cup Winners:** | 1968 |
| **European Cup-Winners' Cup:** | 1991 |
| **European Super Cup Winners:** | 1991 |

## Miscellaneous Records

| | |
|---|---|
| **Record Attendance:** | 76,962 for FA Cup Semi-Final |
| | Wolves v Grimsby Town, 25th March 1939 |
| **Record League Attendance:** | 70,504 v Aston Villa, 27th December 1920 |

## League History

| | | | |
|---|---|---|---|
| 1892 | Elected to Division 1 | 1936-1937 | Division 1 |
| 1894-1906 | Division 2 | 1937-1938 | Division 2 |
| 1906-1922 | Division 1 | 1938-1974 | Division 1 |
| 1922-1925 | Division 2 | 1974-1975 | Division 2 |
| 1925-1931 | Division 1 | 1975-1992 | Division 1 |
| 1931-1936 | Division 2 | 1992 - | FA Premier League |

## Managers and Secretary-Managers

| | | | |
|---|---|---|---|
| 1900-12 | Ernest Magnall | 1944-45 | Walter Crickmer |
| 1914-21 | John Robson | 1945-69 | Matt Busby* |
| 1921-26 | John Chapman | 1969-70 | Wilf McGuinness |
| 1926-27 | Clarence Hildrith | 1971-72 | Frank O'Farrell |
| 1927-31 | Herbert Bamlett | 1972-77 | Tommy Docherty |
| 1931-32 | Walter Crickmer | 1977-81 | Dave Sexton |
| 1932-37 | Scott Duncan | 1981-86 | Ron Atkinson |
| 1938-44 | Jimmy Porter | 1986- | Alex Ferguson |

*continued as GM then Director

# Birth of the Red Devils

Came into being in 1902 changing name from Newton Heath. Predecessors appear to have been formed in 1878 as Newton Heath (LYR) when workers at the Carriage and Wagon Department at the Lancashire and Yorkshire Railway formed a club. This soon outgrew railway competition.

Turned professional in 1885 and founder member of Football Alliance in 1889. In 1892 Alliance runners-up Newton Heath was elected to an enlarged Division One of the Football League. In 1902 the club became Manchester United and, in February 1910, moved from Bank Street, Clayton, to Old Trafford. Premier League founder member 1992.

## Directions:

*From North:*
From the M63 Junction 4 follow the signs for Manchester (A5081). Turn right after 2½ miles into Warwick Road.

*From South:*
From the M6 Junction 19 follow the A556 then the A56 (Altrincham). From Altrincham follow the signs for Manchester turning left into Warwick Road after 6 miles.

*From East:*
From the M62 Junction 17 take the A56 to Manchester. Follow the signs South and then to Chester. Turn right into Warwick Road after 2 miles.

## Telephone Numbers

| | |
|---|---|
| Main Switchboard. | 061-872 1661 |
| Ticket and Match Information: | 061-872 0199 |
| Commercial Enquiries: | 061-872 3488 |
| Developement Association: | 061-872 4676 |
| Membership and Supporters Office: | 061-872 5208 |
| Club Call: | (0891) 121161 |
| Museum: | 061-877 4002 |
| Membership & Travel Info: | 061-873 8303 |
| Executive Suite: | 061-872 3331 |
| Superstore: | 061-872 3398 |

# Arsenal

## Arsenal Stadium, Highbury, London N5

**Nickname:** Gunners

**Colours:** Red/White sleeves, White, Red  **Change:** Yellow, Navy Blue, Yellow

**All-seater Capacity:** 39,497  **Pitch:** 110 yds x 71 yds

## Directions:

*From North:* M1, J2 follow sign for the City. After Holloway Road station (c 6 miles) take third left into Drayton Park. Then right into Aubert Park after ¾ mile and 2nd left into Avenell Road. *From South:* Signs for Bank of England then Angel from London Bridge. Right at traffic lights towards Highbury roundabout. Follow Holloway Road then third right into Drayton Park, thereafter as above. *From West:* A40(M) to A501 ring road. Left at Angel to Highbury roundabout, then as above. *Rail:* Drayton Park/Finsbury Park Tube (Piccadilly line): Arsenal

Telephone: 071-226 0304

# Aston Villa

### Villa Park, Trinity Rd, Birmingham, B6 6HE

**Nickname:** The Villains
**Colours:** Claret/Blue, White, Blue/Claret    **Change:** White, Black, White
**All-seater Capacity:** 40,908    **Pitch:** 115 yds x 75 yds

### Directions:

M6 J6, follow signs for Birminham NE. 3rd exit at roundabout then right into Ashton Hall Rd after ¹/₂ mile.
*Rail:* Witton

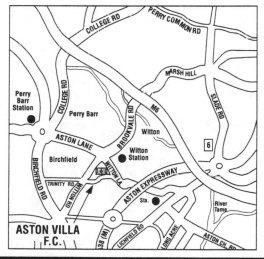

# Blackburn Rovers

Ewood Park, Blackburn, BB2 4JF

**Nickname:** Blue and Whites
**Colours:** Blue/White, White, Blue
**All-seater Capacity:** 30,591

**Change:** Black/Red, Black, Black/Red
**Pitch:** 115yds x 76yds

## Directions:

*From North, South & West:* M6 J31 follow signs for Blackburn then Bolton Road.
Turn left after 1½ miles into Kidder Street.
*From East:* A677 or A679 following signs for Bolton Road, then as above.
*Rail:* Blackburn Central

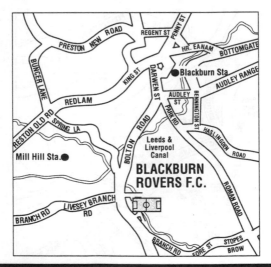

**Telephone: (0254) 55432**

# Chelsea

## Stamford Bridge, London SW6

**Nickname:** The Blues
**Colours:** Royal Blue, Royal Blue, White     **Change:** White/Red, Black, Black
**All-seater Capacity:** 41,050     **Pitch:** 110 yds x 72 yds

## Directions:

*From North & East:* A1 or M1 to central London and Hyde Park corner. Follow signs for Guildford (A3) and then Knightsbridge (A4). After a mile turn left into Fulham Road. *From South:* A219 Putney Bridge then follow signs for West End joining A308 and then into Fulham Road. *From West:* M4 then A4 to central London. Follow A3220 to Westminster, after ¼ mile right at crossroads into Fulham Road.

*Rail/Tube:* Fulham Broadway (District line).

Telephone: 071-385 5545

# Coventry City

Highfield Road Stadium, King Richard Street, Coventry, CV2 4FW

**Nickname:** Sky Blues
**Colours:** All Sky Blue **Change:** Yellow, Blue, Yellow
**All-seater Capacity:** 24,021 **Pitch:** 110 yds x 75 yds

## Directions:

*From North & West:* M6 J3, after 3¹/₂ miles turn left into Eagle Street and straight
on to Swan Lane. *From South & East:* M1 to M45 then A45 to Ryton-on-Dunsmore
where 3rd exit at roundabout is A423. After 1 mile turn right into B4110. Left at T-
junction then right into Swan Lane.
*Rail:* Coventry

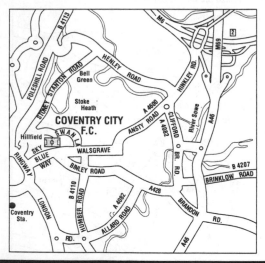

# Crystal Palace

Selhurst Park, London, SE25 6PU

**Nickname:** Eagles
**Colours:** Red/Blue, Red, Red
**All-seater Capacity:** 26,995

**Change:** Yellow, Light Blue, White
**Pitch:** 110 yds x 74 yds

## Directions:

*From North:* M1 or A1 to A406 for Chiswick, then A205 to Wandsworth. A3 and then A214 for Streatham and then A23 to B273 for Whitehorse Lane.
*From South:* A23 and then B266. Turn right into High Street and then as above.
*From East:* A232 and then A215 to B266 for High Street and then as above.
*From West:* M4 to Chiswick and then as for the North.
*Rail:* Norwood Junction, Thornton Heath or Selhurst.

**Telephone: 081-653 4462**

201

# Everton

## Goodison Park, Liverpool, L4 4EL

**Nickname:** The Toffees
**Colours:** Royal Blue, White, Blue   **Change:** Salmon/Dark Blue, Salmon, Salmon
**All-seater Capacity:** 40,160   **Pitch:** 112 yds x 78 yds

### Directions:

*From North:* M6 J8 take A58 to A580 and follow into Walton Hall Avenue.
*From South & East:* M6 J21A to M62, turn right into Queen's Drive then, after 4 miles, left into Walton Hall Avenue.
*From West:* M53 through Wallasey Tunnel, follow signs for Preston on A580. Walton Hall Avenue is signposted.
*Rail:* Liverpool Lime Street

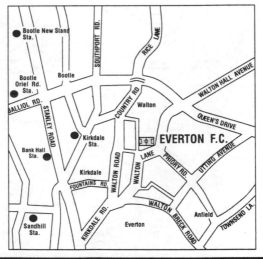

# Ipswich Town

Portman Road, Ipswich, Suffolk, IP1 2DA

**Nickname:** Blues or Town
**Colours:** Blue/White, White, Blue   **Change:** Red/Black, Black, Red/Black
**All-seater Capacity:** 22,823   **Pitch:** 112 yds x 70 yds

## Directions:

Follow A45 and signs for Ipswich West. Through Post House traffic lights and turn
right at second roundabout into West End Road. Ground is situated on the left.
*Rail:* Ipswich

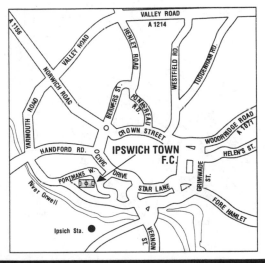

**Telephone: (0473) 219211**

# Leeds United

## Elland Road, Leeds, LS11 0ES

**Nickname:** United

**Colours:** All White      **Change:** All Yellow

**All-seater Capacity:** 39,176      **Pitch:** 117 yds x 76 yds

### Directions:

*From North & East:* A58, A61, A63 or A64 into city centre and then onto M621.
Leave Motorway after 1½ miles onto A643 and Elland Road.

*From West:* take M62 to M621 then as above.

*From South:* M1 then M621 then as above

*Rail:* Leeds City

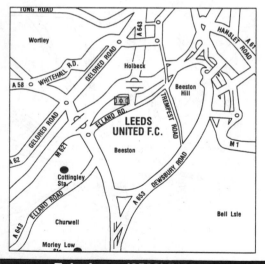

# Leicester City

City Stadium, Filbert Street, Leicester, LE2 7FL

**Nickname:** The Filberts or Foxes
**Colours:** Blue, White, Blue    **Change:** Red, Black, Black
**All-seater Capacity:** 27,722    **Pitch:** 112 yds x 75 yds

## Directions:

*From North:* Leave M1 at J22 or take A46, A607 to town centre. Towards Rugby via Almond Road, Sylestone Road and left into Walnut Street and Filbert Street.
*From South:* M1 or M69 and then A46 to Upperton Road and Filbert Street.
*From East:* A47 into town contre, right along Oxford Street to Aylestone Road and then as North. *From West:* M69 and A50 toAylestone Road and then as North.
*Rail:* Leicester

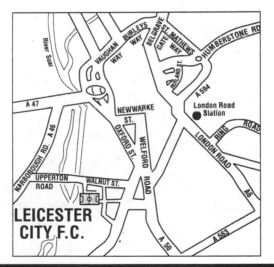

Telephone: (0533) 555000

205

# Liverpool

Anfield Road, Liverpool 4 0TH

**Nickname:** Reds or Pool
**Colours:** All Red/White Trim          **Change:** Racing Green/White Trim
**All-seater Capacity:** 44,243          **Pitch:** 110 yds x 75 yds

## Directions:

*From North:* M6 J8, follow A58 to Walton Hall Avenue and pass Stanley Park turning left into Anfield Road. *From South/East:* To end of M62 and right into Queens Drive (A5058). After 3 miles turn left into Utting Avenue and right after 1 mile into Anfield Road. *From West:* M53 through Wallasey Tunnel, follow signs for Preston then turn into Walton Hall Avenue and right into Anfield Road before Stanley Park. *Rail:* Liverpool Lime Street

**Telephone: 051-263 2361**

# Manchester City

**Maine Road, Moss Side, Manchester, M14 7WN**

**Nickname:** Blues or City
**Colours:** Sky Blue, White, Sky Blue  **Change:** Purple/Candystripe, Purple, Purple
**All-seater Capacity:** 45,053          **Pitch:** 117 yds x 77 yds

## Directions:

*From North & West:* M61 to M63 J9. Follow signs into Manchester (A5103). Right
after 3 miles into Claremont Road. Right after 400 yards into Maine Road.
*From South:* M6 J19 to A556 joining M56. Leave at J3 following A5103 as above.
*From East:* M62 J17 following signs for Manchester Airport (A56 and A57(M)).
Then follow Birmingham signs to A5103. Left into Claremont Road after 1 mile
then right into Maine Road. *Rail:* Manchester Piccadilly

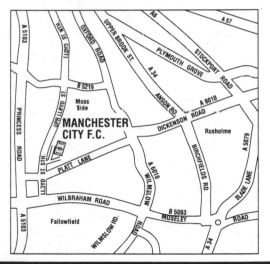

**Telephone: 061-226 1191/2**

207

# Newcastle United

St James' Park, Newcastle-upon-Tyne, NE1 4ST

**Nickname:** Magpies
**Colours:** Black/White, Black, Black    **Change:** All Blue
**All-seater Capacity:** 36,401    **Pitch:** 115 yds x 75 yds.

## Directions:

*From South:* Follow A1, A68 then A6127 to cross the Tyne. At roundabout, first exit into Moseley Street. Left into Neville Street, right at end for Clayton Street and then Newgate Street. Left for Leaze Park Road. *From West:* A69 towards city centre. Left into Clayton Street for Newgate Street, left again for Leaze Park Road. *From North:* A1 then follow signs for Hexham until Percy Street. Right into Leaze Park Road. *Rail:* Newcastle Central (½ mile).

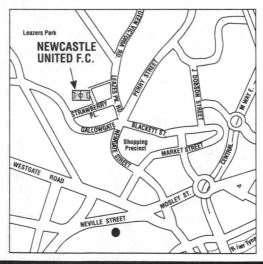

Telephone: 091-232 8361

208

# Norwich City

Carrow Road, Norwich, NR1 1JE

**Nickname:** The Canaries
**Colours:** Yellow, Green, Yellow
**All-seater Capacity:** 25,000

**Change:** All White
**Pitch:** 114yds x 74 yds

## Directions:

*From North:* A140 to ring road and follow signs for Yarmouth A47. Turn right at T junction after 3½ miles then left after ½ mile into Carrow Road.

*From South & West:* A11/A140 onto ring road. Follow signs for Yarmouth A47 etc as for North above.

*From East:* A47 into Norwich then left onto ring road.

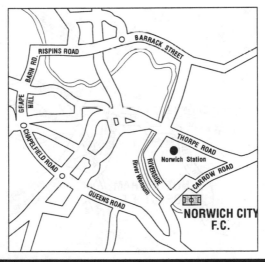

**Telephone: (0603) 612131**

209

# Nottingham Forest

City Ground, Nottingham, NG2 5FJ

**Nickname:** The Reds or Forest
**Colours:** Red, White, Red
**All-seater Capacity:** 30,500

**Change:** White, Black, White
**Pitch:** 115 yds x 78 yds

## Directions:

*From North:* Leave the M1 J26 for the A610 and the A606. Left into Radcliffe Road for the ground. *From South:* Leave the M1 J24 to Trent Bridge, turning right into Radcliffe Road. *From East:* A52 to West Bridgeford and right for the ground. *From West:* A52 to A606 and then as for the North.
*Rail:* Nottingham.

**Telephone: (0602) 822202**

# Queens Park Rangers

South Africa Road, W12 7PA

**Nickname:** Rangers or R's
**Colours:** Blue/White, White, White
**All-seater Capacity:** 19,300

**Change:** Red/Black, Black, Black
**Pitch:** 112 yds x 72 yds

## Directions:

*From North:* M1 to north circular A406 towards Neasden. Left onto A404 for Hammersmith, past White City Stadium then right into South Africa Road. *From South:* A3 across Putney Bridge and signs for Hammersmith. A219 to Shepherds Bush and join A4020 towards Acton. Turn right after ¼ mile into Loftus Road. *From East:* From A40(M) towards M41 roundabout. Take 3rd exit at roundabout to A4020 then as above. *From West:* M4 to Chiswick then A315 and A402 to Shepherd's Bush joining A4020 then as for South. *Rail:* Shepherds Bush *Tube:* White City (Central Line)

# Sheffield Wednesday

Hillsborough, Sheffield, S6 1SW

**Nickname:** The Owls

**Colours:** Blue/White, Blue, Blue    **Change:** All Black with Yellow/Grey trim

**All-seater Capacity:** 40,000    **Pitch:** 115 yds x 75 yds

## Directions:

*From North:* M1 J34 then A6109 to Sheffield. At roundabout after 1½ miles take 3rd exit then turn left after 3 miles into Herries Road.

*From South & East:* M1 J31 or 33 to A57. At roundabout take Prince of Wales Road exit. A further 6 miles then turn left into Herries Road South.

*From West:* A57 to A6101 then turn left after 4 miles at T junction into Penistone Road.

*Rail:* Sheffield Midland

# Southampton

The Dell, Milton Road, Southampton, SO9 4XX

**Nickname:** The Saints
**Colours:** Red/White, Black, Black  **Change:** Turquoise/Blue, Turquoise, Blue
**All-seater Capacity:** 15,288  **Pitch:** 110 yds x 72 yds

## Directions:

*From North:* A33 into The Avenue then right into Northlands Road. Right at the end into Archer's Road. *From East:* M27 then A334 and signs for Southampton along A3024. Follow signs for the West into Commercial Road, right into Hill Lane then first right into Milton Road.

*From West:* Take A35 then A3024 towards city centre. Left into Hill Lane and first right into Milton Road.

*Rail:* Southampton Central

Telephone: (0703) 220505

# Tottenham Hotspur

## 748 High Road, Tottenham, London, N17 0AP

**Nickname:** Spurs
**Colours:** White, Navy Blue, White
**All-seater Capacity:** 30,246

**Change:** All Yellow or all Sky Blue
**Pitch:** 110 yds x 73 yds

### Directions:

A406 North Circular to Edmonton. At traffic lights follow signs for Tottenham
along A1010 then Fore Street for ground.
*Rail:* White Hart Lane (adjacent)
*Tube:* Seven Sisters (Victoria Line) or Manor House (Piccadilly Line).

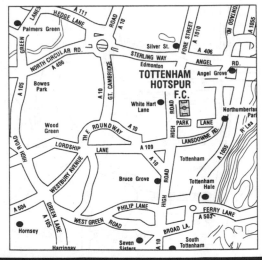

Telephone: 081-808 6666

# West Ham United

Boleyn Ground, Green Street, Upton Park, London E13

**Nickname:** The Hammers

**Colours:** Claret, White, White

**All-seater Capacity:** 24,500

**Change:** All Blue

**Pitch:** 112 yds x 72 yds

## Directions:

*From North & West:* North Circular to East Ham then Barking Rd for 1½ miles until traffic lights. Turn right into Green Street.

*From South:* Blackwall Tunnel then A13 to Canning Town. Then A124 to East Ham, Green Street on left after 2 miles.

*From East:* A13 then A117 and A124. Green Street on right after ¾ miles.

*Rail/Tube:* Upton Park (¼ mile)

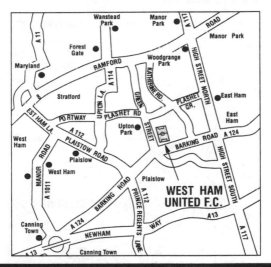

Telephone: 081-472 2740

# Wimbledon

Selhurst Park, South Norwood, London E5

**Nickname:** The Dons

**Colours:** All Blue with Yellow trim        **Change:** All Red

**All-seater Capacity:** 26,995        **Pitch:** 110 yds x 74 yds

## Directions:

*From North:* M1/A1 to North Circular A406 and Chiswick. Follow South Circular A205 to Wandsworth then A3 and A214 towards Streatham and A23. Then left onto B273 for 1 mile and turn left at end into High Street and Whitehorse Lane.
*From South:* On A23 follow signs for Crystal Palace along B266 going through Thornton Heath into Whitehorse Lane. *From East:* A232 Croydon Road to Shirley joining A215, Norwood Road. Turn left after 2½ miles into Whitehorse Lane.
*From West:* M4 to Chiswick then as above.
*Rail:* Selhurst, Norwood Junction or Thornton Heath.

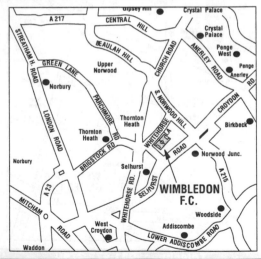

**Telephone: 081-771 2233**

# All-time Records and Statistics

## United Against Other Clubs – *Football Alliance*

| Club | Home | | | | | Away | | | | |
|---|---|---|---|---|---|---|---|---|---|---|
| | P | W | D | L | F | A | W | D | L | F | A |
| Ardwick | 2 | 1 | 0 | 0 | 3 | 1 | 0 | 1 | 0 | 2 | 2 |
| Birmingham St George | 6 | 2 | 0 | 1 | 6 | 4 | 1 | 0 | 2 | 5 | 12 |
| Bootle | 6 | 3 | 0 | 0 | 9 | 1 | 0 | 1 | 2 | 2 | 10 |
| Burton Swifts | 2 | 1 | 0 | 0 | 3 | 1 | 0 | 0 | 1 | 2 | 3 |
| Crewe Alexandra | 6 | 2 | 0 | 1 | 12 | 8 | 2 | 1 | 0 | 5 | 2 |
| Darwen | 4 | 2 | 0 | 0 | 6 | 3 | 0 | 0 | 2 | 2 | 6 |
| Grimsby Town | 6 | 1 | 1 | 1 | 6 | 5 | 0 | 1 | 2 | 3 | 12 |
| Lincoln City | 2 | 1 | 0 | 0 | 10 | 1 | 1 | 0 | 0 | 6 | 1 |
| Long Eaton | 2 | 1 | 0 | 0 | 3 | 0 | 1 | 0 | 0 | 3 | 1 |
| Nottingham Forest | 6 | 0 | 2 | 1 | 2 | 3 | 1 | 0 | 2 | 5 | 12 |
| Sheffield Wednesday | 6 | 0 | 2 | 1 | 3 | 4 | 2 | 0 | 1 | 7 | 6 |
| Small Heath | 6 | 2 | 1 | 0 | 15 | 5 | 0 | 1 | 2 | 4 | 6 |
| Stoke City | 2 | 1 | 0 | 0 | 0 | 1 | 0 | 0 | 1 | 1 | 2 |
| Sunderland Albion | 4 | 1 | 0 | 1 | 5 | 6 | 0 | 0 | 2 | 1 | 4 |
| Walsall Town Swifts | 6 | 2 | 1 | 0 | 10 | 4 | 1 | 0 | 2 | 5 | 7 |
| Total | 66 | 20 | 7 | 6 | 93 | 47 | 9 | 5 | 19 | 53 | 86 |

## United Against Other Clubs – *Football League*

Manchester United met 78 other clubs during their time in the Football League. The following list gives their record against each of those 78 clubs. Where clubs have changed their names, the latest name only is used but the list includes all games against that club under either name (ie Small Heath became Birmingham City, therefore the record shown below in respect of Birmingham City also includes games against Small Heath).

| Club | Home | | | | | | Away | | | | |
|---|---|---|---|---|---|---|---|---|---|---|---|
| | P | W | D | L | F | A | W | D | L | F | A |
| Accrington Stanley | 2 | 0 | 1 | 0 | 3 | 3 | 0 | 1 | 0 | 2 | 2 |
| Arsenal | 146 | 41 | 20 | 12 | 143 | 70 | 18 | 11 | 44 | 84 | 151 |
| Aston Villa | 118 | 37 | 12 | 10 | 127 | 59 | 14 | 15 | 30 | 88 | 128 |
| Barnsley | 30 | 12 | 2 | 1 | 35 | 7 | 5 | 7 | 3 | 20 | 14 |
| Birmingham City | 80 | 23 | 8 | 9 | 60 | 34 | 10 | 15 | 15 | 53 | 62 |
| Blackburn Rovers | 62 | 15 | 8 | 8 | 61 | 38 | 10 | 7 | 14 | 55 | 66 |
| Blackpool | 80 | 26 | 8 | 6 | 83 | 34 | 17 | 9 | 14 | 66 | 60 |
| Bolton Wanderers | 92 | 23 | 9 | 14 | 78 | 53 | 11 | 11 | 24 | 52 | 88 |

| Club | Home | | | | | | Away | | | | |
|---|---|---|---|---|---|---|---|---|---|---|---|
| | P | W | D | L | F | A | W | D | L | F | A |
| Bradford Park Avenue | 18 | 5 | 0 | 4 | 17 | 12 | 3 | 1 | 5 | 13 | 24 |
| Bradford City | 42 | 13 | 6 | 2 | 35 | 9 | 5 | 7 | 9 | 26 | 28 |
| Brentford | 10 | 2 | 1 | 2 | 9 | 7 | 2 | 1 | 2 | 10 | 12 |
| Brighton & Hove Alb | 8 | 3 | 1 | 0 | 7 | 2 | 2 | 1 | 1 | 5 | 2 |
| Bristol City | 34 | 9 | 3 | 5 | 30 | 18 | 5 | 7 | 5 | 17 | 21 |
| Bristol Rovers | 2 | 1 | 0 | 0 | 2 | 0 | 0 | 1 | 0 | 1 | 1 |
| Burnley | 102 | 30 | 8 | 13 | 116 | 66 | 17 | 8 | 26 | 64 | 91 |
| Burton United | 24 | 9 | 3 | 0 | 39 | 6 | 5 | 3 | 4 | 22 | 23 |
| Burton Wanderers | 6 | 1 | 1 | 1 | 5 | 3 | 1 | 0 | 2 | 3 | 7 |
| Bury | 38 | 9 | 2 | 8 | 24 | 23 | 10 | 5 | 4 | 34 | 23 |
| Cardiff City | 26 | 5 | 6 | 2 | 28 | 19 | 8 | 1 | 4 | 22 | 18 |
| Charlton Athletic | 41 | 13 | 4 | 3 | 45 | 20 | 8 | 5 | 8 | 27 | 33 |
| Chelsea | 101 | 21 | 16 | 13 | 81 | 47 | 25 | 12 | 14 | 97 | 75 |
| Chesterfield | 20 | 10 | 0 | 0 | 26 | 7 | 3 | 1 | 6 | 15 | 15 |
| Coventry City | 56 | 15 | 7 | 6 | 49 | 21 | 8 | 12 | 34 | 37 | |
| Crewe Alexandra | 4 | 2 | 0 | 0 | 11 | 1 | 2 | 0 | 0 | 4 | 0 |
| Crystal Palace | 24 | 8 | 2 | 2 | 22 | 7 | 5 | 3 | 4 | 21 | 22 |
| Darwen | 12 | 4 | 1 | 1 | 20 | 5 | 2 | 2 | 2 | 7 | 8 |
| Derby County | 76 | 19 | 10 | 9 | 70 | 39 | 9 | 13 | 16 | 58 | 84 |
| Doncaster Rovers | 8 | 3 | 1 | 0 | 16 | 0 | 1 | 2 | 1 | 3 | 6 |
| Everton | 126 | 32 | 17 | 14 | 107 | 64 | 12 | 16 | 35 | 71 | 140 |
| Fulham | 42 | 17 | 3 | 1 | 44 | 15 | 6 | 7 | 8 | 34 | 32 |
| Gainsborough Trinity | 20 | 8 | 2 | 0 | 26 | 7 | 5 | 3 | 2 | 10 | 7 |
| Glossop North End | 14 | 6 | 1 | 0 | 20 | 5 | 5 | 1 | 1 | 14 | 5 |
| Grimsby Town | 37 | 13 | 2 | 4 | 42 | 26 | 4 | 4 | 10 | 26 | 37 |
| Huddersfield Town | 42 | 11 | 9 | 1 | 46 | 21 | 7 | 6 | 8 | 32 | 39 |
| Hull City | 16 | 7 | 1 | 0 | 22 | 4 | 2 | 2 | 4 | 8 | 13 |
| Ipswich Town | 40 | 13 | 2 | 5 | 31 | 13 | 6 | 4 | 10 | 26 | 40 |
| Leeds City | 2 | 0 | 0 | 1 | 0 | 3 | 1 | 0 | 0 | 3 | 1 |
| Leeds United | 68 | 13 | 13 | 8 | 51 | 32 | 11 | 12 | 11 | 41 | 40 |
| Leicester City | 96 | 32 | 11 | 5 | 115 | 51 | 12 | 11 | 25 | 72 | 90 |
| Leyton Orient | 12 | 3 | 3 | 0 | 13 | 5 | 3 | 1 | 2 | 5 | 3 |
| Lincoln City | 28 | 10 | 3 | 1 | 34 | 12 | 3 | 1 | 10 | 12 | 28 |
| Liverpool | 118 | 27 | 21 | 11 | 100 | 55 | 13 | 16 | 30 | 62 | 103 |
| Loughborough Town | 10 | 5 | 0 | 0 | 23 | 2 | 2 | 2 | 1 | 6 | 5 |
| Luton Town | 38 | 18 | 0 | 1 | 58 | 10 | 9 | 7 | 3 | 30 | 16 |
| Manchester City | 116 | 23 | 21 | 14 | 87 | 74 | 18 | 22 | 18 | 75 | 86 |
| Middlesbrough | 74 | 23 | 6 | 8 | 77 | 47 | 12 | 9 | 16 | 56 | 73 |
| Millwall | 12 | 5 | 1 | 0 | 22 | 3 | 3 | 2 | 1 | 6 | 4 |
| Nelson | 2 | 0 | 0 | 1 | 0 | 1 | 1 | 0 | 0 | 2 | 0 |
| New Brighton Town | 6 | 2 | 0 | 1 | 4 | 3 | 2 | 0 | 1 | 7 | 3 |

| Club | | Home | | | | | | Away | | | |
|---|---|---|---|---|---|---|---|---|---|---|---|
| | P | W | D | L | F | A | W | D | L | F | A |
| Newcastle United | 110 | 33 | 13 | 9 | 125 | 67 | 17 | 12 | 26 | 78 | 111 |
| Northampton Town | 2 | 1 | 0 | 0 | 6 | 2 | 0 | 1 | 0 | 1 | 1 |
| Norwich City | 42 | 13 | 5 | 3 | 34 | 10 | 9 | 6 | 6 | 37 | 28 |
| Nottingham Forest | 86 | 24 | 11 | 8 | 90 | 54 | 13 | 10 | 20 | 55 | 68 |
| Notts County | 48 | 11 | 9 | 4 | 41 | 27 | 9 | 5 | 10 | 33 | 33 |
| Oldham Athletic | 32 | 9 | 3 | 4 | 32 | 17 | 5 | 6 | 5 | 31 | 23 |
| Oxford United | 8 | 4 | 0 | 0 | 13 | 3 | 2 | 0 | 2 | 5 | 4 |
| Plymouth Argyle | 12 | 4 | 1 | 1 | 12 | 7 | 2 | 1 | 3 | 8 | 13 |
| Port Vale | 36 | 16 | 1 | 1 | 52 | 10 | 5 | 4 | 9 | 24 | 27 |
| Portsmouth | 44 | 13 | 3 | 6 | 38 | 21 | 5 | 9 | 8 | 23 | 30 |
| Preston North End | 66 | 15 | 11 | 7 | 51 | 35 | 11 | 9 | 13 | 56 | 55 |
| Queen's Park Rangers | 30 | 12 | 2 | 1 | 33 | 11 | 4 | 6 | 5 | 18 | 22 |
| Rotherham United | 6 | 3 | 0 | 0 | 9 | 2 | 1 | 1 | 1 | 5 | 5 |
| Sheffield United | 82 | 26 | 4 | 11 | 83 | 47 | 11 | 9 | 21 | 49 | 74 |
| Sheffield Wednesday | 96 | 30 | 12 | 6 | 91 | 46 | 11 | 9 | 28 | 62 | 89 |
| Southshields | 6 | 2 | 1 | 0 | 5 | 1 | 2 | 0 | 1 | 5 | 2 |
| Southampton | 64 | 18 | 7 | 7 | 56 | 35 | 9 | 12 | 11 | 38 | 37 |
| Stockport County | 18 | 7 | 2 | 0 | 21 | 7 | 2 | 0 | 7 | 8 | 11 |
| Stoke City | 70 | 17 | 13 | 5 | 63 | 29 | 9 | 11 | 15 | 40 | 60 |
| Sunderland | 96 | 25 | 12 | 11 | 96 | 60 | 12 | 11 | 25 | 61 | 104 |
| Swansea City | 16 | 6 | 2 | 0 | 18 | 6 | 0 | 2 | 6 | 6 | 14 |
| Tottenham Hotspurs | 110 | 34 | 11 | 10 | 104 | 58 | 13 | 20 | 22 | 67 | 99 |
| Walsall | 12 | 5 | 1 | 0 | 24 | 1 | 2 | 3 | 1 | 7 | 7 |
| Watford | 12 | 4 | 2 | 0 | 13 | 4 | 2 | 2 | 2 | 4 | 7 |
| West Bromwich Alb | 100 | 26 | 13 | 11 | 102 | 65 | 13 | 11 | 26 | 72 | 98 |
| West Ham United | 80 | 24 | 6 | 10 | 91 | 48 | 7 | 10 | 23 | 49 | 70 |
| Wimbledon | 12 | 3 | 2 | 1 | 5 | 3 | 2 | 2 | 2 | 9 | 8 |
| Wolverhampton Wndrs | 80 | 26 | 5 | 9 | 80 | 44 | 10 | 9 | 21 | 55 | 81 |
| York City | 2 | 1 | 0 | 0 | 2 | 1 | 1 | 0 | 0 | 1 | 0 |
| Total | 3556 | 1036 | 410 | 332 | 3550 | 1784 | 532 | 462 | 784 | 2406 | 3057 |

# United's Full League Record

| Year | | | | Home | | | | | Away | | | | |
|------|---|---|---|---|---|---|---|---|---|---|---|---|---|
| | P | W | D | L | F | A | W | D | L | F | A | Pts | Pos |
| *Football Alliance* | | | | | | | | | | | | | |
| 1889/90 | 22 | 7 | 0 | 4 | 27 | 11 | 2 | 2 | 7 | 13 | 34 | 20 | 8th |
| 1890/91 | 22 | 5 | 3 | 3 | 25 | 22 | 2 | 0 | 9 | 12 | 31 | 17 | 9th |
| 1891/92 | 22 | 7 | 4 | 0 | 41 | 14 | 5 | 3 | 3 | 28 | 19 | 31 | 2nd |
| *Football League – First Division* | | | | | | | | | | | | | |
| 1892/93 | 30 | 6 | 3 | 6 | 39 | 35 | 0 | 3 | 12 | 11 | 50 | 18 | 16th |
| 1893/94 | 30 | 5 | 2 | 8 | 29 | 33 | 1 | 0 | 14 | 7 | 39 | 14 | 16th |
| *Second Division* | | | | | | | | | | | | | |
| 1894/95 | 30 | 9 | 6 | 0 | 52 | 18 | 6 | 2 | 7 | 26 | 26 | 38 | 3rd |
| 1895/96 | 30 | 12 | 2 | 1 | 48 | 15 | 3 | 1 | 11 | 18 | 42 | 33 | 6th |
| 1896/97 | 30 | 11 | 4 | 0 | 37 | 10 | 6 | 1 | 8 | 19 | 24 | 39 | 2nd |
| 1897/98 | 30 | 11 | 2 | 2 | 42 | 10 | 5 | 4 | 6 | 22 | 25 | 38 | 4th |
| 1898/99 | 34 | 12 | 4 | 1 | 51 | 14 | 7 | 1 | 9 | 16 | 29 | 43 | 4th |
| 1899/1900 | 34 | 15 | 1 | 1 | 44 | 11 | 5 | 3 | 9 | 19 | 16 | 44 | 4th |
| 1900/01 | 34 | 11 | 3 | 3 | 31 | 9 | 3 | 1 | 13 | 11 | 29 | 32 | 10th |
| 1901/02 | 34 | 10 | 2 | 5 | 27 | 12 | 1 | 4 | 12 | 11 | 41 | 28 | 15th |
| 1902/03 | 34 | 9 | 4 | 4 | 32 | 15 | 6 | 4 | 7 | 21 | 23 | 38 | 5th |
| 1903/04 | 34 | 14 | 2 | 1 | 42 | 14 | 6 | 6 | 5 | 23 | 19 | 48 | 3rd |
| 1904/05 | 34 | 16 | 0 | 1 | 60 | 10 | 8 | 5 | 4 | 21 | 20 | 53 | 3rd |
| 1905/06 | 38 | 15 | 3 | 1 | 55 | 13 | 13 | 3 | 3 | 35 | 15 | 62 | 2nd |
| *First Division* | | | | | | | | | | | | | |
| 1906/07 | 38 | 10 | 6 | 3 | 33 | 15 | 7 | 2 | 10 | 20 | 41 | 42 | 8th |
| 1907/08 | 38 | 15 | 1 | 3 | 43 | 19 | 8 | 5 | 6 | 38 | 29 | 52 | 1st |
| 1908/09 | 38 | 10 | 3 | 6 | 37 | 33 | 5 | 4 | 10 | 21 | 35 | 37 | 13th |
| 1909/10 | 38 | 14 | 2 | 3 | 41 | 20 | 5 | 5 | 9 | 28 | 41 | 45 | 5th |
| 1910/11 | 38 | 14 | 4 | 1 | 47 | 18 | 8 | 4 | 7 | 25 | 22 | 52 | 1st |
| 1911/12 | 38 | 9 | 5 | 5 | 29 | 19 | 4 | 6 | 9 | 16 | 41 | 37 | 13th |
| 1912/13 | 38 | 13 | 3 | 3 | 41 | 14 | 6 | 5 | 8 | 28 | 29 | 46 | 4th |
| 1913/14 | 38 | 8 | 4 | 7 | 27 | 23 | 7 | 2 | 10 | 25 | 39 | 36 | 14th |
| 1914/15 | 38 | 8 | 6 | 5 | 27 | 19 | 1 | 6 | 12 | 19 | 43 | 30 | 18th |
| 1919/20 | 42 | 6 | 8 | 7 | 20 | 17 | 7 | 6 | 8 | 34 | 33 | 40 | 12th |
| 1920/21 | 42 | 9 | 4 | 8 | 34 | 26 | 6 | 6 | 9 | 30 | 42 | 40 | 13th |
| 1921/22 | 42 | 7 | 7 | 7 | 25 | 26 | 1 | 5 | 15 | 16 | 47 | 28 | 22nd |
| *Second Division* | | | | | | | | | | | | | |
| 1922/23 | 42 | 10 | 6 | 5 | 25 | 17 | 7 | 8 | 6 | 26 | 19 | 48 | 4th |
| 1923/24 | 42 | 10 | 7 | 4 | 37 | 15 | 3 | 7 | 11 | 15 | 29 | 40 | 14th |
| 1924/25 | 42 | 17 | 3 | 1 | 40 | 6 | 6 | 8 | 7 | 17 | 17 | 57 | 2nd |

| Year | P | W | D | L | F | A | W | D | L | F | A | Pts | Pos |
|------|---|---|---|---|---|---|---|---|---|---|---|-----|-----|
| | | | | Home | | | | | | Away | | | |

| Year | P | W | D | L | F | A | W | D | L | F | A | Pts | Pos |
|------|---|---|---|---|---|---|---|---|---|---|---|-----|-----|
| **First Division** | | | | | | | | | | | | | |
| 1925/26 | 42 | 12 | 4 | 5 | 40 | 26 | 7 | 2 | 12 | 26 | 47 | 44 | 9th |
| 1926/27 | 42 | 9 | 8 | 4 | 29 | 19 | 4 | 6 | 11 | 23 | 45 | 40 | 15th |
| 1927/28 | 42 | 12 | 6 | 3 | 51 | 27 | 4 | 1 | 16 | 21 | 53 | 39 | 18th |
| 1928/29 | 42 | 8 | 8 | 5 | 32 | 23 | 6 | 5 | 10 | 34 | 53 | 41 | 12th |
| 1929/30 | 42 | 11 | 4 | 6 | 39 | 34 | 4 | 4 | 13 | 28 | 54 | 38 | 17th |
| 1930/31 | 42 | 6 | 6 | 9 | 30 | 37 | 1 | 2 | 18 | 23 | 78 | 22 | 22nd |
| **Second Division** | | | | | | | | | | | | | |
| 1931/32 | 42 | 12 | 3 | 6 | 44 | 31 | 5 | 5 | 11 | 27 | 41 | 42 | 12th |
| 1932/33 | 42 | 11 | 5 | 5 | 40 | 24 | 4 | 8 | 9 | 31 | 44 | 43 | 6th |
| 1933/34 | 42 | 9 | 3 | 9 | 29 | 33 | 5 | 3 | 13 | 30 | 52 | 34 | 20th |
| 1934/35 | 42 | 16 | 2 | 3 | 50 | 21 | 7 | 2 | 12 | 26 | 34 | 50 | 5th |
| 1935/36 | 42 | 16 | 3 | 2 | 55 | 16 | 6 | 9 | 6 | 30 | 27 | 56 | 1st |
| **First Division** | | | | | | | | | | | | | |
| 1936/37 | 42 | 8 | 9 | 4 | 29 | 26 | 2 | 3 | 16 | 26 | 52 | 32 | 21st |
| **Second Division** | | | | | | | | | | | | | |
| 1937/38 | 42 | 15 | 3 | 3 | 50 | 18 | 7 | 6 | 8 | 32 | 32 | 53 | 2nd |
| **First Division** | | | | | | | | | | | | | |
| 1938/39 | 42 | 7 | 9 | 5 | 30 | 20 | 4 | 7 | 10 | 27 | 45 | 38 | 14th |
| 1946/47 | 42 | 17 | 3 | 1 | 61 | 19 | 5 | 9 | 7 | 34 | 35 | 56 | 2nd |
| 1947/48 | 42 | 11 | 7 | 3 | 50 | 27 | 8 | 7 | 6 | 31 | 21 | 52 | 2nd |
| 1948/49 | 42 | 11 | 7 | 3 | 40 | 20 | 10 | 4 | 7 | 37 | 24 | 53 | 2nd |
| 1949/50 | 42 | 11 | 5 | 5 | 42 | 20 | 7 | 9 | 5 | 27 | 24 | 50 | 4th |
| 1950/51 | 42 | 14 | 4 | 3 | 42 | 16 | 10 | 4 | 7 | 32 | 24 | 56 | 2nd |
| 1951/52 | 42 | 15 | 3 | 3 | 55 | 21 | 8 | 8 | 5 | 40 | 31 | 57 | 1st |
| 1952/53 | 42 | 11 | 5 | 5 | 35 | 30 | 7 | 5 | 9 | 34 | 42 | 46 | 8th |
| 1953/54 | 42 | 11 | 6 | 4 | 41 | 27 | 7 | 6 | 8 | 32 | 31 | 48 | 4th |
| 1954/55 | 42 | 12 | 4 | 5 | 44 | 30 | 8 | 3 | 10 | 40 | 44 | 47 | 5th |
| 1955/56 | 42 | 18 | 3 | 0 | 51 | 20 | 7 | 7 | 7 | 32 | 31 | 60 | 1st |
| 1956/57 | 42 | 14 | 4 | 3 | 55 | 25 | 14 | 4 | 3 | 48 | 29 | 64 | 1st |
| 1957/58 | 42 | 10 | 4 | 7 | 45 | 31 | 6 | 7 | 8 | 40 | 44 | 43 | 9th |
| 1958/59 | 42 | 14 | 4 | 3 | 58 | 27 | 10 | 3 | 8 | 45 | 39 | 55 | 2nd |
| 1959/60 | 42 | 13 | 3 | 5 | 53 | 30 | 6 | 4 | 11 | 49 | 50 | 45 | 7th |
| 1960/61 | 42 | 14 | 5 | 2 | 58 | 20 | 4 | 4 | 13 | 30 | 56 | 45 | 7th |
| 1961/62 | 42 | 10 | 3 | 8 | 44 | 31 | 5 | 6 | 10 | 28 | 44 | 39 | 15th |
| 1962/63 | 42 | 6 | 6 | 9 | 36 | 38 | 6 | 4 | 11 | 31 | 43 | 34 | 19th |
| 1963/64 | 42 | 15 | 3 | 3 | 54 | 19 | 8 | 4 | 9 | 36 | 43 | 53 | 2nd |
| 1964/65 | 42 | 16 | 4 | 1 | 52 | 13 | 10 | 5 | 6 | 37 | 26 | 61 | 1st |
| 1965/66 | 42 | 12 | 8 | 1 | 50 | 20 | 6 | 7 | 8 | 34 | 39 | 51 | 4th |

| Year | Home | | | | | | Away | | | | | | |
|---|---|---|---|---|---|---|---|---|---|---|---|---|---|
| | P | W | D | L | F | A | W | D | L | F | A | Pts | Pos |
| 1966/67 | 42 | 17 | 4 | 0 | 51 | 13 | 7 | 8 | 6 | 33 | 32 | 60 | 1st |
| 1967/68 | 42 | 15 | 2 | 4 | 49 | 21 | 9 | 6 | 6 | 40 | 34 | 56 | 2nd |
| 1968/69 | 42 | 13 | 5 | 3 | 38 | 18 | 2 | 7 | 12 | 19 | 35 | 42 | 11th |
| 1969/70 | 42 | 8 | 9 | 4 | 37 | 27 | 6 | 8 | 7 | 29 | 34 | 45 | 8th |
| 1970/71 | 42 | 9 | 6 | 6 | 29 | 24 | 7 | 5 | 9 | 36 | 42 | 43 | 8th |
| 1971/72 | 42 | 13 | 2 | 6 | 39 | 26 | 6 | 8 | 7 | 30 | 35 | 48 | 8th |
| 1972/73 | 42 | 9 | 7 | 5 | 24 | 19 | 3 | 6 | 12 | 20 | 41 | 37 | 18th |
| 1973/74 | 42 | 7 | 7 | 7 | 23 | 20 | 3 | 5 | 13 | 15 | 28 | 32 | 21st |
| *Second Division* | | | | | | | | | | | | | |
| 1974/75 | 42 | 17 | 3 | 1 | 45 | 12 | 9 | 6 | 6 | 21 | 18 | 61 | 1st |
| *First Division* | | | | | | | | | | | | | |
| 1975/76 | 42 | 16 | 4 | 1 | 40 | 13 | 7 | 6 | 8 | 28 | 29 | 56 | 3rd |
| 1976/77 | 42 | 12 | 6 | 3 | 41 | 22 | 6 | 5 | 10 | 30 | 40 | 47 | 6th |
| 1977/78 | 42 | 9 | 6 | 6 | 32 | 23 | 7 | 4 | 10 | 35 | 40 | 42 | 10th |
| 1978/79 | 42 | 9 | 7 | 5 | 29 | 25 | 6 | 8 | 7 | 31 | 38 | 45 | 9th |
| 1979/80 | 42 | 17 | 3 | 1 | 43 | 8 | 7 | 7 | 7 | 22 | 27 | 58 | 2nd |
| 1980/81 | 42 | 9 | 11 | 1 | 30 | 14 | 6 | 7 | 8 | 21 | 22 | 48 | 8th |
| 1981/82 | 42 | 12 | 6 | 3 | 27 | 9 | 10 | 6 | 5 | 32 | 20 | 78 | 3rd |
| 1982/83 | 42 | 14 | 7 | 0 | 39 | 10 | 5 | 6 | 10 | 17 | 28 | 70 | 3rd |
| 1983/84 | 42 | 14 | 3 | 4 | 43 | 18 | 6 | 11 | 4 | 28 | 23 | 74 | 4th |
| 1984/85 | 42 | 13 | 6 | 2 | 47 | 13 | 9 | 4 | 8 | 30 | 34 | 76 | 4th |
| 1985/86 | 42 | 12 | 5 | 4 | 35 | 12 | 10 | 5 | 6 | 35 | 24 | 76 | 4th |
| 1986/87 | 42 | 13 | 3 | 5 | 38 | 18 | 1 | 11 | 9 | 14 | 27 | 56 | 11th |
| 1987/88 | 40 | 14 | 5 | 1 | 41 | 17 | 9 | 7 | 4 | 30 | 21 | 81 | 2nd |
| 1988/89 | 38 | 10 | 5 | 4 | 27 | 13 | 3 | 7 | 9 | 18 | 22 | 51 | 11th |
| 1989/90 | 38 | 8 | 6 | 5 | 26 | 14 | 5 | 3 | 11 | 20 | 33 | 48 | 13th |
| 1990/91 | 38 | 11 | 4 | 4 | 34 | 17 | 5 | 8 | 6 | 24 | 28 | 59 | 6th |
| 1991/92 | 42 | 12 | 7 | 2 | 34 | 13 | 9 | 8 | 4 | 29 | 20 | 78 | 2nd |
| *FA Premier League* | | | | | | | | | | | | | |
| 1992/93 | 42 | 14 | 5 | 2 | 39 | 14 | 10 | 7 | 4 | 28 | 17 | 84 | 1st |
| 1993/94 | 42 | 14 | 6 | 1 | 39 | 13 | 13 | 5 | 3 | 41 | 25 | 92 | 1st |

## Players Career Records

NB League appearances/goals entries include games played in the Football Alliance but not in the FA Premier League which has its own column. Where an asterisk * appears in the European Column this denotes the number of "Test Match" appearances made in the early days of the Football League's promotion and relegation method, not European games. The chart does not include wartime games when innumerable players turned out for whichever club they were stationed closest to at the time.

| Player | FAPL App | FAPL Goals | League App | League Goals | FACup App | FACup Goals | LgeCup App | LgeCup Goals | Europe App | Europe Goals | Totals App | Totals Goals |
|---|---|---|---|---|---|---|---|---|---|---|---|---|
| A Ainsworth (1933) | – | – | 2 | – | – | – | – | – | – | – | 2 | – |
| J Aitken (1895) | – | – | 2 | 1 | – | – | – | – | – | – | 2 | 1 |
| G Albison (1920) | – | – | – | – | 1 | – | – | – | – | – | 1 | – |
| AR Albiston (1974/88) | – | – | 364/5 | 6 | 36 | – | 38/2 | 1 | 26/1 | – | 464/18 | 7 |
| JT Allan (1904/06) | – | – | 35 | 21 | 1 | 1 | – | – | – | – | 36 | 22 |
| RA Allen (1950/52) | – | – | 75 | – | 5 | – | – | – | – | – | 80 | – |
| A Allman (1914) | – | – | 12 | – | – | – | – | – | – | – | 12 | – |
| A Ambler (1899/1900) | – | – | 10 | 1 | – | – | – | – | – | – | 10 | 1 |
| G Anderson (1911/14) | – | – | 80 | 37 | 6 | 2 | – | – | – | – | 86 | 39 |
| J Anderson (1947/48) | – | – | 33 | 1 | 6 | 1 | – | – | – | – | 39 | 2 |
| T Anderson (1972/73) | – | – | 13/6 | 2 | – | – | – | – | – | – | 13/6 | 2 |
| VA Anderson (1987/91) | – | – | 50/4 | 2 | 7 | 1 | 6/1 | 1 | 1 | – | 64/5 | 4 |
| WJ Anderson (1963/66) | – | – | 7/2 | 2 | 2 | – | – | – | 1 | – | 10/2 | 2 |
| TA Arkesden (1902/05) | – | – | 70 | 28 | 9 | 5 | – | – | – | – | 79 | 33 |
| B Asquith (1939) | – | – | 1 | – | – | – | – | – | – | – | 1 | – |
| JE Astley (1925/26) | – | – | 2 | – | – | – | – | – | – | – | 2 | – |
| J Aston snr (1946/53) | – | – | 253 | 29 | 29 | 1 | – | – | – | – | 282 | 30 |
| J Aston jnr (1964/71) | – | – | 139/16 | 25 | 5/2 | 1 | 12/3 | – | 8 | 1 | 164/21 | 27 |
| GR Bailey (1978/87) | – | – | 294 | – | 31 | – | 28 | – | 20 | – | 373 | – |
| D Bain (1922/23) | – | – | 22 | 9 | 1 | – | – | – | – | – | 23 | 9 |
| J Bain (1899) | – | – | 2 | 1 | – | – | – | – | – | – | 2 | 1 |
| J Bain (1924/27) | – | – | 4 | – | – | – | – | – | – | – | 4 | – |
| W Bainbridge (1945) | – | – | – | – | 1 | – | – | – | – | – | 1 | – |
| HC Baird (1936/37) | – | – | 49 | 15 | 4 | 3 | – | – | – | – | 53 | 18 |
| T Baldwin (1974) | – | – | 2 | – | – | – | – | – | – | – | 2 | – |

| Player | FAPL | | League | | FACup | | LgeCup | | Europe | | Totals | |
|---|---|---|---|---|---|---|---|---|---|---|---|---|
| | App | Goals | App | Goals | App | Goals | App | Goals | App | Goals | App | Goals |
| J Ball (1947/49) | – | – | 22 | – | 1 | – | – | – | – | – | 23 | – |
| JT Ball (1929/34) | – | – | 47 | 17 | 3 | 1 | – | – | – | – | 50 | 18 |
| WH Ball (1902) | – | – | 4 | – | – | – | – | – | – | – | 4 | – |
| T Bamford (1934/37) | – | – | 98 | 53 | 11 | 4 | – | – | – | – | 109 | 57 |
| J Banks (1901/02) | – | – | 40 | – | 4 | – | – | – | – | – | 44 | – |
| J Bannister (1906/09) | – | – | 57 | 7 | 4 | 1 | – | – | – | – | 61 | 8 |
| J Barber (1922/23) | – | – | 3 | 1 | 1 | 1 | – | – | – | – | 4 | 2 |
| C Barlow (1919/21) | – | – | 29 | 1 | 1 | – | – | – | – | – | 30 | 1 |
| PS Barnes (1985/87) | – | – | 19/1 | 2 | – | – | 4* | 2 | – | – | 24/1 | 4 |
| F Barrett (1896/97) | – | – | 118 | – | 14 | – | – | – | – | – | 136 | – |
| F Barson (1922/27) | – | – | 140 | 4 | 12 | – | – | – | – | – | 152 | 4 |
| A Beardsworth (1902) | – | – | 9 | 1 | 3 | – | – | – | – | – | 12 | 1 |
| RH Beale (1912/14) | – | – | 105 | – | 7 | – | – | – | – | – | 112 | – |
| PA Beardley (1982) | – | – | – | – | – | – | 1 | – | – | – | 1 | – |
| RP Beardsmore (1988/92) | – | – | 30/26 | 4 | 4/4 | – | 3/1 | – | 1/2 | – | 38/33 | 4 |
| T Beckett (1886) | – | – | – | – | 1 | – | – | – | – | – | 1 | – |
| D Beckham (1992/) | – | – | – | – | – | – | -/1 | – | – | – | /1 | – |
| JH Beddow (1904/06) | – | – | 33 | 12 | 1 | 3 | – | – | – | – | 34 | 15 |
| W Behan (1933) | – | – | 1 | – | – | – | – | – | – | – | 1 | – |
| A Bell (1902/12) | – | – | 278 | 10 | 28 | – | – | – | – | – | 306 | 10 |
| SR Bennion (1921/32) | – | – | 286 | 2 | 15 | 1 | – | – | – | – | 301 | 3 |
| G Bent (1954/56) | – | – | 12 | – | – | – | – | – | – | – | 12 | – |
| JJ Berry (1951/57) | – | – | 247 | 37 | 15 | 4 | – | – | 11 | 3 | 273 | 44 |
| W Berry (1906/08) | – | – | 13 | 1 | 1 | – | – | – | – | – | 14 | 1 |
| G Best (1963/73) | – | – | 361 | 137 | 46 | 21 | 25 | 9 | 34 | 11 | 466 | 178 |

| Player | FAPL App | FAPL Goals | League App | League Goals | FACup App | FACup Goals | LgeCup App | LgeCup Goals | Europe App | Europe Goals | Totals App | Totals Goals |
|---|---|---|---|---|---|---|---|---|---|---|---|---|
| PA Bielby (1973) | 2/2 | – | | | | | | | | | 2/2 | – |
| B Birch (1949/51) | – | – | 11 | 4 | 4 | 1 | – | – | – | – | 15 | 5 |
| H Birchenough (1902) | – | – | 25 | – | 5 | – | – | – | – | – | 30 | – |
| C Birkett (1950) | – | – | 9 | 2 | 4 | – | – | – | – | – | 13 | 2 |
| G Birtles (1980/82) | – | – | 57/1 | 11 | 4 | – | 2 | 1 | – | – | 63/1 | 12 |
| G Bissett (1919/21) | – | – | 40 | 10 | 2 | – | – | – | – | – | 42 | 10 |
| R Black (1931/33) | – | – | 8 | 3 | – | – | – | – | – | – | 8 | 3 |
| CG Blackmore (1983/ | 12/2 | – | 138/34 | 19 | 15/6 | 1 | 23/2 | 3 | 12 | 2 | 200/44 | 25 |
| P Blackmore (1899) | – | – | 1 | – | 1 | – | – | – | – | – | 2 | – |
| T Blackstock (1903/06) | – | – | 34 | – | 4 | – | – | – | – | – | 38 | – |
| J Blanchflower (1951/57) | – | – | 105 | 26 | 6 | 1 | – | – | 5 | – | 116 | 27 |
| WH Blew (1905) | – | – | 1 | – | – | – | – | – | – | – | 1 | – |
| SP Blott (1909/12) | – | – | 19 | 2 | – | – | – | – | – | – | 19 | 2 |
| T Bogan (1949/50) | – | – | 29 | 7 | 4 | – | – | – | – | – | 33 | 7 |
| JE Bond (1951/52) | – | – | 20 | 4 | 1 | – | – | – | – | – | 21 | 4 |
| RP Bonthron (1903/06) | – | – | 119 | 3 | 15 | – | – | – | – | – | 134 | 3 |
| W Booth (1900) | – | – | 2 | – | – | – | – | – | – | – | 2 | – |
| M Bosnich (1989/91) | – | – | 3 | – | – | – | – | – | – | – | 3 | – |
| H Boyd (1896/98) | – | – | 52 | 32 | 7 | 1 | – | – | 3* | 2 | 62 | 35 |
| WG Boyd (1934) | – | – | 6 | 4 | – | – | – | – | – | – | 6 | 4 |
| TW Boyle (1928/29) | – | – | 16 | 6 | 1 | – | – | – | – | – | 17 | 6 |
| L Bradbury (1938) | – | – | 2 | 1 | – | – | – | – | – | – | 2 | 1 |
| W Bradley (1958/61) | – | – | 63 | 20 | 3 | 1 | 1 | – | – | – | 66 | 21 |
| H Bratt (1960) | – | – | – | – | – | – | 1 | – | – | – | – | – |
| AB Brazil (1984/85) | – | – | 18/13 | 8 | –/1 | – | 4/3 | 3 | 2 | 1 | 27/17 | 12 |

225

| Player | FAPL App | Goals | League App | Goals | FACup App | Goals | LgeCup App | Goals | Europe App | Goals | Totals App | Goals |
|---|---|---|---|---|---|---|---|---|---|---|---|---|
| DM Brazil (1988/92) | – | – | -/2 | – | – | – | – | – | – | – | -/2 | – |
| J Breedon (1935/39) | – | – | 38 | – | – | – | – | – | – | – | 38 | – |
| T Breen (1936/38) | – | – | 65 | – | 6 | – | – | – | – | – | 71 | – |
| SA Brennan (1957/69) | – | – | 291/1 | 3 | 36 | 3 | 4 | – | 24 | – | 355/1 | 6 |
| FB Brett (1921) | – | – | 10 | – | – | – | – | – | – | – | 10 | – |
| WR Briggs (1960/61) | – | – | 9 | – | 2 | – | – | – | – | – | 11 | – |
| WH Brooks (1898) | – | – | 3 | 3 | – | – | – | – | – | – | 3 | 3 |
| AH Broome (1922) | – | – | 1 | – | – | – | – | – | – | – | 1 | – |
| H Broomfield (1907) | – | – | 9 | – | – | – | – | – | – | – | 9 | – |
| J Brown (1932/33) | – | – | 40 | 17 | 1 | – | – | – | – | – | 41 | 17 |
| J Brown (1935/38) | – | – | 102 | 1 | 8 | – | – | – | – | – | 110 | 1 |
| RB Brown (1947/48) | – | – | 4 | – | – | – | – | – | – | – | 4 | – |
| W Brown (1892) | – | – | 7 | – | – | – | – | – | – | – | 7 | – |
| W Brown (1896) | – | – | 7 | 2 | – | – | – | – | – | – | 7 | 2 |
| SR Bruce (1987/) | 83 | 8 | 162 | 25 | 31 | 1 | 22 | 4 | 14 | 4 | 324/1 | 46 |
| W Bryant (1896/99) | – | – | 109 | 27 | 14 | 6 | – | – | 4* | – | 127 | 33 |
| W Bryant (1934/39) | – | – | 151 | 44 | 9 | – | – | – | – | – | 160 | 44 |
| G Buchan (1973) | – | – | -/3 | – | – | – | -/1 | – | – | – | -/4 | – |
| MM Buchan (1971/82) | – | – | 376 | 4 | 39 | – | 30 | – | 10 | – | 455 | 4 |
| EW Buckle (1946/49) | – | – | 20 | 6 | 4 | 1 | – | – | – | – | 24 | 7 |
| FC Buckley (1906) | – | – | 3 | – | – | – | – | – | – | – | 3 | – |
| KJ Bullock (1930) | – | – | 10 | 3 | – | – | – | – | – | – | 10 | 3 |
| W Bunce (1902) | – | – | 2 | – | – | – | – | – | – | – | 2 | – |
| H Burgess (1906/09) | – | – | 49 | – | 3 | – | – | – | – | – | 52 | – |
| RS Burke (1946/48) | – | – | 28 | 16 | 6 | 6 | – | – | – | – | 34 | 22 |

| Player | FAPL App | FAPL Goals | League App | League Goals | FACup App | FACup Goals | LgeCup App | LgeCup Goals | Europe App | Europe Goals | Totals App | Totals Goals |
|---|---|---|---|---|---|---|---|---|---|---|---|---|
| T Burke (1886) | – | – | 5 | | 1 | | – | – | – | – | 6 | – |
| FS Burns (1967/71) | – | – | 111/10 | 6 | 14/1 | | 10/1 | | 7/1 | | 142/13 | 7 |
| N Butt (1992/ | –/2 | | | | | | | | | | –/3 | |
| D Byrne (1933) | – | – | 4 | 3 | | | | | | | 4 | 3 |
| RW Byrne (1951/57) | – | – | 245 | 17 | 18 | 2 | | | 14 | | 277 | 19 |
| J Cairns (1894/98) | – | – | 2 | | | | | | | | 2 | – |
| WC Campbell (1893) | – | – | 5 | 1 | | | | | | | 5 | 1 |
| E Cantona (1992/ | 55/1 | 27 | | | 6 | 4 | 5 | 1 | 4 | 2 | 70/1 | 34 |
| N Cantwell (1960/66) | – | – | 123 | 6 | 14 | 2 | | | 7 | | 144 | 8 |
| JP Cape (1933/36) | – | – | 59 | 18 | 1 | | | | | | 60 | 18 |
| A Capper (1911) | – | – | 1 | | | | | | | | 1 | – |
| JJ Carey (1937/52) | – | – | 306 | 17 | 38 | 1 | | | | | 344 | 18 |
| J Carman (1897) | – | – | 3 | 1 | | | | | | | 3 | 1 |
| JF Carolan (1958/60) | – | – | 66 | | 4 | | 1 | | | | 71 | – |
| A Carson (1892) | – | – | 13 | 3 | | | | | | | 13 | 3 |
| HR Cartman (1922) | – | – | 3 | | | | | | | | 3 | – |
| WG Cartwright (1895/1903) | – | – | 228 | 8 | 27 | | | | 2* | | 257 | 8 |
| AA Cashmore (1913) | – | – | 3 | | | | | | | | 3 | – |
| J Cassidy (1892/99) | – | – | 152 | 90 | 15 | 9 | | | 7* | 1 | 174 | 100 |
| L Cassidy (1947/51) | – | – | 4 | | | | | | | | 4 | – |
| WS Chalmers (1932/33) | – | – | 34 | 1 | 1 | | | | | | 35 | 1 |
| W Chapman (1926/27) | – | – | 26 | | | | | | | | 26 | – |
| R Charlton (1956/72) | – | – | 604/2 | 199 | 79 | 19 | 24 | 7 | 45 | 22 | 752/2 | 247 |
| RA Chester (1935) | – | – | 13 | 1 | | | | | | | 13 | 1 |
| A Chesters (1929/31) | – | – | 9 | | | | | | | | 9 | – |

| Player | FAPL | | League | | FACup | | LgeCup | | Europe | | Totals | |
|---|---|---|---|---|---|---|---|---|---|---|---|---|
| | App | Goals | App | Goals | App | Goals | App | Goals | App | Goals | App | Goals |
| AC Chilton (1939/54) | – | – | 353 | 3 | 37 | – | – | – | – | – | 390 | 3 |
| JP Chisnall (1961/63) | – | – | 35 | 8 | 8 | 1 | – | – | 4 | 1 | 47 | 10 |
| T Chorlton (1913) | – | – | 4 | – | – | – | – | – | – | – | 4 | – |
| D Christie (1908) | – | – | 2 | – | – | – | – | – | – | – | 2 | – |
| J Christie (1902) | – | – | 1 | – | – | – | – | – | – | – | 1 | – |
| J Clark (1899) | – | – | 9 | – | – | – | – | – | – | – | 9 | – |
| J Clark (1976/77) | – | – | 0/1 | – | – | – | – | – | – | – | 0/1 | – |
| J Clarkin (1893/95) | – | – | 67 | 23 | 5 | – | – | – | 2* | – | 74 | 23 |
| G Clayton (1956) | – | – | 2 | – | – | – | – | – | – | – | 2 | – |
| H Cleaver (1902) | – | – | 1 | – | – | – | – | – | – | – | 1 | – |
| JE Clements (1891/93) | – | – | 72 | 2 | 4 | – | – | – | 2* | – | 78 | 2 |
| F Clempson (1949/52) | – | – | 15 | 2 | – | – | – | – | – | – | 15 | 2 |
| H Cockburn (1946/54) | – | – | 243 | 4 | 32 | – | – | – | – | – | 275 | 4 |
| C Collinson (1946) | – | – | 7 | – | – | – | – | – | – | – | 7 | – |
| J Collinson (1895/1900) | – | – | 62 | 16 | 9 | 1 | – | – | – | – | 71 | 17 |
| E Colman (1955/57) | – | – | 85 | 1 | 9 | – | – | – | 13 | 1 | 107 | 2 |
| J Colville (1892) | – | – | 9 | 1 | 1 | – | – | – | – | – | 10 | 1 |
| J Connachan (1898) | – | – | 4 | – | – | – | – | – | – | – | 4 | – |
| JP Connaughton (1971) | – | – | 3 | – | – | – | – | – | – | – | 3 | – |
| TE Connell (1978) | – | – | 2 | – | – | – | – | – | – | – | 2 | – |
| JM Connelly (1964/66) | – | – | 79/1 | 22 | 13 | 2 | – | – | 19 | 11 | 112/1 | 35 |
| E Connor (1909/10) | – | – | 15 | 2 | – | – | – | – | – | – | 15 | 2 |
| SP Cookson (1914) | – | – | 12 | – | 1 | – | – | – | – | – | 13 | – |
| R Cope (1956/60) | – | – | 93 | 2 | 10 | – | 1 | – | 2 | – | 106 | 2 |
| SJ Coppell (1974/82) | – | – | 320/2 | 54 | 36 | 4 | 25 | 9 | 11/1 | 3 | 392/3 | 70 |

| Player | FAPL App | FAPL Goals | League App | League Goals | FACup App | FACup Goals | LgeCup App | LgeCup Goals | Europe App | Europe Goals | Totals App | Totals Goals |
|---|---|---|---|---|---|---|---|---|---|---|---|---|
| J Coupar (1892/1901) | – | – | 32 | 9 | – | – | – | – | 2* | 1 | 34 | 10 |
| PD Coyne (1975) | – | – | 1/1 | 1 | – | – | – | – | – | – | 1/1 | 1 |
| T Craig (1889/90) | – | – | 25 | 5 | 2 | 1 | – | – | – | – | 27 | 6 |
| C Craven (1938) | – | – | 11 | 2 | – | – | – | – | – | – | 11 | 2 |
| PT Crerand (1962/70) | – | – | 304 | 10 | 43 | 4 | 4 | – | 41 | 1 | 392 | 15 |
| J Crompton (1945/56) | – | – | 191 | – | 20 | – | – | – | – | – | 211 | – |
| GA Crooks (1983) | – | – | 6/1 | 2 | – | – | – | – | – | – | 6/1 | 2 |
| S Crowther (1957/58) | – | – | 13 | – | 5 | – | – | – | 2 | – | 20 | – |
| J Cunningham (1898) | – | – | 15 | 2 | 2 | – | – | – | – | – | 17 | 2 |
| LP Cunningham (1982) | – | – | 3/2 | 1 | – | – | – | – | – | – | 3/2 | 1 |
| JJ Curry (1908/10) | – | – | 13 | – | 1 | – | – | – | – | – | 14 | – |
| A Dale (1890) | – | – | – | – | 1 | – | – | – | – | – | 1 | – |
| J Dale (1947) | – | – | 2 | – | – | – | – | – | – | – | 2 | – |
| W Dale (1928/31) | – | – | 64 | – | 4 | – | – | – | – | – | 68 | – |
| E Dalton (1907) | – | – | 1 | – | – | – | – | – | – | – | 1 | – |
| GA Daly (1973/76) | – | – | 107/4 | 23 | 9/1 | 5 | 17 | 4 | 4 | – | 137/5 | 32 |
| P Davenport (1985/89) | – | – | 72/19 | 22 | 2/2 | – | 8/2 | 4 | 4 | – | 83/23 | 26 |
| WR Davidson (1893/94) | – | – | 40 | 2 | 3 | – | – | – | 1* | – | 44 | 2 |
| A Davies (1981/83) | – | – | 6/1 | – | 2 | – | – | – | –/1 | 1 | 8/2 | 1 |
| JE Davies (1886/89) | – | – | 21 | 2 | 2 | – | – | – | – | – | 23 | 2 |
| J Davies (1892) | – | – | 10 | – | 1 | – | – | – | 2* | – | 13 | – |
| L Davies (1886) | – | – | – | – | 1 | – | – | – | – | – | 1 | – |
| RT Davies (1974) | – | – | –/8 | – | –/2 | – | – | – | – | – | –/10 | – |
| WR Davies (1972) | – | – | 15/1 | 4 | 1 | – | – | – | – | – | 16/1 | 4 |
| AD Dawson (1956/71) | – | – | 80 | 45 | 10 | 8 | 3 | 1 | – | – | 93 | 54 |

| Player | FAPL App | FAPL Goals | League App | League Goals | FACup App | FACup Goals | LgeCup App | LgeCup Goals | Europe App | Europe Goals | Totals App | Totals Goals |
|---|---|---|---|---|---|---|---|---|---|---|---|---|
| H Dean (1931) | – | – | 2 | – | – | – | – | – | – | – | 2 | – |
| J Delaney (1946/50) | – | – | 164 | 25 | 19 | 3 | – | – | – | – | 183 | 28 |
| MJ Dempsey (1983/86) | – | – | 1 | – | – | – | – | – | –/1 | – | 1/1 | – |
| J Denman (1891) | – | – | 6 | – | 1 | – | – | – | – | – | 7 | – |
| W Dennis (1923) | – | – | 3 | – | – | – | – | – | – | – | 3 | – |
| N Dewar (1932/33) | – | – | 36 | 14 | – | – | – | – | – | – | 36 | 14 |
| J Doherty (1952/57) | – | – | 25 | 7 | 1 | – | – | – | – | – | 26 | 7 |
| B Donaghy (1905) | – | – | 3 | – | – | – | – | – | – | – | 3 | – |
| MM Donaghy (1988/92) | – | – | 76/13 | – | 10 | – | 10/4 | – | 2/3 | – | 98/20 | – |
| IR Donald (1972) | – | – | 4 | – | – | – | 2 | – | – | – | 6 | – |
| R Donaldson (1892/97) | – | – | 153 | 76 | 16 | 10 | – | – | 8* | – | 177 | 86 |
| J Donnelly (1890) | – | – | 1 | – | – | – | – | – | – | – | 1 | – |
| A Donnelly (1908/12) | – | – | 34 | – | 3 | – | – | – | – | – | 37 | – |
| T Dougan (1938) | – | – | 4 | – | – | – | – | – | – | – | 4 | – |
| J Doughty (1886/91) | – | – | 26 | 11 | 3 | 3 | – | – | – | – | 29 | 14 |
| R Doughty (1891/96) | – | – | 56 | 3 | 5 | 1 | – | – | 3* | – | 64 | 4 |
| W Douglas (1893/95) | – | – | 55 | – | 1 | – | – | – | 1* | – | 57 | – |
| JM Dow (1893/95) | – | – | 48 | 6 | 1 | – | – | – | 1* | – | 50 | 6 |
| ALB Downie (1902/09) | – | – | 172 | 12 | 19 | 2 | – | – | – | – | 191 | 14 |
| JD Downie (1948/52) | – | – | 110 | 35 | 5 | 1 | – | – | – | – | 115 | 36 |
| WL Draycott (1896/98) | – | – | 81 | 6 | 10 | – | – | – | 4* | – | 95 | 6 |
| D Dublin (1992/) | 4/8 | 2 | – | – | 1/1 | – | 1/1 | 1 | –/1 | – | 6/11 | 3 |
| R Duckworth (1903/12) | – | – | 225 | 11 | 26 | – | – | – | – | – | 251 | 11 |
| W Dunn (1897) | – | – | 10 | – | 2 | – | – | – | – | – | 12 | – |
| AP Dunne (1960/72) | – | – | 414 | 2 | 54/1 | – | 21 | – | 40 | – | 529/1 | 2 |

| Player | FAPL | | League | | FACup | | LgeCup | | Europe | | Totals | |
|---|---|---|---|---|---|---|---|---|---|---|---|---|
| | App | Goals | App | Goals | App | Goals | App | Goals | App | Goals | App | Goals |
| PAJ Dunne (1964/65) | – | – | 45 | – | 7 | – | – | – | 13 | – | 66 | – |
| M Duxbury (1980/90) | – | – | 274/25 | 6 | 20/5 | 1 | 32/2 | – | 17/1 | – | 343/33 | 7 |
| JA Dyer (1905) | – | – | 1 | – | – | – | – | – | – | – | 1 | – |
| J Earp (1886) | – | – | – | – | 1 | – | – | – | – | – | 1 | – |
| A Edge (1891) | – | – | 19 | 6 | 3 | 3 | – | – | – | – | 22 | 9 |
| H Edmonds (1910/11) | – | – | 43 | – | 7 | – | – | – | – | – | 50 | – |
| D Edwards (1952/57) | – | – | 151 | 20 | 12 | 1 | – | – | 12 | – | 175 | 21 |
| PF Edwards (1969/72) | – | – | 52/2 | – | 10 | – | 4 | 1 | – | – | 66/2 | 1 |
| D Ellis (1923) | – | – | 11 | – | – | – | – | – | – | – | 11 | – |
| FC Erentz (1892/1901) | – | – | 280 | 9 | 23 | – | – | – | 7* | – | 310 | 9 |
| H Erentz (1897) | – | – | 6 | – | 3 | – | – | – | – | – | 9 | – |
| G Evans (1890) | – | – | 12 | 5 | 1 | 1 | – | – | – | – | 13 | 6 |
| S Evans (1923) | – | – | 6 | 2 | – | – | – | – | – | – | 6 | 2 |
| JW Fall (1893) | – | – | 23 | – | 3 | – | – | – | 1* | – | 27 | – |
| AH Farman (1889/94) | – | – | 111 | 43 | 7 | 6 | – | – | 3* | 4 | 121 | 53 |
| I Feeman (1949) | – | – | 12 | – | 2 | – | – | – | – | – | 14 | – |
| G Felton (1890) | – | – | 8 | – | 1 | – | – | – | – | – | 9 | – |
| D Ferguson (1927) | – | – | 4 | – | – | – | – | – | – | – | 4 | – |
| D Ferguson (1990/94) | 16/2 | – | 4/5 | – | 1 | – | 1/1 | – | – | – | 22/8 | – |
| J Ferguson (1931) | – | – | 8 | 1 | – | – | – | – | – | – | 8 | 1 |
| RJ Ferrier (1935/37) | – | – | 18 | 4 | 1 | – | – | – | – | – | 19 | 4 |
| WJ Fielding (1946) | – | – | 6 | – | 1 | – | – | – | – | – | 7 | – |
| J Fisher (1900/01) | – | – | 42 | 2 | 4 | 1 | – | – | – | – | 46 | 3 |
| J Fitchett (1902/04) | – | – | 16 | 1 | 2 | – | – | – | – | – | 18 | 1 |
| GA Fitton (1931/32) | – | – | 12 | 2 | – | – | – | – | – | – | 12 | 2 |

| Player | FAPL App | FAPL Goals | League App | League Goals | FACup App | FACup Goals | LgeCup App | LgeCup Goals | Europe App | Europe Goals | Totals App | Totals Goals |
|---|---|---|---|---|---|---|---|---|---|---|---|---|
| JH Fitzpatrick (1964/72) | – | – | 111/6 | 8 | 11 | 1 | 12 | 1 | 7 | – | 141/6 | 10 |
| D Fitzsimmons (1895/99) | – | – | 28 | – | 3 | – | – | – | – | – | 31 | – |
| T Fitzsimmons (1892/93) | – | – | 27 | 6 | 1 | – | – | – | 2* | – | 30 | 6 |
| P Fletcher (1972/73) | – | – | 2/5 | – | – | – | – | – | – | – | 2/5 | – |
| A Foggan (1976) | – | – | –/3 | – | – | – | – | – | – | – | –/3 | – |
| G Foley (1899) | – | – | 7 | 1 | – | – | – | – | – | – | 7 | 1 |
| JB Ford (1908/09) | – | – | 5 | – | – | – | – | – | – | – | 5 | – |
| T Forster (1919/21) | – | – | .35 | – | 1 | – | – | – | – | – | 36 | – |
| A Forsyth (1972/77) | – | – | 99/2 | 4 | 10 | 1 | 7 | – | –/1 | – | 116/3 | 5 |
| WA Foulkes (1952/69) | – | – | 563/3 | 7 | 61 | – | 3 | – | 52 | 2 | 679/3 | 9 |
| W Fox (1914) | – | – | 1 | – | – | – | – | – | – | – | 1 | – |
| T Frame (1932/33) | – | – | 51 | 4 | 1 | – | – | – | – | – | 52 | 4 |
| SH Gallimore (1930/33) | – | – | 72 | 19 | 4 | 1 | – | – | – | – | 76 | 20 |
| CR Gardner (1935/36) | – | – | 16 | 1 | 2 | – | – | – | – | – | 18 | 1 |
| WF Garton (1984/88) | – | – | 39/2 | – | 3 | – | 5/1 | – | –/1 | – | 47/4 | – |
| J Garvey (1900) | – | – | 6 | – | – | – | – | – | – | – | 6 | – |
| JD Gaskell (1957/66) | – | – | 96 | – | 16 | – | 1 | – | 5 | – | 118 | – |
| R Gaudie (1903) | – | – | 7 | – | 1 | – | – | – | – | – | 8 | – |
| CJ Gibson (1985/91) | – | – | 74/5 | 9 | 8/1 | – | 7 | – | – | – | 89/6 | 9 |
| R Gibson (1921) | – | – | 11 | – | 1 | – | – | – | – | – | 12 | – |
| TB Gibson (1985/87) | – | – | 14/9 | 1 | 1/1 | – | –/2 | – | – | – | 15/12 | 1 |
| TRD Gibson (1950/54) | – | – | 108 | – | 6 | – | – | – | – | – | 114 | – |
| J Gidman (1981/86) | – | – | 94/1 | 4 | 9 | – | 5 | – | 7/2 | – | 115/3 | 4 |
| R Giggs (1990/ | 72/7 | 22 | 33/7 | 5 | 11/1 | 3 | 13/5 | 6 | 6 | – | 135/20 | 36 |
| MJ Giles (1959/62) | – | – | 99 | 10 | 13 | 2 | 2 | 1 | – | – | 114 | 13 |

| Player | FAPL App | FAPL Goals | League App | League Goals | FACup App | FACup Goals | LgeCup App | LgeCup Goals | Europe App | Europe Goals | Totals App | Totals Goals |
|---|---|---|---|---|---|---|---|---|---|---|---|---|
| AGD Gill (1986/88) | – | – | 5/5 | 1 | 2/2 | 1 | – | – | – | – | 7/7 | 2 |
| K Gillespie (1992/) | – | – | 1 | – | – | – | – | – | – | – | 1 | 1 |
| M Gillespie (1896/90) | – | – | 74 | 17 | 11 | 4 | – | – | 4* | – | 89 | 21 |
| T Gipps (1912/14) | – | – | 23 | – | – | – | – | – | – | – | 23 | – |
| DJ Givens (1969) | – | – | 4/4 | 1 | – | – | 1 | – | – | – | 5/4 | 1 |
| GWE Gladwin (1936/38) | – | – | 27 | 1 | 1 | – | – | – | – | – | 28 | 1 |
| G Godsmark (1899) | – | – | 9 | 4 | – | – | – | – | – | – | 9 | 4 |
| EH Goldthorpe (1922/24) | – | – | 27 | 15 | 3 | 1 | – | – | – | – | 30 | 16 |
| FJ Goodwin (1954/59) | – | – | 95 | 7 | 8 | – | – | – | 3 | – | 106 | 8 |
| W Goodwin (1920/21) | – | – | 7 | 1 | – | – | – | – | – | – | 7 | 1 |
| J Gotheridge (1886) | – | – | 5 | – | 1 | – | – | – | – | – | 6 | – |
| J Gourlay (1898) | – | – | 1 | – | – | – | – | – | – | – | 1 | – |
| AE Gowling (1967/71) | – | – | 64/7 | 18 | 6/2 | 2 | 7/1 | 1 | – | – | 77/10 | 21 |
| A Graham (1983/84) | – | – | 33/4 | 5 | 1 | – | 6 | 1 | 6/1 | 1 | 46/5 | 7 |
| DWT Graham (1987) | – | – | 1/1 | – | 0/1 | 1 | 0/1 | – | – | – | 1/3 | 1 |
| G Graham (1972/74) | – | – | 41/2 | 2 | 2 | – | 1 | – | – | – | 44/2 | 2 |
| J Graham (1893) | – | – | 4 | – | – | – | – | – | – | – | 4 | – |
| W Grassam (1903/04) | – | – | 29 | 13 | 8 | 1 | – | – | – | – | 37 | 14 |
| ID Greaves (1954/59) | – | – | 67 | – | 6 | – | – | – | 2 | – | 75 | – |
| RE Green (1933) | – | – | 9 | 4 | – | – | – | – | – | – | 9 | 4 |
| B Greenhoff (1973/78) | – | – | 218/3 | 13 | 24 | 2 | 19 | 2 | 6 | – | 267/3 | 17 |
| J Greenhoff (1976/80) | – | – | 94/3 | 26 | 18/1 | 9 | 4 | 1 | 2 | – | 118/4 | 36 |
| W Greenwood (1900) | – | – | 3 | – | – | – | – | – | – | – | 3 | – |
| H Gregg (1957/66) | – | – | 210 | – | 24 | – | 2 | – | 11 | – | 247 | – |
| CL Griffiths (1973) | – | – | 7 | – | – | – | – | – | – | – | 7 | 1 |

| Player | FAPL App | FAPL Goals | League App | League Goals | FACup App | FACup Goals | LgeCup App | LgeCup Goals | Europe App | Europe Goals | Totals App | Totals Goals |
|---|---|---|---|---|---|---|---|---|---|---|---|---|
| J Griffiths (1933/39) | – | – | 168 | 1 | 8 | – | – | – | – | – | 176 | 1 |
| W Griffiths (1898/1904) | – | – | 157 | 27 | 18 | 3 | – | – | – | – | 175 | 30 |
| AA Grimes (1977/82) | – | – | 62/28 | 10 | 5 | 1 | 6 | – | 4/2 | – | 77/30 | 11 |
| A Grimshaw (1975) | – | – | –/1 | – | – | – | –/1 | – | – | – | –/2 | – |
| JB Grimwood (1919/26) | – | – | 196 | 8 | 9 | – | – | – | – | – | 205 | 8 |
| J Grundy (1899/1900) | – | – | 11 | 3 | – | – | – | – | – | – | 11 | 3 |
| H Gyves (1890) | – | – | – | – | 1 | – | – | – | – | – | 1 | – |
| J Hacking (1933/34) | – | – | 32 | – | 2 | – | – | – | – | – | 34 | – |
| J Hall (1933/35) | – | – | 67 | – | 6 | – | – | – | – | – | 73 | – |
| J Hall (1925) | – | – | 3 | – | – | – | – | – | – | – | 3 | – |
| P Hall (1903) | – | – | 8 | 2 | – | – | – | – | – | – | 8 | 2 |
| HJ Halse (1907/11) | – | – | 109 | 41 | 15 | 9 | – | – | – | – | 124 | 50 |
| RL Halton (1936) | – | – | 4 | 1 | – | – | – | – | – | – | 4 | 1 |
| M Hamill (1911/13) | – | – | 57 | 2 | 2 | – | – | – | – | – | 59 | 2 |
| JJ Hanlon (1938/48) | – | – | 64 | 20 | 6 | 2 | – | – | – | – | 70 | 22 |
| C Hannaford (1925/26) | – | – | 11 | – | 1 | – | – | – | – | – | 12 | – |
| J Hanson (1924/29) | – | – | 138 | 47 | 9 | 5 | – | – | – | – | 147 | 52 |
| HP Hardman (1908) | – | – | 4 | – | – | – | – | – | – | – | 4 | – |
| FE Harris (1919/21) | – | – | 46 | 2 | 3 | – | – | – | – | – | 49 | 2 |
| T Harris (1926) | – | – | 4 | 1 | – | – | – | – | – | – | 4 | 1 |
| C Harrison (1889) | – | – | 9 | 1 | 1 | – | – | – | – | – | 10 | 1 |
| WE Harrison (1920/21) | – | – | 44 | 5 | 2 | – | – | – | – | – | 46 | 5 |
| RW Harrop (1957/58) | – | – | 10 | – | 1 | – | – | – | – | – | 11 | – |
| W Hartwell (1903/04) | – | – | 3 | – | 1 | – | – | – | – | – | 4 | – |
| G Haslam (1921/27) | – | – | 25 | – | 2 | – | – | – | – | – | 27 | – |

| Player | FAPL App | Goals | League App | Goals | FACup App | Goals | LgeCup App | Goals | Europe App | Goals | Totals App | Goals |
|---|---|---|---|---|---|---|---|---|---|---|---|---|
| R Haworth (1926) | - | - | 2 | - | - | - | - | - | - | - | 2 | - |
| A Hawksworth (1956) | - | - | 1 | - | - | - | - | - | - | - | 1 | - |
| T Hay (1889) | - | - | 15 | - | 1 | - | - | - | - | - | 16 | - |
| F Haydock (1960/62) | - | - | 6 | - | - | - | - | - | - | - | 6 | - |
| JV Hayes (1900/10) | - | - | 115 | 2 | 13 | - | - | - | - | - | 128 | 2 |
| H Haywood (1932/33) | - | - | 4 | 2 | - | - | - | - | - | - | 4 | 2 |
| JF Haywood (1913/14) | - | - | 26 | - | - | - | - | - | - | - | 26 | - |
| J Heathcote (1899/1900) | - | - | 7 | - | 1 | - | - | - | - | - | 8 | - |
| W Henderson (1921/24) | - | - | 34 | 17 | 2 | - | - | - | - | - | 36 | 17 |
| J Hendry (1892) | - | - | 2 | 1 | - | - | - | - | - | - | 2 | 1 |
| A Henrys (1891/92) | - | - | 23 | - | 3 | - | - | - | - | - | 26 | - |
| DG Herd (1961/67) | - | - | 201/1 | 114 | 35 | 15 | 1 | 1 | 25 | 14 | 262/1 | 144 |
| FTR Heron (1957/60) | - | - | 3 | - | - | - | - | - | - | - | 3 | - |
| W Higgins (1901) | - | - | 10 | - | - | - | - | - | - | - | 10 | - |
| MN Higgins (1985/87) | - | - | 6 | - | 2 | - | - | - | - | - | 8 | - |
| J Higson (1901) | - | - | 5 | 1 | - | - | - | - | - | - | 5 | 1 |
| CG Hidditch (1919/31) | - | - | 301 | 7 | 21 | - | 7 | - | - | - | 322 | 7 |
| GA Hill (1975/77) | - | - | 100/1 | 39 | 17 | 6 | 7 | 4 | 8 | 2 | 132/1 | 51 |
| CE Hillam (1933) | - | - | 8 | - | - | - | - | - | - | - | 8 | - |
| EW Hine (1932/34) | - | - | 51 | 12 | 2 | - | - | - | - | - | 53 | 12 |
| J Hodge (1910/19) | - | - | 79 | 2 | 7 | - | - | - | - | - | 86 | 2 |
| J Hodge (1913/14) | - | - | 30 | - | - | - | - | - | - | - | 30 | - |
| FC Hodges (1919/20) | - | - | 20 | 4 | - | - | - | - | - | - | 20 | 4 |
| L Hofton (1910/20) | - | - | 12 | - | 1 | - | - | - | - | - | 13 | - |
| GJ Hogg (1983/87) | - | - | 82/1 | 1 | 8 | - | 7/1 | - | 10 | - | 107/2 | 1 |

| Player | FAPL | | League | | FACup | | LgeCup | | Europe | | Totals | |
|---|---|---|---|---|---|---|---|---|---|---|---|---|
| | App | Goals | App | Goals | App | Goals | App | Goals | App | Goals | App | Goals |
| RH Holdren (1904/12) | – | – | 106 | – | 11 | – | – | – | – | – | 117 | – |
| J Holt (1899) | – | – | 1 | 1 | – | – | – | – | – | – | 1 | 1 |
| JA Holton (1972/74) | – | – | 63 | 5 | 2 | – | 4 | – | – | – | 69 | 5 |
| TP Homer (1909/11) | – | – | 25 | 14 | – | – | – | – | – | – | 25 | 14 |
| W Hood (1892/93) | – | – | 48 | 11 | 3 | – | – | – | 2* | – | 53 | 11 |
| AH Hooper (1909/13) | – | – | 7 | 1 | – | – | – | – | – | – | 7 | 1 |
| F Hopkin (1919/20) | – | – | 70 | 8 | 4 | – | – | – | – | – | 74 | 8 |
| J Hopkins (1898) | – | – | 1 | – | – | – | – | – | – | – | 1 | – |
| S Hopkinson (1930/33) | – | – | 51 | 10 | 2 | 2 | – | – | – | – | 53 | 12 |
| SM Houston (1973/79) | – | – | 204/1 | 13 | 22 | 1 | 16 | 2 | 6/1 | – | 248/2 | 16 |
| JT Howarth (1921) | – | – | 4 | – | – | – | – | – | – | – | 4 | – |
| E Howells (1886) | – | – | – | – | 1 | – | – | – | – | – | 1 | – |
| EK Hudson (1913/14) | – | – | 11 | – | – | – | – | – | – | – | 11 | – |
| M Hughes (1983/) | 77 | 27 | 227/8 | 85 | 39/1 | 15 | 37/1 | 16 | 25/3 | 7 | 405/13 | 150 |
| A Hulme (1907/08) | – | – | 4 | – | – | – | – | – | – | – | 4 | – |
| GH Hunter (1913/14) | – | – | 22 | 2 | 1 | – | – | – | – | – | 23 | 2 |
| RJ Hunter (1958) | – | – | 1 | – | – | – | – | – | – | – | 1 | – |
| W Hunter (1912) | – | – | 3 | 2 | – | – | – | – | – | – | 3 | 2 |
| DJ Hurst (1902) | – | – | 16 | 4 | 5 | – | – | – | – | – | 21 | 4 |
| R Iddon (1925/26) | – | – | 2 | – | – | – | – | – | – | – | 2 | – |
| PEC Ince (1989/) | 80 | 14 | 87/2 | 6 | 19/1 | 1 | 24/1 | 2 | 14 | – | 224/4 | 23 |
| WW Inglis (1925/28) | – | – | 14 | 1 | – | – | – | – | – | – | 14 | 1 |
| D Irwin (1990/) | 82 | 7 | 70/2 | 4 | 16 | 2 | 25/2 | – | 7 | – | 200/4 | 13 |
| TA Jackson (1975/76) | – | – | 18/1 | – | 3 | – | 4 | – | – | – | 22/1 | – |
| W Jackson (1899/1900) | – | – | 61 | 12 | 3 | 2 | – | – | – | – | 64 | 14 |

| Player | FAPL App | FAPL Goals | League App | League Goals | FACup App | FACup Goals | LgeCup App | LgeCup Goals | Europe App | Europe Goals | Totals App | Totals Goals |
|---|---|---|---|---|---|---|---|---|---|---|---|---|
| SR James (1968/74) | – | – | 129 | 4 | 12 | – | 17/1 | – | 2 | – | 160/1 | 4 |
| CAL Jenkyns (1896/97) | – | – | 35 | 5 | 8 | – | – | – | 4* | 1 | 47 | 6 |
| WR John (1936) | – | – | 15 | – | – | – | – | – | – | – | 15 | – |
| SC Johnson (1900) | – | – | 1 | – | – | – | – | – | – | – | 1 | – |
| WG Johnston (1927/31) | – | – | 71 | 24 | 6 | 3 | – | – | – | – | 77 | 27 |
| D Jones (1937) | – | – | 1 | – | – | – | – | – | – | – | 1 | – |
| EP Jones (1957) | – | – | 1 | – | – | – | – | – | – | – | 1 | – |
| M Jones (1950/57) | – | – | 103 | 1 | 7 | – | – | – | 10 | – | 120 | 1 |
| OJ Jones (1898) | – | – | 2 | – | – | – | – | – | – | – | 2 | – |
| T Jones (1924/36) | – | – | 189 | – | 11 | – | – | – | – | – | 200 | – |
| TJ Jones (1934) | – | – | 20 | 4 | 2 | – | – | – | – | – | 22 | 4 |
| J Jordan (1977/80) | – | – | 109 | 37 | 11/1 | 2 | 4 | 2 | 1 | – | 125/1 | 41 |
| N Jovanovich (1979/80) | – | – | 20/1 | 4 | 1 | – | 2 | – | 2 | – | 25/1 | 4 |
| A Kanchelskis (1990/) | 42/15 | 9 | 29/6 | 5 | 12 | 5 | 12 | 2 | 2 | – | 97/21 | 21 |
| R Keane (1993-) | 34/3 | 5 | – | – | 6 | 1 | 6/1 | – | 3 | 2 | 49/4 | 8 |
| JW Kelly (1975) | – | – | -/1 | – | – | – | – | – | – | – | -/1 | – |
| F Kennedy (1923/24) | – | – | 17 | 4 | 1 | – | – | – | – | – | 18 | 4 |
| PA Kennedy (1954) | – | – | 1 | – | – | – | – | – | – | – | 1 | – |
| WJ Kennedy (1895/96) | – | – | 30 | 11 | 3 | 1 | – | – | – | – | 33 | 12 |
| H Kerr (1903) | – | – | 2 | – | – | – | – | – | – | – | 2 | – |
| B Kidd (1967/73) | – | – | 195/8 | 52 | 24/1 | 8 | 20 | 7 | 16 | 3 | 255/9 | 70 |
| J Kinloch (1892) | – | – | 1 | – | 1 | 1 | – | – | – | – | 2 | 1 |
| AJ Kinsey (1964) | – | – | – | – | 1 | – | – | – | – | – | 1 | – |
| F Knowles (1911/14) | – | – | 46 | 1 | 1 | – | – | – | – | – | 47 | 1 |
| F Kopel (1967/68) | – | – | 8/2 | – | 1 | – | – | – | 1 | – | 10/2 | – |

| Player | FAPL | | League | | FACup | | LgeCup | | Europe | | Totals | |
|---|---|---|---|---|---|---|---|---|---|---|---|---|
| | App | Goals | App | Goals | App | Goals | App | Goals | App | Goals | App | Goals |
| JG Lancaster (1949) | – | – | 2 | – | 2 | – | – | – | – | – | 4 | 1 |
| T Lang (1935/36) | – | – | 12 | 1 | 1 | – | – | – | – | – | 13 | 1 |
| L Langford (1934/35) | – | – | 15 | – | – | – | – | – | – | – | 15 | – |
| HH Lappin (1900/02) | – | – | 27 | 4 | – | – | – | – | – | – | 27 | 4 |
| D Law (1961/72) | – | – | 305/4 | 171 | 44/2 | 34 | 11 | 3 | 33 | 28 | 393/6 | 236 |
| RR Lawson (1900) | – | – | 3 | – | – | – | – | – | – | – | 3 | – |
| N Lawton (1959/62) | – | – | 36 | 6 | 7 | – | 1 | – | – | – | 44 | 6 |
| E Lee (1898/99) | – | – | 11 | 5 | – | – | – | – | – | – | 11 | 5 |
| T Leigh (1899/1900) | – | – | 43 | 15 | 3 | – | – | – | – | – | 46 | 15 |
| J Leighton (1988/91) | – | – | 73 | – | 14 | – | 7 | – | – | – | 94 | – |
| HD Leonard (1920) | – | – | 10 | 5 | – | – | – | – | – | – | 10 | 5 |
| E Lewis (1952/55) | – | – | 20 | 9 | 4 | 2 | – | – | – | – | 24 | 11 |
| L Lievesley (1931) | – | – | 2 | – | – | – | – | – | – | – | 2 | – |
| W Lievesley (1922) | – | – | 2 | – | 1 | – | – | – | – | – | 3 | – |
| OHS Linkson (1908/12) | – | – | 55 | – | 4 | – | – | – | – | – | 59 | – |
| GT Livingstone (1908/13) | – | – | 43 | 4 | 3 | – | – | – | – | – | 46 | 4 |
| AW Lochhead (1921/25) | – | – | 147 | 50 | 6 | – | – | – | – | – | 153 | 50 |
| W Longair (1894) | – | – | 1 | – | – | – | – | – | – | – | 1 | – |
| W Longton (1886) | – | – | – | – | 1 | – | – | – | – | – | 1 | – |
| T Lowrie (1947/49) | – | – | 13 | – | 1 | – | – | – | – | – | 14 | – |
| G Lydon (1930/31) | – | – | 3 | – | – | – | – | – | – | – | 3 | – |
| D Lyner (1922) | – | – | 3 | – | – | – | – | – | – | – | 3 | – |
| S Lynn (1947/49) | – | – | 13 | – | – | – | – | – | – | – | 13 | – |
| G Lyons (1903/05) | – | – | 4 | – | 1 | – | – | – | – | – | 5 | – |
| L Macari (1972/83) | – | – | 311/18 | 78 | 31/3 | 8 | 22/5 | 10 | 9/1 | 1 | 373/27 | 97 |

| Player | FAPL | | League | | FACup | | LgeCup | | Europe | | Totals | |
|---|---|---|---|---|---|---|---|---|---|---|---|---|
| | App | Goals | App | Goals | App | Goals | App | Goals | App | Goals | App | Goals |
| N McBain (1921/22) | – | – | 42 | 2 | 1 | – | – | – | – | – | 43 | 2 |
| J McCalliog (1973/74) | – | – | 31 | 7 | 1 | – | 5/1 | – | – | – | 37/1 | 7 |
| P McCarthy (1911) | – | – | 1 | – | – | – | – | – | – | – | 1 | – |
| W McCartney (1903) | – | – | 13 | – | – | – | – | – | – | – | 13 | – |
| WJ McCartney (1894) | – | – | 18 | 1 | 1 | – | – | – | 1* | – | 20 | 1 |
| BJ McClair (1987) | 53/15 | 10 | 190/3 | 70 | 28/4 | 12 | 37/1 | 18 | 15 | 5 | 323/23 | 115 |
| J McClelland (1936) | – | – | 5 | 1 | – | – | – | – | – | – | 5 | 1 |
| JJ McCrae (1925) | – | – | 9 | – | 4 | – | – | – | – | – | 13 | – |
| D McCreery (1974/78) | – | – | 48/39 | 7 | 1/6 | – | 4/4 | 1 | 4/3 | – | 57/52 | 8 |
| K MacDonald (1922/23) | – | – | 9 | 2 | – | – | – | – | – | – | 9 | 2 |
| W McDonald (1931/33) | – | – | 27 | 4 | – | – | – | – | – | – | 27 | 4 |
| EJ MacDougall (1972) | – | – | 18 | 5 | – | – | – | – | – | – | 18 | 5 |
| NW McFarlane (1953) | – | – | 1 | – | – | – | – | – | – | – | 1 | – |
| R McFarlane (1891) | – | – | 18 | 1 | 3 | – | – | – | – | – | 21 | 1 |
| D McFetteridge (1894) | – | – | 1 | – | – | – | – | – | – | – | 1 | – |
| ST McGarvey (1891/92) | – | – | 13/12 | 3 | – | – | – | – | – | – | 13/12 | 3 |
| C McGillivray (1933) | – | – | 8 | – | 1 | – | – | – | – | – | 9 | – |
| J McGillivray (1907/08) | – | – | 3 | – | 1 | – | – | – | – | – | 4 | – |
| W McGlen (1946/51) | – | – | 110 | 2 | 12 | – | – | – | – | – | 122 | 2 |
| P McGrath (1982/89) | – | – | 159/4 | 12 | 15/3 | 2 | 13 | 2 | 4 | 2 | 191/7 | 16 |
| W McGuinness (1955/59) | – | – | 81 | 2 | 2 | – | 2 | – | 2 | – | 85 | 2 |
| SB McIlroy (1971/81) | – | – | 320/22 | 57 | 35/3 | 6 | 25/3 | – | 10 | 2 | 390/28 | 71 |
| E McIlvenny (1950) | – | – | 2 | – | – | – | – | – | – | – | 2 | – |
| W McKay (1933/39) | – | – | 171 | 15 | 13 | – | – | – | – | – | 184 | 15 |
| C Mckee (1994- | 1 | – | – | – | – | – | – | – | – | – | 1 | – |

| Player | FAPL App | FAPL Goals | League App | League Goals | FACup App | FACup Goals | LgeCup App | LgeCup Goals | Europe App | Europe Goals | Totals App | Totals Goals |
|---|---|---|---|---|---|---|---|---|---|---|---|---|
| C Mackie (1904) | – | – | 5 | 3 | 2 | 1 | – | – | – | – | 7 | 4 |
| GH McLachlan (1929/32) | – | – | 110 | 4 | 6 | – | – | – | – | – | 116 | 4 |
| H McLenahan (1929/32) | – | – | 112 | 11 | 4 | 1 | – | – | – | – | 116 | 12 |
| A Macmillan (1890) | – | – | 2 | – | – | – | – | – | – | – | 2 | – |
| ST McMillan (1961/62) | – | – | 15 | 6 | – | – | – | – | – | – | 15 | 6 |
| WS McMillen (1933/34) | – | – | 27 | 2 | 2 | – | – | – | – | – | 29 | 2 |
| JR McNaught (1893/97) | – | – | 140 | 12 | 17 | – | – | – | 5* | – | 162 | 12 |
| T McNulty (1949/53) | – | – | 57 | – | 2 | – | – | – | – | – | 59 | – |
| FC McPherson (1923/27) | – | – | 159 | 45 | 16 | 7 | – | – | – | – | 175 | 52 |
| G McQueen (1977/84) | – | – | 184 | 20 | 21 | 2 | 16 | 4 | 7 | – | 228 | 26 |
| H McShane (1950/53) | – | – | 56 | 8 | 1 | – | – | – | – | – | 57 | 8 |
| G Maiorana (1988/) | – | – | 2/5 | – | – | – | –/1 | – | – | – | 2/6 | – |
| T Manley (1931/38) | – | – | 188 | 40 | 7 | 1 | – | – | – | – | 195 | 41 |
| FD Mann (1922/29) | – | – | 180 | 5 | 17 | – | – | – | – | – | 197 | 5 |
| H Mann (1931) | – | – | 13 | 2 | – | – | – | – | – | – | 13 | 2 |
| T Manns (1933) | – | – | 2 | – | – | – | – | – | – | – | 2 | – |
| AE Marshall (1902) | – | – | 6 | – | – | – | – | – | – | – | 6 | – |
| LA Martin (1987/) | 1 | – | 55/17 | 1 | 13/1 | 1 | 8/2 | – | 6/5 | – | 83/25 | 2 |
| MP Martin (1972/74) | – | – | 33/7 | 2 | 2 | – | 1 | – | – | – | 36/7 | 2 |
| W Mathieson (1892/93) | – | – | 13 | 3 | – | – | – | – | – | – | 13 | 3 |
| T Meehan (1919/20) | – | – | 51 | 6 | 2 | – | – | – | – | – | 53 | 6 |
| J Mellor (1930/36) | – | – | 116 | – | 6 | – | – | – | – | – | 122 | – |
| AW Menzies (1906/07) | – | – | 23 | 4 | 2 | – | – | – | – | – | 25 | 4 |
| WH Meredith (1906/20) | – | – | 303 | 35 | 29 | – | – | – | – | – | 332 | 35 |
| JW Mew (1912/25) | – | – | 186 | – | 13 | – | – | – | – | – | 199 | – |

| Player | FAPL App | FAPL Goals | League App | League Goals | FACup App | FACup Goals | LgeCup App | LgeCup Goals | Europe App | Europe Goals | Totals App | Totals Goals |
|---|---|---|---|---|---|---|---|---|---|---|---|---|
| R Milarvie (1890) | – | – | 22 | 4 | 1 | 1 | – | – | – | – | 23 | 4 |
| G Millar (1894) | – | – | 6 | 5 | 1 | – | – | – | – | – | 7 | 5 |
| J Miller (1923) | – | – | 4 | 1 | – | – | – | – | – | – | 4 | 1 |
| T Miller (1920) | – | – | 25 | 7 | 2 | 1 | – | – | – | – | 27 | 8 |
| R Milne (1988/91) | – | – | 19/4 | 3 | 7 | – | – | – | – | – | 26/4 | 3 |
| A Mitchell (1886/93) | – | – | 90 | – | 7 | – | – | – | 3* | – | 90 | – |
| A Mitchell (1932) | – | – | 1 | – | – | – | – | – | – | – | 1 | – |
| C Mitten (1946/49) | – | – | 142 | 50 | 19 | 11 | – | – | – | – | 161 | 61 |
| HH Moger (1903/11) | – | – | 242 | – | 22 | – | – | – | – | – | 264 | – |
| I Moir (1960/64) | – | – | 45 | 5 | – | – | – | – | – | – | 45 | 5 |
| A Montgomery (1905) | – | – | 3 | – | – | – | – | – | – | – | 3 | – |
| J Montgomery (1914/20) | – | – | 27 | 1 | – | – | – | – | – | – | 27 | 1 |
| J Moody (1931/32) | – | – | 50 | – | 1 | – | – | – | – | – | 51 | – |
| CW Moore (1919/29) | – | – | 309 | – | 19 | – | – | – | – | – | 328 | – |
| G Moore (1963) | – | – | 18 | 4 | 1 | – | – | – | – | – | 19 | 5 |
| KR Moran (1978/88) | – | – | 228/3 | 21 | 18 | 1 | 24/1 | 2 | 13/1 | – | 283/5 | 24 |
| H Morgan (1900) | – | – | 20 | 4 | 3 | – | – | – | – | – | 23 | 4 |
| W Morgan (1896/19(2) | – | – | 143 | 6 | 9 | 1 | – | – | – | – | 152 | 7 |
| W Morgan (1968/75) | – | – | 236/2 | 25 | 27 | 4 | 24/1 | 3 | 4 | 1 | 291/3 | 33 |
| KG Morgans (1957/60) | – | – | 17 | – | 2 | – | – | – | 4 | – | 23 | – |
| J Morris (1946/48) | – | – | 83 | 32 | 9 | 3 | – | – | – | – | 92 | 35 |
| T Morrison (1902/03) | – | – | 29 | 7 | 7 | 1 | – | – | – | – | 36 | 8 |
| BW Morton (1935) | – | – | 1 | – | – | – | – | – | – | – | 1 | – |
| RM Moses (1981/88) | – | – | 143/7 | 7 | 11 | 1 | 22/2 | 4 | 12/1 | – | 188/10 | 12 |
| AJH Muhren (1982/84) | – | – | 65/5 | 13 | 8 | 1 | 11 | 1 | 8 | 3 | 92/5 | 18 |

| Player | FAPL App | FAPL Goals | League App | League Goals | FACup App | FACup Goals | LgeCup App | LgeCup Goals | Europe App | Europe Goals | Totals App | Totals Goals |
|---|---|---|---|---|---|---|---|---|---|---|---|---|
| RD Murray (1937) | – | – | 4 | – | – | – | – | – | – | – | 4 | – |
| G Mutch (1934/37) | – | – | 112 | 46 | 8 | 3 | – | – | – | – | 120 | 49 |
| J Myerscough (1920/22) | – | – | 33 | 8 | 1 | – | – | – | – | – | 34 | 8 |
| G Neville (1992/) | 1 | – | – | – | – | – | – | – | /3 | – | 1/3 | – |
| GW Nevin (1933) | – | – | 4 | – | – | – | – | – | – | – | 5 | – |
| P Newton (1933) | – | – | 2 | – | – | – | – | – | – | – | 2 | – |
| JM Nicholl (1974/81) | – | – | 188/9 | 3 | 22/4 | 1 | 14 | 1 | 10 | 1 | 234/13 | 6 |
| JJ Nicholson (1960/65) | – | – | 58 | 5 | 7 | – | 3 | – | – | – | 68 | 6 |
| G Nichol (1927/28) | – | – | 6 | 2 | – | – | – | – | – | – | 7 | 2 |
| R Noble (1965/66) | – | – | 31 | 2 | 2 | – | – | – | – | – | 33 | 2 |
| JP Norton (1913/14) | – | – | 37 | 3 | – | – | – | – | – | – | 37 | 3 |
| TA Nuttall (1911/12) | – | – | 16 | 4 | – | – | – | – | – | – | 16 | 4 |
| LF O'Brien (1986/88) | – | – | 16/15 | 2 | –/2 | – | 1/2 | – | – | – | 17/19 | 2 |
| W O'Brien (1901) | – | – | 1 | – | – | – | – | – | – | – | 1 | – |
| P O'Connell (1914) | – | – | 34 | 2 | 1 | – | – | – | – | – | 35 | 2 |
| RL Olive (1952) | – | – | 2 | – | – | – | – | – | – | – | 2 | – |
| J Olsen (1984/89) | – | – | 119/20 | 21 | 13/3 | 2 | 10/3 | 1 | 6/1 | – | 148/27 | 24 |
| TP O'Neil (1970/72) | – | – | 54 | – | 7 | – | 7 | – | – | – | 68 | – |
| W O'Shaughnessy (1890) | – | – | 1 | – | 1 | – | – | – | – | – | 1 | – |
| A Owen (1898) | – | – | 1 | – | – | – | – | – | – | – | 1 | – |
| G Owen (1889) | – | – | 12 | 2 | 1 | – | – | – | – | – | 13 | 2 |
| J Owen (1889/91) | – | – | 52 | 3 | 6 | – | – | – | – | – | 58 | 3 |
| W Owen (1934/35) | – | – | 17 | 1 | – | – | – | – | – | – | 17 | 1 |
| LA Page (1931/32) | – | – | 12 | – | – | – | – | – | – | – | 12 | – |
| GA Pallister (1989/) | 82 | 2 | 108/3 | 4 | 24 | – | 32 | 1 | 17/1 | 1 | 264/4 | 7 |

| Player | FAPL App | FAPL Goals | League App | League Goals | FACup App | FACup Goals | LgeCup App | LgeCup Goals | Europe App | Europe Goals | Totals App | Totals Goals |
|---|---|---|---|---|---|---|---|---|---|---|---|---|
| AA Pape (1924/25) | – | – | 18 | 5 | – | – | – | – | – | – | 18 | 5 |
| B Parker (1893) | – | – | 11 | – | 1 | – | – | – | – | – | 12 | – |
| P Parker (1991/ | 70/2 | 1 | 24/2 | – | 13 | – | 14 | – | 14/3 | – | 125/19 | 4 |
| TA Parker (1930/31) | – | – | 17 | – | – | – | – | – | – | – | 17 | – |
| R Parkinson (1899) | – | – | 15 | 7 | – | – | – | – | – | – | 15 | 7 |
| AE Partridge (1920/28) | – | – | 148 | 16 | 12 | 2 | – | – | – | – | 160 | 18 |
| SW Paterson (1976/79) | – | – | 3/3 | 1 | – | – | 2 | – | /2 | – | 5/5 | 1 |
| E Payne (1908) | – | – | 2 | 1 | – | – | – | – | – | – | 2 | 1 |
| S Pears (1984) | – | – | 4 | – | 1 | – | – | – | – | – | 5 | – |
| M Pearson (1957/62) | – | – | 68 | 12 | 7 | 1 | 3 | 1 | 2 | – | 80 | 14 |
| SC Pearson (1937/53) | – | – | 315 | 128 | 30 | 21 | – | – | 2 | – | 345 | 149 |
| JS Pearson (1974/77) | – | – | 138/1 | 55 | 22 | 5 | 12 | 5 | 6 | 1 | 178/1 | 66 |
| JH Peddie (1902/06) | – | – | 112 | 52 | 9 | 6 | – | – | – | – | 121 | 58 |
| J Peden (1893) | – | – | 28 | 7 | 3 | 1 | – | – | 1* | – | 32 | 8 |
| J Pedley (1889) | – | – | 1 | – | – | – | – | – | – | – | 1 | – |
| D Pegg (1952/57) | – | – | 127 | 24 | 9 | – | – | – | 12 | 4 | 148 | 28 |
| E Pegg (1902/03) | – | – | 41 | 13 | 10 | 7 | – | – | – | – | 51 | 20 |
| JK Pegg (1947) | – | – | 2 | – | – | – | – | – | – | – | 2 | – |
| F Pepper (1898) | – | – | 7 | – | 1 | – | – | – | – | – | 8 | – |
| G Perrins (1892/95) | – | – | 92 | – | 6 | – | – | – | 4* | – | 102 | – |
| J Peters (1894/95) | – | – | 46 | 13 | 4 | 1 | – | – | 1* | – | 51 | 14 |
| M Phasey (1891) | – | – | 1 | – | – | – | – | – | – | – | 1 | – |
| MC Phelan (1989/ | 5/7 | 1 | 82/7 | 2 | 10 | 1 | 14/2 | – | 14/3 | – | 125/19 | 4 |
| JB Picken (1905/10) | – | – | 113 | 39 | 8 | 7 | – | – | – | – | 121 | 46 |
| MJ Pinner (1960) | – | – | 4 | – | – | – | – | – | – | – | 4 | – |

| Player | FAPL App | FAPL Goals | League App | League Goals | FACup App | FACup Goals | LgeCup App | LgeCup Goals | Europe App | Europe Goals | Totals App | Totals Goals |
|---|---|---|---|---|---|---|---|---|---|---|---|---|
| W Porter (1934/37) | – | – | 61 | – | 4 | – | – | – | – | – | 65 | – |
| AA Potts (1913/19) | – | – | 27 | 5 | 1 | – | – | – | – | – | 28 | 5 |
| J Powell (1886/90) | – | – | 21 | – | 4 | – | – | – | – | – | 25 | – |
| JH Prentice (1919) | – | – | 1 | – | – | – | – | – | – | – | 1 | – |
| S Preston (1901/02) | – | – | 33 | 14 | 1 | – | – | – | – | – | 34 | 14 |
| AJ Prince (1914) | – | – | 1 | – | – | – | – | – | – | – | 1 | – |
| D Prince (1893) | – | – | 2 | – | – | – | – | – | – | – | 2 | – |
| J Pugh (1921/22) | – | – | 2 | – | – | – | – | – | – | – | 2 | – |
| JJ Quinn (1908/09) | – | – | 2 | – | – | – | – | – | – | – | 2 | – |
| A Quixall (1958/63) | – | – | 165 | 50 | 14 | 4 | 1 | 2 | 3 | – | 183 | 56 |
| G Radcliffe (1898) | – | – | 1 | – | – | – | – | – | – | – | 1 | – |
| C Radford (1920/23) | – | – | 91 | 1 | 5 | – | – | – | – | – | 96 | 1 |
| CW Ramsden (1927/30) | – | – | 14 | 3 | 2 | – | – | – | – | – | 16 | 3 |
| R Ramsey (1890) | – | – | 22 | 5 | 1 | – | – | – | – | – | 23 | 5 |
| P Rattigan (1890) | – | – | 1 | – | – | – | – | – | – | – | 1 | – |
| WE Rawlings (1927/29) | – | – | 35 | 19 | 1 | – | – | – | – | – | 36 | 19 |
| TH Read (1902/03) | – | – | 35 | – | 7 | – | – | – | – | – | 42 | – |
| W Redman (1950/53) | – | – | 36 | – | 2 | – | – | – | – | – | 38 | – |
| H Redwood (1935/39) | – | – | 89 | 3 | 7 | 1 | – | – | – | – | 96 | 4 |
| T Reid (1928/32) | – | – | 96 | 63 | 5 | 4 | – | – | – | – | 101 | 67 |
| C Rennox (1924/26) | – | – | 60 | 24 | 8 | 1 | – | – | – | – | 68 | 25 |
| CH Richards (1902) | – | – | 8 | – | 3 | – | – | – | – | – | 11 | – |
| W Richards (1901) | – | – | 9 | 1 | – | – | – | – | – | – | 9 | 1 |
| LH Richardson (1925/28) | – | – | 38 | – | 4 | – | – | – | – | – | 42 | – |
| W Ridding (1931/33) | – | – | 42 | 14 | 2 | – | – | – | – | – | 44 | 14 |

| Player | FAPL App | FAPL Goals | League App | League Goals | FACup App | FACup Goals | LgeCup App | LgeCup Goals | Europe App | Europe Goals | Totals App | Totals Goals |
|---|---|---|---|---|---|---|---|---|---|---|---|---|
| JA Ridgway (1895/97) | - | - | 14 | - | 3 | - | - | - | - | - | 17 | - |
| JJ Rimmer (1967/72) | - | - | 34 | - | 3 | - | 6 | - | 2/1 | - | 45/1 | - |
| AT Ritchie (1977/80) | - | - | 26/7 | 13 | 3/1 | - | 3/2 | - | - | - | 32/10 | 13 |
| J Roach (1945) | - | - | - | - | 2 | - | - | - | - | - | 2 | - |
| DM Robbie (1935) | - | - | 1 | - | - | - | - | - | - | - | 1 | - |
| B Roberts (1898/99) | - | - | 9 | 2 | 1 | - | - | - | - | - | 10 | 2 |
| C Roberts (1903/12) | - | - | 271 | 22 | 28 | 1 | - | - | - | - | 299 | 23 |
| RHA Roberts (1913) | - | - | 2 | - | - | - | - | - | - | - | 2 | - |
| A Robertson (1903/05) | - | - | 33 | 1 | 2 | - | - | - | - | - | 35 | 1 |
| A Robertson (1903/04) | - | - | 28 | 10 | 6 | - | - | - | - | - | 34 | 10 |
| T Robertson (1903) | - | - | 3 | - | - | - | - | - | - | - | 3 | - |
| WS Robertson (1933/35) | - | - | 47 | 1 | 3 | - | - | - | - | - | 50 | 1 |
| MG Robins (1988/91) | - | - | 19/29 | 11 | 4/4 | 3 | -/7 | 2 | 4/2 | 1 | 27/42 | 17 |
| JW Robinson (1919/21) | - | - | 21 | 3 | - | - | - | - | - | - | 21 | 3 |
| M Robinson (1931) | - | - | 10 | - | - | - | - | - | - | - | 10 | - |
| B Robson (1981/94) | 15/14 | 2 | 310/5 | 72 | 33/1 | 10 | 50/2 | 5 | 26/1 | 8 | 434/23 | 97 |
| PJ Roche (1974/81) | - | - | 46 | - | 4 | - | 3 | - | - | - | 53 | - |
| M Rogers (1977) | - | - | 1 | - | - | - | - | - | - | - | 1 | - |
| C Rothwell (1893/96) | - | - | 2 | 1 | 1 | 2 | - | - | - | - | 3 | 3 |
| H Rothwell (1902) | - | - | 22 | - | 6 | - | - | - | - | - | 28 | - |
| WG Roughton (1936/38) | - | - | 86 | - | 6 | - | - | - | - | - | 92 | - |
| E Round (1909) | - | - | 2 | - | - | - | - | - | - | - | 2 | - |
| J Rowe (1913) | - | - | 1 | - | - | - | - | - | - | - | 1 | - |
| HB Rowley (1928/36) | - | - | 173 | 55 | 7 | - | - | - | - | - | 180 | 55 |
| JF Rowley (1937/54) | - | - | 380 | 182 | 42 | 26 | - | - | - | - | 422 | 208 |

| Player | FAPL | | League | | FACup | | LgeCup | | Europe | | Totals | |
|---|---|---|---|---|---|---|---|---|---|---|---|---|
| | App | Goals | App | Goals | App | Goals | App | Goals | App | Goals | App | Goals |
| EJ Royals (1912/13) | – | – | 7 | – | – | – | – | – | – | – | 7 | – |
| J Ryan (1965/69) | – | – | 21/3 | 4 | 1 | – | – | – | 2 | – | 24/3 | 4 |
| D Sadler (1963/73) | – | – | 266/6 | 22 | 22/1 | 1 | 22 | 1 | 16 | 3 | 326/7 | 27 |
| T Sadler (1890) | – | – | 1 | – | – | – | – | – | – | – | 1 | – |
| C Sagar (1905/06) | – | – | 30 | 20 | 3 | 4 | – | – | – | – | 33 | 24 |
| GD Sapsford (1919/21) | – | – | 52 | 16 | 1 | 1 | – | – | – | – | 53 | 17 |
| C Sartori (1968/71) | – | – | 26/13 | 4 | 9 | 1 | 3/2 | – | 2 | 1 | 40/15 | 6 |
| W Sarvis (1922) | – | – | 1 | – | – | – | – | – | – | – | 1 | – |
| J Saunders (1901/02) | – | – | 12 | – | 1 | – | – | – | – | – | 13 | – |
| RE Savage (1937) | – | – | 4 | – | 1 | – | – | – | – | – | 5 | – |
| F Sawyer (1899/1900) | – | – | 6 | – | – | – | – | – | – | – | 6 | – |
| AJ Scanlon (1954/60) | – | – | 115 | 34 | 6 | 1 | 3 | – | 3 | – | 127 | 35 |
| P Schmeichel (1991/) | 82 | – | 40 | – | 13 | – | 16 | – | 8 | – | 159 | – |
| A Schofield (1900/06) | – | – | 157 | 30 | 22 | 5 | – | – | – | – | 179 | 35 |
| GW Schofield (1920) | – | – | 1 | – | – | – | – | – | – | – | 1 | – |
| J Schofield (1903) | – | – | 2 | – | – | – | – | – | – | – | 2 | – |
| P Schofield (1921) | – | – | 23 | – | 1 | – | – | – | – | – | 24 | – |
| J Scott (1921) | – | – | 3 | – | – | – | – | – | – | – | 3 | – |
| J Scott (1952/56) | – | – | 33 | – | – | – | – | – | – | – | 33 | – |
| LJ Sealey (1989/94) | – | – | – | – | 4/1 | – | 9 | – | 8 | – | 21/1 | – |
| ME Setters (1959/64) | – | – | 159 | 12 | 25 | 1 | 2 | – | 7 | 1 | 193 | 14 |
| LS Sharpe (1988/) | 53/4 | 10 | 59/17 | 4 | 12/4 | 1 | 13/6 | 9 | 10/2 | 1 | 147/33 | 24 |
| WH Sharpe (1890/91) | – | – | 25 | 6 | – | – | – | – | – | – | 25 | 6 |
| J Sheldon (1910/12) | – | – | 26 | 1 | – | – | – | – | – | – | 26 | 1 |
| A Sidebottom (1972/73) | – | – | 16 | – | 2 | – | 2 | – | – | – | 20 | – |

| Player | FAPL | | League | | FACup | | LgeCup | | Europe | | Totals | |
|---|---|---|---|---|---|---|---|---|---|---|---|---|
| | App | Goals | App | Goals | App | Goals | App | Goals | App | Goals | App | Goals |
| J Silcock (1919/33) | – | – | 423 | 2 | 26 | – | – | – | – | – | 449 | 2 |
| J Siveback (1985/87) | – | – | 29/2 | 1 | 2 | – | 1 | – | – | – | 32/2 | 1 |
| JF Slater (1890/91) | – | – | 41 | – | 4 | – | – | – | – | – | 45 | – |
| T Sloan (1978/80) | – | – | 4/7 | – | – | – | –/1 | – | – | – | 4/8 | – |
| AC Smith (1926) | – | – | 5 | 1 | – | – | – | – | – | – | 5 | 1 |
| J Smith (1937/45) | – | – | 37 | 14 | 5 | 1 | – | – | – | – | 42 | 15 |
| L Smith (1902) | – | – | 3 | 1 | 7 | – | – | – | – | – | 10 | 1 |
| R Smith (1894/1900) | – | – | 93 | 35 | 7 | 2 | – | – | 1* | – | 101 | 37 |
| TG Smith (1923/26) | – | – | 83 | 12 | 7 | 4 | – | – | – | – | 90 | 16 |
| W Smith (1901) | – | – | 16 | – | 1 | – | – | – | – | – | 17 | – |
| J Sneddon (1891) | – | – | 21 | 6 | 3 | 1 | – | – | – | – | 24 | 7 |
| JW Spence (1919/32) | – | – | 481 | 158 | 29 | 10 | – | – | – | – | 510 | 168 |
| CW Spencer (1928/29) | – | – | 46 | – | 2 | – | – | – | – | – | 48 | – |
| W Spratt (1914/19) | – | – | 13 | – | – | – | – | – | – | – | 13 | – |
| G Stacey (1907/14) | – | – | 241 | 9 | 26 | – | – | – | – | – | 267 | 9 |
| H Stafford (1895/1902) | – | – | 183 | – | 17 | – | – | – | – | – | 200 | – |
| FA Stapleton (1981/87) | – | – | 204/19 | 60 | 21 | 7 | 26/1 | 6 | 14/1 | 5 | 265/21 | 78 |
| R Stephenson (1895) | – | – | 1 | 1 | – | – | – | – | – | – | 1 | 1 |
| AC Stepney (1966/77) | – | – | 433 | 2 | 44 | – | 35 | – | 23 | – | 535 | 2 |
| A Steward (1920/31) | – | – | 309 | – | 17 | – | – | – | – | – | 326 | – |
| W Stewart (1932/33) | – | – | 46 | 7 | 3 | – | – | – | – | – | 49 | 7 |
| WS Stewart (1890/94) | – | – | 138 | 23 | 9 | – | – | – | 2* | – | 149 | 23 |
| NP Stiles (1960/70) | – | – | 311 | 17 | 38 | – | 7 | – | 36 | 2 | 392 | 19 |
| H Stone (1893/94) | – | – | 6 | – | 1 | – | – | – | – | – | 7 | – |
| I Storey-Moore (1971/73) | – | – | 39 | 11 | – | – | 4 | 1 | 1* | – | 43 | 12 |

| Player | FAPL | | League | | FACup | | LgeCup | | Europe | | Totals | |
|---|---|---|---|---|---|---|---|---|---|---|---|---|
| | App | Goals | App | Goals | App | Goals | App | Goals | App | Goals | App | Goals |
| GD Strachan (1984/89) | – | – | 155/5 | 33 | 22 | 2 | 12/1 | 1 | 6 | 2 | 195/6 | 38 |
| E Street (1902) | – | – | 1 | – | – | – | – | – | – | – | 3 | – |
| JW Sutcliffe (1903) | – | – | 21 | – | 7 | – | – | – | – | – | 28 | – |
| EE Sweeney (1925/29) | – | – | 27 | 6 | 5 | 1 | – | – | – | – | 32 | 7 |
| T Tait (1889/90) | – | – | 7 | – | – | – | – | – | – | – | 7 | – |
| NH Tapken (1938) | – | – | 14 | – | 2 | – | – | – | – | – | 16 | – |
| C Taylor (1924/29) | – | – | 28 | 6 | 2 | 1 | – | – | – | – | 30 | 7 |
| E Taylor (1957/58) | – | – | 22 | 2 | 6 | – | – | – | 2 | 1 | 30 | 4 |
| T Taylor (1952/57) | – | – | 166 | 112 | 9 | 5 | – | – | 14 | 11 | 189 | 128 |
| W Taylor (1921) | – | – | – | – | – | – | – | – | – | – | 1 | – |
| H Thomas (1921/29) | – | – | 128 | 12 | 7 | 1 | – | – | – | – | 135 | 13 |
| MR Thomas (1978/80) | – | – | 90 | 11 | 13 | 2 | 5 | 2 | 2 | – | 110 | 15 |
| A Thomson (1929/30) | – | – | 3 | 1 | 2 | – | – | – | – | – | 5 | 1 |
| E Thomson (1907/08) | – | – | 4 | – | – | – | – | – | – | – | 4 | – |
| J Thompson (1913) | – | – | 6 | 1 | – | – | – | – | – | – | 6 | 1 |
| JE Thompson (1936/37) | – | – | 3 | 1 | – | – | – | – | – | – | 3 | 1 |
| W Thompson (1893) | – | – | 3 | – | – | – | – | – | – | – | 3 | – |
| B Thornley (1994/ | –/1 | – | – | – | – | – | – | – | – | – | –/1 | – |
| WE Toms (1919/20) | – | – | 13 | 3 | 1 | – | – | – | – | – | 14 | 4 |
| HW Topping (1932/34) | – | – | 12 | 1 | – | – | – | – | – | – | 12 | 1 |
| WJ Tranter (1963) | – | – | – | – | – | – | – | – | – | – | 1 | – |
| GE Travers (1913/14) | – | – | 21 | 4 | – | – | – | – | – | – | 21 | 4 |
| A Turnbull (1906/14) | – | – | 220 | 90 | 25 | 10 | – | – | – | – | 245 | 100 |
| JM Turnbull (1907/09) | – | – | 67 | 36 | 9 | 6 | – | – | – | – | 76 | 42 |
| B Turner (1890) | – | – | 1 | – | – | – | – | – | – | – | 1 | – |

| Player | FAPL App | FAPL Goals | League App | League Goals | FACup App | FACup Goals | LgeCup App | LgeCup Goals | Europe App | Europe Goals | Totals App | Totals Goals |
|---|---|---|---|---|---|---|---|---|---|---|---|---|
| CR Turner (1985/88) | – | – | 64 | – | 8 | – | 7 | – | – | – | 79 | – |
| J Turner (1898/1902) | – | – | 3 | – | 1 | – | – | – | – | – | 4 | – |
| R Turner (1898) | – | – | 2 | – | – | – | – | – | – | – | 2 | – |
| S Tyler (1923) | – | – | 1 | 1 | – | – | – | – | – | – | 1 | 1 |
| JF Ure (1969/70) | – | – | 47 | – | 8 | – | 10 | – | – | – | 65 | – |
| R Valentine (1904/05) | – | – | 10 | – | – | – | – | – | – | – | 10 | – |
| J Vance (1895/96) | – | – | 11 | – | – | – | – | – | – | – | 11 | – |
| E Vincent (1931/33) | – | – | 64 | – | 1 | – | – | – | – | – | 65 | – |
| DS Viollet (1952/61) | – | – | 259 | 159 | 18 | 5 | 2 | 1 | 12 | 13 | 291 | 178 |
| G Vose (1933/39) | – | – | 197 | 1 | 14 | – | – | – | – | – | 211 | 1 |
| C Waldron (1976) | – | – | 3 | – | 1 | – | – | – | – | – | 4 | – |
| DA Walker (1962) | – | – | 1 | – | – | – | – | – | – | – | 1 | – |
| R Walker (1898) | – | – | 2 | – | – | – | – | – | – | – | 2 | – |
| G Wall (1905/14) | – | – | 287 | 89 | 29 | 9 | – | – | – | – | 316 | 98 |
| DL Wallace (1989/93) | 12 | – | 36/9 | 6 | 7/2 | 2 | 4/3 | 3 | 5/2 | – | 52/18 | 11 |
| G Walsh (1986/ | 2/1 | – | 37 | – | – | – | 4 | – | 3 | – | 44 | – |
| JA Walton (1951) | – | – | 2 | – | – | – | – | – | – | – | 2 | – |
| JW Walton (1945/47) | – | – | 21 | 10 | 2 | – | – | – | – | – | 23 | 10 |
| A Warburton (1929/⊞) | – | – | 35 | – | 4 | – | – | – | – | – | 39 | – |
| J Warner (1892) | – | – | 22 | – | – | – | – | – | – | – | 22 | – |
| J Warner (1938/47) | – | – | 105 | 1 | 13 | – | – | – | – | – | 118 | 2 |
| JV Wassall (1935/39) | – | – | 46 | 6 | 2 | – | – | – | – | – | 48 | 6 |
| W Watson (1970/72) | – | – | 11 | – | – | – | 3 | – | – | – | 14 | – |
| JA Wealands (1982/⊞) | – | – | 7 | – | – | – | – | – | 1 | – | 8 | – |
| NJ Webb (1989/92) | 7/1 | – | 70/4 | 8 | 9 | 1 | 14 | 1 | 11 | 1 | 104/5 | 11 |

249

| Player | FAPL App | FAPL Goals | League App | League Goals | FACup App | FACup Goals | LgeCup App | LgeCup Goals | Europe App | Europe Goals | Totals App | Totals Goals |
|---|---|---|---|---|---|---|---|---|---|---|---|---|
| C Webster (1953/58) | – | – | 65 | 26 | 9 | 4 | – | – | 5 | 1 | 79 | 31 |
| FE Wedge (1897) | – | – | 2 | 2 | – | – | – | – | – | – | 2 | 2 |
| EJ West (1910/14) | – | – | 166 | 72 | 15 | 8 | – | – | – | – | 181 | 80 |
| J Wetherell (1896) | – | – | 2 | – | – | – | – | – | – | – | 2 | – |
| A Whalley (1909/19) | – | – | 97 | 6 | 9 | – | – | – | – | – | 106 | 6 |
| H Whalley (1935/46) | – | – | 33 | – | 6 | – | – | – | – | – | 39 | – |
| AG Whelan (1980) | – | – | –/1 | – | – | – | – | – | – | – | –/1 | – |
| LA Whelan (1954/57) | – | – | 79 | 43 | 6 | 4 | – | – | 11 | 5 | 96 | 52 |
| J Whitefoot (1949/55) | – | – | 93 | – | 2 | – | – | – | – | – | 95 | – |
| J Whitehouse (1900/02) | – | – | 59 | – | 5 | – | – | – | – | – | 64 | – |
| W Whitehurst (1955) | – | – | 1 | – | – | – | – | – | – | – | 1 | – |
| KD Whiteside (1907) | – | – | – | – | – | – | – | – | – | – | – | – |
| N Whiteside (1981/89) | – | – | 193/13 | 47 | 24 | 10 | 26/3 | 9 | 11/2 | 1 | 254/18 | 67 |
| J Whitney (1895/1900) | – | – | 3 | – | – | – | – | – | – | – | 3 | – |
| W Whittaker (1895) | – | – | 3 | – | – | – | – | – | – | – | 3 | – |
| J Whittle (1931) | – | – | 1 | – | – | – | – | – | – | – | 1 | – |
| N Whitworth (1990/91) | – | – | 2 | – | – | – | – | – | – | – | 2 | – |
| TWJ Wilcox (1908) | – | – | – | – | – | – | – | – | – | – | – | – |
| RC Wilkins (1979/83) | – | – | 158/2 | 7 | 10 | 1 | 14/1 | 1 | 8 | 1 | 190/3 | 10 |
| H Wilkinson (1903) | – | – | 8 | – | 1 | – | – | – | – | – | 9 | – |
| IM Wilkinson (1991) | – | – | – | – | – | – | 1 | – | – | – | 1 | – |
| DR Williams (1927/28) | – | – | 31 | 2 | 4 | – | – | – | – | – | 35 | 2 |
| F Williams (1902) | – | – | 8 | – | 2 | 4 | – | – | – | – | 10 | 4 |
| F Williams (1930) | – | – | 3 | – | – | – | – | – | – | – | 3 | – |
| H Williams (1922) | – | – | 5 | 2 | – | – | – | – | – | – | 5 | 2 |

| Player | FAPL App | FAPL Goals | League App | League Goals | FACup App | FACup Goals | LgeCup App | LgeCup Goals | Europe App | Europe Goals | Totals App | Totals Goals |
|---|---|---|---|---|---|---|---|---|---|---|---|---|
| H Williams (1904/05) | – | – | 33 | 7 | 4 | 1 | – | – | – | – | 37 | 8 |
| J Williams (1906) | – | – | 3 | 1 | – | – | – | – | – | – | 3 | 1 |
| W Williams (1901) | – | – | 4 | – | – | – | – | – | – | – | 4 | – |
| J Williamson (1919) | – | – | 2 | – | – | – | – | – | – | – | 2 | – |
| DG Wilson (1988) | – | – | /4 | – | /2 | – | – | – | – | – | /6 | – |
| E Wilson (1889) | – | – | 19 | 6 | 1 | – | – | – | – | – | 20 | 6 |
| JT Wilson (1926/31) | – | – | 130 | 3 | 10 | – | – | – | – | – | 140 | 3 |
| T Wilson (1907) | – | – | 1 | – | – | – | – | – | – | – | 1 | – |
| W Winterbottom (1936/37) | – | – | 25 | – | 2 | – | – | – | – | – | 27 | – |
| R Wombwell (1904/06) | – | – | 47 | 3 | 4 | – | – | – | – | – | 51 | 3 |
| J Wood (1922) | – | – | 15 | 1 | 1 | – | – | – | – | – | 16 | 1 |
| NA Wood (1985/86) | – | – | 2/1 | – | – | – | –/1 | – | – | – | 2/2 | – |
| RE Wood (1949/58) | – | – | 178 | – | 15 | – | – | – | 12 | – | 205 | – |
| W Woodcock (1913/19) | – | – | 58 | 20 | 3 | 1 | – | – | – | – | 61 | 21 |
| H Worrall (1946/47) | – | – | 6 | – | – | – | – | – | – | – | 6 | – |
| P Wratten (1990/91) | – | – | /2 | – | – | – | – | – | – | – | /2 | – |
| W Wrigglesworth (1936/46) | – | – | 30 | 8 | 7 | 2 | – | – | – | – | 37 | 10 |
| W Yates (1906) | – | – | 3 | – | – | – | – | – | – | – | 3 | – |
| J Young (1906) | – | – | 2 | – | – | – | – | – | – | – | 2 | – |
| TA Young (1970/75) | – | – | 59/14 | 1 | 5 | – | 5/4 | – | – | – | 79/18 | 1 |

# Players International Appearances Whilst with United

## England

VA Anderson   – 1987 W Germany, 1988 Hungary, Columbia (3)

J Aston       – 1948 Denmark, Wales, Switzerland; 1949 Scotland, Sweden, Norway, France, Rep of Ireland, Wales,N Ireland, Italy; 1950 Scotland, Portugal, Belgium, Chile, USA, N Ireland(17)

GR Bailey     – 1985 Rep of Ireland, Mexico (2)

JJ Berry      – 1953 Argentina, Chile, Uruguay, 1956 Sweden (4)

W Bradley     – 1959 Italy, Mexico, USA, (3)

RW Byrne      – 1954 Scotland, Yugoslavia, Hungary, Belgium, Switzerland, Uruguay, N Ireland, Wales, West Germany; 1955 Scotland, France, Spain, Portugal, Denmark, Wales, N Ireland, Spain; 1956 Scotland, Sweden, Brazil, Finland, West Germany, N Ireland, Wales, Yugoslavia, Denmark; 1957 Scotland, Rep of Ireland, Denmark, Rep of Ireland, Wales, N Ireland, France(33)

R Charlton    – 1958 Scotland, Portugal, Yugoslavia, N Ireland, USSR, Wales; 1959 Scotland, Italy, Brazil, Peru, Mexico, USA, Wales, Sweden; 1960 Scotland, Yugoslavia, Spain, Hungary, N Ireland, Luxembourg, Spain, Wales; 1961 Scotland, Mexico, Portugal, Italy, Austria, Luxembourg, Wales, Portugal, N Ireland; 1962 Austria, Scotland, Switzerland, Peru, Hungary, Argentina, Bulgaria, Brazil; 1963 France, Scotland, Brazil, Czechoslovakia, East Germany, Switzerland, Wales, Rest of World, N Ireland; 1964 Scotland, Uruguay, Portugal, Rep of Ireland, USA, Brazil, Argentina, N Ireland, Holland; 1965 Scotland, Wales, Austria, N Ireland, Spain ; 1966 West Germany, Scotland. Yugoslavia, Finland, Norway, Poland, Uruguay, Mexico, France, Argentina, Portugal, West Germany, N Ireland, Czechoslovakia, Wales; 1967 Scotland, Wales, N Ireland, USSR; 1968 Scotland, Spain, Spain, Sweden, Yugoslavia, USSR, Romania, Bulgaria; 1969 Romania, N Ireland, Wales, Scotland, Mexico, Brazil, Holland, Portugal; 1970 Holland, Wales, N Ireland, Colombia, Ecuador, Romania, Brazil, Czechoslovakia, West Germany (106)

AC Chilton    – 1950 N Ireland; 1951 France (2)

H Cockburn    – 1946 N Ireland, Rep of Ireland, Wales; 1948 Scotland, Italy, Denmark, N Ireland, Switzerland; 1949 Scotland, Sweden; 1951 Argentina, Portugal, France (13)

JM Connelly   – 1965 Hungary, Yugoslavia, Sweden, Wales, Austria, N Ireland; 1966 Scotland, Norway, Denmark, Uruguay (10)

SJ Coppell – 1977 Italy; 1978 West Germany, Brazil, Wales, N Ireland, Scotland, Hungary, Denmark, Rep of Ireland, Czechoslovakia; 1979 N Ireland (twice), Wales, Scotland, Bulgaria, Austria, Denmark, N Ireland; 1980 Rep of Ireland, Spain, Argentina, Wales, Scotland, Belgium, Italy, Romania, Switzerland; 1981 Romania, Brazil, Wales, Scotland, Switzerland, Hungary (twice), 1982 Scotland, Finland, France, Czechoslovakia, Kuwait, West Germany, Luxembourg; 1983 Greece (42)

M Duxbury – 1983 Luxembourg; 1984, France, Wales, Scotland, USSR, Brazil, Uruguay, Chile, East Germany, Finland (10)

D Edwards – 1955 Scotland, France, Spain, Portugal; 1956 Scotland, Brazil, Sweden, Finland, West Germany, N Ireland, Denmark; 1957 Scotland, Rep of Ireland, Denmark, Rep of Ireland, Wales, N Ireland, France (18)

WA Foulkes – 1954 N Ireland (1)

B Greenhoff – 1976 Wales, N Ireland, Rep of Ireland, Finland, Italy; 1977 Holland, N Ireland, Wales, Scotland, Brazil, Argentina, Uruguay; 1978 Brazil, Wales, N Ireland, Scotland, Hungary (17)

HJ Halse – 1909 Austria (1)

GA Hill – 1976 Italy, Rep of Ireland, Finland; 1977 Luxembourg, Switzerland, Luxembourg (6)

P Ince – 1992 Spain, Norway, Turkey, 1993 Turkey, Holland, Poland, USA, Brazil, Germany; 1994 Poland, Holland, San Marino, (Norway?), Denmark (13/14?)

B Kidd – 1970 N Ireland, Ecuador (2)

W McGuinness – 1958 N Ireland; 1959 Mexico (2)

JW Mew – 1920 Ireland (1)

GA Pallister – 1991 Cameroon, Turkey, Germany; 1993 Norway, USA, Brazil, Germany; 1994 Poland, Holland, San Marino, Denmark (11)

P Parker – 1991 Germany; 1994 Holland, Denmark (3)

JS Pearson – 1976 Wales, N Ireland, Scotland, Brazil, Finland, Rep of Ireland; 1977 Holland, Wales, Scotland, Brazil, Argentina, Uruguay, Italy; 1978 West Germany, N Ireland (15)

SC Pearson – 1948 Scotland, N Ireland; 1949 Scotland, N Ireland, Italy; 1951 Portugal; 1952 Scotland, Italy (8)

D Pegg – 1957 Rep of Ireland (1)

MC Phelan – 1989 Italy (1)

C Roberts – 1905 Ireland, Wales, Scotland (3)

B Robson       – 1981 Hungary; 1982 N Ireland, Wales, Holland, Scotland,
                 Finland, France, Czechoslovakia, West Germany, Spain,
                 Denmark, Greece, Luxembourg; 1983 Scotland, Hungary,
                 Luxembourg; 1984 France, N Ireland, Scotland, USSR, Brazil,
                 Uruguay, Chile, East Germany, Finland, Turkey; 1985 Rep of
                 Ireland, Romania, Finland, Scotland, Italy, Mexico, West
                 Germany, USA, Romania, Turkey; 1986 Israel, Mexico,
                 Portugal, Morocco, N Ireland; 1987 Spain, N Ireland, Turkey,
                 Brazil, Scotland, Turkey, Yugoslavia; 1988 Holland, Hungary,
                 Scotland, Columbia, Switzerland, Rep of Ireland, Holland,
                 USSR, Denmark, Sweden, Saudi Arabia; 1989 Greece, Albania,
                 Albania, Chile, Scotland, Poland, Denmark, Poland, Italy,
                 Yugoslavia; 1990 Czechoslovakia, Uruguay, Tunisia, Rep of
                 Ireland, Holland; 1991 Cameroon, Rep of Ireland, Turkey (77)

JF Rowley      – 1948 Switzerland; 1949 Sweden, France, N Ireland, Italy; 1952
                 Scotland (6)

D Sadler       – 1967 N Ireland, USSR; 1970 Ecuador, East Germany (4)

LS Sharpe      – 1991 Rep of Ireland; 1993 Turkey, Norway, USA, Brazil,
                 Germany; 1994 Poland (7)

J Silcock      – 1921 Wales, Scotland; 1923 Sweden (3)

JW Spence      – 1926 Belgium, N Ireland (2)

AC Stepney     – 1968 Sweden

NP Stiles      – 1965 Scotland, Hungary, Yugoslavia, Sweden, Wales, Austria,
                 N Ireland, Spain; 1966 Poland, West Germany, Scotland,
                 Norway, Denmark, Poland, Uruguay, Mexico, France,
                 Argentina, Portugal, West Germany, N Ireland, Czechoslovakia,
                 Wales; 1967 Scotland; 1968 USSR; 1969 Romania; 1970 N
                 Ireland, Scotland (28)

T Taylor       – 1953 Argentina, Chile, Uruguay; 1954 Belgium, Switzerland;
                 1956 Scotland, Brazil, Sweden, Finland, West Germany, N
                 Ireland, Yugoslavia, Denmark; 1957 Rep of Ireland, Denmark,
                 Rep of Ireland, Wales, N Ireland, France (19)

DS Viollet     – 1960 Hungary; 1961 Luxembourg (2)

G Wall         – 1907 Wales; 1908 Ireland; 1909 Scotland; 1910 Wales,
                 Scotland; 1912 Scotland; 1913 Ireland (7)

NJ Webb        – 1989 Sweden; 1990 Italy; 1992 France, Hungary, Brazil (5)

RG Wilkins     – 1979 Denmark, N Ireland, Bulgaria; 1980 Spain, Argentina,
                 Wales, N Ireland, Scotland, Belgium, Italy, Spain; 1981 Spain,
                 Romania, Brazil, Wales, Scotland, Switzerland, Hungary; 1982
                 N Ireland, Wales, Holland, Scotland, Finland, France,
                 Czechoslovakia, Kuwait, West Germany, Spain, Denmark, West

|  | Germany; 1983 Denmark; 1984 N Ireland, Wales, Scotland, USSR, Brazil, Uruguay, Chile (38) |
| RE Wood | – 1954 N Ireland, Wales; 1956 Finland (3) |

*Northern Ireland (and Ireland prior to 1924)*

| T Anderson | – 1973 Cyprus, England, Scotland, Wales, Bulgaria, Portugal (6) |
| G Best | – 1964 Wales, Uruguay, England, Switzerland, Switzerland, Scotland; 1965 Holland, Holland, Albania, Scotland, England, Albania; 1966 England; 1967 Scotland; 1968 Turkey; 1969 England, Scotland, Wales, USSR; 1970 Scotland, England, Wales, Spain; 1971 Cyprus, Cyprus, England, Scotland, Wales, USSR; 1972 Spain, Bulgaria; 1973 Portugal (32) |
| J Blanchflower | – 1954 Wales, England, Scotland; 1955 Scotland; 1956 Wales, England, Scotland; 1957 Portugal, Scotland, England, Italy; 1958 Italy (12) |
| T Breen | – 1937 Wales, England, Scotland; 1938 Scotland; 1939 Wales (5) |
| WR Briggs | – Wales (1) |
| JJ Carey | – 1946 England, Scotland; 1947 Wales, England; 1948 England, Scotland; 1949 Wales (7) |
| W Crooks | – 1922 Wales (1) |
| MM Donaghy | – 1988 Spain; 1989 Spain, Malta, Chile, Rep of Ireland; 1990 Norway, Yugoslavia, Denmark; 1991 Poland, Yugoslavia, Faroe Islands, Faroe Islands, Austria, Denmark; 1992 Scotland, Lithuania (18) |
| H Gregg | – 1958 Wales, Czechoslovakia, Argentina, West Germany, France, England; 1959 Wales, Scotland, England; 1960 Wales, England, Scotland; 1961 Scotland, Greece; 1963 Scotland, England (16) |
| M Hamill | – 1912 England; 1914 England, Scotland (3) |
| TA Jackson | – 1975 Sweden, Norway, Yugoslavia; 1976 Holland, Belgium; 1977 West Germany, England, Scotland, Wales, Iceland (10) |
| D Lyner | – 1922 England (1) |
| D McCreery | – 1976 Scotland, England, Wales, Holland, Belgium; 1977 West Germany, England, Scotland, Wales, Iceland, Iceland, Holland, Belgium; 1978 Scotland, England, Wales, Rep of Ireland, Denmark, Bulgaria; 1979 England, Bulgaria, Wales, Denmark (23) |
| RC McGrath | – 1976 Belgium; 1977 West Germany, England, Scotland, Wales, Iceland, Iceland, Holland, Belgium; 1978 Scotland, England, |

Wales, Bulgaria; 1979 England, England (15)

SB McIlroy – 1972 Spain, Scotland; 1974 Scotland, England, Wales, Norway, Sweden; 1975 Yugoslavia, England, Scotland, Wales, Sweden, Norway, Yugoslavia; 1976 Scotland, England, Wales, Holland, Belgium; 1977 England, Scotland, Wales, Iceland, Iceland, Holland, Belgium; 1978 Scotland, England, Wales, Rep of Ireland, Denmark, Bulgaria; 1979 England, Bulgaria, England, Scotland, Wales, Denmark, England, Rep of Ireland; 1980 Israel, Scotland, England, Wales, Australia, Australia, Australia, Sweden, Portugal; 1981 Scotland, Portugal, Svotland, Sweden, Scotland, Israel (52)

ST McMillan – 1962 England, Scotland (2)

WS McMillen – 1933 England; 1934 Scotland; 1936 Scotland (3)

JM Nicholl – 1976 Israel. Wales, Holland, Belgium; 1977 England, Scotland, Wales, Iceland, Iceland, Holland, Belgium; 1978 Scotland, England, Wales, Rep of Ireland, Denmark, Bulgaria; 1979 Emgland, Bulgaria, Engalnd, Scotland, Wales, Denmark, England, Rep of Ireland; 1980 Israel, Scotland, England, Wales, Sweden, Australia, Australia, Australia, Sweden, Portugal; 1981 Scotland, Portugal, Scotland, Sweden, Scotland, Israel; 1982 England (41)

JJ Nicholson – 1960 Scotland; 1961 Wales, Greece, England; 1962 Wales, Holland, Poland, England, Scotland, Poland (10)

T Sloan – 1979 Scotland, Wales, Denmark (3)

N Whiteside – 1982 Yugoslavia, Honduras, Spain, Austria, France, West Germany, Albania; 1983 Turkey, Austria, Turkey, West Germany, Scotland; 1984 England, Wales, Finland, Romania, Israel, Finland; 1985 England, Spain, Turkey, Romania, England; 1986 France, Denmark, Morocco, Algeria, Spain,Brazil, England; 1987 Israel, England, Yugoslavia, Turkey; 1988 Poland, France (36)

## Scotland

A Albiston – 1982 N Ireland; 1983 Uruguay, Belgium, East Germany; 1984 Wales, England, Yugoslavia, Iceland, Spain; 1985 Spain, Wales, East Germany; 1986 Holland. Uruguay (14)

A Bell – 1912 Ireland (1)

MM Buchan – 1972 Wales, Yugoslavia, Czechoslovakia, Brazil, Denmark, Denmark; 1973 England; 1974 West Germany, N Ireland, Wales, Norway, Brazil, Yugoslavia, East Germany; 1975 Spain, Portugal, Denmark, Romania; 1976 Finland, Czechoslovakia;

256

|  |  |
|---|---|
|  | 1977 Chile, Argentina, Brazil, East Germany, Wales; 1978 N Ireland, Peru, Iran, Holland, Austria, Norway, Portugal(32) |
| FS Burns | – 1969 Austria (1) |
| PT Crerand | – 1963 N Ireland; 1965 England, Poland, Finland, Poland (5) |
| J Delaney | – 1947 England, N Ireland, Wales; 1948 England (4) |
| A Forsyth | – 1973 England; 1974 East Germany, Spain; 1975 N Ireland, Romania, Denmark (6) |
| G Graham | – 1973 England, Wales, N Ireland, Switzerland, Brazil (5) |
| JA Holton | – 1973 Wales, N Ireland, England, Switzerland, Brazil, Czechoslovakia, West Germany; 1974 N ireland, Wales, England, Norway, Zaire, Brazil, Yugoslavia, East Germany (15) |
| SM Houston | – 1975 Denmark (1) |
| J Jordan | – 1978 Bulgaria, N Ireland, England, Peru, Iran, Holland, Austria, Portugal; 1979 Wales, N Ireland, England, Norway, Belgium; 1980 N Ireland, Wales, England, Poland; 1981 Israel, Wales, England (20) |
| D Law | – 1962 Wales, N Ireland; 1963 England, Austria, Norway, Rep of Ireland, Spain, Norway, Wales; 1964 England, West Germany, Wales, Finland, N Ireland; 1965 England, Spain, Poland, Finland, N Ireland, Poland; 1966 England, Wales; 1967 England, USSR, N Ireland; 1968 Austria; 1969 West Germany, N Ireland; 1972 Peru, N Ireland, Wales, England, Yugoslavia, Czechoslovakia, Brazil (35) |
| J Leighton | – 1988 Colombia, England, Norway; 1989 Cyprus, France, Cyprus, England, Chile, Yugoslavia, France, Norway; 1990 Argentina, Malta, Costa Rica, Sweden, Brazil (16) |
| N McBain | – 1922 England (1) |
| BJ McClair | – 1987 Bulgaria; 1988 Malta, Spain, Norway, Yugoslavia, Italy; 1989 Cyprus, France, Norway; 1990 Argentina, Bulgaria; 1991 Bulgaria, San Marino, Switzerland, Romania; 1992 Northern Ireland, USA, Canada (18) |
| G McQueen | – 1978 Bulgaria, N Ireland, Wales, Austria, Norway, Portugal; 1979 N Ireland, England, Norway, Peru, Austria, Belgium; 1981 Wales (13) |
| L Macari | – 1973 England, Wales, N Ireland, England; 1975 Sweden, Portugal, Wales, England, Romania; 1977 N Ireland, England, Chile, Argentina, East Germany, Wales; 1978 Bulgaria, Peru, Iran (18) |
| T Miller | – 1921 Ireland, England (2) |

W Morgan        –   1972 Peru, Yugoslavia, Czechoslovakia, Brazil, Denmark,
                    Denmark; 1973 England, Wales, N Ireland, England,
                    Switzerland, Brazil, Czechoslovakia, Czechoslovakia, West
                    Germany; 1974 West Germany, N Ireland, Belgium, Brazil,
                    Yugoslavia (20)

GD Strachan     –   1985 Spain, England, Iceland, Wales, Australia; 1986 Romania,
                    Denmark, West Germany, Uruguay, Bulgaria, Rep of Ireland;
                    1987 Rep of Ireland, Hungary; 1989 France (14)

*Wales*
_____

SR Bennison     –   1925 Scotland; 1926 Scotland; 1927 Scotland, England; 1928 N
                    Ireland, Scotland, England; 1929 N Ireland, Scotland; 1931 N
                    Ireland (10)

CG Blackmore    –   1985 Norway, Scotland, Hungary; 1986 Saudi Arabia, Rep of
                    Ireland, Uruguay, Finland; 1987 USSR, Finland,
                    Czechoslovakia, Denmark, Denmark, Czechoslovakia; 1988
                    Yugoslavia, Sweden, Malta, Italy, Holland, Finland; 1989
                    Israel, West Germany, Finland, Holland, West Germany; 1990
                    Costa Rica, Belgium, Luxembourg; 1992 Rep of Ireland,
                    Austria, Romania, Holland, Argentina, Japan; 1993 Faroe
                    Islands, Cyprus, Belgium, Czechoslavakia (37)

T Burke         –   1887 England, Scotland, 1888 Scotland (3)

A Davies        –   1983 N Ireland, Brazil; 1984 England, N Ireland, Iceland,
                    Iceland; 1985 Norway (7)

J Davies        –   1888 England, Ireland, Scotland; 1889 Scotland; 1890 England
                    (5)

R W Davies      –   1972 England; 1973 Scotland, N Ireland (3)

J Doughty       –   1887 Ireland, Scotland; 1888 England, Ireland, Scotland; 1889
                    Scotland; 1890 England (7)

R Doughty       –   1888 Ireland, Scotland (2)

RJ Giggs        –   1991 Germany, Luxembourg; 1992 Romania, Faroe Islands,
                    Belgium; 1993 Czechoslavakia, Belgium, Faroe Islands (8)

LM Hughes       –   1984 England, N Ireland, Iceland, Spain, Iceland; 1985 Norway,
                    Scotland, Spain, Norway, Scotland, Hungary; 1986 Uruguay;
                    1988 Holland, Finland; 1989 Israel, Sweden, West Germany,
                    Finland, West Germany; 1990 Costa Rica, Denmark, Belgium,
                    Luxembourg; 1991 Belgium, Iceland, Poland, Germany, Brazil,
                    Germany, Luxembourg; 1992 Rep of Ireland, Romania,
                    Holland, Argentina, Japan, 1993 Faroe Islands, Belgium,
                    Czechoslavakia. Cyprus, Eire, Belgium, Faroe Islands; 1994
                    Norway (43)

| CAL Jenkyns | – 1897 Ireland (1) |
|---|---|
| T Jones | – 1926 N Ireland; 1927 England, N Ireland; 1930 N Ireland (4) |
| WH Meredith | – 1907 Ireland, Scotland, England; 1908 England, Ireland; 1909 Scotland, England, Ireland; 1910 Scotland, England, Ireland; 1911 Ireland, Scotland, England; 1912 Scotland, England, Ireland; 1913 Ireland, Scotland, England; 1914 Ireland, Scotland, England; 1920 Ireland, Scotland, England (26) |
| G Moore | – 1963 Scotland; 1964 N Ireland (2) |
| G Owen | – 1889 Scotland, Ireland (2) |
| J Owen | – 1892 England (1) |
| W Owen | – 1888 England; 1889 England, Scotland, Ireland (4) |
| J Powell | – 1887 England, Scotland; 1888 England, Ireland, Scotland (5) |
| H Thomas | – 1927 England |
| MR Thomas | – 1978 Turkey; 1979 West Germany, Malta, Rep of Ireland, West Germany, Turkey; 1980 England, Scotland, N Ireland, Czechoslovakia; 1981 Scotland, England, USSR (13) |
| J Warner | – 1939 France (1) |
| C Webster | – 1957 Czechoslovakia; 1958 Hungary, Mexico, Brazil (4) |
| DR Williams | – 1928 Scotland, England (2) |

## *Republic of Ireland*

| T Breen | – 1937 Switzerland, France (2) |
|---|---|
| SA Brennan | – 1965 Spain, Spain, 1966 Austria, Belgium, Spain, Turkey, Spain; 1969 Czechoslovakia, Denmark, Hungary, Scotland, Czechoslovakia, Denmark, Hungary; 1970 Poland, West Germany (16) |
| N Cantwell | – 1961 Scotland, Scotland, Czechoslovakia, Czechoslovakia; 1962 Austria, Iceland, Iceland; 1963 Scotland, Austria; 1964 Spain, England, Poland; 1965 Spain, Spain, Spain; 1966 Austria, Belgium, Spain; 1967 Turkey (19) |
| B Carey | – 1992 USA, 1993 Wales (2) |
| JJ Carey | – 1937 Norway; 1938 Czechoslovakia, Poland, Switzerland, Poland; 1939 Hungary, Hungary, Germany; 1946 Portugal, Spain, England; 1947 Spain, Portugal; 1948 Portugal, Spain, Switzerland; 1949 Belgium, Portugal, Sweden, Spain, Finland, England, Finland, Sweden; 1950 Norway; 1951 Argentina, Norway; 1952 France; 1953 Austria (29) |
| JE Carolan | – 1959 Sweden; 1960 Chile (2) |

GA Daly  – 1973 Poland, Norway; 1974 Brazil, Uruguay; 1975 West Germany, Switzerland; 1976 England, Turkey, France (9)

AP Dunne  – 1962 Austria, Iceland; 1963 Scotland, Austria; 1964 Spain, Norway, England, Norway, England, Poland; 1965 Spain, Spain, Spain; 1966 Austria, Belgium, Spain, Turket, Spain; 1968 Poland, Denmark; 1969 Hungary, Hungary; 1970 Sweden; 1971 Italy, Austria (24)

PAJ Dunne  – 1965 Spain, Spain, Spain; 1966 West Germany, Turkey (5)

MJ Giles  – 1959 Sweden; 1960 Chile, Wales, Norway; 1961 Scotland, Scotland, Czechoslovakia, Czechoslovakia; 1962 Austria, Iceland; 1963 Scotland (11)

DJ Givens  – 1969 Denmark, Hungary, Scotland, Czechoslovakia, Denmark, Hungary (6)

AA Grimes  – 1978 Turkey, Poland, Norway, England; 1979 Bulgaria, USA, N Ireland; 1980 England, Cyprus; 1981 Czechoslovakia, West Germany, Poland; 1982 Algeria, Spain; 1983 Spain (15)

DJ Irwin  – 1990 Morocco, Turkey; 1991 Wales, England, Poland, USA, Hungary, Poland; 1992 Wales, USA, Albania, USA, Italy; 1993 Latvia, Denmark, Spain, N. Ireland, Denmark, Albania, Latvia, Lithunia (21)

R Keane  – ????

P McGrath  – 1985 Italy, Israel, England, Norway, Switzerland, Switzerland, Denmark; 1986 Wales, Iceland, Czechoslovakia, Belgium, Scotland, Poland; 1987 Scotland, Bulgaria, Belgium, Brazil, Luxembourg, Luxembourg, Bulgaria; 1988 Yugoslavia, Poland, Norway, England, Holland, N Ireland; 1989 France, Hungary, Spain, Malta, Hungary (31)

MP Martin  – 1973 USSR, Poland, France, Norway, Poland; 1974 Brazil, Uruguay, Chile, USSR, Turkey; 1975 West Germany, Switzerland, USSR, Switzerland (14)

KR Moran  – 1980 Switzerland, Argentina, Belgium, France, Cyprus; 1981 Wales, Belgium, Czechoslovakia, West Germany, Poland, France; 1982 Algeria, Iceland, Holland, Malta; 1984 Israel, Mexico; 1985 Denmark, Iceland, Czechoslovakia, Belgium, Scotland, Poland; 1987 Scotland, Bulgaria, Belgium, Brazil, Luxembourg, Luxembourg, Bulgaria, Israel; 1988 Romania, Yugoslavia, Poland, Norway, England, USSR, Holland (38)

LF O'Brien  – 1987 Brazil, Israel; 1988 Romania, Yugoslavia, Poland, Tunisia (6)

PJ Roche  – 1974 USSR, Turkey; 1975 West Germany, Switzerland, USSR, Switzerland, Turkey (7)

| FA Stapleton | – 1981 Holland, France; 1982 Algeria, Holland, Iceland, Spain; 1983 Malta, Spain, Iceland, Holland, Malta; 1984 Israel, Poland, China, Norway, Denmark; 1985 Italy, Israel, England, Norway, Switzerland, Switzerland, USSR, Denmark; 1986 Uruguay, Iceland, Czechoslovakia, Belgium, Scotland, Poland; 1987 Scotland, Bulgaria, Belgium, Luxembourg (34) |
|---|---|
| L A Whelan | – 1956 Holland, Denmark; 1957 England, England (4) |

*France*

| E Cantona | – 1994 Italy (1) |
|---|---|

*Denmark*

| J Olsen | – 1984 Austria, Norway, Switzerland; 1985 East Germany, USSR, Rep of Ireland; 1986 N Ireland, Bulgaria, Poland, Paraguay, Scotland, Uruguay, West Germany, Spain, East Germany, West Germany, Czechoslovakia; 1987 Czechoslovakia, Sweden, West Germany, Wales; 1988 Austria, Hungary, Czechoslovakia, Belgium (25) |
|---|---|
| P Schmeichel | – 1991 Italy, Sweden, Faroe Islands, Austria, N Ireland; 1992 England, Sweden, France, Holland, Germany; 1994 England (11) |
| J Siveback | – 1986 N Ireland, Bulgaria, Norway, Poland, Scotland, West Germany, East Germany, Finland, West Germany; 1987 Finland, Czechoslovakia (11) |

*USSR/Russia*

| A Kanchelskis | – 1991 Hungary, England, Argentina, Cyprus, Sweden, Italy, Norway, Hungary, Italy, Cyprus; 1992 Spain, England |
|---|---|

*Yugoslavia*

| N Jovanovic | – 1980 Luxembourg, Denmark; 1982 N Ireland, Spain, Honduras (5) |
|---|---|

*Rest of the World*

| D Law | – 1963 England (1) |
|---|---|

*Rest of Europe*

| JJ Carey | – 1947 Great Britain (1) |
|---|---|
| R Charlton | – 1964 Scandinavia (1) |
| D Law | – 1964 Scandinavia (1) |

**1886/87**

| 1st Round | v Fleetwood Rangers | (a) | 2-2 | Doughty 2 |
|---|---|---|---|---|

*(tie awarded to Fleetwood as Newton Heath refused to play extra-time)*

**1889/90**

| 1st Round | v Preston North End | (a) | 1-6 | Craig |
|---|---|---|---|---|

**1890/91**

| 1st Qual Round | v Higher Walton | (h) | 2-0 | Farman, Evans |
|---|---|---|---|---|
| 2nd Qual Round | v Bootle Reserves | (a) | 0-1 | |

*(both teams fielded virtual Reserve teams)*

**1891/92**

| 1st Qual Round | v Ardwick | (h) | 5-1 | Farman 2, Doughty, Sneddon, Edge |
|---|---|---|---|---|
| 2nd Qual Round | v Heywood | | | *(Heywood withdrew)* |
| 3rd Qual Round | v South Shore | (a) | 2-0 | Farman, Doughty, |
| 4th Qual Round | v Blackpool | (h) | 3-4 | Farman, Edge 2 |

**1892/93**

| 1st Round | v Blackburn Rovers | (a) | 0-4 | |
|---|---|---|---|---|

**1893/94**

| 1st Round | v Middlesborough | (h) | 4-0 | Farman, Pedden Donaldson 2, |
|---|---|---|---|---|
| 2nd Round | v Blackburn Rovers | (h) | 0-0† | |
| Replay | v Blackburn Rovers | (a) | 1-5 | Donaldson |

**1894/95**

| 1st Round | v Stoke City | (h) | 2-3 | Smith, Peters |
|---|---|---|---|---|

**1895/96**

| 1st Round | v Kettering Town | (h) | 2-1 | Donaldson, Smith |
|---|---|---|---|---|
| 2nd Round | v Derby County | (h) | 1-1 | Kennedy |
| Replay | v Derby County | (a) | 1-5 | Donaldson |

**1896/97**

| 3rd Qual Round | v West Manchester | (h) | 7-0 | Cassidy 2, Gillespie 2, Rothwell 2, Bryant |
|---|---|---|---|---|
| 4th Qual Round | v Nelson | (h) | 3-0 | Cassidy, Donaldson, Gillespie |
| 5th Qual Round | v Blackpool | (h) | 2-2 | Gillespie, Donaldson |
| Replay | v Blackpool | (a) | 2-1 | Boyd, Cassidy |
| 1st Round | v Kettering Town | (h) | 5-1 | Cassidy, Donaldson |

| | | | | |
|---|---|---|---|---|
| 2nd Round | v Southampton | (a) | 1-1 | Donaldson |
| Replay | v Southampton | (h) | 3-1 | Bryant 2, Cassidy |
| 3rd Round | v Derby County | (a) | 0-2 | |

**1897/98**

| | | | | |
|---|---|---|---|---|
| 1st Round | v Walsall | (h) | 1-0 | Own Goal |
| 2nd Round | v Liverpool | (h) | 0-0 | |
| Replay | v Liverpool | (a) | 1-2 | Collinson |

**1898/99**

| | | | | |
|---|---|---|---|---|
| 1st Round | v Tottenham Hotspur | (a) | 1-1 | Cassidy |
| Replay | v Tottenham Hotspur | (h) | 3-5 | Bryant 3 |

**1899/00**

| | | | | |
|---|---|---|---|---|
| 3rd Qual Round | v South Shore | (a) | 1-3 | Jackson |

**1900/01**

| | | | | |
|---|---|---|---|---|
| Prelim Round | v Portsmouth | (h) | 3-0 | Griffiths, Jackson, Stafford |
| 1st Round | v Burnley | (h) | 0-0 | |
| Replay | v Burnley | (a) | 1-7 | Schofield |

**1901/02**

| | | | | |
|---|---|---|---|---|
| Prelim Round | v Lincoln City | (h) | 1-2 | Fisher |

**1902/03**

| | | | | |
|---|---|---|---|---|
| 3rd Qual Round | v Accrington Stanley | (h) | 7-0 | Williams 3, Peddie, Richards, Pegg, Morgan |
| 4th Qual Round | v Oswaldtwistle Rovers | (h) | 3-2 | Pegg, Beardsworth, Williams |
| 5th Qual Round | v Southport Central | (h) | 4-1 | Pegg 3, Banks |
| 6th Qual Round | v Burton United | (h) | 1-1 | Griffiths |
| Replay | v Burton United | (h) | 3-1 | Schofield, Pegg, Peddie |
| 1st Round | v Liverpool | (h) | 2-1 | Peddie 2 |
| 2nd Round | v Everton | (a) | 1-3 | Griffiths |

**1903/04**

| | | | | |
|---|---|---|---|---|
| Prelim Round | v Small Heath | (h) | 1-1 | Schofield |
| Replay | v Small Heath | (a) | 1-1† | Arkesden |
| 2nd Replay | v Small Heath | (n) | 1-1† | Schofield |
| 3rd Replay | v Small Heath | (n) | 3-1 | Arkesden 2, Grassam |
| 1st Round | v Notts County | (a) | 3-3 | Downie, Schofield, Arkesden |
| Replay | v Notts County | (h) | 2-1 | Morrison, Pegg |
| 2nd Round | v Sheffield Wednesday | (a) | 0-6 | |

**1904/05**

| | | | | |
|---|---|---|---|---|
| Prelim Round | v Fulham | (h) | 2-2 | Mackie, Arkesden |
| Replay | v Fulham | (a) | 0-0† | |
| 2nd Replay | v Fulham | (n) | 0-1 | |

**1905/06**

| | | | | |
|---|---|---|---|---|
| 1st Round | v Staple Hill | (h) | 7-2 | Beddow 3, Picken 2, Allen, Williams |
| 2nd Round | v Norwich City | (h) | 3-0 | Downie, Peddie, Sagar |
| 3rd Round | v Aston Villa | (h) | 5-1 | Picken 3, Sagar 2 |
| 4th Round | v Woolwich Arsenal | (h) | 2-3 | Peddie, Sagar |

**1906/07**

| | | | | |
|---|---|---|---|---|
| 1st Round | v Portsmouth | (a) | 2-2 | Picken, Wall |
| Replay | v Portsmouth | (h) | 1-2 | Wall |

**1907/08**

| | | | | |
|---|---|---|---|---|
| 1st Round | v Blackpool | (h) | 3-1 | Wall 2, Bannister |
| 2nd Round | v Chelsea | (h) | 1-0 | A.Turnbull |
| 3rd Round | v Aston Villa | (a) | 2-0 | A.Turnbull, Wall |
| 4th Round | v Fulham | (a) | 1-2 | J.Turnbull |

**1908/09**

| | | | | |
|---|---|---|---|---|
| 1st Round | v Brighton & H.A | (h) | 1-0 | Halse |
| 2nd Round | v Everton | (h) | 1-0 | Halse |
| 3rd Round | v Blackburn Rovers | (h) | 6-1 | A.Turnbull 3, J.Turnbull 3 |
| 4th Round | v Burnley | (a) | 3-2 | J Turnbull 2, Halse |
| Semi Final | v Newcastle United | (n) | 1-0 | Halse |
| Final | v Bristol City | (n) | 1-0 | A.Turnbull |

**1909/10**

| | | | | |
|---|---|---|---|---|
| 1st Round | v Burnley | (a) | 0-2 | |

**1910/11**

| | | | | |
|---|---|---|---|---|
| 1st Round | v Blackpool | (a) | 2-1 | Picken, West |
| 2nd Round | v Aston Villa | (h) | 2-1 | Halse, Wall |
| 3rd Round | v West Ham United | (a) | 1-2 | A.Turnbull |

**1911/12**

| | | | | |
|---|---|---|---|---|
| 1st Round | v Huddersfield Town | (h) | 3-1 | West 2, Halse |
| 2nd Round | v Coventry City | (a) | 5-1 | Halse 2, West, Turnbull, Wall |
| 3rd Round | v Reading | (a) | 1-1 | West |
| Replay | v Reading | (h) | 3-0 | A.Turnbull 2, Halse |
| 4th Round | v Blackburn Rovers | (h) | 1-1 | Own Goal |
| Replay | v Blackburn Rovers | (a) | 2-4† | West 2 |

**1912/13**

| | | | | |
|---|---|---|---|---|
| 1st Round | v Coventry City | (h) | 1-1 | Wall |
| Replay | v Coventry City | (a) | 2-1 | Anderson, Roberts |
| 2nd Round | v Plymouth Argyle | (a) | 2-0 | Anderson, Wall |
| 3rd Round | v Oldham Athletic | (a) | 0-0 | |
| Replay | v Oldham Athletic | (h) | 1-2 | West |

**1913/14**

| | | | | |
|---|---|---|---|---|
| 1st Round | v Swindon Town | (a) | 0-1 | |

**1914/15**

| | | | | |
|---|---|---|---|---|
| 1st Round | v Sheffield Wednesday | (a) | 0-1 | |

**1919/20**

| | | | | |
|---|---|---|---|---|
| 1st Round | v Port Vale | (a) | 1-0 | Toms |
| 2nd Round | v Aston Villa | (h) | 1-2 | Woodcock |

**1920/21**

| | | | | |
|---|---|---|---|---|
| 1st Round | v Liverpool | (a) | 1-1 | Miller |
| Replay | v Liverpool | (h) | 1-2 | Partridge |

**1921/22**

| | | | | |
|---|---|---|---|---|
| 1st Round | v Cardiff City | (h) | 1-4 | Sapsford |

**1922/23**

| | | | | |
|---|---|---|---|---|
| 1st Round | v Bradford City | (a) | 1-1 | Partridge |
| Replay | v Bradford City | (h) | 2-0 | Barber, Goldthorpe |
| 2nd Round | v Tottenham Hotspurs | (a) | 0-4 | |

**1923/24**

| | | | | |
|---|---|---|---|---|
| 1st Round | v Plymouth Argyle | (h) | 1-0 | McPherson |
| 2nd Round | v Huddersfield Town | (h) | 0-3 | |

**1925/25**

| | | | | |
|---|---|---|---|---|
| 1st Round | v Sheffield Wednesday | (a) | 0-2 | |

**1925/26**

| | | | | |
|---|---|---|---|---|
| 3rd Round | v Port Vale | (a) | 3-2 | Spence 2, McPherson |
| 4th Round | v Tottenham Hotspurs | (a) | 2-2 | Spence, Thomas |
| Replay | v Tottenham Hotspurs | (h) | 2-0 | Spence, Rennox |
| 5th Round | v Sunderland | (a) | 3-3 | Smith 2, McPherson |
| Replay | v Sunderland | (h) | 2-1 | Smith, McPherson |
| 6th Round | v Fulham | (a) | 2-1 | Smith, McPherson |
| Semi Final | v Manchester City | (n) | 0-3 | |

**1926/27**

| | | | | |
|---|---|---|---|---|
| 3rd Round | v Reading | (a) | 1-1 | Bennion |
| Replay | v Reading | (h) | 2-2 | Spence, Sweeney |
| 2nd Replay | v Reading | (n) | 1-2 | McPherson |

**1927/28**

| | | | | |
|---|---|---|---|---|
| 3rd Round | v Brentford | (h) | 7-1 | Hanson 4, Spence, McPherson, Johnston |
| 4th Round | v Bury | (a) | 1-1 | Johnston |
| Replay | v Bury | (h) | 1-0 | Spence |
| 5th Round | v Birmingham | (h) | 1-0 | Johnston |
| 6th Round | v Blackburn Rovers | (a) | 0-2 | |

**1928/29**

| | | | | |
|---|---|---|---|---|
| 3rd Round | v Port Vale | (a) | 3-0 | Spence, Hanson, Taylor |
| 4th Round | v Bury | (h) | 0-1 | |

**1929/30**

| | | | | |
|---|---|---|---|---|
| 3rd Round | v Swindon Town | (h) | 0-2 | |

**1930/31**

| | | | | |
|---|---|---|---|---|
| 3rd Round | v Stoke City | (a) | 3-3 | Reid 3 |
| Replay | v Stoke City | (h) | 0-0† | |
| 2nd Replay | v Stoke City | (n) | 4-2 | Hopkinson 2, Spence, Gallimore |
| 4th Round | v Grimsby Town | (a) | 0-1 | |

**1931/32**

| | | | | |
|---|---|---|---|---|
| 3rd Round | v Plymouth Argyle | (a) | 1-4 | Reid |

**1932/33**

| | | | | |
|---|---|---|---|---|
| 3rd Round | v Middlesbrough | (h) | 1-4 | Spence |

**1933/34**

| | | | | |
|---|---|---|---|---|
| 3rd Round | v Portsmouth | (h) | 1-1 | McLenahan |
| Replay | v Portsmouth | (a) | 1-4 | Ball |

**1934/35**

| | | | | |
|---|---|---|---|---|
| 3rd Round | v Bristol Rovers | (a) | 3-1 | Bamford 2, Mutch |
| 4th Round | v Nottingham Forest | (a) | 0-0 | |
| Replay | v Nottingham Forest | (h) | 0-3 | |

**1935/36**

| | | | | |
|---|---|---|---|---|
| 3rd Round | v Reading | (a) | 3-1 | Mutch 2, Manley |
| 4th Round | v Stoke City | (a) | 0-0 | |
| Replay | v Stoke City | (h) | 0-2 | |

**1936/37**

| | | | | |
|---|---|---|---|---|
| 3rd Round | v Reading | (h) | 1-0 | Bamford |
| 4th Round | v Arsenal | (a) | 0-5 | |

**1937/38**

| | | | | |
|---|---|---|---|---|
| 3rd Round | v Yeovil Town | (h) | 3-0 | Baird, Bamford, Pearson |

| | | | | |
|---|---|---|---|---|
| 4th Round | v Barnsley | (a) | 2-2 | Baird, Carey |
| Replay | v Barnsley | (h) | 1-0 | Baird |
| 5th Round | v Brentford | (a) | 0-2 | |

**1938/39**

| | | | | |
|---|---|---|---|---|
| 3rd Round | v West Bromwich Alb | (a) | 0-0 | |
| Replay | v West Bromwich Alb | (h) | 1-5 | Redwood |

**1945/46**

| | | | | |
|---|---|---|---|---|
| 3rd Round(leg1) | v Accrington Stanley | (a) | 2-2 | Smith, Wrigglesworth |
| 3rd Round(leg2) | v Accrington Stanley | (h) | 5-1(7-3) | Rowley 2, Bainbridge, Wrigglesworth, Own goal |
| 4th Round(leg1) | v Preston North End | (h) | 1-0 | Hanlon |
| 4th Round(leg2) | v Preston North End | (a) | 1-3(2-3) | Hanlon |

**1946/47**

| | | | | |
|---|---|---|---|---|
| 3rd Round | v Bradford | (a) | 3-0 | Rowley 2, Buckle |
| 4th Round | v Nottingham Forest | (h) | 0-2 | |

**1947/48**

| | | | | |
|---|---|---|---|---|
| 3rd Round | v Aston Villa | (a) | 6-4 | Pearson 2, Morris 2, Delaney, Rowley |
| 4th Round | v Liverpool | (h) | 3-0 | Morris, Rowley, Mitten |
| 5th Round | v Charlton Athletic | (h) | 2-0 | Warner, Mitten |
| 6th Round | v Preston North End | (h) | 4-1 | Pearson 2, Rowley, Mitten |
| Semi Final | v Derby County | (n) | 3-1 | Pearson 3 |
| Final | v Blackpool | (n) | 4-2 | Rowley 2, Pearson, Anderson |

**1948/49**

| | | | | |
|---|---|---|---|---|
| 3rd Round | v Bournemouth | (h) | 6-0 | Burke 2, Rowley 2, Pearson, Mitten |
| 4th Round | v Bradford | (h) | 1-1 | Mitten |
| Replay | v Bradford | (a) | 1-1† | Mitten |
| 2nd Replay | v Bradford | (h) | 5-0 | Burke 2, Rowley 2, Pearson |
| 5th Round | v Yeovil Town | (h) | 8-0 | Rowley 5, Burke 2, Mitten |
| 6th Round | v Hull City | (a) | 1-0 | Pearson |
| Semi Final | v Wolves | (n) | 1-1† | Mitten |
| Replay | v Wolves | (n) | 0-1 | |

**1949/50**

| | | | | |
|---|---|---|---|---|
| 3rd Round | v Weymouth | (h) | 4-0 | Rowley 2, Pearson, Delaney |
| 4th Round | v Watford | (a) | 1-0 | Rowley |
| 5th Round | v Portsmouth | (h) | 3-3 | Mitten 2, Pearson |
| Replay | v Portsmouth | (a) | 3-1 | Delaney, Downie, Mitten |
| Round 6 | v Chelsea | (a) | 0-2 | |

**1950/51**

| | | | | |
|---|---|---|---|---|
| 3rd Round | v Oldham Athletic | (h) | 4-1 | Pearson, Aston, Birch, Whyte og |
| 4th Round | v Leeds United | (h) | 4-0 | Pearson 3, Rowley |
| 5th Round | v Arsenal | (h) | 1-0 | Pearson |
| 6th Round | v Birmingham City | (a) | 0-1 | |

**1951/52**

| | | | | |
|---|---|---|---|---|
| 3rd Round | v Hull City | (h) | 0-2 | |

**1952/53**

| | | | | |
|---|---|---|---|---|
| 3rd Round | v Millwall | (a) | 1-0 | Pearson |
| 4th Round | v Walthamstow Avenue | (h) | 1-1 | Lewis |
| Replay | v Walthamstow Avenue | (n) | 5-2 | Rowley, Byrne, Lewis, Pearson |
| 5th Round | v Everton | (a) | 1-2 | Rowley |

**1953/54**

| | | | | |
|---|---|---|---|---|
| 3rd Round | v Burnley | (a) | 3-5 | Blanchflower, Taylor, Viollet |

**1954/55**

| | | | | |
|---|---|---|---|---|
| 3rd Round | v Reading | (a) | 1-1 | Webster |
| Replay | v Reading | (h) | 4-1 | Webster 2, Viollet, Rowley |
| 4th Round | v Manchester City | (a) | 0-2 | |

**1955/56**

| | | | | |
|---|---|---|---|---|
| 3rd Round | v Bristol Rovers | (a) | 0-4 | |

**1956/57**

| | | | | |
|---|---|---|---|---|
| 3rd Round | v Hartlepools United | (a) | 4-3 | Whelan 2, Berry, Taylor |
| 4th Round | v Wrexham | (a) | 5-0 | Whelan 2, Taylor 2, Byrne |
| 5th Round | v Everton | (h) | 1-0 | Edwards |
| 6th Round | v Bournemouth | (a) | 2-1 | Berry 2 |
| Semi Final | v Birmingham City | (n) | 2-0 | Berry, Charlton |
| Final | v Aston Villa | (n) | 1-2 | Taylor |

**1957/58**

| | | | | |
|---|---|---|---|---|
| 3rd Round | v Workington | (a) | 3-1 | Viollet 3 |
| 4th Round | v Ipswich Town | (h) | 2-0 | Charlton 2 |
| 5th Round | v Sheffield Wednesday | (h) | 3-0 | Brennan 2, Dawson |
| 6th Round | v West Bromwich Alb | (a) | 2-2 | E.Taylor, Dawson |
| Replay | v West Bromwich Alb | (h) | 1-0 | Webster |
| Semi Final | v Fulham | (n) | 2-2 | Charlton 2 |
| Replay | v Fulham | (n) | 5-3 | Dawson 3, Charlton, Brennan |
| Final | v Bolton Wanderers | (n) | 0-2 | |

**1958/59**

| | | | | |
|---|---|---|---|---|
| 3rd Round | v Norwich City | (a) | 0-3 | |

**1959/60**

| | | | | |
|---|---|---|---|---|
| 3rd Round | v Derby County | (a) | 4-2 | Goodwin, Charlton, Scanlon, Own goal |
| 4th Round | v Liverpool | (a) | 3-1 | Charlton 2, Bradley |
| 5th Round | v Sheffield Wednesday | (h) | 0-1 | |

**1960/61**

| | | | | |
|---|---|---|---|---|
| 3rd Round | v Middlesbrough | (h) | 3-0 | Dawson 2, Cantwell |
| 4th Round | v Sheffield Wednesday | (a) | 1-1 | Cantwell |
| Replay | v Sheffield Wednesday | (h) | 2-7 | Dawson, Pearson |

**1961/62**

| | | | | |
|---|---|---|---|---|
| 3rd Round | v Bolton Wanderers | (h) | 2-1 | Nicholson, Herd |
| 4th Round | v Arsenal | (h) | 1-0 | Setters |
| 5th Round | v Sheffield Wednesday | (h) | 0-0 | |
| Replay | v Sheffield Wednesday | (a) | 2-0 | Charlton, Giles |
| 6th Round | v Preston North End | (a) | 0-0 | |
| Replay | v Preston North End | (h) | 2-1 | Herd, Charlton |
| Semi Final | v Tottenham Hotspurs | (n) | 1-3 | Herd |

**1962/63**

| | | | | |
|---|---|---|---|---|
| 3rd Round | v Huddersfield Town | (h) | 5-0 | Law 3, Giles, Quixall |
| 4th Round | v Aston Villa | (h) | 1-0 | Quixall |
| 5th Round | v Chelsea | (h) | 2-1 | Quixall, Law |
| 6th Round | v Coventry City | (a) | 3-1 | Charlton 2, Quixall |
| Semi Final | v Southampton | (n) | 1-0 | Law |
| Final | v Leicester City | (n) | 3-1 | Herd 2, Law |

**1963/64**

| | | | | |
|---|---|---|---|---|
| 3rd Round | v Southampton | (a) | 3-2 | Crerand, Moore, Herd |
| 4th Round | v Bristol City | (h) | 4-1 | Law 3, Herd |
| 5th Round | v Barnsley | (a) | 4-0 | Law 2, Best, Herd |

| 6th Round | v Sunderland | (h) | 3-3 | Charlton, Best, Own goal |
|---|---|---|---|---|
| Replay | v Sunderland | (a) | 2-2† | Charlton, Law |
| 2nd Replay | v Sunderland | (n) | 5-1 | Law 3, Chisnall, Herd |
| Semi Final | v West Ham United | (n) | 1-3 | Law |

**1964/65**

| 3rd Round | v Chester | (h) | 2-1 | Kinsey, Best |
|---|---|---|---|---|
| 4th Round | v Stoke City | (a) | 0-0 | |
| Replay | v Stoke City | (h) | 1-0 | Herd |
| 5th Round | v Burnley | (h) | 2-1 | Crerand, Law |
| 6th Round | v Wolves | (a) | 5-3 | Law 2, Crerand, Herd, Best |
| Semi-Final | v Leeds United | (n) | 0-0 | |
| Replay | v Leeds United | (n) | 0-1 | |

**1965/66**

| 3rd Round | v Derby County | (a) | 5-2 | Best 2, Law 2, Herd |
|---|---|---|---|---|
| 4th Round | v Rotherham United | (h) | 0-0 | |
| Replay | v Rotherham United | (a) | 1-0† | Connelly |
| 5th Round | v Wolves | (h) | 4-2 | Law 2, Herd, Best |
| 6th Round | v Preston North End | (a) | 1-1 | Herd |
| Replay | v Preston North End | (h) | 3-1 | Law 2, Connelly |
| Semi Final | v Everton | (n) | 0-1 | |

**1966/67**

| 3rd Round | v Stoke City | (h) | 2-0 | Law, Herd |
|---|---|---|---|---|
| 4th Round | v Norwich City | (h) | 1-2 | Law |

**1967/68**

| 3rd Round | v Tottenham Hotspurs | (h) | 2-2 | Best, Charlton |
|---|---|---|---|---|
| Replay | v Tottenham Hotspurs | (a) | 0-1† | |

**1968/69**

| 3rd Round | v Exeter City | (a) | 3-1 | Fitzpatrick, Kidd, Own goal |
|---|---|---|---|---|
| 4th Round | v Watford | (h) | 1-1 | Law |
| Replay | v Watford | (a) | 2-0 | Law 2 |
| 5th Round | v Birmingham City | (a) | 2-2 | Law, Best |
| Replay | v Birmingham City | (h) | 6-2 | Law 3, Kidd, Morgan, Crerand |
| 6th Round | v Everton | (h) | 0-1 | |

**1969/70**

| 3rd Round | v Ipswich Town | (a) | 1-0 | Own goal |
|---|---|---|---|---|
| 4th Round | v Manchester City | (h) | 3-0 | Kidd 2, Morgan |
| 5th Round | v Northampton Town | (a) | 8-2 | Best 6, Kidd 2 |

| | | | | |
|---|---|---|---|---|
| 6th Round | v Middlesbrough | (a) | 1-1 | Sartori |
| Replay | v Middlesbrough | (h) | 2-1 | Charlton, Morgan |
| Semi Final | v Leeds United | (n) | 0-0 | |
| Replay | v Leeds United | (n) | 0-0† | |
| 2nd Replay | v Leeds United | (n) | 0-1 | |
| 3rd Place p/o | v Watford | (n) | 2-0 | Kidd 2 |

**1970/71**

| | | | | |
|---|---|---|---|---|
| 3rd Round | v Middlesbrough | (h) | 0-0 | |
| Replay | v Middlesbrough | (a) | 1-2 | Best |

**1971/72**

| | | | | |
|---|---|---|---|---|
| 3rd Round | v Southampton | (a) | 1-1 | Charlton |
| Replay | v Southampton | (h) | 4-1† | Best 2, Sadler, Aston |
| 4th Round | v Preston North End | (a) | 2-0 | Gowling 2 |
| 5th Round | v Middlesbrough | (h) | 0-0 | |
| Replay | v Middlesbrough | (a) | 3-0 | Morgan, Charlton, Best |
| 6th Round | v Stoke City | (h) | 1-1 | Best |
| Replay | v Stoke City | (a) | 1-2† | Best |

**1972/73**

| | | | | |
|---|---|---|---|---|
| 3rd Round | v Wolves | (a) | 0-1 | |

**1973/74**

| | | | | |
|---|---|---|---|---|
| 3rd Round | v Plymouth Argyle | (h) | 1-0 | Macari |
| 4th Round | v Ipswich Town | (h) | 0-1 | |

**1974/75**

| | | | | |
|---|---|---|---|---|
| 3rd Round | v Walsall | (h) | 0-0 | |
| Replay | v Walsall | (a) | 2-3† | McIlroy, Daly |

**1975/76**

| | | | | |
|---|---|---|---|---|
| 3rd Round | v Oxford United | (h) | 2-1 | Daly 2 |
| 4th Round | v Peterborough United | (h) | 3-1 | Forsyth, McIlroy, Hill |
| 5th Round | v Leicester City | (a) | 2-1 | Daly, Macari |
| 6th Round | v Wolves | (h) | 1-1 | Daly |
| Replay | v Wolves | (a) | 3-2† | B.Greenhoff, McIlroy, Pearson |
| Semi Final | v Derby County | (n) | 2-0 | Hill 2 |
| Final | v Southampton | (n) | 0-1 | |

**1976/77**

| | | | | |
|---|---|---|---|---|
| 3rd Round | v Walsall | (h) | 1-0 | Hill |
| 4th Round | v Queens Park Rangers | (h) | 1-0 | Macari |
| 5th Round | v Southampton | (a) | 2-2 | Macari, Hill |

| | | | | | |
|---|---|---|---|---|---|
| Replay | v Southampton | (h) | 2-1 | J.Greenhoff 2 |
| 6th Round | v Aston Villa | (h) | 2-1 | Houston, Macari |
| Semi Final | v Leeds United | (n) | 2-1 | Coppell, J.Greenhoff |
| Final | v Liverpool | (n) | 2-1 | Pearson, J.Greenhoff |

**1977/78**

| | | | | | |
|---|---|---|---|---|---|
| 3rd Round | v Carlisle United | (a) | 1-1 | Macari |
| Replay | v Carlisle United | (h) | 4-2 | Pearson 2, Macari 2 |
| 4th Round | v West Bromwich Alb | (h) | 1-1 | Coppell |
| Replay | v West Bromwich Alb | (a) | 2-3 | Pearson, Hill |

**1978/79**

| | | | | | |
|---|---|---|---|---|---|
| 3rd Round | v Chelsea | (h) | 3-0 | Coppell, J.Greenhoff, Grimes |
| 4th Round | v Fulham | (a) | 1-1 | J.Greenhoff |
| Replay | v Fulham | (h) | 1-0 | J.Greenhoff |
| 5th Round | v Colchester United | (a) | 1-0 | J.Greenhoff |
| 6th Round | v Tottenham Hotspurs | (a) | 1-1 | Thomas |
| Replay | v Tottenham Hotspurs | (h) | 2-0 | McIlroy, Jordan |
| Semi Final | v Liverpool | (n) | 2-2 | Jordan, B.Greenhoff |
| Replay | v Liverpool | (n) | 1-0 | J.Greenhoff |
| Final | v Arsenal | (n) | 2-3 | McQueen, McIlroy |

**1979/80**

| | | | | | |
|---|---|---|---|---|---|
| 3rd Round | v Tottenham Hotspurs | (a) | 1-1 | McIlroy |
| Replay | v Tottenham Hotspurs | (h) | 0-1† | |

**1980/81**

| | | | | | |
|---|---|---|---|---|---|
| 3rd Round | v Brighton & Hove Alb | (h) | 2-2 | Duxbury, Thomas |
| Replay | v Brighton & Hove Alb | (a) | 2-0 | Nicholl, Birtles |
| 4th Round | v Nottingham Forest | (a) | 0-1 | |

**1981/82**

| | | | | | |
|---|---|---|---|---|---|
| 3rd Round | v Watford | (a) | 0-1 | |

**1982/83**

| | | | | | |
|---|---|---|---|---|---|
| 3rd Round | v West Ham United | (h) | 2-0 | Stapleton, Coppell |
| 4th Round | v Luton Town | (a) | 2-0 | Moses, Moran |
| 5th Round | v Derby County | (a) | 1-0 | Whiteside |
| 6th Round | v Everton | (h) | 1-0 | Stapleton |
| Semi Final | v Arsenal | (n) | 2-1 | Robson, Whiteside |
| Final | v Brighton & Hove Alb | (n) | 2-2† | Stapleton, Wilkins |
| Replay | v Brighton & Hove Alb | (n) | 4-0 | Robson 2, Muhren, Whiteside |

**1983/84**

| | | | | | |
|---|---|---|---|---|---|
| 3rd Round | v AFC Bournemouth | (a) | 0-2 | |

**1984/85**

| | | | | |
|---|---|---|---|---|
| 3rd Round | v AFC Bournemouth | (h) | 3-0 | Strachan, McQueen, Stapleton |
| 4th Round | v Coventry City | (h) | 2-1 | Hughes, McGrath |
| 5th Round | v Blackburn Rovers | (a) | 2-0 | Strachan, McGrath |
| 6th Round | v West Ham United | (h) | 4-2 | Whiteside 3, Hughes |
| Semi Final | v Liverpool | (n) | 2-2† | Robson, Stapleton |
| Replay | v Liverpool | (n) | 2-1 | Robson, Hughes |
| Final | v Everton | (n) | 1-0† | Whiteside |

**1985/86**

| | | | | |
|---|---|---|---|---|
| 3rd Round | v Rochdale | (h) | 2-0 | Stapleton, Hughes |
| 4th Round | v Sunderland | (a) | 0-0 | |
| Replay | v Sunderland | (h) | 3-0 | Olsen 2, Whiteside |
| 5th Round | v West Ham United | (a) | 1-1 | Stapleton |
| Replay | v West Ham United | (h) | 0-2 | |

**1986/87**

| | | | | |
|---|---|---|---|---|
| 3rd Round | v Manchester City | (h) | 1-0 | Whiteside |
| 4th Round | v Coventry City | (h) | 0-1 | |

**1987/88**

| | | | | |
|---|---|---|---|---|
| 3rd Round | v Ipswich Town | (a) | 2-1 | Own goal, Anderson |
| 4th Round | v Chelsea | (h) | 2-0 | Whiteside, McClair |
| 5th Round | v Arsenal | (a) | 1-2 | McClair |

**1988/89**

| | | | | |
|---|---|---|---|---|
| 3rd Round | v Queens Park Rangers | (h) | 0-0 | |
| Replay | v Queens Park Rangers | (a) | 2-2† | Gill, Graham |
| 2nd Replay | v Queens Park Rangers | (h) | 3-0 | McClair 2(1pen), Robson |
| 4th Round | v Oxford United | (h) | 4-0 | Hughes, Bruce, Own goal, Robson |
| 5th Round | v AFC Bournemouth | (a) | 1-1 | Hughes |
| Replay | v AFC Bournemouth | (h) | 1-0 | McClair |
| 6th Round | v Nottingham Forest | (h) | 0-1 | |

**1989/90**

| | | | | |
|---|---|---|---|---|
| 3rd Round | v Nottingham Forest | (a) | 1-0 | Robins |
| 4th Round | v Hereford United | (a) | 1-0 | Blackmore |
| 5th Round | v Newcastle United | (a) | 3-2 | Robins, Wallace, McClair |
| 6th Round | v Sheffield United | (a) | 1-0 | McClair |
| Semi Final | v Oldham Athletic | (n) | 3-3aet | Robson, Webb, Wallace |
| Replay | v Oldham Athletic | (n) | 2-1aet | McClair, Robins |

| | | | | |
|---|---|---|---|---|
| Final | v Crystal Palace | (n) | 3-3aet | Hughes 2, Robson |
| Replay | v Crystal Palace | (n) | 1-0 | Martin |

**1990/91**

| | | | | |
|---|---|---|---|---|
| 3rd Round | v Queens Park Rangers | (h) | 2-1 | Hughes, McClair |
| 4th Round | v Bolton Wanderers | (h) | 1-0 | Hughes |
| 5th Round | v Norwich City | (a) | 1-2 | McClair |

**1991/92**

| | | | | |
|---|---|---|---|---|
| 3rd Round | v Leeds United | (a) | 1-0 | Hughes |
| 4th Round | v Southampton | (a) | 0-0 | |
| Replay | v Southampton | (h) | 2-2 | Kanchelskis, McClair |

*(Southampton won 4-2 on penalties)*

**1992/93**

| | | | | |
|---|---|---|---|---|
| 3rd Round | v Bury | (h) | 2-0 | Gillespie, Phelan |
| 4th Round | v Brighton & Hove Alb | (h) | 1-0 | Giggs |
| 5th Round | v Sheffield United | (a) | 1-3 | Giggs |

**1993/94**

| | | | | |
|---|---|---|---|---|
| 3rd Round | v Sheffield United | (a) | 1-0 | Hughes |
| 4th Round | v Norwich City | (a) | 2-0 | Keane, Cantona |
| 5th Round | v Wimbledon | (a) | 3-0 | Cantona, Bruce, Irwin |
| 6th Round | v Charlton Athletic | (h) | 3-1 | Hughes, Kanchelskis 2 |
| S/F | v Oldham Athletic | (n) | 1-1 | Hughes |
| S/F | v Oldham Athletic | (n) | 4-1 | Ince, Kanchelskis, Robson, Giggs |
| Final | v Chelsea | (n) | 4-0 | Cantona 2pen, Hughes, McClair |

## Full record in Domestic Cup Competitions – *League Cup*

**1960/61**

| | | | | |
|---|---|---|---|---|
| 1st Round | v Exeter City | (a) | 1-1 | Dawson |
| Replay | v Exeter City | (h) | 4-1 | Quixall 2(1pen), Giles, Pearson |
| 2nd Round | v Bradford City | (a) | 1-2 | Viollet |

**1966/67**

| | | | | |
|---|---|---|---|---|
| 2nd Round | v Blackpool | (a) | 1-5 | Herd |

**1969/70**

| | | | | |
|---|---|---|---|---|
| 2nd Round | v Middlesbrough | (h) | 1-0 | Sadler |
| 3rd Round | v Wrexham | (h) | 2-0 | Kidd, Best |

| | | | | |
|---|---|---|---|---|
| 4th Round | v Burnley | (a) | 0-0 | |
| Replay | v Burnley | (h) | 1-0 | Best |
| 5th Round | v Derby County | (a) | 0-0 | |
| Replay | v Derby County | (h) | 1-0 | Kidd |
| Semi Final(leg1) | v Manchester City | (a) | 1-2 | Charlton |
| Semi Final(leg2) | v Manchester City | (h) | 2-2 (3-4) | Edwards, Law |

## 1970/71

| | | | | |
|---|---|---|---|---|
| 2nd Round | v Aldershot | (a) | 3-1 | Law, Kidd, Best |
| 3rd Round | v Portsmouth | (h) | 1-0 | Charlton |
| 4th Round | v Chelsea | (h) | 2-1 | Best, Charlton |
| 5th Round | v Crystal Palace | (h) | 4-2 | Kidd 2, Charlton, Fitzpatrick |
| Semi Final(leg1) | v Aston Villa | (h) | 1-1 | Kidd |
| Semi Final(leg2) | v Aston Villa | (a) | 1-2 (2-3) | Kidd |

## 1971/72

| | | | | |
|---|---|---|---|---|
| 2nd Round | v Ipswich Town | (a) | 3-1 | Best 2, Morgan |
| 3rd Round | v Burnley | (h) | 1-1 | Charlton |
| Replay | v Burnley | (a) | 1-0 | Charlton |
| 4th Round | v Stoke City | (h) | 1-1 | Gowling |
| Replay | v Stoke City | (a) | 0-0† | |
| 2nd Replay | v Stoke City | (a) | 1-2 | Best |

## 1972/73

| | | | | |
|---|---|---|---|---|
| 2nd Round | v Oxford United | (a) | 2-2 | Charlton, Law |
| Replay | v Oxford United | (h) | 3-1 | Best 2, Storey-Moore |
| 3rd Round | v Bristol Rovers | (a) | 1-1 | Morgan |
| Replay | v Bristol Rovers | (h) | 1-2 | McIlroy |

## 1973/74

| | | | | |
|---|---|---|---|---|
| 2nd Round | v Middlesbrough | (h) | 0-1 | |

## 1974/75

| | | | | |
|---|---|---|---|---|
| 2nd Round | v Charlton Athletic | (h) | 5-1 | Macari 2, Houston, McIlroy, Own goal |
| 3rd Round | v Manchester City | (h) | 1-0 | Daly |
| 4th Round | v Burnley | (h) | 3-2 | Macari 2, Morgan |
| 5th Round | v Middlesbrough | (a) | 0-0 | |
| Replay | v Middlesbrough | (h) | 3-0 | McIlroy, Pearson, Macari |
| Semi Final(leg1) | v Norwich City | (h) | 2-2 | Macari 2 |
| Semi Final(leg2) | v Norwich City | (a) | 0-1(2-3) | |

**1975/76**

| | | | | |
|---|---|---|---|---|
| 2nd Round | *v* Brentford | (h) | 2-1 | McIlroy, Macari |
| 3rd Round | *v* Aston Villa | (a) | 2-1 | Coppell, Macari |
| 4th Round | *v* Manchester City | (a) | 0-4 | |

**1976/77**

| | | | | |
|---|---|---|---|---|
| 2nd Round | *v* Tranmere Rovers | (h) | 5-0 | Daly 2, Pearson, Macari, Hill |
| 3rd Round | *v* Sunderland | (h) | 2-2 | Pearson, Own goal |
| Replay | *v* Sunderland | (a) | 2-2† | Daly, B.Greenhoff |
| 2nd Replay | *v* Sunderland | (h) | 1-0 | B.Greenhoff |
| 4th Round | *v* Newcastle United | (h) | 7-2 | Hill 3, Nicholl, Houston, Coppell, Pearson |
| 5th Round | *v* Everton | (h) | 0-3 | |

**1977/78**

| | | | | |
|---|---|---|---|---|
| 2nd Round | *v* Arsenal | (a) | 2-3 | McCreery, Pearson |

**1978/79**

| | | | | |
|---|---|---|---|---|
| 2nd Round | *v* Stockport County | (a) | 3-2 | McIlroy, J.Greenhoff, Jordan |
| 3rd Round | *v* Watford | (h) | 1-2 | Jordan |

**1979/80**

| | | | | |
|---|---|---|---|---|
| 2nd Round (leg1) | *v* Tottenham Hotspurs | (a) | 1-2 | Thomas |
| 2nd Round (leg2) | *v* Tottenham Hotspurs | (h) | 3-1(4-3) | Coppell, Thomas, Miller |
| 3rd Round | *v* Norwich City | (a) | 1-4 | McIlroy |

**1980/81**

| | | | | |
|---|---|---|---|---|
| 2nd Round (leg1) | *v* Coventry City | (h) | 0-1 | |
| 2nd Round (leg2) | *v* Coventry City | (a) | 0-1(0-2) | |

**1981/82**

| | | | | |
|---|---|---|---|---|
| 2nd Round (leg1) | *v* Tottenham Hotspurs | (a) | 0-1 | |
| 2nd Round (leg2) | *v* Tottenham Hotspurs | (h) | 0-1(0-2) | |

**1982/83**

| | | | | |
|---|---|---|---|---|
| 2nd Round (leg1) | *v* AFC Bournemouth | (h) | 2-0 | Own goal, Stapleton |
| 2nd Round (leg2) | *v* AFC Bournemouth | (a) | 2-2 | Muhren, Coppell |
| 3rd Round | *v* Bradford City | (a) | 0-0 | |
| Replay | *v* Bradford City | (h) | 4-1 | Moses, Albiston, Moran, Coppell |
| 4th Round | *v* Southampton | (h) | 2-0 | McQueen, Whiteside |
| 5th Round | *v* Nottingham Forest | (h) | 4-0 | McQueen 2, Coppell, Robson |

| | | | | |
|---|---|---|---|---|
| Semi Final (leg1) | v Arsenal | (a) | 4-2 | Coppell 2, Whiteside, Stapleton |
| Semi Final (leg2) | v Arsenal | (h) | 2-1(6-3) | Coppell, Moran |
| Final | v Liverpool | (n) | 1-2† | Whiteside |

**1983/84**

| | | | | |
|---|---|---|---|---|
| 2nd Round (leg1) | v Port Vale | (a) | 1-0 | Stapleton |
| 2nd Round (leg2) | v Port Vale | (h) | 2-0(3-0) | Whiteside, Wilkins |
| 3rd Round | v Colchester United | (a) | 2-0 | McQueen, Moses |
| 4th Round | v Oxford United | (a) | 1-1 | Hughes |
| Replay | v Oxford United | (h) | 1-1† | Stapleton |
| 2nd Replay | v Oxford United | (a) | 1-2aet | Graham |

**1984/85**

| | | | | |
|---|---|---|---|---|
| 2nd Round (leg1) | v Burnley | (h) | 4-0 | Hughes 3, Robson |
| 2nd Round (leg2) | v Burnley | (a) | 3-0 (7-0) | Brazil 2, Olsen |
| 3rd Round | v Everton | (h) | 1-2 | Brazil |

**1985/86**

| | | | | |
|---|---|---|---|---|
| 2nd Round (leg1) | v Crystal Palace | (a) | 1-0 | Barnes |
| 2nd Round (leg2) | v Crystal Palace | (h) | 1-0 (2-0) | Whiteside |
| 3rd Round | v West Ham United | (h) | 1-0 | Whiteside |
| 4th Round | v Liverpool | (a) | 1-2 | McGrath |

**1986/87**

| | | | | |
|---|---|---|---|---|
| 2nd Round (leg1) | v Port Vale | (h) | 2-0 | Stapleton, Whiteside |
| 2nd Round (leg2) | v Port Vale | (a) | 5-2 (7-2) | Moses 2, Stapleton, Barnes, Davenport |
| 3rd Round | v Southampton | (h) | 0-0 | |
| Replay | v Southampton | (a) | 1-4 | Davenport |

**1987/88**

| | | | | |
|---|---|---|---|---|
| 2nd Round (leg1) | v Hull City | (h) | 5-0 | McGrath, Davenport, Whiteside, Strachan, McClair |
| 2nd Round (leg2) | v Hull City | (a) | 1-0 (6-0) | McClair |
| 3rd Round | v Crystal Palace | (h) | 2-1 | McClair 2 |
| 4th Round | v Bury | (a) | 2-1 | Whiteside, McClair |
| 5th Round | v Oxford United | (a) | 0-2 | |

**1988/89**

| | | | | |
|---|---|---|---|---|
| 2nd Round (leg1) | v Rotherham United | (a) | 1-0 | Davenport |
| 2nd Round (leg2) | v Rotherham United | (h) | 5-0 (6-0) | McClair 3, Robson, Bruce |
| 3rd Round | v Wimbledon | (a) | 1-2 | Robson |

**1989/90**

| | | | | |
|---|---|---|---|---|
| 2nd Round (leg1) | v Portsmouth | (a) | 3-2 | Ince 2, Wallace |
| 2nd Round (leg2) | v Portsmouth | (h) | 0-0 (3-2) | |
| 3rd Round | v Tottenham Hotspurs | (h) | 0-3 | |

**1990/91**

| | | | | |
|---|---|---|---|---|
| 2nd Round (leg1) | v Halifax Town | (a) | 3-1 | Blackmore, McClair, Webb |
| 2nd Round (leg2) | v Halifax Town | (h) | 2-1 (5-2) | Bruce, Anderson |
| 3rd Round | v Liverpool | (h) | 3-1 | Bruce, Hughes, Sharpe |
| 4th Round | v Arsenal | (a) | 6-2 | Sharpe 3, Blackmore, Hughes, Wallace |
| 5th Round | v Southampton | (a) | 1-1 | Hughes |
| Replay | v Southampton | (h) | 3-2 | Hughes 3 |
| Semi Final (leg1) | v Leeds United | (h) | 2-1 | Sharpe, McClair |
| Semi Final (leg2) | v Leeds United | (a) | 1-0 (3-1) | Sharpe |
| Final | v Sheffield Wednesday | (n) | 0-1 | |

**1991/92**

| | | | | |
|---|---|---|---|---|
| 2nd Round (leg1) | v Cambridge United | (h) | 3-0 | Giggs, McClair, Bruce |
| 2nd Round (leg2) | v Cambridge United | (a) | 1-1 (4-1) | McClair |
| 3rd Round | v Portsmouth | (h) | 3-1 | Robins 2, Robson |
| 4th Round | v Oldham Athletic | (h) | 2-0 | McClair, Kanchelskis |
| 5th Round | v Leeds United | (a) | 3-1 | Blackmore, Kanchelskis, Giggs |
| Semi Final (leg1) | v Middlesbrough | (a) | 0-0 | |
| Semi Final (leg2) | v Middlesbrough | (h) | 2-1 (2-1) | Sharpe, Giggs |
| Final | v Nottingham Forest | (n) | 1-0 | McClair |

**1992/93**

| | | | | |
|---|---|---|---|---|
| 2nd Round (leg1) | v Brighton & Hove Alb | (h) | 1-1 | Hughes |
| 2nd Round (leg2) | v Brighton & Hove Alb | (a) | 1-0 | Wallace |
| 3rd Round | v Aston Villa | (a) | 0-1 | |

**1993/94**

| | | | | |
|---|---|---|---|---|
| 2nd Round (leg1) | v Stoke City | (a) | 1-2 | Dublin |
| 2nd Round (leg2) | v Stoke City | (h) | 2-0 | Sharpe, McClair |
| 3rd Round | v Leicester City | (h) | 5-1 | Bruce 2, McClair, Sharpe, Hughes |
| 4th Round | v Everton | (a) | 2-0 | Huges, Giggs |
| 5th Round | v Portsmouth | (h) | 2-2 | Giggs, Cantona |
| Replay | v Portsmouth | (a) | 1-0 | McClair |

| Semi Final (leg1) | v Sheffield Wednesday | (h) | 1-0 | Giggs |
| Semi Final (leg2) | v Sheffield Wednesday | (a) | 4-1 | Hughes 2, McClair, Kanchelskis |
| Final | v Aston Villa | (n) | 1-3 | Hughes |

## Cup Final Squads – *FA Cup*

| Date | Opponents | Venue | Score | Att. |
|------|-----------|-------|-------|------|
| 24/4/09 | v Bristol City | The Crystal Palace | Won 1-0 | 71,401 |

*Team:* Moger, Stacey, Hayes, Duckworth, Roberts, Bell, Meredith, Halse, J Turnbull, A Turnbull, Wall Scorer: A Turnbull

24/4/48  v Blackpool  Wembley  Won 4-2  100,000
*Team:* Crompton, Carey, Aston, Anderson, Chilton, Cockburn, Delaney, Morris, Rowley, Pearson, Mitten Scorers: Rowley 2, Pearson, Anderson

5/5/57  v Aston Villa  Wembley  Lost 1-2  100,000
*Team:* Wood, Foulkes, Byrne, Colman, Blanchflower, Edwards, Berry, Whelan, T Taylor, Charlton, Pegg Scorer: Taylor

3/5/58  v Bolton Wanderers  Wembley  Lost 0-2  100,000
*Team:* Gregg, Foulkes, Greaves, Goodwin, Cope, Crowther, Webster, E Taylor, Dawson, Charlton, Brennan
*Stan Crowther having played for Aston Villa twelve months earlier thus played against and for United in consecutive FA Cup Finals..*

25/5/63  v Leicester City  Wembley  Won 3-1  100,000
*Team:* Gaskell, Dunne, Cantwell, Crerand, Foulkes, Setters, Giles, Stiles, Quixall, Herd, Law, Charlton Scorers: Herd 2, Law

1/5/75  v Southampton  Wembley  Lost 0-1  100,000
*Team:* Stepney, Forsyth, Houston, Daly, B Greenhoff, Buchan, Coppell, McIlroy, Pearson, Macari, Hill (McCreery)

21/5/76  v Liverpool  Wembley  Won 2-1  100,000
*Team:* Stepney, Nicholl, Albiston, McIlroy, B Greenhoff, Buchan, Coppell, J Greenhoff, Pearson, Macari, Hill (McCreery) Scorers: Pearson, J Greenhoff
*This was Arthur Albiston's FA Cup debut. Martin Buchan became the first player ever to captain both an English and a Scottish Cup winning side.*

12/5/79  v Arsenal  Wembley  Lost 2-3  100,000
*Team:* Bailey, Nicholl, Albiston, McIlroy, McQueen, Buchan, Coppell, J.Greenhoff, Jordan, Macari, Thomas Scorers; McQueen, McIlroy

21/5/83  v Brighton & Hove Albion  Wembley  Drew 2-2 aet 100,000
*Team:* Bailey, Duxbury, Albiston, Wilkins, Moran, McQueen, Robson, Muhren, Stapleton, Whiteside, Davies Scorers: Stapleton, Wilkins
*Like Albiston seven years earlier, this was Alan Davies' FA Cup debut.*

26/5/83    *v* Brighton & Hove Albion    Wembley          Won 4-0    92,000
*Team:* Bailey, Duxbury, Albiston, Wilkins, Moran, McQueen, Robson, Muhren,
Stapleton, Whiteside, Davies Scorers: Robson 2, Muhren, Whiteside
*In this game Davies created the unusual career record of only ever playing two FA*
*Cup ties for United, both of which were FA Cup Finals. He compounded this record*
*further 12 months later when he made his only European appearance. He certainly*
*knew how to pick his games for he came on as substitute against Juventus in the*
*semi-final of the Cup-winners Cup and scored United's equaliser in a 1-1 draw!*
*Norman Whiteside also set the record in this game of becoming the youngest ever*
*player to score in the Finals of both League Cup and FA Cup.*

18/5/85    *v* Everton              Wembley          Won 1-0 aet 100,000
*Team:* Bailey, Gidman, Albiston (Duxbury), Whiteside, McGrath, Moran, Robson,
Strachan, Hughes, Stapleton, Olsen Scorer: Whiteside
*Kevin Moran was the first player ever to be dismissed in a FA Cup Final.*

12/5/90    *v* Crystal Palace        Wembley          Drew 3-3 aet 80,000
*Team:* Leighton, Ince, Martin (Blackmore), Bruce, Phelan, Pallister (Robins),
Robson, Webb, McClair, Hughes, Wallace Scorers: Hughes 2, Robson

17/5/90    *v* Crystal Palace        Wembley          Won 1-0    80,000
*Team:* Sealey, Ince, Martin, Bruce, Phelan, Pallister, Robson, Webb, McClair,
Hughes, Wallace Scorer: Martin
*This FA Cup winning goal was the only goal Martin ever scored in the competition.*
14/5/94    *v* Chelsea             Wembley          Won 4-0    80,000
*Team:* Schmeichel, Parker, Irwin (Sharpe), Bruce, Pallister, Ince, Keane, Cantona,
Kanchelskis (McClair), Hughes, Giggs. Scorers: Cantona 2 pens, Hughes, McClair

## Cup Final Squads – *League Cup*

| Date | Opponents | Venue | Score | Att. |
|---|---|---|---|---|
| 26/3/83 | *v* Liverpool | Wembley | Lost 1-2 aet | 100,000 |

*Team:* Bailey, Duxbury, Albiston, Moses, Moran (Macari), McQueen, Wilkins,
Muhren, Stapleton, Whiteside, Coppell Scorer: Whiteside

| 21/4/91 | *v* Sheffield Wednesday | Wembley | Lost 0-1 | 80,000 |
|---|---|---|---|---|

*Team:* Sealey, Irwin, Blackmore, Bruce, Webb (Phelan), Pallister, Robson, Ince,
McClair, Hughes, Sharpe

| 12/4/92 | *v* Nottingham Forest | Wembley | Won 1-0 | 76,810 |
|---|---|---|---|---|

*Team:* Schmeichel, Parker, Irwin, Bruce, Phelan, Pallister, Kanchelskis (Sharpe),
Ince, McClair, Hughes, Giggs Scorer: McClair

| 27/3/94 | *v* Aston Villa | Wembley | Lost 1-3 | 77,231 |
|---|---|---|---|---|

*Team:* Sealy, Parker, Irwin, Bruce (McClair), Pallister, Cantona, Ince, Hughes,
Giggs (Sharpe), Kanchelskis, Keane. Scorer: Hughes

## Cup Final Squads – *European Champions' Cup*

| Date | Opponents | Venue | Score | Att. |
|------|-----------|-------|-------|------|
| 29/5/68 | v Benfica | Wembley | Won 4-1 aet | 100,000 |

*Team:* Stepney, Dunne, Burns, Crerand, Foulkes, Stiles, Best, Kidd, Charlton, Sadler, Aston Scorers: Charlton 2, Best, Kidd

## Cup Final Squads – *European Cup-Winners' Cup*

| Date | Opponents | Venue | Score | Att. |
|------|-----------|-------|-------|------|
| 15/5/91 | v Barcelona | Rotterdam | Won 2-1 | 45,000 |

*Team:* Schmeichel, Irwin, Blackmore, Bruce, Phelan, Pallister, Robson, Ince, McClair, Hughes, Sharpe Scorer: Hughes 2

## United in Europe – *European Champions' Cup*

**1956/57**

| | | | | |
|---|---|---|---|---|
| Prelim (1) | v Anderlecht | (a) | 2-0 | Viollet, Taylor |
| Prelim (2) | v Anderlecht | (h) | 10-0 | Viollet 4, Taylor 3, Whelan 2, Berry |
| Round 1(1) | v Borussia Dortmund | (h) | 3-2 | Viollet 2, Pegg |
| Round 1(2) | v Borussia Dortmund | (a) | 0-0 | |
| Q Final(1) | v Athletic Bilbao | (a) | 3-5 | Taylor, Viollet, Whelan |
| Q Final(2) | v Athletic Bilbao | (h) | 3-0 | Viollet, Taylor, Berry |
| S Final(1) | v Real Madrid | (a) | 1-3 | Taylor |
| S Final(2) | v Real Madrid | (h) | 2-2 | Taylor, Charlton |

**1957/58**

| | | | | |
|---|---|---|---|---|
| Prelim (1) | v Shamrock Rovers | (a) | 6-0 | Taylor 2, Whelan 2, Pegg, Berry |
| Prelim (2) | v Shamrock Rovers | (h) | 3-2 | Viollet 2, Pegg |
| Round 1(1) | v Dukla Prague | (h) | 3-0 | Webster, Taylor, Pegg |
| Round 1(2) | v Dukla Prague | (a) | 0-1 | |
| Q Final(1) | v Red Star Belgrade | (h) | 2-1 | Colman, Charlton |
| Q Final(2) | v Red Star Belgrade | (a) | 3-3 | Charlton 2, Viollet |
| S Final(1) | v AC Milan | (h) | 2-1 | Taylor(pen), Viollet |
| S Final(2) | v AC Milan | (a) | 0-4 | |

**1965/66**

| | | | | |
|---|---|---|---|---|
| Prelim (1) | v HJK Helsinki | (a) | 3-2 | Connelly, Herd, Law |

| | | | | |
|---|---|---|---|---|
| Prelim (2) | v HJK Helsinki | (h) | 6-0 | Connelly 3, Best 2, Charlton |
| Round 1(1) | v ASK Vorwaerts | (a) | 2-0 | Law, Connelly |
| Round 1(2) | v ASK Vorwaerts | (h) | 3-1 | Herd 3 |
| Q Final(1) | v Benfica | (h) | 3-2 | Herd, Law, Foulkes |
| Q Final(2) | v Benfica | (a) | 5-1 | Best 2, Charlton, Connelly, Crerand. |
| S Final(1) | v FK Partizan Belgrade | (a) | 0-2 | |
| S Final(2) | v FK Partizan Belgrade | (h) | 1-0 | Stiles |

**1967/68**

| | | | | |
|---|---|---|---|---|
| Round 1(1) | v Hibernians (Malta) | (h) | 4-0 | Sadler 2, Law 2 |
| Round 1(2) | v Hibernians (Malta) | (a) | 0-0 | |
| Round 2(1) | v FK Sarajevo | (a) | 0-0 | |
| Round 2(2) | v FK Sarajevo | (h) | 2-1 | Best, Aston |
| Q Final(1) | v Gornik Zabre | (h) | 2-0 | Kidd, own goal |
| Q Final(2) | v Gornik Zabre | (a) | 0-1 | |
| S Final(1) | v Real Madrid | (h) | 1-0 | Best |
| S Final(2) | v Real Madrid | (a) | 3-3 | Foulkes, Sadler, Own goal |
| Final | v Benfica | (n) | 4-1 | Charlton 2, Best, Kidd |

**1968/69**

| | | | | |
|---|---|---|---|---|
| Round 1(1) | v Waterford | (a) | 3-1 | Law 3 |
| Round 1(2) | v Waterford | (h) | 7-1 | Law 4, Stiles, Burns, Charlton |
| Round 2(1) | v RSC Anderlecht | (h) | 3-0 | Law 2, Kidd |
| Round 2(2) | v RSC Anderlecht | (a) | 1-3 | Sartori |
| Q Final(1) | v Rapid Vienna | (h) | 3-0 | Best 2, Morgan |
| Q Final(2) | v Rapid Vienna | (a) | 0-0 | |
| S Final(1) | v AC Milan | (a) | 0-2 | |
| S Final(2) | v AC Milan | (h) | 1-0 | Charlton |

**1993/94**

| | | | | |
|---|---|---|---|---|
| Round 1(1) | v Honved | (a) | 3-2 | Keane 2, Cantona |
| Round 1(2) | v Honved | (h) | 2-1 | Bruce 2 |
| Round 2(1) | v Galatasary | (h) | 3-3 | Robson, own goal, Cantona |
| Round 2(2) | v Galatasary | (a) | 0-0 | |

# United in Europe – *European Cup-Winners' Cup*

**1963/64**

| | | | | |
|---|---|---|---|---|
| Round 1(1) | v Willem II | (a) | 1-1 | Herd |
| Round 1(2) | v Willem II | (h) | 6-1 | Law 3, Charlton, Chisnall, Setters |
| | | | | |
| Round 2(1) | v Tottenham Hotspurs | (a) | 0-2 | |
| Round 2(2) | v Tottenham Hotspurs | (h) | 4-1 | Charlton 2, Herd 2 |
| Q Final(1) | v Sporting Club Lisbon | (h) | 4-1 | Law 3, Charlton |
| Q Final(2) | v Sporting Club Lisbon | (a) | 0-5 | |

**1977/78**

| | | | | |
|---|---|---|---|---|
| Round 1(1) | v AS Saint-Etienne | (a) | 1-1 | Hill |
| Round 1(2) | v AS Saint-Etienne | (h) | 2-0 | Coppell, Pearson |
| Round 2(1) | v FC Porto | (a) | 0-4 | |
| Round 2(2) | v FC Porto | (h) | 5-2 | Coppell 2, Nicholl, 2 own goals |

**1983/84**

| | | | | |
|---|---|---|---|---|
| Round 1(1) | v Dukla Prague | (h) | 1-1 | Wilkins |
| Round 1(2) | v Dukla Prague | (a) | 2-2 | Robson, Stapleton |
| Round 2(1) | v Spartak Varna | (a) | 2-1 | Robson, Graham |
| Round 2(2) | v Spartak Varna | (h) | 2-0 | Stapleton 2 |
| Q Final(1) | v FC Barcelona | (a) | 0-2 | |
| Q Final(2) | v FC Barcelona | (h) | 3-0 | Robson 2, Stapleton |
| S Final(1) | v Juventus | (h) | 1-1 | Davies |
| S Final(2) | v Juventus | (a) | 1-2 | Whiteside |

**1990/91**

| | | | | |
|---|---|---|---|---|
| Round 1(1) | v Pecsi Munkas | (h) | 2-0 | Blackmore, Webb |
| Round 1(2) | v Pecsi Munkas | (a) | 1-0 | McClair |
| Round 2(1) | v Wrexham | (h) | 3-0 | McClair, Bruce, Pallister |
| Round 2(2) | v Wrexham | (a) | 2-0 | Robins, Bruce |
| Q Final(1) | v Montpellier | (h) | 1-1 | McClair |
| Q Final(2) | v Montpellier | (a) | 2-0 | Blackmore, Bruce |
| S Final(1) | v Legia Warsaw | (a) | 3-1 | McClair, Hughes, Bruce |
| S Final(2) | v Legia Warsaw | (h) | 1-1 | Sharpe |
| Final | v Barcelona | (n) | 2-1 | Hughes 2 |

**1991/92**

| | | | | |
|---|---|---|---|---|
| Round 1(1) | v Panathinaikos | (a) | 0-0 | |
| Round 1(2) | v Panathinaikos | (h) | 2-0 | Hughes, McClair |
| Round 2(1) | v Athletico Madrid | (a) | 0-3 | |
| Round 2(2) | v Athletico Madrid | (h) | 1-1 | Hughes |

# United in Europe – *Inter-Cities Fairs Cup*

**1964/65**

| | | | | |
|---|---|---|---|---|
| Round 1(1) | *v* Djurgardens IF | (a) | 1-1 | Herd |
| Round 1(2) | *v* Djurgardens IF | (h) | 6-1 | Law 3, Charlton 2, Best |
| Round 2(1) | *v* Borussia Dortmund | (a) | 6-1 | Charlton 3, Herd, Law, Best |
| Round 2(2) | *v* Borussia Dortmund | (h) | 4-0 | Charlton 2, Connelly, Law |
| Round 3(1) | *v* Everton | (h) | 1-1 | Connelly |
| Round 3(2) | *v* Everton | (a) | 2-1 | Connelly, Herd |
| Q Final(1) | *v* RC Strasbourg | (a) | 5-0 | Law 2, Connelly, Charlton, Herd. |
| Q Final(2) | *v* RC Strasbourg | (h) | 0-0 | |
| S Final(1) | *v* Ferencvaros | (h) | 3-2 | Herd 2, Law |
| S Final(2) | *v* Ferencvaros | (a) | 0-1 | |
| Play Off | *v* Ferencvaros | (a) | 1-2 | Connelly |

# United in Europe – *UEFA Cup*

**1976/77**

| | | | | |
|---|---|---|---|---|
| Round 1(1) | *v* Ajax Amsterdam | (a) | 0-1 | |
| Round 1(2) | *v* Ajax Amsterdam | (h) | 2-0 | McIlroy, Macari |
| Round 2(1) | *v* Juventus | (h) | 1-0 | Hill |
| Round 2(2) | *v* Juventus | (a) | 0-3 | |

**1980/81**

| | | | | |
|---|---|---|---|---|
| Round 1(1) | *v* Widzew Lodz | (h) | 1-1 | McIlroy |
| Round 1(2) | *v* Widzew Lodz | (a) | 0-0 | |

**1982/83**

| | | | | |
|---|---|---|---|---|
| Round 1(1) | *v* Valencia CF | (h) | 0-0 | |
| Round 1(2) | *v* Valencia CF | (a) | 1-2 | Robson |

**1984/85**

| | | | | |
|---|---|---|---|---|
| Round 1(1) | *v* Raba Vasas ETO | (h) | 3-0 | Robson, Muhren, Hughes |
| Round 1(2) | *v* Raba Vasas ETO | (a) | 2-2 | Brazil, Muhren |
| Round 2(1) | *v* PSV Eindhoven | (a) | 0-0 | |
| Round 2(2) | *v* PSV Eindhoven | (h) | 1-0 | Strachan |
| Round 3(1) | *v* Dundee United | (h) | 2-2 | Strachan, Robson |
| Round 3(2) | *v* Dundee United | (a) | 3-2 | Hughes, Muhren, Own goal |

| Q Final(1) | v Videoton | (h) | 1-0 | Stapleton |
| Q Final(2) | v Videoton | (a) | 0-1 | |
| | | | *Lost 5-4 on penalties* | |

**1992/93**

| Round 1(1) | v Moscow Torpedo | (h) | 0-0 | |
| Round 1(2) | v Moscow Torpedo | (a) | 0-0 | |
| | | | *Lost 4-3 on penalties* | |

## United in Europe – *European Super Cup*

**1991**

| Final | v Red Star Belgrade | (h) | 1-0 | McClair |

## United in Europe – *World Club Championship*

**1968**

| 1st Leg | v Estudiantes de la Plata | (a) | 0-1 | |
| 2nd Leg | v Estudiantes de la Plata | (h) | 1-1 | Morgan |

## Other Competitions – *World Club Championships*

| Date | Round/Leg | Opponents | Venue | Score | Att. |
|---|---|---|---|---|---|
| 25/9/68 | First Leg | v Estudiantes | (a) | lost 0-1 | 55,000 |

*Team:* Stepney, Dunne, Burns, Crerand, Foulkes, Stiles, Morgan, Sadler, Charlton, Law, Best.

| 16/10/68 | Second Leg | v Estudiantes | (h) | drew 1-1 | 63,500 |

*Team:* Stepney, Brennan, Dunne, Crerand, Foulkes, Sadler, Morgan, Kidd, Charlton, Law (Sartori), Best.

## Other Competitions – *European Super Cup*

| Date | Round/Leg | Opponents | Venue | Score | Att. |
|---|---|---|---|---|---|
| 19/11/91 | | v Red Star Belgrade | | won 1-0 | 22,110 |

*Team;* Schmeichel, Irwin, Martin (Giggs), Bruce, Webb, Pallister, Kanchelskis, Ince, **McClair,** Hughes, Blackmore.

## Other Competitions – *Anglo-Italian Cup*

Group 1
21st February 1973     v Fiorentina (h)     drew 1-1     Att: 23,951

| 21st March 1973 | v Lazio (a) | drew 0-0 | Att: 52,834 |
| 4th April 1973 | v Bari (h) | won 3-1 | Att: 14,303 |
| 2nd May 1973 | v Verona (a) | won 4-1 | Att: 8,168 |

*Despite remaining unbeaten United failed to qualify for the semi-final stages.*

## Other Competitions – *Watney Cup*

| Date | Round/Leg | Opponents | Venue | Score | Att. |
|------|-----------|-----------|-------|-------|------|
| 1970/71 | 1st Round | v Reading | (a) | Won 3-2 | |
| | Semi-Final | v Hull City | (a) | 1-1aet | |

*Won 4-3 on penalties. This is thought to be the first occasion any first class game in England was decided by penalties.*

| | Final | v Derby County | (a) | Lost 1-4 | |
| 1971/72 | 1st Round | v Halifax Town | (a) | Lost 1-2 | |

*Of the thirteen United players to take part in this game, eleven – Stepney, Dunne, Crerand, Burns, Sadler, Morgan, Kidd, Charlton, Law and Best – were full internationals whilst Gowling was an Under 23 International.*

## United in the FA Charity Shield

27/4/08 · v Queen's Park Rangers   Stamford Bridge  1-1     6,000
Scorer: Meredith
*Team:* Moger, Stacey, Burgess, Duckworth, Roberts, Bell, **Meredith**, Bannister, J Turnbull, A Turnbull, Wall

29t/8/08 · v Queen's Park Rangers   Stamford Bridge  4-0     6,000
*Team:* Moger, Stacey, Burgess, Duckworth, Roberts, Bell, Meredith, Bannister, J **Turnbull (3)**, Picken, **Wall**

25t/9/11 · v Swindon Town   Stamford Bridge  8-4     10,000
*Team:* Edmonds, Hofton, Stacey, Duckworth, Roberts, Bell, Meredith, Hamill, **Halse (6)**, **Turnbull**, **Wall**

6/10/48 · v Arsenal   Highbury  3-4     31,000
*Team:* Crompton, Carey, Aston, Anderson, Chilton, Warner, Delaney, Morris, **Burke, Rowley,** Mitten – **Smith (o.g)**

24/9/52 · v Newcastle United   Old Trafford  4-2     11,381
*Team:* Wood, McNulty, Aston, Carey, Chilton, Gibson, Berry, **Downie, Rowley (2)**, Pearson, **Byrne**

24/10/56 · v Manchester City   Maine Road  1-0     30,495
*Team:* Wood (Gaskell), Foulkes, Byrne, Colman, Jones, Edwards, Berry, Whelan, Taylor, **Viollet**, Peg

22/10/57    *v* Aston Villa                    Old Trafford      4-0        27,923
*Team:* Wood, Foulkes, Byrne, Goodwin, Blanchflower, Edwards, **Berry,** Whelan,
**Taylor (3),** Viollet, Pegg

17/8/63    *v* Everton                         Goodison Park     0-4        54,840
*Team:* Gaskell, A Dunne, Cantwell, Crerand, Foulkes, Setters, Giles, Quixall, Herd,
Law, Charlton

14/8/65    *v* Liverpool                       Old Trafford      2-2        48,502
*Team:* P Dunne, Brennan, A Dunne, Crerand, Cantwell, Stiles, **Best** (Anderson),
Charlton, **Herd,** Law, Aston

12/8/67    *v* Tottenham Hotspurs              Old Trafford      3-3        54,106
*Team:* Stepney, Brennan, A Dunne, Crerand, Foulkes, Stiles, Best, Kidd, **Charlton
(2), Law,** Aston

13/8/77    *v* Liverpool                       Wembley           0-0        82,000
*Team:* Stepney, Nicholl, Albiston, McIlroy, B Greenhoff, Buchan, Coppell, J
Greenhoff (McCreery), Pearson, Macari, Hill

20/8/83    *v* Liverpool                       Wembley           2-0        92,000
*Team:* Bailey, Duxbury, Albiston, Wilkins, Moran, McQueen, **Robson (2),** Muhren
(Gidman), Stapleton, Whiteside, Graham

10/8/85    *v* Everton                         Wembley           0-2        82,000
Bailey, Gidman, Albiston, Whiteside, McGrath, Hogg, Robson, Duxbury (Moses),
Hughes, Stapleton, Olsen

19/8/90    *v* Liverpool                       Wembley           1-1        66,558
*Team:* Sealey, Irwin, Donaghy, Bruce, Phelan, Pallister, **Blackmore,** Ince, McClair,
Hughes, Wallace (Robins)

7/8/93     *v* Arsenal                         Wembley           1-1        60,000
                                               *United won 5-4 on penalties*
*Team:* Schemeichel, Parker, Irwin, Bruce, Kanchelskis, Pallister, Cantona, Ince,
Keane, **Hughes,** Giggs (Robson)

## United in FA Youth Cup Finals

4/5/53     1st Leg        *v* Wolves           Old Trafford      7-1        20,934
*Team:* Clayton, Fulton, Kennedy, Colman, Cope, Edwards, **McFarlane (2),
Whelan, Lewis (2), Pegg, Scanlon**

9/5/53     2nd Leg        *v* Wolves           Molineux          2-2        14,290
*Team:* Clayton, Fulton, Kennedy, Colman, Cope, Edwards, McFarlane, **Whelan,
Lewis,** Pegg, Scanlon                                *Aggregate: 9-3*

23/4/54    1st Leg        *v* Wolves           Old Trafford      4-4        18,246
*Team:* Hawksworth, Beswick, Rhodes, Colman, Harrop, McGuinness, Littler,
**Edwards (2),** Charlton, **Pegg (2 – 1 via penalty),** Scanlon

26/4/54    2nd Leg    v Wolves    Molineux    1-0    28,651
*Team:* Hawksworth, Beswick, Rhodes, Colman, Harrop, McGuinness, Littler, Edwards, Charlton, **Pegg (penalty)**, Scanlon    *Aggregate: 5-4*

27/4/55    1st Leg    v West Brom    Old Trafford    4-1    16,696
*Team:* Hawksworth, Queenan, Rhodes, **Colman (2)**, Jones, McGuinness, **Beckett,** Brennan, Edwards, **Charlton,** Fidler

30/4/55    2nd Leg    v West Brom    The Hawthorns    3-0    8,335
*Team:* Hawksworth, Queenan, Rhodes, Colman, Jones, McGuinness, Beckett, Brennan, **Edwards, Charlton,** Fidler – **Cooke (og)**    *Aggregate: 7-1*

30/4/56    1st Leg    v Chesterfield    Old Trafford    3-2    25,544
*Team:* Hawksworth, Queenan, Jones, **Carolan,** Holland, McGuinness, Morgans, **Pearson,** Dawson. **Charlton,** Fidler

7/5/56    2nd Leg    v Chesterfield    Recreation Grnd    1-1    15,838
*Team:* Hawksworth, Queenan, Jones, Carolan, Holland, McGuinness, Morgans, Pearson, Dawson, Charlton, **Fidler**    *Aggregate: 4-3*
*Gordon Banks kept goal for Chesterfield in both games*

2/5/57    1st Leg    v West Ham Utd    Upton Park    3-2    14,000
*Team:* Gaskell, Smith, Madison, English, Holland, Bratt, Morgans, **Lawton, Dawson,** Pearson, **Hunter**

7/5/57    2nd Leg    v West Ham Utd    Old Trafford    5-0    23,349
*Team:* Gaskell, Smith, Madison, English, Holland, Bratt, **Morgans,** Lawton, Dawson, **Pearson (3), Hunter**    *Aggregate: 8-2*

27/5/64    1st Leg    v Swindon Town    County Ground    1-1    17,000
*Team:* Rimmer, Duff, Noble, McBride, Farrar, Fitzpatrick, Anderson, **Best,** Sadler, Kinsey, Aston.

30t/4/64    2nd Leg    v Swindon Town    Old Trafford)    4-1    25,563
*Team:* Rimmer, Duff, Noble, McBride, Farrar, Fitzpatrick, Anderson, Best, **Sadler (3),** Kinsey, **Aston**    *Aggregate: 5-2*

26/4/82    1st Leg    v Watford    Old Trafford    2-3    7,280
*Team:* P Hughes, Hill, Scott, Hogg, Garton, **Blackmore,** Pearson, **Dempsey,** Whiteside, M Hughes, Docherty (Woods)

6/5/82    2nd Leg    v Watford    Vicarage Road    4-4†    8,000
*Team:* P Hughes, Hill, Scott, Hogg, Garton, Williams (Wood), Blackmore, **Dempsey, Whiteside, M Hughes (2),** Docherty    *Aggregate: 6-7*

24/4/86    1st Leg    v Manchester City    Old Trafford    1-1    7,602
*Team:* Walsh, Gill, Martin, Scott, Gardner, Bottomley, Murphy, Todd, Cronin, Wilson (Hopley), **Harvey**

29/5/86    2nd leg    v Manchester City    Maine Road    0-2    18,158
*Team:* Walsh, Gill, Martin, Scott, Gardner, Harvey, Murphy, Todd, Cronin, Bottomley (Hopley), Goddard    *Aggregate: 1-3*

14/4/92   1st Leg   *v* Crystal Palace   Selhurst Park   3-1   7,825
*Team:* Pilkington, O'Kane, Switzer, Casper, G Neville, **Beckham, Butt (2),** Davies, McKee, Savage (Roberts), Thornley

15/5/92   2nd Leg   *v* Crystal Palace   Old Trafford   3-2   14,681
*Team:* Pilkington, O'Kane, Switzer, Casper, G Neville, Beckham, Butt, Davies (Gillespie), McKee, Giggs, Thonley (Savage)   *Aggregate: 6-3*

10/4/93   1st Leg   *v* Leeds Utd   Old Trafford   0-2   30,562
*Team:* Whitmarsh, O'Kane, Riley, Casper, G Neville, Gillespie, Butt, Beckham (Savage), Irving (Murdock), Scholes, Thornley

13/5/93   2ndLeg   *v* Leeds Utd   Elland Road   1-2   31,037
*Team:* Whitmarsh, P.Neville, Riley, Casper, G Neville, Gillespie, Scholes, Beckham, Irving (Murdock), Savage, Thornley   *Aggregate: 1-4*

# Miscellaneous

## *Managers*

**Ernest Mangnall (1903-1912)**

| | |
|---|---|
| Football League champions | 1907/8, 1910/11 |
| Division Two runners-up | 1905/06 |
| FA Cup winners | 1909 |

**John Robson (1914-1921)**

The first person to assume the title of Manager – Mangnall's official title had been Secretary.

**John Chapman (1921-1926)**

| | |
|---|---|
| Division Two runners-up | 1924/25 |

Although full details were never made known, the FA suspended Chapman from football in 1926.

**Clarence Hilditch (1926-1927)**

The only player-manager in United's history.

**Herbert Bamlett (1927-1931)**

Made history by being the youngest man ever to referee an FA Cup Final – in 1914 aged 32. As a manager he guided United into their worst ever spell.

**Walter Crickmer (1931-1932)**

Another never to assume the title of manager although he was responsible for team selection. Crickmer was one of the victims of the Munich Air Crash.

**Scott Duncan (1932-1937)**

| | |
|---|---|
| Division Two champions | 1935/36 |

**Walter Crickmer (1937-1945)**

**Sir Matt Busby (1945-1969)**

| | |
|---|---|
| Football League champions | 1951/52, 1955/56, 1956/57, 1964/65, 1966/67 |
| Division One runners-up | 1946/47, 1947/48, 1948/49, 1950/51, 1958/59, 1963/64, 1967/68 |
| FA Cup winners | 1948, 1963 |
| FA Cup runners-up | 1957 |
| European champions | 1967/68 |

**Jimmy Murphy (1958)**

In the absence of Matt Busby, seriously injured in the Munich Air Crash, Jimmy Murphy took over for six months from February to August 1958. During that time he led the makeshift team to an FA Cup Final appearance.

| | |
|---|---|
| FA Cup runners-up | 1958 |

**Wilf McGuinness (1969-70)**

United's only attempt to promote from within. Two League Cup semi-finals and one FA Cup semi-final were not sufficient to keep him in the job.

**Frank O'Farrell (1971-72)**

At Christmas of his first season in charge, United were five points clear at the top of the league when there were only two points for a win but they slumped to finish eighth. He soon paid the penalty.

**Tommy Docherty (1972-77)**

| | |
|---|---|
| Division Two champions | 1974/75 |
| FA Cup winners | 1977 |
| FA Cup runners-up | 1976 |

**Dave Sexton (1977-1981)**

| | |
|---|---|
| FA Cup runners-up | 1979 |
| First Division runners-up | 1979/80 |

Tommy Docherty was the first manager to offer Dave Sexton a chance in management when he appointed Sexton as his coach at Stamford Bridge. Sexton was later to replace Docherty at both Chelsea and Manchester United.

**Ron Atkinson (1981-1986)**

| | |
|---|---|
| FA Cup winners | 1983, 1985 |
| League Cup runners-up | 1983 |

Looked likely to succeed in bringing the Holy Grail back to Old Trafford when his side began the 1985/86 campaign with ten straight league victories but it wasn't to be.

**Alex Ferguson (1986-)**

| | |
|---|---|
| FA Premier League champions | 1992/93, 1993/94 |
| Division One runners-up | 1987/88, 1991/92 |
| FA Cup winners | 1990, 1994 |
| League Cup winners | 1992 |
| League Cup runners-up | 1991, 1994 |
| European Cup Winners Cup winners | 1991 |

---

## Reds in Management

1993/94 saw a quite extraordinary number of former United players in management positions. Brian Kidd, of course, was very much at home as Assistant Manager to Alex Ferguson at Old Trafford whilst another former Red to hold an Assistant Manager position was David McCreery at Carlisle United. Arsenal and Bradford City were both totally "United" in their management teams with George Graham and Stewart Houston teaming at Highbury whilst Frank Stapleton had Stuart Pearson as his second in command at the Yorkshire club.

Lou Macari was the last manager to beat United before they set off on their long unbeaten run when he was with Stoke City before his move to Celtic whilst another Scot, Joe Jordan, took over the reins from Macari at Stoke. Barry Fry started the campaign with Barnet, had a short sojourn at Southend United and then moved to Birmingham City but Viv Anderson just made do with Barnsley.

In Scotland, Jimmy Nicholl had revamped Raith Rovers to claim a place in the Premier Division for the first time ever and over the channel in Ireland, Scott McGarvey had a spell in charge of Derry City.

On the non-league scene, Sammy McIlroy was in demand and, after spells at Northwich Victoria and Ashton United in the previous campaign, he was to be found at the giant-killers of old, Macclesfield Town with John Gidman completing a formidable total at Kings Lynn.

# Post War Average Attendances

| Season | Home | Away | Season | Home | Away |
|--------|------|------|--------|------|------|
| 46/47 | 43,615 | 31,364 | 70/71 | 44,754 | 41,695 |
| 47/48 | 53,660 | 40,493 | 71/72 | 45,999 | 44,085 |
| 48/49 | 46,023 | 44,720 | 72/73 | 48,623 | 41,171 |
| 49/50 | 41,455 | 46,172 | 73/74 | 42,721 | 35,337 |
| 50/51 | 37,159 | 38,091 | 74/75 | 48,388 | 25,556 |
| 51/52 | 41,870 | 40,945 | 75/76 | 54,750 | 37,037 |
| 52/53 | 35,737 | 37,068 | 76/77 | 53,710 | 35,357 |
| 53/54 | 33,637 | 37,096 | 77/78 | 51,938 | 30,424 |
| 54/55 | 34,077 | 35,865 | 78/79 | 46,687 | 30,498 |
| 55/56 | 38,880 | 32,872 | 79/80 | 51,562 | 34,101 |
| 56/57 | 45,192 | 39,772 | 80/81 | 45,055 | 29,849 |
| 57/58 | 45,583 | 45,352 | 81/82 | 44,685 | 27,214 |
| 58/59 | 53,258 | 44,028 | 82/83 | 41,583 | 25,294 |
| 59/60 | 47,288 | 41,026 | 83/84 | 42,534 | 24,936 |
| 60/61 | 37,807 | 34,139 | 84/85 | 43,010 | 27,884 |
| 61/62 | 33,490 | 33,964 | 85/86 | 44,422 | 28,204 |
| 62/63 | 40,317 | 34,894 | 86/87 | 40,625 | 25,221 |
| 63/64 | 43,753 | 38,697 | 87/88 | 39,155 | 23,041 |
| 64/65 | 45,990 | 41,377 | 88/89 | 36,488 | 23,713 |
| 65/66 | 38,456 | 38,171 | 89/90 | 39,078 | 26,666 |
| 66/67 | 53,984 | 45,577 | 90/91 | 43,241 | 25,020 |
| 67/68 | 57,759 | 45,802 | 91/92 | 44,985 | 27,893 |
| 68/69 | 51,121 | 44,295 | 92/93 | 35,132 | 28,254 |
| 69/70 | 51,115 | 43,997 | 93/94 | 44,240 | 28,868 |

# The Cost of Post War Championship Sides

These costs are not necessarily exact as they depend on newspaper reports which may not have been 100% accurate. Also it has to borne in mind that some of the cost will have been offset by outgoing transfers.

### *1951/52*                                                                *Total Cost £61,000*

Reg Allen (QPR) £6,000, John Downie (Bradford PA) £20,000,
Johnny Berry (Birmingham City) £25,000, Harry McShane £5,000.
*NB Johnny Carey and Jack Rowley had been signed before the Second World War for nominal fees.*

### *1955/56 and 1956/57*                                           *Total Cost £60,999*

Ray Wood (Darlington) £6,000, Tommy Taylor (Barnsley) £29,999,
Johnny Berry (Birmingham City) £25,000.

### *1964/65*                                                              *Total Cost £283,000*

Tony Dunne (Shelbourne) £6,000, David Herd (Arsenal) £40,000,
Denis Law (Torino) £115,000, Pat Crerand (Celtic) £56,000,
John Connolly (Burnley) £56,000, Pat Dunne £10,000 (Shamrock Rovers).

### *1966/67*                                                              *Total Cost £269,750*

Tony Dunne (Shelbourne) £6,000, Denis Law (Torino) £115,000,
David Herd £40,000, Pat Crerand (Celtic) £56,000, David Sadler (Maidstone) £750,
Alex Stepney (Millwall) £52,000.

### *1992/93*                                                            *Total Cost £21,800,000*

Peter Schmeichel (Brondby) £850,000, Paul Parker (QPR) £2,000,000,
Denis Irwin (Oldham Athletic) £625,000, Steve Bruce (Norwich City) £800,000,
Gary Pallister (Middlesborough) £2,300,000, Lee Sharpe (Torquay United)
£185,000, Paul Ince (West Ham United) £1,250,000 plus £5,000 a game,
Mark Hughes (Barcelona) £1,500,000, Eric Cantona (Leeds United) £1,000,000,
Bryan Robson (West Bromwich Albion) £1,500,000, Mike Phelan (Norwich City)
£750,000, Brian McClair (Celtic) £850,000, Dion Dublin (Cambridge Utd)
£1,000,000

### *1993/94*                                                            *Total Cost £25,800,000*

As above plus Roy Keane (Notts Forest) £3,750,000, Ince played approx 50 games.

*European Champions' Cup winning side.*          *Total Cost £114,750*

Alex Stepney (Millwall) £52,000, Tony Dunne (Shelbourne) £6,000,
Pat Crerand (Celtic) £56,000, David Sadler (Maidstone) £750.

## *Important Dates in the History of Old Trafford*

| | | |
|---|---|---|
| 1909 | – | After winning the FA Cup, United are given the then huge sum of £60,000 to purchase a new site and build a modern (for the times) stadium. |
| 19/02/1910 | – | United leave their old ground in Clayton and play their first ever game at Old Trafford. The visitors are Liverpool and 45,000 fans turn up but go home disappointed as United lose 4-3 after twice leading by two goals. |
| 29/04/1911 | – | United beat Sunderland 5-1 on the final day of the season at Old Trafford to take the First Division title by one point. Two World Wars would be waged before it landed back at Old Trafford again. |
| 1911 | – | The new stadium is quickly rewarded as the Football Association choose it for the FA Cup replay between Bradford City and Newcastle United. The Yorkshire club win their one and only FA Cup, beating the Geordies 1-0. |
| 1915 | – | Old Trafford hosts the FA Cup Final to end a 19 year association with Crystal Palace as the venue. With war clouds over Europe, the Final became known as "The Khaki Final" as the terraces were packed with soldiers at home on leave for the weekend. Sheffield United beat Chelsea 3-0. |
| 27/12/1920 | – | The record attendance for a League game is set at 70,504 for the visit of Aston Villa who win 3-1. |
| 1922 | – | Old Trafford stages the FA Charity Shield match between Huddersfield Town and Liverpool which goes to the Yorkshire side 1-0. |
| 17/04/1926 | – | The last England v. Scotland full International to be played in England outside of Wembley Stadium takes place at Old Trafford. The Scots win with the only goal of the game from Jackson. |
| Sept 1930 | – | United concede thirteen goals in successive home games four days apart when Huddersfield hit them for six and Newcastle United knock in seven. In the worst ever start by any Football League club, United's first point of the campaign does not come until November when Birmingham City are beaten 2-0 at Old |

Trafford after twelve straight defeats.

16/11/1938 — The ground witnesses the fastest ever hat-trick in International football as Willie Hall (Spurs) nets a treble inside three and a half minutes against Ireland. He goes on to score five times in succession thus equalling the England record in a 7-0 rout.

25/03/1939 — The ground's record attendance of 76,962 is set when Old Trafford stages the FA Cup semi-final between Portsmouth and Grimsby Town. The "Mariners" lose their 'keeper very early in the match and Portsmouth take full advantage to win 5-0.

11/03/1941 — The ground, situated on the perimeter of Manchester's vast Trafford Park industrial complex, is virtually demolished as Hitler's bombs target the area to halt engineering production for Britain's war effort.

8/01/1949 — United play their first FA Cup tie at Old Trafford for ten years when they hammer Bournemouth 6-0. Their last tie at Old Trafford had been a Third Round replay on 11th January 1939 when West Bromwich Albion had beaten the Reds 5-1.

1951 — The first foreign team to play United at Old Trafford are Red Star Belgrade in a fixture organised to celebrate the Festival of Britain. The match finishes 1-1 with Jack Rowley equalising from the penalty spot late in the game.

26/04/1952 — United swamp Arsenal, the only team who can catch them, 6-1 in the final game of the season to capture the title for the first time since 1911. Rowley nets a hat-trick.

24/01/1955 — The longest ever FA Cup tie is finally resolved at Old Trafford when Stoke City eventually beat Bury 3-2 after nine hours twenty-two minutes.

07/04/1956 — United clinch their third ever First Division title by beating Blackpool 2-1 at Old Trafford in front of their biggest crowd of the season, 62,277.

30/04/1956 — The programme for the First Leg of the FA Youth Cup Final at Old Trafford against Chesterfield contains the following pen picture of a Chesterfield youngster. *"Gordon Banks (Goalkeeper), a Sheffield boy in his second year at the club. Has played several games in the Reserves recently and acquitted himself well"*.

6/10/1956 — In a strange coincidence, Bobby Charlton makes his debut at Old Trafford against his namesake team, Charlton Athletic. He scores twice and in the return game hits a hat-trick!

20/10/1956 — United lose 5-2 to Everton at Old Trafford where they had been unbeaten for eighteen months. The last team to beat them at

|  |  | home had also been Everton in March 1955. |
|---|---|---|
| 25/03/1957 | – | United play their first ever game at Old Trafford under floodlights but fail to celebrate as they go down 2-0 in a league match to Bolton Wanderers. |
| 08/04/1957 | – | United's Youth team lose 3-2 to Southampton at Old Trafford in the semi-final of the FA Youth Cup. It is their first ever defeat in the competition since it was formed in 1952 but they still go on to win it again as they had won the first leg at the Dell 5-1. |
| 25/04/1957 | – | Old Trafford stages its first ever European cup tie as Real Madrid provide stiff resistance in a 2-2 draw which sees them through to the Final having beaten United 3-1 in Spain. All United's previous home games in the European Cup had been played at Maine Road. |
| 2/10/1957 | – | Shamrock Rovers become United's first ever Old Trafford European victims when they are beaten 3-2 in the European Cup. |
| 30/10/1957 | – | Brian Clough becomes the second player to score five goals in a Representative game at Old Trafford when he goes "nap" for an FA XI against the Army. |
| 30/11/1957 | – | Having never been beaten by a London club at Old Trafford since October 1938 when Charlton Athletic won 2-0, United finally lose 4-3 to Spurs. United then proceeded to lose their very next home game to another London outfit, Chelsea! |
| 19/02/1958 | – | United's first game after the Munich Air Crash takes place in an emotional atmosphere at Old Trafford. The FA Cup Fifth Round tie is won 3-0 with a make shift team of youngsters. Shay Brennan's opening goal was in fact United's first ever FA Cup goal against Wednesday as the Yorkshire side had been victorious in all the previous encounters by scores of 6-0, 1-0 and 2-0. |
| 14/01/1961 | – | United beat Spurs 2-0 at Old Trafford – the only occasion that the famous Tottenham "double" side failed to score all season. |
| 1961 | – | Old Trafford stages the first ever League Cup semi-final replay when Aston Villa beat Burnley 2-1. |
| 1966 | – | Old Trafford is selected to host three of the Group games in the World Cup. Portugal, who England went on to defeat in the semi-final score their first ever goal in World Cup Finals stages when Augusto nets in a 3-1 win over Hungary at Old Trafford. |
| 26/11/1966 | – | David Herd scores one of the most unusual hat-tricks ever when Sunderland visit Old Trafford. Each of his three goals was put past a different 'keeper! He scored first of all against Jim |

Montgomery who was injured and then against his replacement, central defender Charlie Hurley. The Sunderland management then decided the team pattern was better served by Hurley reverting to his outfield position and he was replaced by John Parke against whom Herd completed his treble!

| | | |
|---|---|---|
| 1967/68 | – | United, with Best, Law and Charlton in the side set an average attendance record for the season at Old Trafford (and the Football League) of 57,758. |
| 17/12/1969 | – | Old Trafford sets a record attendance for the League Cup when United draw 2-2 with neighbours Manchester City in the second leg of a semi-final tie. A crowd of 63,418 see City reach the Final, having won the first leg 2-1. |
| 1970 | – | Old Trafford stages its third FA Cup Final when Leeds United and Chelsea replay there after a 2-2 draw at Wembley. The game finishes 2-1 to Chelsea after extra-time. |
| 1972 | – | Bobby Moore saves a penalty at Old Trafford in the League Cup 2nd Replay between West Ham United and Stoke City. He had to go in net when the "Hammers" 'keeper Ferguson was taken off injured but although Moore saved the spot kick, Bernard followed up to convert. When Conroy scored the winner for Stoke, the tie had been underway for seven hours. |
| 1977 | – | Old Trafford sees League Cup history made when Aston Villa beat Everton in a League Cup Final 2nd Replay by 3-2. They become the first club to win the trophy three times. |
| 1978 | – | The League Cup Final is back again at Old Trafford with Nottingham Forest defeating Liverpool 1-0 via a hotly disputed John Robertson penalty. |
| 22/03/1980 | – | The 100th "Derby" match with Manchester City takes place at Old Trafford. A Micky Thomas goal gives the Reds victory. |
| 14/10/1980 | – | Old Trafford hosts the England "B" international with the United States. The home side win 1-0. |
| 12/12/1984 | – | Celtic are ordered to replay their European tie with Rapid Vienna at Old Trafford after crowd trouble on their own ground and are well beaten by the Austrians. |
| 22/04/1989 | – | The Women's FA Cup Final takes place at Old Trafford and is televised for the first time. Leasowe Pacific beat Fulham 3-2. |
| 21/10/1989 | – | Rugby League history is made at Old Trafford when Paul Newlove becomes the youngest Great Britain international at the age of 18 years and 72 days in the 24-16 reverse at the hands of New Zealand. |

# The History of Manchester United

Although now a household name in most countries of the world where football is played, Manchester United's beginnings were, extremely humble and on at least two occasions they were nearly forced out of business. The origins of the club can be traced back to 1878 and a railway carriage making department at the Newton Heath works of the Lancashire and Yorkshire Railway Company. Not surprisingly, the workmen who formed the first side called themselves Newton Heath Lancashire and Yorkshire Railway.

The first ground was by the side of a clay pit in North Road, Newton Heath but there was no running straight out on to the pitch in those days. The players changed in a pub called the Three Crowns about eight hundred yards up the road from the ground but, nevertheless, the side were easily the best railway side in the area at that time and other works teams failed to give the Newton Heath side a decent game on most occasions. Soon, Newton Heath were looking further afield for matches. By the time professionalism was legalised in 1885, Newton Heath were on the fringe of the better class of sides in the area such as Bootle and Bolton Wanderers. In order to progress, Newton Heath decided to begin recruiting professionals who could also be offered work in the carriage department to boost their soccer earnings. This double–barrelled bargaining point enabled Newton Heath to attract some quite decent players including several Welsh internationals.

Indeed, no fewer than five Newton Heath players appeared for Wales in an international against Scotland in 1888. No matter that the Welsh side were beaten 5-1 in that game, the fact was that Newton Heath were growing in stature. Jack and Roger Doughty had been recruited from the top Welsh side of the day, Druids, whilst Jack Powell, who signed in 1886, became captain. Many is the player these days who says he would *"walk to Old Trafford for the privilege of playing for United"*. In the late 1880's a Scot by the name of Patrick O'Donnell did just that (except of course it was then Newton Heath). The distance from Glasgow to Manchester, however, was the same those days as a century later and he was rewarded for his epic walk with a job at the railway as well as playing football.

It may seem nonsensical now but, on the first occasion United (Newton Heath) applied for membership of the Football League in 1891, they received just one vote. They therefore turned their attentions in the direction of the Football Alliance and were promptly accepted. They won their first game against Sunderland Albion 4-1 and beat Small Heath 9-1 in their first campaign but struggled away, winning just twice on their travels, a feat they were to repeat in their second season. The third term of Alliance soccer got under way with yet another away beating but this disguised the course of events that lay ahead. When a second application to join the Football League was made, they could hardly have fared worse than on the first occasion but they did with Newton Heath not receiving a single vote of support. After this set back and an opening day defeat at Burton, few could have forecast the success that was to arrive in the 1891/92 season. After the loss at Burton, Newton

Heath remained unbeaten in their next fifteen outings and lost only twice more all season to secure runners-up spot behind Notts Forest who drew a crowd of 16,000 to North Road on New Year's Day 1892. At the end of that season, the Football League decided to enlarge and the Football Alliance were virtually encompassed en bloc. Newton Heath and Forest, as the Alliance's top two teams, went straight into the First Division and, now in the big time, the LYR was dropped from the club's title and the first full time Secretary, A.H.Albut appointed.

Thus, United began their Football League life under the name Newton Heath with a 4-3 defeat at Blackburn Rovers and, a week later, First Division football came to Manchester for the first time when Burnley visited North Road and went home with a 1-1 draw under their belts. It took Newton Heath seven games to notch their first ever Football League victory but it was done in some style. Strangely, their first ever win, 10-1 against Wolves remains today, well over 3,600 games later, their record score in the Football League! The big victory, however, was just a flash in the pan and Newton Heath finished rock bottom to be saved from relegation only by a "Test Match" defeat of Small Heath. Newton Heath were, however, out of their depth in the First Division and finished bottom yet again the following campaign. They were relegated after losing their "Test Match" to a side that were going to become, a century later, one of United's chief protagonists, Liverpool.

By now, Newton Heath had moved to pastures new at Bank Street but crowds were disappointing and, starved of cash, Newton Heath remained by and large a struggling Second Division outfit. There were highlights, however, including what almost was a record Football League scoreline of 14-0 over Walsall. The Midlanders, though, were obviously gluttons for punishment as they put in a protest, which was upheld, and when the game was replayed, Newton Heath could only find the net nine times!

Although nowadays a fashionable shirt to wear, the green and gold halves were dropped and the team kitted out in white but the side still languished in the lower reaches. By the turn of the century, the club were in serious financial trouble but were saved in bizarre fashion at a Bazaar by a St Bernard dog. The Bazaar had been organised to raise much needed money for the club and the captain of the side, Harry Stafford, tied a collection box to the neck of his St Bernard and allowed it to roam freely about the hall. Unfortunately, or, as it turned out, very fortunately, the dog wandered off out of the building and was eventually found by a wealthy businessman, John Davies. He became the club's first saviour.

On hearing of Newton Heath's plight, Davies paid off the club's debts of £2,500 (an astronomical sum in those days) and put in a further £500 to get some new players. He immediately became Chairman, decreed a change of name to Manchester United and bought a new kit – the famous red and white!

The first game under the new name was at Gainsborough Trinity in September 1902 and ended in a 1-0 victory. The season was to see another, much more, significant development, however, with the appointment of James Mangall as Secretary. Although his official title was Secretary, Mangnall was accepted as the first manager of the club as he was responsible for team selection and policy. It is a sign of how significant this move was, that Mangnall ranks with Sir Matt Busby and, latterly, Alex Ferguson in the top three managers the club has ever had.

In modern day parlance, Mangnall quite simply *"turned the club round"*. After finishing fifth in the Second Division in his first season (Manchester City, unfortunately for United supporters, won it) a crowd of over 40,000 turned out for the opening game of the 1903/04 campaign. For the next two seasons United were to just miss out on promotion but in 1905/06, after twice finishing third, United returned to the top flight after an absence of twelve years. They were about to embark on their most successful era and one that would not be repeated until another forty years had elapsed.

The strength of the team lay in the midfield, or half back line as it was then known, with Duckworth, Bell and Roberts acknowledged as the finest to be seen in English football until the 1940s. Mangnall(whichspelling?) also recruited the unrelated Sandy and James Turnbull along with Harold Halse and the legendary Billy Meredith. Halse was to play in FA Cup Finals for three different clubs in a seven year period (United, Villa and Chelsea) and it was his goal that brought United an FA Cup Final appearance for the first time in 1909. Meredith and Sandy Turnbull were part of a deal that saw United sign five players from Manchester City in 1906 with suspensions still to be served until 1907 over an illegal payments row. It wasn't, therefore, until the start of the 1907/08 season that Mangnall could at last get the team he wanted out on to the field but when he did, it was to prove a resounding success.

They won 14 of their first 15 league games in 1907/08, the only set back being a 2-1 reverse at Middlesborough in the third game of the campaign. In those 15 games, Sandy Turnbull found the net 19 times, Meredith 8 and Jack Turnbull scored six after missing the opening five matches through injury. United dominated the Championship, finishing nine points (when there were only two points awarded for a win) clear of second placed Aston Villa who themselves were only thirteen points off bottom spot! Given that domination, United surprisingly didn't figure at all in the following season's Championship but they did put their appaling FA Cup record behind them by lifting the famous trophy for the first time.

United had never been beyond the quarter-final stage, indeed they had only reached the last eight on three occasions, and they needed an inordinate slice of luck to get past that stage on their way to capturing the Cup. They were losing 1-0 at Burnley with only eighteen minutes play left when a blizzard put paid to the game. When the replay took place, United won 3-2 and were then fortunate to tackle in the semi-final the most successful FA Cup side of that era, Newcastle United, when the Geordies were reduced to ten men with Halse scoring the only goal. Halse also had a big role to play in the final, for it was his shot that hit the Bristol City crossbar before bouncing down for Sandy Turnbull to score the only goal.

Satisfied with the success that his money had brought, John Davies now put in a further £60,000, a colossal amount in that period, to build a new stadium that would match the brilliance of the team his money had enabled Mangnall to establish.

United played their last game at Clayton, ending with a 5-0 victory against Spurs and in February 1910, Old Trafford was born. The last game at Clayton was witnessed by a crowd of only 7,000 but in true Old Trafford tradition the opening of the new stadium attracted 45,000!

The first game was a hard pill to swallow as arch enemies Liverpool spoiled the party with a 4-3 success after United had led 3-1. The first full campaign in the stadium, which matched the best anywhere in the country, saw the crowds flock to Old Trafford to watch United take their second Championship, but whereas their first title had been all over bar the shouting a long way from home, this one went right to the finishing line. Again, Villa were the nearest challengers and going into the penultimate game of the season United had a two point lead. They lost at Villa Park which put Villa level on 50 points and a game in hand, a game which they proceeded to draw. The final day saw United at home to Sunderland whilst Villa, with a superior goal average, played Liverpool who were languishing in the bottom half of the table and with nothing to play for. United had to win and Villa lose, or alternatively, United win by a large score whilst Villa drew. The public showed what they thought of United's chances when only 10,000 turned up but United did their bit by winning 5-1 and then, with communications not as good as they are today, it was a case of sit and wait. For once, probably to their eternal sorrow, Liverpool did United a favour by beating Villa 3-1 and the title came to Old Trafford. But two World Wars were to pass before Old Trafford saw success again.

Mangnall left in 1912 as he saw his great team beginning to age and United were not to appoint a successor until John Robson in December 1914. The First World War, however, then intervened but when the country opened for football again in 1919, Old Trafford was inundated with crowds and the record league gate, 70,504 was set in 1920 for the visit of Aston Villa who won 3-1. United, however, were only a shadow of their former selves and Robson resigned after two seasons of mid-table mediocrity. His replacement, John Chapman, would doubtless have settled for a mid-table position as his first season in charge saw United relegated to the Second Division!

The relegation brought one of football's most famous names of the time, Frank Barson, to Old Trafford in an effort to regain a place in the top flight and a change of colours to all white with a red "V". But success was not achieved overnight and United had to wait until 1925 before gaining promotion behind Leicester City setting, in the process, a defensive record of just 23 goals conceded, a total never beaten before or since in the Second Division. Once again, however, the issue was not settled until the very last game of the campaign with United needing a point from their game with Barnsley to secure promotion in front of Derby County. They got the necessary point in a goalless draw at Barnsley but, in the event, County failed to win so United would have gone up anyway.

Back in the First Division, United had a reasonable season finishing ninth but they also had some bitter disappointments. There was a 5-0 hiding at Huddersfield and an even bigger 7-0 trouncing (then a record, later equalled but never surpassed) at Blackburn. Manager Chapman was quickly dismissed when the FA suspended him over a charge of "improper conduct", the exact details of which were never made known but, perhaps, the biggest blow of all was the FA Cup semi-final defeat at Bramall Lane against Manchester City. Another little piece of Old Trafford history was made with the appointment of Clarrie Hilditch as player/manager to replace Chapman, the only occasion the club have ever had such a position. No sooner was 1926 out of the way than the death of John Davies, who had done so much to first of all save, then resurrect, United was announced. The appointment of Hilditch had never been intended as anything other than temporary and 1927 saw the appointment of Herbert Bartlett along with a return to the familiar red shirts.

All these changes put United firmly on a downward road and the club headed towards oblivion. After four terms of being bottom half material, United had probably their worst ever season, being relegated back to the Second Division with a paltry 22 points and also set a Football League record that still exists when they lost all their first twelve games of 1930/31 season. In consecutive home games against Huddersfield Town and Newcastle United, the Reds conceded thirteen goals whilst in an away game at Stamford Bridge immediately prior to those two home disasters, Chelsea had also breached the United defence, if one could call it that, six times. Later in the season, Huddersfield Town and Derby County were also to find the net six times against United who, altogether, conceded 115 goals. Bamlett resigned but with the poor form, allied to the recession, attendances plummeted and the club was again financially crippled. With no John Davies to turn to, United were now saved by another local businessman, James Gibson, whose son Alan is still a Vice-President of the club.

He cleared the more pressing debts, paid the outstanding wages, injected a reported £20,000 to buy players and hired a new manager, Scott Duncan at a salary rumoured to be almost £1,000 a year. Duncan quickly spent the £20,000 recruiting his players mainly from his homeland, Scotland. Despite the vast expenditure he incurred, Duncan's early stewardship was a disaster and in 1933/34 they reached an all time low when they were just one game away from relegation to the Third Division North. United travelled to play Millwall in their final match of the season knowing they had to win in order to avert relegation. Lincoln City were already down but the Reds were in 21st spot with 32 points. Immediately above United were Millwall with 33 points but their problem had been picking up points away from home. At the Den they had a good home record, better in fact than the Champions, Grimsby Town and, as United travelled to London, the unthinkable was very much on the cards. Despite, or because of, using no fewer than 38 players (no substitutes in those days) during the campaign United looked doomed. In the event, United surprised everybody, including most probably themselves, and won 2-0 with goals from Cape and Manley. The Reds had, in fact, gone five games unbeaten at the end of the campaign to save themselves.

Immediately after this escape, Duncan made probably his best buy, capturing George Mutch from Arbroath for £800. He was leading scorer in his first term and when, twelve months later, United won the Second Division title thanks to an unbeaten run of 19 games stretching from 4th January, when Bradford City beat them 1-0, until the end of the season, it was Mutch's 21 goals that led the way. Mutch went on to be transferred for £5,000 to Preston North End and is still shown on television scoring the only goal of the 1938 FA Cup Final from the penalty spot in the last minute. Duncan was rewarded with a new five year contract for gaining promotion but the directors should have waited – twelve months later the Reds were back in the Second Division! Almost as bad was the fact that Manchester City had won the First Division title! Duncan resigned and moved to Ipswich Town whom he immediately proceeded to take into the Football League.

As the saying goes, football is a funny old game. The following season United won promotion back to the First whilst, almost unbelievably, Manchester City created history by being the first, and to date, only Champions to be immediately relegated. The boot was very firmly on the other foot! But, once again, it was a nailbiting climax that went to the last day. Aston Villa were up as Champions and Sheffield United were second with 53 points having finished their programme. United and Coventry City were level in third place, two points behind Sheffield, with United's goal average just the better. A crowd of over 50,000 saw United clinch promotion with a 2-0 victory whilst Coventry finished fourth when they only drew their last fixture. In this new look United were several unknowns who were not to remain unknown after World War Two – the era of Johnny Carey, Stan Pearson and Jack Rowley was beginning to unfold.

By the end of the war, Matt Busby had been named as manager but United had no ground. Old Trafford, situated in the heart of Manchester's main industrial complex, Trafford Park, had been destroyed as the Germans targeted factories in the area for almost daily bombings. Whilst in the Army, Busby had been in charge of an army side in Italy and had been helped out by Jimmy Murphy. Busby immediately turned to his war-time colleague and invited him to become his assistant. The partnership was to take United to great heights.

United had arguably the best team in the land but couldn't prove it with a title as they finished runners-up four times in the first five post-war championships. They did, however, lift the FA Cup for the second time nearly forty years after their first success in 1909. The 1948 Wembley victory came without playing anybody outside of the top flight. The Third Round tie against Aston Villa was a classic as the home side went in front in under 20 seconds only for United to lead 5-1 at half-time. Anybody who thought the game was over had another think coming. The Reds scraped home 6-4 in one of the classic FA Cup confrontations of all time. By the time they reached the Twin Towers, the Reds had scored eighteen goals but so had their opponents, Blackpool. With just over twenty minutes left it looked like United were going to be bridesmaids as Blackpool led 2-1 but Rowley equalised and goals from Pearson and Anderson secured the coveted trophy.

The crowds were returning in dramatic fashion and United, with their ground rebuilt, left their temporary home at Maine Road to return to Old Trafford in the knowledge that they had repaid all debts. The way was clear for progress. Despite being invited to take over the Italian National side, Busby remained at Old Trafford and by 1952 had landed his first Championship. It then seemed as if United could follow City in to the record books by getting relegated immediately after winning the title when, at the end of October they were bottom – not that City fans were laughing – they were next to bottom! To halt the rot, Busby introduced many of his young reserve team, Whitefoot, Pegg, Edwards, Viollett, Foulkes, Jones and Blanchflower. In addition he bought Tommy Taylor from Barnsley for £29,999, the missing £1 being because Busby didn't want the youngster being burdened with the tag of becoming the first £30,000 player. Another youngster, Roger Byrne, who had played in the Championship side as a left winger was switched to left back on the retirement of Carey and was to become one of the most astute captains ever to lead United.

The youngsters learned their trade under Busby and Murphy for two years, finishing fourth and fifth, before becoming the most dominant team of their era. The 1955/56 title was a one horse race when they took the title by eleven points (in the days of two points for a win) from Blackpool. There was no nail biting finish this time with the Championship nicely wrapped up as early as 7th April when the Reds beat their nearest rivals 2-1 at Old Trafford in front of almost 63,000 adoring fans. Only winger Johnny Berry and Roger Byrne, still a youngster himself, remained from the team that won the title just four years earlier and the average age was an incredible 22. Just Berry and Taylor had cost sizeable fees with almost the entire squad having come through the Youth ranks. Indeed, it was not uncommon for crowds of over 25,000 to turn out to watch the Youth team as it won the FA Youth Cup in each of the first five occasions it was competed for. The aggregate scores of 9-3, 7-1 and 8-2 in three of the Finals demonstrated how outclassed the opposition were in this competition whilst it took great goalkeeping by an unknown youngster, Gordon Banks, to keep United down to four in the 1956 Final against Chesterfield. Indeed, although the 25,000 plus crowd at that Final didn't realise it at the time, they were watching two players who were to become household names throughout the world, let alone England, in Banks and Bobby Charlton.

United ignored an FA request not to enter the newly instituted European Cup (Chelsea had obliged the FA the previous season) and, without floodlights, they played their home games at Maine Road. Having won the First Leg against Belgian champions, Anderlecht, barely 40,000 turned up to see one of most polished performances given by any team in the world. Anderlecht were not a bad team but they had no answer to United on that evening as the Reds ran riot scoring ten which would have been significantly more had several players refused to score, preferring instead to try to give a goal to Pegg, who didn't get on the scoresheet despite setting up many chances for his colleagues. In the league, United took their unbeaten run of fourteen games at the end of the previous campaign to 26 before Everton surprisingly put five past the Reds at Old Trafford. The title was wrapped up by eight points and there were high hopes of a treble as United reached the FA Cup Final and the semi-finals of the European Cup thanks to a momentous night at Maine Road. United were trailing by two goals to Spanish champions, Atletico Bilbao, from the first leg but overcame the deficit in an electric atmosphere.

United were now to embark on nine months that was nothing but grief. A truly

305

great Real Madrid side containing players such as Di Stefano, Gento, Santamaria and Kopa drew 2-2 in Old Trafford's first European competitive game to knock United out 5-3 on aggregate. In the FA Cup Final, United's hopes were dashed by what today would have been an automatic sending off but McParland, after breaking 'keeper Wood's jaw stayed on to score both Aston Villa's goals against stand in custodian, Jackie Blanchflower. United were left with just the Championship in a season which marked the two goal debut of Bobby Charlton against, strangely, Charlton Athletic, whom he scored a hat-trick against in the return fixture!

United didn't quite dominate the 1957/58 title race as they had in the previous two seasons but, after winning a classic 5-4 encounter at Arsenal on 1st February, after putting seven past Bolton Wanderers in the previous match, everything seemed on course for a third successive championship. The Reds left Arsenal in good spirits to travel to Red Star Belgrade confident of protecting a 2-1 First Leg lead to reach the semi-finals of the European Cup for a second successive time. The game finished 3-3 but, as the whole football world knows, tragedy was to wipe out most of the team at a stroke. Attempting to take off for a third time following a refuelling stop at Munich, an iced up wing caused the plane to veer off the runway and crash. Roger Byrne, Eddie Colman, Mark Jones, David Pegg, Billy Whelan, Tommy Taylor and a reserve player, Geoff Bent were amongst those killed instantly. Duncan Edwards, as one would expect from such a giant, fought for life against overwhelming odds for almost two weeks before losing the one sided battle. When he died in his 21st year, he already held 18 full caps, two championship medals and an FA Cup Final medal.

Miraculously, United beat AC Milan 2-1 in the first leg of the European Cup semi-final and reached the FA Cup Final, but won only one more league match (against Sunderland 2-1, away) as not surprisingly they fell down the table to finish ninth. As Matt Busby fought successfully for his life, Jimmy Murphy, who had not been on the ill fated trip due to his commitments with the Welsh national side, took charge and produced a team for the first match after Munich, a 5th Round FA Cup-tie against Sheffield Wednesday, containing only two players, Harry Gregg and Billy Foulkes, who had played in the previous round, three weeks earlier against Ipswich Town. Ian Greaves, Ronnie Cope, Mark "Pancho" Pearson, Shay Brennan and Alex Dawson were boys who became men overnight. Two reserve players who had played in the first team previously, Colin Webster and Freddie Goodwin made up the side along with two signings, Ernie Taylor and Stan Crowther, who were given special dispensation by the FA to play as they had already appeared for Blackpool and Aston Villa in that season's competition. Carried along on a wave of emotion, the cobbled together side won 3-0 with two goals from Brennan and one from Dawson. The Sixth Round saw a Colin Webster goal dispose of West Bromwich Albion on another emotional night after a 2-2 draw at the Hawthorns in a match that saw the arrival back of Bobby Charlton – little could he have known then what responsibility he was going to have thrust on him over the next few years. Fulham (and a young Jimmy Hill) almost put United out in the semi-final but two Charlton goals saved the day and a Dawson treble in the Highbury replay did the rest. Incredibly, the ravaged United were in the FA Cup Final.

Unbelievably, United were to have their 'keeper injured for the second Final in succession when Lofthouse quite blatantly bundled both Gregg and the ball into the net for Bolton's second and decisive goal. Charlton had hit the post for United and had had another fine effort saved by England 'keeper Eddie Hopkinson but the Reds became the first side in the 20th century to lose two successive FA Cup Finals. Eleven days later, their European dreams also crashed when they lost 4-0 in Milan.

Amazingly, the following season United finished runners-up to Wolverhampton Wanderers as Denis Viollet broke the club scoring record for a campaign with 32 strikes. But the momentum began to wane and United had some average seasons finishing seventh twice and then 15th as well as being humiliated 7-2 at home in the FA Cup by Sheffield Wednesday. In 1963 it looked for much of the time as if they would be relegated but a draw in the third last game of the season at Maine Road virtually kept the Reds up and City down. The FA Cup, however, redeemed an otherwise forgettable year with United completely outclassing Leicester City who had finished fifteen places above them in the First Division. Goals from David Herd (two) and Denis Law brought the Cup back to Old Trafford.

Just as almost thirty years earlier when the near drop into the Third Division galvanised United, so did the threat of relegation in 1963. The following year saw the introduction of a youngster from Northern Ireland, George Best, who became an instant hit with the fans. United finished runners-up to Liverpool and reached the semi-final of the FA Cup only to be beaten by a Bobby Moore inspired West Ham on a quagmire at Hillsborough just days after finally overcoming Sunderland at the third attempt on another bog at Leeds Road, Huddersfield. But the biggest disappointment was reserved for the Cup-winners Cup where everyone went home after a 4-1 first-leg victory over Sporting Lisbon thinking all United had to do was to turn up in Portugal. Apparently, the players also thought along those lines for they crashed 5-0 in one of the biggest ever turn rounds in European history.

The crowds flocked back to Old Trafford as United boasted three of the world's best players, Law, Best and Charlton on display every Saturday afternoon. United won the 1964/65 title on goal difference from Leeds United although it wasn't quite as close as that as they already had the title sewn up when they lost their last game at Aston Villa. Leeds had the last laugh, however, when they beat United in the semi-final of the FA Cup after two games. United were also destined to lose in the semi-final of the Inter-Cities Fairs Cup over three matches to the Hungarian outfit, Ferencvaros.

United were now back on the big stage of the European Cup itself and the dream was shortly to become reality but not before more disappointment. Best became christened "El Beatle" after demolishing Benfica 5-1 in the Stadium of Light. After such a performance United were considered very serious contenders for the European crown but the soldiers of Partisan Belgrade surprised everybody with a 2-0 home win that United could not overcome in the return. Busby presumably thought his dream had vanished for ever. But his side bounced back to grab the title once more in 1966/67 with a relentless run of twenty games unbeaten to the end of the season culminating in a 6-1 celebration at Upton Park. The boys were back!

The following season they lost their title of Champions but the fact that it was Manchester City who deprived them of top spot made it hurt just that little bit more. However, there was a glittering prize that was more than ample consolation. Comparatively easy wins over Hibernians of Malta, Sarajevo, and Gornik saw United up against Real Madrid in the semi-final. A George Best goal gave United a slender advantage to take to the Bernabeau Stadium but surely it wasn't enough. And so it looked with a quarter of an hour left as United trailed 3-1 but then, as in all fairy stories, came the unlikeliest of heroes. Billy Foulkes had started down the European road in United's first ever tie in 1956. Twelve years later he was to inspire United from adversity to their golden goal. In a career spanning almost 700 games, Foulkes rarely ventured over the half way line and scored just nine goals in a 17 year career. Suddenly, he rose above the Madrid defence to head a Crerand free-kick on for Sadler to convert and, then, three minutes later appeared from nowhere to stab home the equaliser on the night and the winner on aggregate.

On a nostalgic night that nobody who was present will ever forget, United finally overcame Benfica 4-1 in extra time at Wembley. Even that game, however, could have gone the other way had Stepney not made a great save from Eusebio in normal time. Best was a wizard, Charlton scored a rare goal with his head, and Kidd celebrated his 19th birthday with a goal but the lad who played the game of his life that night was the one who was the target of the boo boys for much of the campaign, John Aston, whose pace tore the Portuguese side apart.

United were unable to retain their new title the following year when they lost 2-1 to AC Milan and Busby handed over the reins to Wilf McGuinness. It heralded an era of managerial change at Old Trafford and with McGuinness soon departed, Busby took over again temporarily before Frank O'Farrell experienced an even worse time than McGuinness. In 1972, with relegation once more a very real prospect, Tommy Docherty was brought in. He saved them from the immediate threat but couldn't keep them up the following season which had a sting in the tail, for it was former United hero Denis Law, now returned to Manchester City, who back heeled the goal at Old Trafford that confirmed the relegation. Law took no pleasure from the act and did not join in the City celebrations. The following day he announced his retirement – his last league goal had put United down. At least the Board kept faith with Docherty and he rewarded them with probably the best "flair" team to play between Busby's 1967 championship side and Ferguson's 1992 Champions. Gordon Hill and Steve Coppell patrolled the wings and scored goals at the same time, Martin Buchan had developed into a fine defender as well as a fine leader and there were talents such as Macari and McIlroy. They were lucky with injuries and, by the end of the season, no fewer than ten players had played over 30 games. They won their first game at Orient and were never headed.

Back in the First Division, Docherty saw his young side more than hold their own and they also reached Wembley where they were hot favourites to dispose of

Southampton, then a mid-table Division Two side. On the day, United never performed and a good strike by Bobby Stokes sealed victory for the "Saints". The following year they were back at the Twin Towers but very much in the role that Southampton had adopted twelve months previously. Liverpool had won the League and Wembley was merely a stopping off point on the way to a unique treble as they were also to take the European crown. Unfortunately for the Anfield club, nobody had given United a copy of the script and two goals in a five minute second half spell gave United a victory as unexpected as their defeat in the previous final. Two months after this success, Docherty was dismissed for undertaking a relationship with the wife of the United 'physio, Laurie Brown.

After flirting in more ways than one with the outgoing personality of Docherty, United turned back to the quiet and unassuming type in Dave Sexton even though their experience with O'Farrell should have been sufficient to let the Board know it was not what the fans wanted. Sexton, to an extent, was unlucky for he saw his team come second in one of the best modern FA Cup Finals. United fought back from 2-0 down to level against Arsenal in the last four minutes of the 1979 Wembley spectacular only to immediately concede a third goal themselves. The following campaign saw United level with Liverpool at the top of the First Division on the final Saturday of the season but Liverpool beat Villa whilst United lost at Elland Road. 1980/81 saw the end of Sexton's reign and he must look back and think it was a case of so near, yet so far. Sadly, for a man of immense integrity, he left with the millstone of his £1 million plus signing, striker Gary Birtles, around his neck – Birtles had failed to find the net in the 25 league games he played under Sexton.

United's hierarchy realised they had to give the fans someone with charisma and in those stakes they didn't come much bigger than Ron Atkinson. Where Sexton and O'Farrell had struggled in communication with the fans, Atkinson, like Docherty, loved the publicity and banter. He also had a flair for producing attractive sides and United looked good again. He took twelve months to settle in and then gave the Reds their first ever League Cup Final but it ended in defeat against Liverpool after extra-time. Just weeks later the Red hordes were back at Wembley for the FA Cup Final against Brighton. That, too, almost finished in disaster as Bailey made a great reflex save to deny Brighton the winner with virtually the last kick of the match. Brighton had their opportunity and paid heavily in the replay, losing to a 4-0 scoreline that flattered them. In these games Alan Davies created what will surely be a record that stands for all time. He only played two FA Cup ties for United, both of which were FA Cup Finals! Two years later United made FA Cup history again when Kevin Moran became the first player to be sent off in a FA Cup Final as United beat Everton with a Norman Whiteside goal in extra-time.

The coveted title still eluded United but, in 1985, it looked to be on its way as United won their first ten matches. It all went sadly wrong, however, and a bad start to the next campaign left Atkinson to rue that two Cup wins in three seasons was no compensation for not winning the Championship. United appointed Alex Ferguson, destined to become the first man since Busby to land the title, but it took him six years to end the obsession. In November 1986, just weeks after Ferguson's arrival, United were in 21st position but had recovered to finish 11th by the end of the season. In 1987/88 they improved to finish second but near misses were no good to United followers and 1988/89 brought only disappointment. Indeed, many United fans were beginning to see Ferguson in the mould of Sexton and O'Farrell and there were distant rumblings. The league performance in 89/90 was tantamount to disillusionment for many Old Trafford faithful and the rumblings were getting very much closer to home and almost reached a crescendo when a United side that had cost Ferguson £11m were crushed like schoolboys 5-1 by Manchester City. Off the field, United were almost becoming a laughing stock with Robert Maxwell expressing interest in buying the club and then a ball juggling Michael Knighton appearing out of the blue in a bid to become Chairman. United finished 13th but Ferguson was probably saved by an incredible cup run. United were drawn away in every round, drew 3-3 with Oldham Athletic in the semi-final and, amazingly, drew by the same scoreline in the Final itself with Crystal Palace. In the replay, the only FA Cup goal ever scored by Lee Martin brought Ferguson his first trophy.

Having broken his duck at last, Ferguson collected prizes for fun. Although they slipped up badly against Sheffield Wednesday (and Ron Atkinson) in the Final of the Rumbelows' League Cup, United lifted their second European honour when they beat Barcelona 2-1 in Rotterdam in the Cup-Winners Cup. The next year it was the League Cup with Nottingham Forest the victims but the Reds let the league title slip away to Leeds. Still the ultimate prize eluded them but then in the late autumn of 1992 with his side again failing to set the world alight, Ferguson, quite out of character, took an immense gamble. He purchased from Leeds United the volatile Frenchman, Eric Cantona. Most pundits agreed that Ferguson had flipped his lid but, in fact, the last piece of the jigsaw had just been slotted into place. On a stage fit for world class acts, Cantona became one. The bald statistics show just what a bargain Ferguson landed for £1m. In the Frenchman's first fifty games, United lost just twice! The title was won at last, and by ten points, but it was never that easy. Indeed, at 4.45 on 10th April 1993, United appeared to have lost the lead to Aston Villa for they trailed Sheffield Wednesday by 1-0 at Old Trafford whilst title rivals Villa (and Ron Atkinson) were winning. In the next minute Villa dropped two valuable points and United gained three as Steve Bruce scored twice in time added on for injury to the referee! The five point turn around in that decisive moment proved vital and United went on to win their last seven games as Villa fell away. Strangely, just twenty four hours earlier, central defender Bruce had said on TV that it was about time he started scoring again following a run of over 30 games without finding the net! The Holy Grail came back to Old Trafford in a carnival atmosphere as United entertained Blackburn Rovers on 3rd May but nobody mentioned Harry Stafford and his dog!

# *Names for the Future*

If the present first team squad show any signs of being on the wane, United not only have the money in the bank to bring in replacements, but also have a full team of youngsters knocking at the door from their successful FA Youth Cup team of 1993. The star of that team, of course, is already a household name in Ryan Giggs but there are also several others who are bound to make it to the top. No fewer than eight of the side that beat Crystal Palace 6-3 on aggregate in the 1993 Final were awarded contracts, an extremely high percentage and manager Alex Ferguson has since gone on record as saying at least five, maybe six will be good enough to play in United's first team. Already several of them have been included in first team training sessions and have accompanied the team to away matches to "get the feeling of things".

Besides Giggs, several others have tested first team football although three of these have only done so away from Old Trafford. The captain of the successful 1993 side, stylish midfielder Simon Davies, made a big impression when on loan at Exeter City under Alan Ball, whilst Keith Gillepie was also a hit while at Wigan Athletic on a similar deal to give him experience he could not get at Old Trafford. A third Player to go out on loan was Neil Whitworth who was loaned to Barnsley, Rotherham United and Blackpool. Gary Neville, who like his brother Phil was good enough for both football and cricket to be offered contracts at both Old Traffords, has tested first action as a substitute in European combat and was given his FAPL debut in the last game of the campaign against Coventry along with Colin McKee who is something of a rarity at Old Trafford these days – he is the only other Scot besides Brain McClair on the books. Neville's younger brother, incidentally is also progressing quickly in the "A" and "B" teams and has figured in the Reserves on occasions. Neville's defensive partner, Chris Casper son of former Burnley Star Frank Casper, has been seen regularly alongside Neville in the Reserves and they also formed the defensive strength in England's youth team.

Yet another youth international is Nicky Butt and, again, there are extremely high hopes for him and he has been included in away trips on several occasions with the first team squad and got on as a substitute against Spurs and in the FA Cup semi final against Oldham. Ben Thornley, John O'Kane and David Beckham (a free kick specialist) have played regularly in the Reserves with Thornley making his first team debut at Westham in February but his season was brought to a premature halt by injury at Blackburn. The 'keeper' of the team, Kevin Pilkington has found his way blocked by the superb form of Peter Schmeichel which in turn means that Les Sealey and Gary Walsh need the Reserve outings to keep them on the ball. The only two players released from th e 1993 youth Cup side was Geoge Switzer and Raphael Burke who went to Darlington and Bristol City respectively on free transfers. All in all United are well placed to continue at the top for a long time to come.

# Obituaries

## JIM HOLTON

Jim Holton was not long at Old Trafford but he became a legend in his own time as a United player, a quite staggering feat when ranged alongside the likes of Carey, Byrne, Edwards, Best, Law, Charlton etc. It is even more remarkable when one considers the fact that he played only 69 games in total for the Reds, was virtually unheard of before he signed and quickly disappeared once he left Old Trafford, and that in two of the three seasons he was with the club they finished 18th and 21st! Yet, in that short time, the crowd grew to love him. Born in a small village just outside Glasgow, Holton didn't make the grade at West Bromwich as an apprentice but was picked up by Shrewsbury Town for whom he made over 150 appearances before being signed by Tommy Docherty for £80,000 in January 1973 making his debut in the same game as Lou Macari, a 2-2 draw with West Ham in which Macari scored.

Although United's fortunes were at a low ebb, the crowd recognised the effort that Holton put in and loved to chant "Six foot two, eyes of blue, watch out, Big Jim Holton's after you" at the opposition's centre forward. His talents, once recognised by Docherty quickly brought Holton international recognition and he won the first of his fifteen Scottish caps in May 1973 against Wales. He went to Germany with the Scotland squad for the 1974 World Cup Finals and played in all three of their games before they were knocked out without losing a game. Then, with United running away with the Second Division title, Holton broke his leg and never played for the first team again. Nine months after his first break, he broke the same leg in a Reserve match and eventually moved to Sunderland for a knock down £40,000.

During his time at Old Trafford, Holton carved out for himself a little niche in football's Hall of Fame by becoming the first player playing for an English club to be voted the Scottish Football Writer's Player of the Year. When he left the English scene, he played in America for Miami Toros and Detroit Express before returning home to run a pub, an occupation he was still pursuing when struck down by a heart attack returning from a jogging session on 4th October 1993. "Six foot two, eyes of blue, we'll remember you".

## Sir MATT BUSBY

Sir Matt Busby had been at Old Trafford for almost fifty years when he passed away in his sleep on 20th January 1994. It was testament to his vision that when he departed, Sir Matt left a club that stands shoulder to shoulder with the best in the world with a stadium to match after inheriting a club in 1945 that had no ground and finished the last pre-war season 14th in Division One.

He himself had masterminded the building of three separate great sides that between them won five Championships, seven times been runners-up, appeared in four FA Cup Finals and lifted the European Cup. After giving up the managerial reins, he joined the Board and was then elevated to President from where he presided over the team that Alex Ferguson built to rival Sir Matt's great sides. Nothing would have given Busby greater pleasure than to see Ferguson's team achieve their success with the style and flair always associated with his own superb footballing creations.

Born in May 1909, a son of a miner in Lanarkshire, a hot bed for football managers with the names of Jock Stein and Bill Shankly also springing immediately to mind, Busby himself won a FA Cup Winners medal in 1934 and was capped by Scotland against Wales the same year. Strangely his playing career involved turning out mainly for two of United's arch rivals, Manchester City and Liverpool after beginning his working life as a miner.

During his time on earth, he experienced joy and sorrow that nobody can ever imagine. His life was not always a bed of roses and he was to taste grief at the tender age of six when his father was killed in the First World War. He was, of course, to lose many of "his" youngsters in the Munich Air Crash where his own life hung in the balance for many days. Indeed, whilst in hospital at Munich, Sir Matt was twice given the Last Rites. When he recovered he vowed to walk away from football but his loyal wife, Jean, persuaded him otherwise – she told him he had to carry on for the people who had perished.

Whilst the newspapers of the day, looking for a scapegoat for the accident, tried to pin the blame on the pilot, Captain Thain, not so Busby. He merely told, many years later, of how he still felt "such sorrow for Captain Thain". That was typical of a man whose Christianity was very important to him.

As a manager, he had great vision but his vision was just as great as an administrator. When the FA misguidedly advised against the English Champions entering in to the European Cup, Busby defied them seeing the step as the only way forward. As an old man, he could not believe that clubs could not see that three points for a win would bring more open play. Just when it looked as if the proposal would get squashed, Busby spoke out and it was passed and the formula is now to be used in the World Cup.

Matt Busby spent sixty-five years of his life in a sport where jealousy is rife. In that time not one person had a bad word to say about the man. Many people say Sir Matt created a legend, they are wrong – he was the legend.

# Awards

## European Footballer of the Year

| 1964 | Denis Law | 1966 | Bobby Charlton | 1968 | George Best |

*(NB – The only other British club to have had a player voted European Footballer of the Year are Blackpool whose Stanley Matthews won the first award in 1956).*

## Footballer of the Year

| 1949 | Johnnie Carey | 1966 | Bobby Charlton | 1968 | George Best |

## PFA Player of the Year

| 1989 | Mark Hughes | 1991 | Mark Hughes | 1992 | Gary Pallister |
| 1994 | Eric Cantona |

*(NB – Mark Hughes is the only player to have won this award on more than one occasion)*

## PFA Young Player of the Year

| 1985 | Mark Hughes | 1991 | Lee Sharpe | 1992 | Ryan Giggs |
| 1993 | Ryan Giggs |

*(NB – Ryan Giggs is the only player to have won this award in successive seasons. United are the only club to have had three successive winners)*

## PFA Merit Awards

| 1974 | Bobby Charlton | 1975 | Denis Law | 1980 | Sir Matt Busby |
| 1993 | 1968 Manchester United team |

## Manager of the Year

| 1968 | Sir Matt Busby | 1993 | Alex Ferguson | 1994 | Alex Ferguson |

## Barclay's Young Eagle of the Year

| 1992 | Ryan Giggs |

*Eric Cantona – The Players' Player of the Year.*

# Squad Performances 1993-94

## "A" Team

*Lancashire League Division 1*

| Date | Opponent | | Score | Scorers |
|---|---|---|---|---|
| 21/08/93 | v Liverpool "A" | (a) | 3-1 | Irving, Davies(pen),McKee |
| 28/08/93 | v Crewe Alexandra Res | (h) | 2-1 | Irving, Gillespie, |
| 11/09/93 | v Chester City "A" | (h) | 2-2 | Irving, Beckham |
| 25/09/93 | v Everton "A" | (h) | 0-2 | |
| 9/10/93 | v Crewe Alexandra "A" | (a) | 0-0 | |
| 15/10/93 | v Morecambe Res | (a) | 1-0 | Rawlinson |
| 23/10/93 | v Liverpool "A" | (h) | 3-1 | Irving, Davies 2 |
| 6/11/93 | v Blackburn Rovers "A" | (a) | 4-1 | Irving, Thornley, Ferguson, Rawlinson, |
| 13/11/93 | v Blackpool "A" | (h) | 5-0 | Irving, P.Neville(pen), Savage(2),Cooke |
| 20/11/93 | v Manchester City "A" | (h) | 1-1 | Scholes |
| 27/11/93 | v Morecambe Res | (h) | 3-0 | Gillespie, McGibbon, Beckham |
| 18/12/93 | v Blackburn Rovers "A" | (h) | 1-2 | Beckham |
| 15/01/94 | v Tranmere Rovers "A" | (h) | 3-1 | Rawlinson, Beckham, Irving |
| 22/01/94 | v Bury Res | (a) | 4-0 | Irving 2, Roberts, Rawlinson |
| 29/01/94 | v Rochdale Res | (h) | 3-0 | Irving, Cooke, og. |
| 5/02/94 | v Burnley "A" | (a) | 2-2 | G.Neville, Gillespie |
| 12/02/94 | v Blackpool "A" | (a) | 3-3 | Roberts, Irving, Beckham |
| 19/02/94 | v Manchester City | (a) | 1-1 | Johnson |
| 5/03/94 | v Oldham Athletic "A" | (a) | 4-0 | |
| 7/03/94 | v Chester City "A" | (a) | 1-1 | |
| 12/03/94 | v Oldham Athletic "A" | (h) | 0-3 | |
| 19/03/94 | v Marine Reserves | (a) | 3-1 | Roberts, P.Neville, Beckham |
| 16/04/94 | v Everton "A" | (a) | 0-2 | |
| 23/04/94 | v Bury Res | (h) | 1-4 | |
| 25/04/94 | v Rochdale Reserves | (a) | 4-2 | |
| 30/04/94 | v Marine Res | (h) | 2-1 | |
| 2/05/94 | v Burnley "A" | (h) | 1-2 | |
| 7/05/94 | v Tranmere Rovers "A" | (a) | 1-0 | Irving |

# "B" Team

*Lancashire League Division 2*

| 21/08/93 | v Bolton Wanderers "A" | (a) | 0-3 | |
|---|---|---|---|---|
| 28/08/93 | v Manchester City "B" | (h) | 4-2 | Mustoe 2, Mitten, Mulryne |
| 4/09/93 | v Oldham Athletic "B" | (a) | 8-0 | Mustoe 2, Mitten 2, Hart 2, Twynham, Appleton. |
| 11/09/93 | v Tranmere Rovers "B" | (h) | 8-0 | Mustoe, Hart 3, Cooke 3, Twynham |
| 18/09/93 | v Marine Youth | (h) | 11-0 | Mustoe 3, Baker 2, Hart 2, Appleton, Cooke, Heckingbotham, Lee |
| 25/09/93 | v Marine Youth | (a) | 4-1 | Twynham, Mitten, Mustoe, Heckingbotham |
| 2/10/93 | v Stockport County "A" | (h) | 1-1 | Heckingbotham |
| 9/10/93 | v Blackburn Rovers "B" | (h) | 2-2 | Twynham, Macken |
| 16/10/93 | v Preston North End "B" | (h) | 2-2 | Mustoe, Twynham |
| 23/10/93 | v Carlisle United "A" | (a) | 3-1 | Hart 2, Whittam |
| 30/10/93 | v Blackpool "B" | (a) | 5-2 | Irving 3, Whittam, Hart |
| 6/11/93 | v Preston North End "B" | (a) | 2-1 | Cooke, Barnes |
| 27/11/93 | v Bury "A" | (a) | 3-1 | Dean, Kirovski, Hart |
| 4/12/93 | v Rochdale "A" | (h) | 9-0 | Roberts 2, Hart 2, Whittam, Mitten, Clegg, Gardner, Cooke |
| 11/12/93 | v Bury "A" | (h) | 5-1 | Irving 2, Westwood 2, Roberts |
| 18/12/93 | v Carlisle United "B" | (a) | 3-3 | Hart, Mustoe, Cooke |
| 8/01/94 | v Blackpool "B" | (h) | 4-1 | Beckham 2, Mustoe, Cooke |
| 22/01/94 | v Liverpool "B" | (h) | 2-2 | Hart 2 |
| 29/01/94 | v Crewe Alexandra "A" | (h) | 5-1 | Johnson 3, Gardner 2. |
| 5/02/94 | v Bolton Wanderers | (h) | 3-0 | Cooke, Mustoe, Whittam |
| 19/02/94 | v Burnley "B" | (h) | 0-0 | |
| 26/02/94 | v Everton "B" | (h) | 2-3 | Kirovski, Irving |
| 5/03/94 | v Everton "B" | (a) | 0-2 | |
| 12/03/94 | v Wigan Athletic "A" | (a) | 1-2 | Mustoe |
| 19/03/94 | v Manchester City "B" | (a) | 2-1 | Sharpe, Johnson |
| 26/03/94 | v Tranmere Rovers "B" | (a) | 3-4 | Cooke, Johnson, Hart |
| 30/03/94 | v Burnley "B" | (a) | 0-0 | |
| 2/04/94 | v Stockport County "A" | (a) | 4-1 | Roberts, Gardner, Mustoe, McGibbon |
| 9/04/94 | v Wigan Athletic "A" | (h) | 1-0 | Appleton |

317

| 16/04/94 | v Blackburn Rovers "B" | (a) | 1-1 | Kirovski |
| 27/04/94 | v Rochdale "A" | (a) | 6-0 | |
| 30/04/94 | v Liverpool "B" | (a) | 2-1 | |
| 4/05/94 | v Oldham Athletic "B" | (h) | 4-1 | |
| 7/05/94 | v Crewe Alexandra "A" | (a) | 1-4 | |

## Reserves

*Pontins League Division 1.*

| 19/08/93 | v Blackburn Rovers | (a) | 1-0 | Sharpe |
| 26/08/93 | v Notts County | (h) | 5-0 | McKee 3, Dublin, Gallagher og. |
| 4/09/93 | v Leeds United | (h) | 3-1 | Robson, McClair, Dublin |
| 8/09/93 | v Newcastle United | (h) | 3-2 | Martin 2 (1pen), McKee |
| 13/09/93 | v Leicester City | (h) | 4-3 | McKee, O'Kane, Scholes, Butt (pen) |
| 23/09/93 | v Notts Forest | (a) | 3-2 | Wallace, Blackmore, Scholes |
| 2/10/93 | v Everton | (h) | 2-0 | Casper, McKee |
| 13/10/93 | v Aston Villa | (a) | 1-1 | Wallace |
| 27/10/93 | v Wolverhampton Wanderers | (a) | 3-2 | Savage 2, Thornley |
| 10/11/93 | v Liverpool | (h) | 0-0 | |
| 13/11/93 | v Sheffield United | (h) | 2-1 | McKee, Dublin |
| 17/11/93 | v Coventry City | (h) | 2-1 | Beckham, Dublin |
| 25/11/93 | v Bolton Wanderers | (a) | 4-2 | Phelan, Butt, Dublin, McKee |
| 1/12/93 | v Derby County | (a) | 2-3 | Davies, Dublin |
| 5/01/94 | v Sheffield Wednesday | (h) | 1-0 | Dublin |
| 25/01/94 | v Wolverhampton Wanderers | (h) | 1-0 | Irving |
| 31/01/94 | v Everton | (a) | 2-1 | McKee, Scholes |
| 1/02/94 | v Sheffield United | (a) | 4-0 | McKee 2, Dublin, Thornley |
| 12/02/94 | v Leicester City | (a) | 1-3 | Dublin |
| 2/03/94 | v York City | (a) | 0-0 | |
| 8/03/94 | v Derby County | (h) | 0-2 | |
| 14/03/94 | v Notts County | (a) | 2-1 | Thornley, Scholes pen. |
| 23/03/94 | v Leeds United | (a) | 7-0 | Scholes 3, Dublin 2, Davies, Blackmore |
| 31/03/94 | v Sheffield Wednesday | (a) | 6-0 | Dublin 2, Butt 2, Thornley, Beckham |
| 6/04/94 | v Blackburn Rovers | (h) | 3-0 | Butt 2, Morrison og. |
| 13/04/94 | v Sunderland | (h) | 1-3 | Casper |
| 19/04/94 | v Liverpool | (a) | 1-0 | Dublin |
| 23/04/94 | v Notts Forest | (h) | 2-1 | Dublin, Phelan |

| 25/04/94 | v Aston Villa | (h) | 1-1 | Scholes |
| 27/04/94 | v Bolton Wanderers | (h) | 3-0 | Scholes, Dublin, og. |
| 3/05/94 | v Coventry City | (a) | 1-1 | Maiorana |
| 5/05/94 | v York City | (h) | 2-2 | Scholes 2 |
| 9/05/94 | v Sunderland | (a) | 1-2 | Scholes |
| 16/05/94 | v Newcastle United | (a) | | |

# Youth Team

### LANCASHIRE FA YOUTH CUP

| 22/09/93 | v Preston North End | (h) | 5-1 | Irving 2, Twynham 2, Hart |
| 5/02/94 | v Wigan Athletic | (h) | 2-1 | Hart, Johnson |

**FINAL**

| 21/04/94 | v Burnley | (a) | 4-2 | Appleton, P.Neville, |
| Kirovski, Irving | | | | |

### FA YOUTH CUP

| 22/11/93 | v Bradford City | (a) | 0-2 | |

# "Ton Up Boys"

A select band of just fourteen players have scored a century or more goals for United. They are:

| | | | | | |
|---|---|---|---|---|---|
| J | Cassidy | (1892-99) | D | Herd | (1961-67) |
| A | Turnbull | (1906-14) | D | Law | (1961-72) |
| J | Spence | (1919-32) | G | Best | (1963-73) |
| S | Pearson | (1937-53) | B | Robson | (1981- |
| T | Taylor | (1952-57) | M | Hughes | (1983 - |
| D | Viollet | (1952-61) | B | Mcclair | (1987- |
| R | Charlton | (1956-72) | | | |

*There is a long list of "One goal wonders" but since the Second World War, the following players have scored on just one occasion for United;*

| W Bainbridge | 9/01/46 | v Accrington Stanley (FA Cup) | (h) | Won 5-1 |
|---|---|---|---|---|
| P Coyne | 24/04/76 | v Leicester City | (a) | Lost 1-2 |
| L Cunningham | 23/04/83 | v Watford | (h) | Won 2-0 |
| A Davies | 11/04/83 | v Juventus | (h) | Drew 1-1 |
| P Edwards | 17/12/69 | v Man.City (League Cup) | (h) | Drew 2-2 |
| T Gibson | 24/01/87 | v Arsenal | (h) | Won 2-0 |
| D Givens | 30/08/69 | v Sunderland | (h) | Won 3-1 |
| D Graham | 11/01/87 | v QPR (FA Cup) | (a) | Drew 2-2 aet |
| G Hogg | 7/02/84 | v Birmingham City | (a) | Drew 2-2 |
| M Jones | 17/12/55 | v Birmingham City | (h) | Won 2-1 |
| A Kinsey | 9/01/65 | v Chester FA Cup | (h) | Won 2-1 |
| R McGrath | 10/12/77 | v West Ham Utd | (a) | Lost 1-2 |
| J Sivebaek | 22/11/86 | v QPR | (h) | Won 1-0 |
| I Ure | 13/12/69 | v Liverpool | (a) | Won 4-1 |
| T Young | 3/11/73 | v Chelsea | (h) | Drew 2-2 |

*Strangely, Bainbridge, Graham, and Kinsey all scored their only goals for United in the only FA Cup-ties they ever played. Davies scored his goal in the only European match he played in, and Coyne scored his solitary goal in the his only full appearance*